Exporting Democracy

Exporting Democracy

THE UNITED STATES AND LATIN AMERICA

Case Studies

Edited by Abraham F. Lowenthal

The Johns Hopkins University Press

Baltimore and London

© 1991 The Johns Hopkins University Press
All rights reserved
Printed in the United States of America

The Johns Hopkins University Press
701 West 40th Street
Baltimore, Maryland 21211
The Johns Hopkins Press Ltd., London

The paper used in this book meets the minimum requirements
of American National Standards for Information Sciences—
Permanence of Paper for Printed Library Materials,
ANSI Z39.48–1984.

Library of Congress Cataloging-in-Publication Data

Exporting democracy : the United States and Latin America.
Case studies / edited by Abraham F. Lowenthal.
        p.   cm.
    Includes bibliographical references and index.
    ISBN 0–8018–4133–X (pbk.)
        1. Latin America—Foreign relations—United States.
2. United States—Foreign relations—Latin America.
3. United States—Foreign relations—20th century.
4. Representative government and representation—Latin
America—History—20th century. 5. Latin America—Politics
and government—20th century.
I. Lowenthal, Abraham F.
F1418.E892   1991
327.7308—dc20   90–24062
                                                CIP

Contents

Preface and Acknowledgments

FROM THE mid-1970s through the late 1980s and into the 1990s, Latin America has moved broadly from authoritarianism of various kinds toward democratic politics, also of varying types. Of all the countries in Central and South America in 1976, elected civilian governments ruled only in Costa Rica, Colombia, Venezuela, and Suriname. By the end of 1989, almost every government in Central and South America was civilian and had been elected under reasonably competitive circumstances. The direct presidential elections in December 1989 in Brazil and Chile—the first such polls since 1962 and 1970, respectively—seemed to culminate this dramatic trend. Then, in February 1990, it was carried one dramatic step further with the electoral victory of the Nicaraguan opposition in the most free and fair national election in that country's history.

Latin America's democratic opening has been uneven and fragile, and summarizing it in the aggregate may obscure as much as it reveals. Elected regimes are not necessarily democratic, for instance; much depends on the extent and the conditions of popular participation and on the protection of basic civil rights. But there can be no denying that the past dozen years have seen a considerable swing toward democratic politics in one Latin American country after another.

Under successive administrations of both political parties, the U.S. government since the mid-1970s has frequently expressed its support for Latin America's democratic transitions. Presidents Carter, Reagan, and Bush have all stated explicitly that the promotion of democracy is a central aim of U.S. policy in the Western Hemisphere. Washington has employed various instruments to push for what U.S. officials have regarded as movement toward democracy in countries as different as Chile and Nicaragua, El Salvador and Paraguay, Haiti and Panama. Although not everyone would assign equal importance to the role of U.S. policy, there is broad bipartisan agreement in Washington today that fostering democracy in Latin America—and elsewhere, for that matter—is a legitimate and significant goal of the U.S. policy and that the United States can be effective in pursuing that aim.

With such widespread agreement on the goal of promoting Latin American democracy, there have been strong pressures to step up such efforts and to expand the resources devoted to them. After a generation of strenuous internal debate in the United States on various foreign policy issues and a decade of particularly bitter divisions over Latin American policy, the idea that the United States should and can export democracy is virtually unchallenged in the Washington policy-making community of the early 1990s.

This is not the first time that democratic opening has occurred in Latin American politics or that the U.S. government has proclaimed its desire for a democratic hemisphere. In fact, U.S. support for Latin American democracy has been frequently expressed since the early nineteenth century, and especially since the time of Woodrow Wilson. Some such expressions have no doubt been merely rhetorical, and there have been notable instances when the United States has actually opposed democratic regimes and contributed to their overthrow, propped up dictators, or promoted democratization for ulterior motives. It is clear, however, that on various occasions and in several countries, long before the 1980s, the United States *has* used its influence to promote what U.S. officials sincerely conceived of as democratic politics. Yet no systematic and comparative study of past U.S. attempts to promote Latin American democracy has ever been published, and the Washington policy community seems remarkably unaware of this long history.

This volume is motivated by the collective amnesia that affects both academia and contemporary Washington regarding prior U.S. attempts to promote Latin American democracy. We believe this is the first book in any language to focus sharply and comparatively on the historic influence of the United States on Latin America's prospects for democracy. The extensive literature on Latin America's transition from authoritarian rule devotes little explicit attention to the U.S. role, or to external influence more generally. Despite the powerful influence of *dependencia* and "hegemony" as major concepts for analyzing United States–Latin American relations, the impact of the United States and of U.S. policy on Latin America's democratic prospects has not been emphasized.

Our project (involving scholars from the United States, Latin America, and the United Kingdom) seeks to help fill that gap by analyzing the sources, concepts, instruments, and impact of the recurrent impulse in the United States to export its national political values and institutions. Our methods and purposes are scholarly, but we also want to derive insights from history that may illuminate contemporary policy choices.

More specifically, we have set out to analyze *when* and *where* the United States has sought to promote Latin American democracy, *why, how,* and *with what consequences.* We have sought to assess the meaning and significance of various declared U.S. attempts to promote democracy, and to discern what motivated the U.S. interest in each case. We have specified the prevailing concepts and main instruments the United States employed, and have evaluated their effects. Where relevant, we have studied what caused the U.S. concern with democracy eventually to wane or be abandoned.

Our project has proceeded on the basis of several shared premises and approaches. We have analyzed primarily those instances in which U.S. officials took an active interest in promoting Latin American democracy, rather than repeatedly document the fact that this oft-expressed concern has frequently been ignored and even contradicted. Without denying that the indirect effects of the United States on Latin America—because of its cultural influence, its role in the world economy, and its hegemonic power—may often be more important than deliberate policies, we have concentrated mostly on purposive U.S. actions, both by governmental and nongovernmental actors. We have sought to disaggregate both "the United States" and "Latin America" by asking what groups, forces, and actors in the United States have been concerned with Latin American democracy and what significant differences have existed among U.S. government agencies and officials, and also by analyzing the variance among U.S. policies toward distinct countries. And we have understood Latin America not as a passive arena simply being acted in or upon, but rather as a region characterized by complex political struggles, in which some groups have often sought, with varying degrees of success, to mobilize U.S. involvement.

Our methodology has been self-consciously eclectic and comparative.

• Four authors—Paul Drake, Leslie Bethell, Tony Smith, and Thomas Carothers—concentrate on specific periods when U.S. efforts to promote Latin American democracy were particularly notable: from World War I to the Great Depression; the years immediately following World War II; the Alliance for Progress interlude; and the Reagan era.

• Five chapters—by Carlos Escudé, Heraldo Muñoz, Jonathan Hartlyn, Lorenzo Meyer, and Joseph Tulchin and Knut Walter—focus on countries in which the declared U.S. interest in promoting democracy has recurred several times over an extended period: Argentina, Chile, the Dominican Republic, Mexico, and Nicaragua. In each of these cases, U.S. efforts to build local democracy have been particularly notable, if not always successful.

• Elizabeth Cobbs and Paul Buchanan analyze the extent to which major U.S. interest groups—business enterprises and organized labor—have been concerned with Latin American democracy, and they evaluate the impact these groups have had, particularly by comparison with governmental efforts.

• John Sheahan corrects our emphasis on political concepts and instruments by asking what effects U.S. economic policies have had on Latin America's prospects for democracy, and whether the political impact of U.S. economic policy could somehow be made more positive.

• Laurence Whitehead and I, in separate chapters, draw conclusions about the U.S. capacity to promote Latin American democracy. Whitehead focuses on three cases in which the U.S. track record is long and the extent of U.S. involvement has been great, and shows that even in these settings the

U.S. ability to impose democracy has usually been sharply circumscribed. My own chapter summarizes the volume's contents and then comments on the implications of this history for U.S. foreign policy choices in the 1990s. By way of anticipation, let me simply say here that this book tells a cautionary tale. Past U.S. attempts to promote Latin American democracy have met with little enduring success. Although the idea that the United States knows how to export democracy is widely accepted today, the historical record strongly suggests reasons for skepticism.

On behalf of all contributors to this symposium, I wish to express our great appreciation to those who made this book possible. For the necessary financial support, we owe thanks to the World Peace Foundation and its director, Ambassador Richard J. Bloomfield; the Social Science Research Council and the American Council of Learned Societies and their Joint Committee on Latin American Studies; the Exxon Educational Foundation; the California Council for the Humanities; and the University of Southern California (USC). Ambassador Bloomfield and the World Peace Foundation provided more than financial backing, and indeed helped us conceptualize the project and convey its first results to the Washington policy community. The Joint Committee's support for a preliminary workshop, drawing in turn on support from the Ford Foundation and the Andrew W. Mellon Foundation, enabled us to plan the volume with some care.

For superb research assistance and project coordination, we are grateful to Phillip Pearson, an advanced graduate student at USC. Stephen Brager of the University of California, San Diego, and Shelly McConnell of Stanford University assisted Mr. Pearson with the rapporteurial chores. Tina Gallop of the School of International Relations at USC handled the project's logistics and finances with skill and grace.

I owe a great deal to my fellow contributors to the volume, who made the task of editing less a chore than a pleasant challenge. Special thanks are also due to a few other persons with whom I have discussed these issues at one time or another: Genaro Arriagada, Harry Barnes, Peter D. Bell, Sergio Bitar, Cole Blasier, Paul Boeker, Jorge G. Castañeda, Edwin Corr, Julio Cotler, John Crimmins, Larry Diamond, Albert Fishlow, Adam Garfinkle, Manuel Antonio Garretón, Carl Gershman, Peter Hakim, Albert O. Hirschman, Michael Hunt, Samuel P. Huntington, Terry Karl, Walter Lafeber, Bolivar Lamounier, Cynthia McClintock, Guillermo O'Donnell, Robert Packenham, Robert Pastor, Paulo Sergio Pinheiro, Steve Ropp, Sally Shelton-Colby, Paul Sigmund, Viron Vaky, Francisco Weffort, Howard Wiarda, and especially Peter Winn. Others who have contributed to my understanding of these issues include the members of the Inter-American Dialogue, and the participants in the Carter Center's 1986 conference on "Reinforcing Democracy in the Americas." Finally, I happily acknowledge the continuing help and inspiration of Jane S. Jaquette.

Part One

Case Studies

1 | Argentina: The Costs of Contradiction

Carlos Escudé

THROUGHOUT the twentieth century there have been episodes of gross violations of human rights in Argentina; however, two periods stand out for the blatant and systematic way in which these rights were trampled upon by the state over the course of several years. First and foremost is the period from 1976 to 1983, during which a military dictatorship made the term *desaparecidos* tragically associated with the name *Argentina*. Lagging considerably behind the 1976–83 period in terms of the intensity of the crimes committed by the state (there were no massive disappearances) lie the years between 1946 and 1955, when the constitutionally elected government of Juan Perón systematically annulled civil liberties and violated constitutional rights to a very considerable extent.[1]

This chapter analyzes the U.S. drive to export democracy or human rights vis-à-vis Argentina during both of these periods, extending the treatment of the Perón regime to its military prelude of 1943–46.[2] Notwithstanding the enormous contextual differences between these periods, the comparison is worthwhile for six reasons:

1. During both periods, the U.S. government said, externally and internally, that it was promoting democracy and human rights in Argentina.

2. During both periods, U.S. policy was internally contradictory. Both periods can be subdivided into stages during which opposing U.S. policies prevailed. Furthermore, during the 1947–49 subperiod, as well as during the Carter years, the political dimension of policy was contradicted by its economic dimension.

3. During both periods, there was intense, sometimes uncontrolled ideological and bureaucratic competition within the U.S. government with respect to policy toward Argentina.

4. During both periods, U.S. policy not only was unsuccessful in its promotion of democracy but actually had unintended consequences of a negative character that further polarized an already deeply divided society.

5. During both periods, the sharp contradictions in U.S. policy were facilitated by Argentina's uncommon stature in U.S. foreign policy. Argentina is a country sufficiently large and visible as to give it some salience, internationally and domestically in the United States, yet is sufficiently marginal to the vital interests of the United States to allow ideological, bureaucratic, and even personality conflicts to play a much greater role than would be tolerated in more relevant policy arenas. Argentina is thus a perfect target for bureaucratic, ideological, and personal competitions. Less significant countries are less attractive for such frays, whereas the cost of policy errors or unintended policy consequences remains low in the Argentine case because of the country's relative irrelevance to the vital interests of the United States.

6. Last, both periods were lost opportunities for Wilsonianism. Precisely because of its relative irrelevance to the vital interests of the United States, Argentina is a country with respect to which the United States *could* afford to sacrifice pragmatism and devote itself almost exclusively to the promotion of democracy. However, despite these structural conditions, this opportunity was wasted because the pragmatists nevertheless competed with the idealists in the making of U.S. policy toward Argentina. Thus, not only were the opportunities for Wilsonianism frustrated, but they were translated into greater contradictions, with considerable counterproductive consequences from both an idealistic and a pragmatic point of view.

For each of these periods, I seek to analyze the courses, motives and degree of sincerity and coherence of the announced U.S. policy to promote Argentine democracy; to evaluate the instruments used by the United States; to assess the impact, intended and unintended, of U.S. policy; and to sketch some modest and tentative theoretical hypotheses with respect to the nature of the relations between the United States and a state such as Argentina.*

---

*An additional word should be said about the relative irrelevance of Argentina to the vital interests of the United States. Argentina is, by world standards, a medium-ranking country with a huge, underpopulated territory and a very considerable resource endowment in per capita terms. However, Argentina is and has been less important to the United States (at least in positive terms) than a good number of countries intrinsically far less important than it. Argentina's main source of wealth stems from its significance as a producer of temperate-climate foodstuffs, and the United States is the world's largest producer of such foodstuffs. The United States does not *need* Argentina economically (contrariwise to the case of Britain vis-à-vis the River Plate country before and during World War II). Technically speaking, the U.S. and the Argentine economies are competitive, not complementary. Argentina has at times become a nuisance to U.S. interests and an obstacle to the

The 1943–1955 Period

The period for 1943–55 can be divided into two main stages. The first, from 1943 to 1949, involved an intense boycott and efforts at destabilization, a policy that really began in 1942, while the constitutional government of Castillo was still in power. In contrast, the second stage, 1950–55, was characterized by the U.S. government's acknowledgment of the failure of its previous policies, and by a full-fledged effort to seduce Perón and make him a friend of the United States. In this second stage, the democratizing and human rights policies of the United States became basically rhetorical and ceased to be a real U.S. priority in Argentina.

The United States and Argentina during World War II

The story of U.S.-Argentine relations during most of the 1942–53 period is one of almost continuous diplomatic conflict.[3] It is also one in which extremely self-destructive Argentine policies can be seen side by side with extremely contradictory U.S. policies toward Argentina, setting in motion a most perverse dynamics in which the weaker party was necessarily the loser. The self-destructiveness of Argentine policies lay in the continuous defiance of U.S. policy objectives under circumstances in which no benefits could accrue to Argentina from such attitudes, and in which, indeed, great costs were almost guaranteed. The contradictory character of U.S. policy stemmed from acute bureaucratic and ideological conflict with respect to policy toward Argentina and led to activating and deactivating the democratization of Argentina as a U.S. policy objective, according both to the behavior of the Argentine government (vis-à-vis other U.S. policy objectives perceived as more important in the United States) and to changing priorities within the U.S. government.

---

pursuit of some U.S. policy objectives, but its importance to the United States has never arisen from being needed in a positive, tangible sense, for what it could provide, and its capacity for doing damage to the United States has been limited by its relative weakness and remoteness. Argentina does not produce any goods that have had, for the United States, the economic importance of Chilean copper, Venezuelan or Mexican oil, Brazilian rubber, or even Bolivian tin. Furthermore, Argentina is geographically remote. Mexican stability (a positive condition to be maintained) is much more important, for the United States, than Argentine stability. Moreover, Argentina could not be further from the center of the East-West conflict. For geostrategic reasons, during the cold war Turkey has been much more important to the United States than Argentina, although Turkey was less developed. Finally, Argentina does not have a crucially important accumulation of U.S. investments, as does Brazil. A U.S. policy error vis-à-vis Mexico, Brazil, Venezuela, or even Panama is of considerably more serious consequences to the United States than a policy error toward Argentina. This means that, in the making of policy toward Argentina, there is more room for bureaucratic conflict, contradictions, and even testing and experimentation. There is also an opportunity for Wilsonianism, which has been frustrated and perverted by the competing objectives of pragmatists. This chapter illustrates the point.

In 1942 Argentina had a constitutional government, albeit one flawed by electoral fraud. The country was traditionally isolationist, neutral with respect to world conflicts, and European-oriented in terms of its export trade and foreign policy. It had developed a tradition of diplomatic conflict with the United States, which went back all the way to 1889 and the first Pan American Conference. Nevertheless, almost two years before the Rio Conference of January 1942, in which the U.S. government would demand the support of the Latin American republics, Argentina had made a strong overture to the United States, suggesting that both countries abandon neutrality to support the Allies. The U.S. reply had been that this was unthinkable, that the United States was truly neutral, and that U.S. public opinion would disapprove such a measure, which would require an act of Congress. The Argentine government was advised not to abandon neutrality for the sake of "hemispheric unity." News of the Argentine proposal was leaked to the press, and this was a heavy blow to the democratic and Allied-oriented faction of the Argentine government.[4] When the time came for the United States to seek the support of Argentina, that support was not forthcoming, for reasons that are related to the country's traditional neutralism, to the altered balance-of-power within the government (which had been partly a product of the previous U.S. rebuff), and to a prestige-oriented attitude that was and still is characteristic of Argentine foreign policy (which appears to make it almost mandatory to answer haughtily to a rebuff).[5] In turn, Argentina's refusal to break relations with the Axis set off an intense diplomatic attack and economic boycott against that country by the U.S. government.[6]

In June 1943, the constitutional government of Argentina was overthrown, for reasons that were only partly a consequence of U.S. policy. Nevertheless, according to British sources, the U.S. embassy celebrated the coup as its own success, believing that it would lead to a rupture of Argentine relations with the Axis.[7] This was also the belief of the U.S. Board of Economic Warfare, which took steps to lift some of its discriminatory measures against Argentina.[8]

However, they were soon to be disappointed. As a consequence, Cordell Hull became obsessed with the conviction that the Argentine officials were Nazi agents aiming at the Nazification of the whole of South America. During the next two years, the continuous destabilization efforts waged against the military regime from the United States led to the successive ousting of the more moderate elements from the government, to the overthrow of its first military president, and finally to the democratic election of Colonel Perón.[9] Notwithstanding the fact that Argentina was a major supplier of meat, wheat, hydes, tungsten, and other vital raw materials to the Allies throughout the war, from 1942 to 1945 the U.S. government used virtually every available tactic except military attack to destabilize three Argentine governments and to force the nation to accept U.S. government directives in extrahemispheric affairs.[10] This was the result of a combination of ideological motivations, sphere-of-influence considerations, and chronically conflictive diplomatic relations. Despite the fact that the constitutional government had been overthrown partly as a consequence of U.S. policy, from that moment on the U.S. government acted in the name of democracy.[11] Concomitantly, the wildest claims were used to justify the hard line taken against Argentina, to the point that, in 1943, U.S. vice-president Henry Wallace declared that Germany considered World War II lost and was preparing Argentina for World War III.[12] The idea took flight and as late as 1945 a "Society for the Prevention of World War III" was advocating all-out measures against Argentina.[13]

Nevertheless, although the anti-Nazi element was always present, the fact remains that, during the first stage of the conflict, the constitutional government of Argentina was destabilized politically and economically boycotted because it did not respond to U.S. policy directives, whereas in the second stage of the conflict the fact that the government was a military dictatorship (which was partly a product of U.S. policy) was used as an additional reason for the desirability of destabilization and boycott. The attitude of the U.S. government during the brief period (only weeks) in which it thought that the military dictatorship would cooperate with its foreign policy—a period of celebration and of preparations to cooperate with the regime—shows on the other hand (and without a recourse to counterfactual reasoning) that had the dictatorship acquiesced with the State Department's policy, the nature of the regime would have been no obstacle to good relations. As will be seen later on, this pattern was identical to the one found in far less dire circumstances, the 1950–55 period, in which a "cold" war had replaced a very hot one.

On the other hand, that the essence of the post–1943 U.S. destabilization and boycott of Argentina was at least partly ideological, basically unrelated to the war effort, and (apparently) linked intrinsically to the U.S. drive to export democracy (and obliterate fascism) is clearly seen (among many other documents) in the State Department warning of September 1944, when it was stated that: "If that Fascist government survives the war our opposition to it will remain. We can give no assurances for the future of American investments there."[14] And these words are also witness to the intensity of the boycott: very rarely does the U.S. democratization drive reach the point of officially discouraging private investment.

This intensity is further illustrated by the "Export Policy I" of February 3, 1945: "Export of capital goods should be kept at present minimums. It is essential to prevent the expansion of Argentine heavy industry."[15] Even fuel was denied to Argentina—the British being pressed by the State Department to refrain from supplying it—with the explicit objective of either forcing major political concessions or overthrowing the government.[16]

This policy was basically an ideological crusade to export democracy and eliminate fascism. However, if compared with the U.S. attitude toward other fascist or quasi-fascist states not directly committed to the Axis camp, it was also a clear case of application of double standards. And though an ideological crusade it was, it also carried a pragmatic camouflage, insofar as Hull and others sold it to the White House with the argument that Argentina was a threat to the security of the Western Hemisphere and the United States itself. The assertion that World War III could come from Argentina if it was not subdued was such a gross exaggeration that this pragmatic rationale cannot be taken seriously in its own terms and must be considered as probably no more than a strong selling argument for a basically ideologically oriented policy.[17]

Nonetheless, and notwithstanding the extreme character of this rationale, this policy was not without sharp, unpredictable, albeit brief interruptions and contradictions. From approximately March to June 1945, Assistant Secretary Nelson Rockefeller was able to reverse it and begin a U.S.-Argentine rapprochement, which was abruptly put to an end by Ambassador Spruille Braden's renewed anti-Argentine crusade. This culminated in Rockefeller's resignation and Braden's promotion to the former's post. Bureaucratic and ideological conflict, not rational action, explains these counterproductive and harmful contradictions.

The Postwar Boycott of Argentina

The end of the war was not the end of the U.S. boycott of Argentina. Nor was the democratic election of the not-so-democratic colonel Perón the end of it. The first half of this period was characterized first by Braden's personal attacks against Perón, and after the latter's success and the former's promotion, by the internal battle between Braden and the new U.S. ambassador, George Messersmith. Braden's rationale was that the election of Perón could not really be deemed democratic, although there had been no direct fraud, because of the severe limitations placed on the opposition's electioneering: it had very little access to radio, it suffered press censorship, and its meetings were repeatedly attacked by hoodlums or fired upon by the police. In this respect, one can readily agree: Perón was no democrat. But in his "Memorandum on the Argentine situation" of mid-1946, Braden went into a frenzy that can only be understood as the exaggerations he thought necessary to continue selling his policy of boycott to his superiors in the State Department and the White House. He explicitly expounded on the possibility that "a southern bloc of nations led by a totalitarian Argentine state . . . would constitute a dangerous threat to our security in the event of war."[18]

On the other hand, Messersmith's opinion about Argentina could not have been more opposed to Braden's. In a memorandum to Secretary of State James Byrnes of late 1946, he complained bitterly about Braden's policy. Very much a pragmatist, he did not mention violations of human rights at all. Messersmith stated that the government was constitutional, and attacked the U.S. press for creating a hostile atmosphere toward Argentina and alienating Perón. And in a memorandum of January 1947 he went further, arguing that *not* selling arms to Argentina would generate a potential threat to U.S. security because of the arms race it would generate in European countries anxious to fill the vacuum left in the Argentine market.[19]

Messersmith finally had his way, insofar as relations with Argentina were normalized officially in early 1947, thus clearing the way for the Río Conference and its product, the Inter-American Treaty of Reciprocal Assistance. Braden turned in his resignation and Messersmith's mission in Argentina was declared "successfully terminated." Nevertheless, the U.S. government did not forget overnight the transgressions of the Perón regime. The State Department's Argentine Committee stressed that the methods utilized by Perón were reminiscent of fascist-falangist procedures. The committee mentioned the opposition of the Confederación de Trabajadores de America Latina (CTAL; the Confederation of Latin American Workers) to Perón-dominated labor unions, its condemnation of the Argentine government, and its admission of underground labor delegates from Argentina to its sessions. It also called the 1946 elections not free because of the suppression of the opposition press and organizations.[20]

Neither was the economic boycott interrupted, although official State Department policy called for the end of all discriminatory treatment of Argentina. The powerful Economic Cooperation Administration (ECA), which was in charge of the implementation of the Marshall Plan, set out from its very inception, intentionally and discriminatorily, to place obstacles to Argentina's export trade with Europe. This last episode of the economic boycott was ignored by the new U.S. ambassador, James Bruce, who was dismayed when minor ECA officials made public anti-Argentine statements. He then ordered a State Department investigation of ECA policy toward Argentina, which documented over thirty instances of direct discrimination against that country.[21]

Nevertheless, despite these sanctions, the affirmation of human rights in Argentina ceased to be a priority for the State Department. For example, in a memorandum of early January 1948, which is a typical period piece, the U.S. embassy appears to be making an apology of Perón. Chargé d'affaires Guy W. Ray defended the regime, saying that, although "civil liberties and the Constitution have suffered some severe shocks," Perón was not really the absolute dictator he was thought to be, that there was dissension within the party, and that congress "could not be described as completely subservient to the will of the President." In this and other documents of the 1947–50 period, the main problems analyzed with respect to U.S.-Argentine relations were clearly economic, in addition to the ratification of the Río Pact of 1947. Violations of human rights were acknowledged but had only a very minor impact on relations. According to the chargé Ray: "The mentality of most of the people in the present administration is such that we would waste our time by preaching principle to them. If we really want to accomplish something, we must make them see that certain advantages will accrue to Argentina under certain conditions."[22]

As will be seen later, these "certain conditions" would not be primarily related to the promotion of democracy but to the ratification of the Río Pact. Toward late 1948 the climate of U.S.-Argentine relations tended to deteriorate, due not so much to the state of human rights in Argentina but instead to the Perón regime's overall uncooperative attitude in foreign affairs. This attitude included intervention in the domestic affairs of other Latin American states; an intense anti–United States propaganda, which, increasingly, it began to disseminate both in Argentina and abroad through its labor attachés; and what Perón called the "third position"—that is, a policy of neutralism or ambiguity vis-à-vis the cold war. In a State Department memorandum listing issues to be discussed with the Argentine foreign minister, Atilio Bramuglia, and dated December 9, 1948, the first point relates to the charges of Argentine intervention in the affairs of neighboring states. Other priority points include Communism, the Río Pact (which Argentina had signed but not yet ratified), and the Antarctic. Point five was the only one related to human rights, and very conservative language is used therein: the U.S. government realized that freedom of the press in Argentina was a domestic affair, but it wished to point out "in a friendly way" that violations of that right created unfavorable publicity in the United States, thus generating "difficulties in our friendly relations."[23] The points related to the anti–United States propaganda of the Perón regime and to the "third position" would, on the other hand, become increasingly important in the coming months as factors of a deteriorating relationship. This is illustrated in similar memoranda produced on December 16 and February 10.[24]

It is thus clear that the explicit crusade for democracy ended in 1947, although the economic boycott, which was its main instrument, was not terminated—paradoxically—until more than two years later. From 1947 to 1949 we have a period in which the issue of human rights was a secondary State Department objective in the context of officially friendly and non-discriminatory relations, while a covert boycott continued at the ECA level, making U.S. policy toward Argentina the epitome of contradiction. In contrast, by 1950 all discrimination appears to have ceased, and U.S. policy concentrated basically on the seduction of Perón, in an attempt to make a friend out of this formerly loathed and much-besieged dictator.

The Quest for a Free Press and Free Labor Unions

The State Department Policy Statement for Argentina of March 21, 1950, is a cold-war–inspired document in which, notwithstanding the overriding interest of "obtaining Argentina's collaboration in the defense of the Western Hemisphere," the democratization of Argentina is mentioned twice in a brief list of four principal U.S. policy objectives toward that country.[25] Nevertheless, it is only necessary to read further on to be fully conscious of the limits set by U.S. policy to this quest, which was really a policy only at the rhetorical level:

> While it is our policy to attempt in every appropriate way to persuade the Argentine government to abandon its restrictions on civil liberties, the measures which the US can take to achieve this purpose are limited by its policy and international commitment not to intervene in the affairs of other states. Through diplomatic channels we have attempted to point out to Perón the advantages of a free press. He does not agree with our viewpoint.[26]

In truth, the principal concern of U.S. policy in 1950 was to bribe Argentina into ratifying the Río Pact, an entirely realistic objective considering its dire need of U.S. dollars (a consequence of a balance-of-payments crisis that had been *partly* generated by the ECA boycott).[27] The Argentine military was also greatly concerned about the South American balance of power, which had been altered during World War II in favor of Brazil, thanks to U.S. lend-lease equipment.[28] Ratification of the Río Pact meant qualifying for U.S. arms sales, and it also meant getting a badly needed Eximbank credit of $125 million, for the payment of commercial arrears.[29] When news of the Eximbank credit was released, the State Department started receiving loud complaints, both from U.S. and Latin American quarters. The chairman on Latin American affairs of the Congress of Industrial Organizations, Jacob S. Potofsky, wrote to the assistant secretary, Edward G. Miller, that: "The Perón dictatorship is opposed to everything we cherish. . . . It has imposed an atmosphere of fear, terror and suspicion on one of the great nations of South America. . . . Leaders of free labor are crushed, imprisoned or banished. . . . Ironically, the proposed loan from our great democracy will help tighten the iron grip of Perón upon the people of Argentina."[30] Miller's reply is enlightening: it warned that "over-zealousness respecting the political complexion of governments of other Western Hemisphere countries" would give "comfort and pleasure" to the enemies of the United States.[31]

Thus, the loan was authorized and the Río Pact ratified, but Perón disappointed the U.S. government by not being willing to send soldiers to Korea, by continuing to preach the "third position" (which was in theory contradictory with Argentina's newly acquired obligations under the Río Pact), and by increasing the pitch of his anti–United States propaganda. During 1951 and 1952, by far the foremost concern of U.S. policy toward Argentina was getting Perón to cooperate with "U.S. world objectives." On the other hand, Perón's measures were whimsical, and were greatly determined by his resentment of the frequent attacks against him made by the

U.S. press and labor.[32] Nevertheless, the U.S. government was always soothing and conciliatory, and intentionally avoided "placing Argentina in an embarrassing position."[33] This was the opposite of what had happened before 1947, when there had been no way of appeasing it.

In order to make this state of affairs intelligible, it must be noted that Perón's policy was highly ambiguous. For example, at one point in 1952, Perón made an emphatic public pronouncement to the effect that not one Argentine soldier would ever leave Argentine soil and that the country had not and would not sign any treaty that would require it to do so. At the same time, a high official of Argentina's defense establishment suggested to the Pentagon that his government might be interested in bilateral military conversations, and the foreign minister said he was delighted that Argentina should have accepted the Inter-American Defense Board's plan. An embassy official concluded: "How much method there is in this madness is yet to be determined."[34] The State Department had to choose whether to definitely alienate Perón or to attempt to seduce him, and it chose the latter course. On the other hand, neither was it being overly generous: after the 1950 Eximbank credit, no more relevant official U.S. government loans were disbursed during Perón's government,[35] and Argentina was not made eligible for grant military aid, as were several Latin American countries, including Brazil, Chile, and Uruguay.[36]

Nonetheless, two human rights issues increasingly annoyed the U.S. government: the lack of a free press and Perón's manipulation of the labor movement (which included his attempts to create a Peronist-oriented Latin American labor organization). The closing and later expropriation of *La Prensa* (depicted by the U.S. Embassy as "one of the great newspapers of the world") sent shock waves through the U.S. press and, therefore, through the State Department. The problem of a free press was placed as number one on a list of unfulfilled Argentine promises prepared by the Department on February 14, 1951, and the closing of *La Prensa* specifically was placed number three among "current problems," coming after the lack of Argentine cooperation against Communist aggression and the very frequent attacks on the United States by Argentina's official press.[37] On a list of unfavorable Argentine actions vis-à-vis the United States made a few days later, the closing of *La Prensa* was placed second.[38] Former U.S. ambassador Messersmith, who traveled to Buenos Aires in February 1951, preached the principle of a free press directly to Perón during a long conversation held on February 9.[39] And Assistant Secretary Miller stated publicly that his government was "finding it necessary to restrict its policy of cooperation" with Argentina, as a "possible effect of the closing of the newspaper *La Prensa*."[40]

It was a lot of fuss, no doubt, for the closing and expropriation of a newspaper, if we consider the context in which it was taking place. Restrictions of civil liberties and restraint of freedom of the press had been perpetrated since 1943 on a systematic basis. Men were imprisoned without trial and tortured into insanity. The opposition repeatedly read a long list of alleged political murders. By mid-1950, at least thirteen opposition periodicals had been closed down by the government.[41] *Time* and *Newsweek* had long been denied entry. All radio programs were censored for political content. U.S. citizens, including news correspondents, had been imprisoned on fictitious charges. The government had censored reports of foreign correspondents and some correspondents had been expelled. Speaking or writing disrespectfully of public officials was a crime (called *desacato*) subject to a penalty of three years in prison. Opposition representatives were ousted from the Argentine Congress for "disrespect" toward President Perón. At times the right to assembly was denied to opposition groups. Anti-Peronist judges had been removed. Telephone lines were tapped. Teachers had to propagate the Peronist faith or risk almost certain dismissal. Yet, as an embassy memo stated explicitly in June 1950: "Where attacks on civil liberties are clearly matters of Argentine domestic concern, we do not intervene."[42]

The case of *La Prensa* was different basically because this daily was the most important foreign client of the United Press and, according to a statement made by Perón to Ambassador Nufer, its (Argentine) owner was one of the main shareholders of this news agency. Two years after *La Prensa* was expropriated, Thomas Curran, United Press's vice-president and correspondent for South America, half-threatened Ambassador Nufer that the attitude of the U.S. press toward Perón would make U.S.-Argentine rapprochement very difficult unless *La Prensa* were restored to its rightful owners.[43] On the other hand, Nufer acknowledged to Perón that other dictators, such as Franco and Tito, were much better treated by the U.S. press, although he attributed this (before Perón) to the fact that they had given ample evidence of their desire to be friends of the United States, and that the U.S. public had become convinced that they were staunch U.S. allies against Soviet aggression.[44]

Thus, a very specific *material* interest and a very powerful lobby were behind this ideological appeal to civil liberties and the principles of Western civilization, in a context in which much more serious violations went by unnoticed in terms of their impact upon U.S.-Argentine relations. And—although to a lesser degree—the same was true of the only other human rights issue to which the U.S. government paid attention in terms of its policy objectives, which was that of Perón's domination of the labor movement.

State Department concern over this issue arose because of the bitter antagonism that had developed between U.S. and Argentine organized labor. U.S. unions had successfully created an inter-American federation, Organización Regional Interamericana de Trabajadores (ORIT), to neutralize the Communist-dominated Latin American federation, Confedera-

ción de Trabajadores de America Latina (CTAL), led by Lombardo Tole-
dano of Mexico. Argentina was not a member of either organization, dedi-
cating itself instead to proselyting activities with the objective of creating a
third, Peronist-oriented federation of Latin American labor, the Agrupación
de Trabajadores Latinoamericanos Sindicalistas (ATLAS).[45] The position
of U.S. organized labor was that Perón, as the dictator of a totalitarian state,
represented everything opposed by the democracies; that organized labor in
Argentina was completely dominated by the government; that democratic
trade union liberties had been wiped out; and that human rights in general
had been crushed. The U.S. unions had successfully barred Argentine membership in ORIT and in its predecessor, Confederación Interamericana de
Trabajadores (CIT, which had been organized in Lima in 1948). Argentina
had fought back by condemning CIT and ORIT as instruments of "Wall
Street capitalism." It had organized a corps of labor attachés appointed to
its embassies and used them to spread Peronist propaganda, successfully
creating Peronist-oriented groups in several countries, which were deemed
dangerous by U.S. labor.[46]

The war that ensued could not but have a strong impact on the State
Department: this second and last human rights issue, which was systematically listed by State Department papers in relation to policy objectives, was
also linked to a powerful U.S. lobby. Moreover, it was connected directly to
the political interests of U.S. policy insofar as those very same Argentine
labor attachés were actively dedicated to disseminating anti–United States
propaganda. Thus, not one of the post-1947 human rights concerns vis-à-
vis Argentina was "pure" or disinterested: they were a weapon used to
advance material interests in the context of a pragmatic policy, or else the
inevitable reaction to lobby pressures, rather than a true U.S. government
objective in and of itself.

The Instrumental Use of Principle

The stubbornly anti–United States character of Perón's policy and rhetoric, which (after the end of the boycott in 1949) was irrational insofar as it
could generate no benefit for Argentina, led to a deterioration of relations
and to a change of U.S. policy in 1952. Already in 1951 there were officials
advocating such a change. After much discussion, a meeting was held on
June 23, 1952, at the State Department, in which policy changes vis-à-vis
the Statement of October 1951 were agreed. It was decided to continue
with a "generally correct policy towards Argentina," but at the same time to
use every profitable opportunity to counter that country's anti–United
States propaganda and its "political penetration" of Latin America. It was
pointed out that the interest of Latin American countries should be aroused
to "the danger to them and to Latin American unity" present in Argentine
policies, each country being "encouraged to adopt its measures to oppose
Argentine penetration."[47]

ATLAS was the foremost example of "Argentine penetration." Another important case was Perón's projected economic unions with neighboring countries. An August 26, 1952, State Department memorandum to U.S. diplomatic officials in the other American republics set the line to be taken when dealing with local nationals. It instructed diplomats to subtly underline the ridiculousness of Argentina's bombastic claims about itself ("Argentina is, in fact, much less important economically, politically and militarily than her ego permits her to believe"), and to underscore how Ecuador had recently declared the Argentine ambassador persona non grata for interfering in internal affairs; how Panama had forced the withdrawal of the labor attaché; and yet other governments had placed Argentine diplomats under surveillance. In this very context, part of the suggested anti-Argentine line lay in emphasizing "principle," especially freedom of the press: "It behooves free men—and especially publishers and journalists, since their survival is directly involved—to defend the bases of freedom of information by repudiating falsified news and exposing its purveyors." In the terms of this line of argument, the dissemination of false news, the misrepresentation of news sources and datelines, and the subsidization of the unscrupulous news agency, Agencia Latina (which spread lies throughout the continent), were a serious threat that undermined the ethics of journalism, and thus "reinforced upon our shores the attack waged from behind the Iron Curtain upon our great Western institution of the free press."[48]

Clearly thus—in this instance—principle lay at the service of a U.S. policy that was pragmatically inspired: the ideological discourse was activated because the State Department had not only given up hope of getting Perón to cooperate with U.S. objectives but had also reached the conclusion that he would continue to be actively dedicated to attacking these objectives. Principle (democracy, civil liberties, and human rights) was not truly an objective end but basically an instrument at the service of other more self-interested ends. In 1950, principle had clearly been sacrificed for the sake of rapprochement. But rapprochement had failed due to the dictator's moods and whims. As a consequence, an active policy of thwarting "Argentine penetration" was adopted and, in this context, principle was again introduced in the discourse, as a part of a pragmatic strategy.

The Final Seduction of a Dictator

What happened next is something that no social scientist would ever have predicted, but that might have been foreseen by a wise and old-fashioned knower of men. General Dwight Eisenhower was elected president of the United States. Perón, in the recorded perception of most of the foreign diplomats who dealt with him, was a very sensitive man who "craved for recognition," was easily offended, took everything personally, and confused statesmanship with his private affairs.[49] Perón did not yet feel offended by

General Eisenhower, and as long as this remained the case, everything was possible. And Eisenhower decided to flatter him.

First, there was a message sent to Perón from John Foster Dulles. It was a routine statement with one key sentence: "Argentina and the United States are both recognized leaders (of the) American community."[50] Perón melted. According to Nufer's memorandum of conversation, he was unable to conceal his pleasure: "He actually flushed with pride and turned to (foreign minister) Remorino remarking, in effect, 'See what they think of us!'"[51] And three months later, Eisenhower sent his brother Milton on a goodwill trip to Latin America. Juan and Milton became buddies (or so Perón felt). And that was the end of Perón's enmity with the United States and his anti–United States policies. Immediately after the visit, Nufer described him as "anxious to reminisce" the event and "literally bubbling over with good will and enthusiasm." Perón now had, "for the first time, he said, the definite impression that the government of the United States was not ill-disposed toward his government and that there was, therefore, a real opportunity to improve relations."[52]

For the State Department, no better news could have come from Argentina. Already with Dulles's message to Perón, instructions to the ambassador had been issued that listed the obstacles to friendly relations with Argentina as: Argentina's neutralism (the "third position"); official and officially inspired Peronist attacks on the United States; apprehension of other Latin American countries that an eventual U.S.-Argentine rapprochement might affect their own friendship with the United States; Peronist actions against the free press and radio; and government control of Argentine labor. But the telegram made it clear that the last two points were domestic Argentine matters and that the United States was not in a position to insist on changes therein as a basis for official rapprochement.[53] Similarly, an embassy despatch dated July 31, 1953, states that "Argentina's form of government is of secondary importance to our purpose."[54] The same concept was repeated in the October 1953 instructions to U.S. diplomats in the Latin American region.[55]

The U.S. government was successful in keeping Perón's trust of its desire for friendly relations, despite continued U.S. press attacks. In order to attain this goal, Nufer went as far as to suggest that U.S. labor leaders should be indoctrinated with the department's view of Argentine realities vis-à-vis the United States, as a first step toward the generation of a more favorable public opinion toward that country. From there on, U.S.-Perón relations entered a long honeymoon, until his lamented overthrow in September 1955. Shortly before the coup, on April 4, 1955, the *New York Times* had said: "There is probably no phase of U.S. policy toward Latin America that has aroused so much controversy as the openly and strongly pro-Peronist attitude of the State Department and the U.S. Embassy in Buenos Aires." On March 10, 1955, the Eximbank had announced a credit for $60 million for a steel mill at San Nicolás (suspended because of the coup); on April 25, a contract for oil exploitation had been signed with the Standard Oil Company of California (annulled by the "provisional government" of Argentina immediately after the coup); and on June 7 the "Atoms for Peace" agreement between Argentina and the United States had also been signed.[56]

Thus, what until 1947 had been a clear and forceful antifascist policy of the United States government vis-à-vis the Argentine regime, and what from that year until 1949 had been a mixed policy of apparent collaboration with a covert economic boycott, had by 1955 become a policy of pragmatic support for a regime that was no more democratic than it had ever been. In order to arrive to this point, Perón's harassment of the United States had first to be checked. But the U.S. decision to attempt to seduce Perón was taken long before the latter's change of attitude. U.S. policy vis-à-vis Perón changed before Perón's policy vis-à-vis the United States. And the former change was not the product of success in the democratization of Argentina but rather quite the contrary. It was the result of the experience-generated conviction that the country could not be made democratic through external pressure, plus the activation of a cold war logic that made quasi-fascist regimes less undesirable from a pragmatic point of view.

The 1976–1983 Period

In 1955 a military government took over, outlawing the Peronist party. During the following eighteen years, this majority yet authoritarian party was proscribed. As a consequence, there was no real democracy. At least partly as a result of this, the civilian governments of Frondizi and Illía were overthrown by the military with the excuse that they were not really legitimate after all, and a leftist guerrilla movement was born and prospered, until finally Perón was allowed to return to electoral politics and his party won the elections of 1973 with an overwhelming popular vote. Violence escalated, with terrorist bombings and kidnappings both on the side of the leftist guerrillas and the paramilitary organization of the "Triple A," mounted by the Peronist regime. Finally, the military took over once again in March 1976, unleashing a repression with systematic abductions, tortures, and murders of not only guerrilla members but also their associates and suspected associates, a condition that, under circumstances of absolute lack of accountability, could apply to almost anyone. How did this situation affect U.S.-Argentine relations? Was the U.S. democratization drive vis-à-vis Argentina subject to similar contradictions during the 1976–83 period as during the 1943–55 years, or was it more consistent and efficient with respect to its professed objectives?

As in the case of 1943–55, the 1976–83 period can also be divided into stages from the point of view of U.S. human rights policy. In this case, however, the stages were determined by the changes in the U.S. administration. The differences between Ford, Carter, and Reagan were much more marked, with respect to the subject under study, than those between Truman and Eisenhower. Thus, March–December 1976, 1977–80, and 1981–83 are the main stages, from the point of view of U.S. human rights policy. But the Reagan period (which from the wider perspective of U.S.-Argentine relations must be divided into pre- and post–Falkland war subperiods) was, in terms of human rights policy, merely a stage of dismantlement. It was characterized by the ideological distinction between "authoritarian" and "totalitarian" regimes (the latter being, in actual practice, only the U.S.S.R. and its allies), and it was marked by the U.S. administration's political efforts to recuperate its "true" friends, in a way similar to the post-1950 efforts to seduce Perón (which proved to be a far more difficult objective than the "recuperation" of the previously "misunderstood" dictatorship of 1976–83). In truth, the military junta was so easily and rapidly seduced that the Reagan period, until the Falkland war, resembled more the post-1953—that is, post seduction—phase of U.S.-Argentine relations in the earlier period than it did the difficult and tortuous 1950–53 process that I have described. The Reagan dismantlement of the human rights policy appears to have been basically a U.S. domestic affair that can be followed largely through congressional hearings; its impact, at least vis-à-vis Argentina, was almost immediate, so there is little to say about it except that the junta was delighted from the very start. Thus, I will concentrate on the Carter years, with only brief references, when relevant, to the process of dismantlement during the Reagan subperiod.

Briefly summarized, conventional wisdom claims that after a pragmatic Ford prelude, the Wilsonian spirit prevailed during the Carter period, while Reagan sacrificed principle to security interests, befriending the military regime until its bewildering attack on the Falkland Islands made the U.S. government think twice about what its true interests vis-à-vis such an unpredictable regime really were. This story, however, is only partly true. Vis-à-vis Argentina there is both a reality and a myth with respect to the Carter policy.

The Story That Has Been Told

During the 1976–80 period, human rights abuses were the most important (albeit not the only) cause of tension between Argentina and the United States; dealing with the issue brought out the most intense passions. Nevertheless, the first stage of this period was simply a brief interlude during which the Ford administration adopted a policy of discreet but firm approval of the new dictatorship. There were warnings against violations of human rights, but Videla's promises were taken at face value and the administration recommended $49 million in military aid for the fiscal year 1977.[57]

However, as soon as Jimmy Carter was inaugurated, Patricia Derian was appointed head of the new Office of Human Rights of the State Department, and Argentina was singled out for special treatment as a human rights violator that was devoid of the strategic relevance of Iran or South Korea. Nonetheless, there were signs of intense ideological and bureaucratic competition throughout the period. Ford's ambassador to Buenos Aires, Robert C. Hill, was only replaced in August 1977, and publicly pronounced himself against the human rights policy on at least two occasions before that date.[58] Terence Todman's appointment as assistant secretary for inter-American affairs, in mid-1977, was perceived by the Argentine dictatorship as a welcome success of the U.S. diplomatic establishment vis-à-vis the liberal sector of Carter's team.[59] Likewise, Todman's 1978 replacement, after a public pronouncement against the human rights policy, spelled bad news for the regime. Meanwhile, Derian had been making public statements about human rights in Argentina that made the headlines in Buenos Aires, and Secretary of State Cyrus Vance had announced the curtailment of military aid to Argentina on account of human rights violations.[60]

Vance's declaration was followed immediately by a nationalistic reaction in Argentina. On March 1, 1977, the junta announced that it would reject all U.S. aid linked to the observance of human rights. This rejection underscored a deeper reality: the effect of the military aid curtailment had been to unite the dominant political elite in Argentina, rallying it in the defense of national autonomy and sovereignty. As J. S. Tulchin remarks in his recently published book, Videla was successful stacking his nationalist chips on this issue. Interviews by Tulchin bring out the fact that, by the end of the Carter administration, the professionals in the State Department believed that increasing public pressure on the Argentine government did not necessarily produce the desired results.[61]

The most critical moment in U.S.-Argentine relations during this period, however, came when an Eximbank guarantee for the financing of hydroelectric turbines was vetoed by the State Department on the grounds of human rights abuses. This decision was the consequence of an early 1978 agreement between Deputy Secretary of State Cristopher and Eximbank's President Moore to suspend Eximbank activity in Argentina.[62] As soon as the veto was announced, however, there was an avalanche of lobby pressures. The president of the U.S. firm that was to sell the turbines said that 18 million working hours for U.S. laborers were at stake. Gen. Gordon Summers, former president of the Inter-American Defense Board, said before a House subcommittee that only the Communists would profit from such a policy. The vice-president of the Association of U.S. Chambers of Commerce in Latin America stated that the policy would cost the United States from $2.5 to $5 billion, and that $1.25 billion in exports would be lost in Argentina alone: only U.S. firms would be penalized by the U.S. human rights policy. Thus, although it is impossible to ascertain that the veto's later reversal was exclusively the product of these pressures, that reversal cannot be considered surprising.[63] Eximbank continued operating with Argentina. And perhaps as a consequence of that frustrated attempt, Carter's human rights policy toward Argentina never had an economic-sanctions dimension. The popularity of Argentina's economics minister, José Martínez de Hoz, with U.S. business and with the Treasury Department, probably also had an impact on this result: after all, the Treasury is less politically minded than the State Department, and the minister, who had many influential friends, engaged in almost permanent lobbying in Washington.

Nevertheless, one aspect of U.S. economic policy toward Argentina that was related to human rights was widely publicized and attracted a great deal of attention. Legislation was enacted to the effect that U.S. representatives at the multilateral development banks (MDBs) would vote against credits to countries that engaged "in a consistent pattern of gross violations of human rights." As a consequence, the September 1981 issue of the periodical *Update,* edited by the Washington Office on Latin America, published an article sensationalistically titled "Argentina Today: Coming Apart," in which it was stated that, of the thirty-two credits applied for by Argentina to the World Bank and the Inter-American Development Bank (IDB) between 1976 and 1980, twenty-eight had been rejected by representatives of the Carter administration.[64] This was interpreted by most scholars who wrote on U.S. policy toward Argentina to mean that a "*de facto* 'stop' to all credits from the international financial institutions (IDB and World Bank)" had been placed by the United States against Argentina.[65] The notion that the Carter administration had effectively vetoed credits from the MDBs to Argentina became the conventional wisdom on the subject, unquestioned by scholars, and thus it is that, successively, Jorge I. Domínguez (1982), W. Grabendorff (1982), R. Russell (1987), and A. Vacs (1988) disseminated this false information in papers and publications.[66]

It should be very clear that I am not trying to pick holes in my colleagues' pioneering and useful work (from which I have profited so much) but simply to show just how successful the Carter administration was in projecting for itself a human rights crusading image, which (as will be seen) was largely contradicted by its economic policy. Most specialized scholars were impressed by the Carter policy because it was perceived to discriminate against the Argentine dictatorship not only in terms of military equipment but also in such effective economic terms as would be implied by a "*de facto*" veto to MDB credits. This was sadly not true. The Carter administration's efforts to promote the cause of human rights in Argentina were always overrated. Carter's policy, however vocal it may have been and however it may have offended the military junta, was basically focused on a diplomatic level, with such publicity that it resembled more a public relations campaign than a serious exercise of pressure on an Argentine dictatorship, which reacted nationalistically against the campaigns, rallying with it most rightist and right-of-center forces.

The Story That Has Not Been Told

If we refer to the Congressional hearings in which the Reagan administration was attempting to justify its unilateral decision to put a stop to the U.S. representatives' vote against credits for human rights abuses at the MDBs, we get a very different picture of this publicized but ineffective policy. For example, on July 21, 1981, Ernest B. Johnson, Jr., the senior deputy assistant secretary of state for economic and business affairs, declared to a House subcommittee that: "In recent years the United States voted negatively or abstained on 118 loans to 15 countries because of human rights concerns. On no occasion have we received sufficient support from other countries to prevent a loan."[67] And if we refer to the State Department data sheet presented together with the statement by the under secretary of state for economic affairs, Myer Rashish, before the Joint Economic Committee on July 14, we can determine the amount of aid to Argentina from the MDBs during the years 1978, 1979, and 1980:

	1978	1979	1980
	(in millions of dollars)		
IBRD (World Bank)	165.0	96.0	237.0
IFC	27.0	6.0	15.0
IBD	356.2	280.7	232.2

When we place these figures in the context of the total assistance received by Argentina from these sources, from their inception until 1980—that is, during their entire history—we get the full picture:

	(in millions of dollars)
Total IBRD	1239.4
Total IFC	108.1
Total IDB	1893.5

We thus come to the somewhat shocking conclusion that it was (partly) thanks to an MDB policy that was awarding Argentina, in three years, 50.2 percent of what the World Bank had awarded it in its entire history, 44.4 percent of what IFC had awarded it since its inception, and 46.9 percent of what the IDB had awarded it during its history, that the regime was to "fall apart." Even allowing for inflation, these are historically disproportionate figures. And although it is true that the United States had only 18 percent of the voting power of the World Bank (to take the least favorable example), it is also true that the industrialized "first world" summed 62 percent of that voting power, so to say the least, the lobbying efforts displayed by the U.S. representatives were not impressive. This is even more the case for the IDB. It must be borne in mind that even though the European and Latin American countries may not share the United States' inclination to defend human rights, neither were they inclined, in principle, to give the Videla dictatorship a disproportionate amount of money.

The same State Department data sheet presented Eximbank credits authorized to Argentina as $27.4 million in 1978, $32.7 million in 1979, and $79.2 million in 1980.[68] This leads us to a crucial point, and that is that normal Eximbank activity continued in Argentina throughout the Carter years, a fact that was also obscured by the publicity given to the human rights policy, which also misled scholars on this score. There is no sign of a human rights policy in terms of U.S. government credits, which remained at more or less the same level through the military regime on to the democratic government established in December 1983. Treasury Department statistics reveal, for example, that on June 30, 1975 (nine months before the coup) the outstanding principal indebtedness of Argentina on U.S. government credits amounted to $335.9 million, while on June 30, 1979 (well into the Carter period) it was equal to $339.9 million, and on June 30, 1985 (one and a half years after Alfonsín had taken over) it summed $337 million. Dictatorship and democracy made absolutely no difference in terms of this instrument of U.S. government economic support.

The same Treasury Department data show, on the other hand, that U.S. government guarantees for credits, as well as investment support insurance to Argentina, were at a very high level during those years, and indeed reached a record peak in September 1980. Moreover, Argentina occupied a highly privileged position worldwide in terms of such U.S. government contingent liabilities. On March 31, 1979, for example, the ranking of the most privileged countries was as follows: Republic of Korea, Brazil, Israel, Taiwan, Philippines, Mexico, Argentina. On the same date, Argentina was getting approximately one-seventeenth of total U.S. government contingent liabilities in foreign countries worldwide, a very important share of this type of U.S. government assistance, and one of the *least visible* types of assistance granted by that government. Yet the publicity given to the human rights policy was so successful that in his recent study on U.S.-Argentine relations during the junta's dictatorship, M. Falcoff states point-blank that "the United States refused Export-Import Bank financing for Argentine purchases in the United States."[69]

The issue of the visibility of different types of U.S. government foreign assistance is, I think, of some relevance. The assistance given under such programs as the Agricultural Trade Development and Assistance Act, the Foreign Assistance Act (and related acts), and the Commodity Credit Corporation has a high degree of visibility. Eximbank credits are less visible. Despite the fact that the Eximbank is included in the yearly foreign assistance acts (and its activity is thus rightly acknowledged as having a foreign assistance dimension), Congress only sets limits to total worldwide amounts, and generally does not intrude in Eximbank's lending or guarantee-awarding decisions. Partly as a consequence, Eximbank assistance is not included in such comprehensive publications as the Congressional Research Service (CRS) Report for Congress on U.S. foreign aid programs,[70] and the figures there printed are absolutely misleading. And Eximbank guarantees are far less visible than Eximbank credits: they are as good as a credit, but they are not listed anywhere except in highly specialized Treasury microfiche publications. The same is true for Overseas Private Investment Corporation (OPIC) Investment Support insurance. It is not secret, to be sure, but its visibility is sufficiently low as to let an administration get away with publicly chastising a foreign government while giving it economic support of a kind that usually goes by unnoticed without generating negative reactions or a public awareness of a contradiction in policy. Thus it is that while in June 1979 the ratio of outstanding U.S. government credits vis-à-vis contingent liabilities—that is, guarantees and investment insurance—worldwide was 47:13, the ratio of credits to Argentina versus contingent liabilities in that country was 340:472; there was more support in terms of the less visible contingent liabilities than in terms of the more visible credits (Table 5.1). I am not saying that this was a conscious U.S. government tactic designed for deceiving the public. I am only stating that the normal ratio of more visible aid to less visible aid was inverted in the case of Argentina and that, as a consequence, the public tended to get the wrong impression with respect to U.S. government policy toward the country.

The relevance of this ratio for the measurement of what could be labeled the "rhetoric factor" in a human rights policy comes out clearly again when we look at the figures for Chile, where during the Carter years we find a rapidly decreasing credit indebtedness while the contingent liabilities held their own and did not suffer the impact of the righteous wrath of Carter's policy—as a matter of fact, U.S. government contingent liabilities to Chile went up from $128.3 million in December 1979 to $337.4 million in March 1980, illustrating that it was the visible sanctions that counted for the Carter administration. Most of this increase in the Carter administration's economic support of Pinochet came by way of the OPIC-Investment Support program, which from only four operations in Chile in December was upgraded to twelve operations by March. Indeed, the economic data seem to yell out loud that it was not human rights violations that the U.S. government castigated, nor was democracy what it supported. It is very obvious that U.S. government contingent liabilities in Argentina fell drastically with the Falkland Islands war, and that the reestablishment of democracy did nothing to reverse that trend: by December 1986, U.S. government contingent liabilities in Alfonsín's Argentina had sunk to $39 million, while those for Pinochet's Chile had ballooned to $660 million.

Table 5.1 Comparison of U.S. Aid to Argentina in the Form of Credits and Contingent Liabilities

Argentina	Outstanding Long-term Principal Indebtedness on U.S. Government Credits	Contingent Liabilities of U.S. Government
	(in millions of dollars)	
June 30, 1975	335.9	—
September 30, 1977	357.1	—
December 31, 1977	—	550.2
June 30, 1978	—	523.0
September 30, 1978	365.6	504.8
March 31, 1979	—	490.9
June 30, 1979	339.9	472.3
September 30, 1979	—	479.0
December 31, 1979	322.4	469.0
March 31, 1980	322.4	497.4
June 30, 1980	300.4	548.4
September 30, 1980	295.4	575.6
December 31, 1980	292.4	536.3
March 31, 1981	285.4	472.9
June 30, 1981	278.2	442.0
September 30, 1981	279.0	459.1
March 31, 1982	280.0	425.6
September 30, 1982	284.5	306.8
December 31, 1982	296.8	258.3
June 30, 1983	315.1	208.8
September 30, 1983	319.2	156.5
December 31, 1983	322.8	119.4
December 31, 1984	339.0	78.0
June 30, 1985	337.0	—
December 31, 1985	—	45.0
December 31, 1986	437.0	39.0

Sources: See n. 69.

Finally, another important and indeed complementary piece of data is that, in 1980, Argentina was listed as one of the "principal beneficiaries" of the U.S. Generalized System of Preferences (GSP) and exported to the United States a total of $231 million that entered the country duty free. Surely *this* was not done to protect an eroding U.S. trade balance, as the rationale for not tampering with U.S. export credits and guarantees claimed in relation with Eximbank operations in countries where human rights were being abused. With a GSP product list subject to negotiation, and country eligibility dependent upon the U.S. president's authority to "withdraw, suspend or limit duty-free treatment," the place of relative privilege reached by Argentina in 1980 implied at least a sin of omission. And the Argentine regime was grateful. According to the *Report to the Congress in the first five years operation of the U.S. Generalized System of Preferences,* "Many beneficiary countries cited examples of major export expansion as a result of GSP. Such was the case of Argentina, Brazil," and so on. Indeed, during the Carter years Argentina's duty-free GSP exports, in millions of dollars, showed a promising trend:[71]

1976	$72
1977	$77
1978	$148
1979	$102
1980	$231

Once again, this was economic support with a low degree of visibility. Thus, policy toward the Argentine dictatorship during the Carter years was, to say the least, contradictory. Contradictions were not limited to State Department policy, but were much more marked when considering the contrast between that policy and U.S. commercial and financial policy. The Treasury, at best, promoted Argentine economic policies perceived as sound, while the liberal wing of the State Department promoted democracy with very feeble means.

But the human rights campaign of 1977–80 did exist, it was very loud, it generated a great deal of diplomatic tension between the U.S. and the Argentine governments, and every informed person in the world knew of the bloodshed that was taking place in Argentina. The contradiction is clear, and it is also clear that the economic support that Argentina was in fact receiving from the U.S. government was not widely publicized, and that what *was* publicized loudly was the negative vote of the U.S. representatives to the MDBs, while its utter ineffectiveness was never at all mentioned in the relevant media or in academic papers.

With the sole purpose of fully illustrating the negative consequences of these contradictions, let us for one moment imagine being given the task of engineering long-term conditions for dividing a society. In that case, the best possible strategy might well be to:

1. Feed right-of-center public opinion with:

    a. a rally-round-the-flag mystique produced by what they perceive as offensive intromission in the country's domestic affairs, and

    b. a feeling of economic contentment with approval of the regime, through little publicized U.S. government credits, guarantees and investment insurance, MDB credits, privileged GSP treatment, and massive private funding.

2. Feed left-of-center public opinion concomitantly with an intense resentment and hatred of the regime, through loud public denunciations of its savage violations of human rights (which are basically against the political left), thus further concealing the unpublicized economic support of the regime.

This is precisely what appears to have happened during the Carter years. Needless to say, there was no such brilliant engineer of destruction. The aggregate policy, which was contradictory and divisive, was not the responsibility of the liberals who desired to defend the cause of human rights. Neither was it the responsibility of the conservatives who were not willing to let the cause of human rights overshadow the security and economic interests of the United States. Rather, it was the unintended consequence of the dynamics generated by the competition between generous liberals and pragmatic conservatives. Basically, it appears to have been the perverse product of uncontrolled bureaucratic competition and internal (U.S.) political and ideological conflict in a policy arena that is objectively of only secondary importance to the vital interests of the United States.

But the problem was very serious indeed, and the additional polarization that the phenomenon produced in a society that was already deeply divided cannot be determined yet should not be underestimated. In his recent book, J. S. Tulchin states that "certainly until 1980, the majority of the Argentine people was disposed to accept the . . . regime, with its horrible repression, as the best possible alternative. For the acquiescent majority, external pressure on their government prompted a hostile reaction and self-defense."[72]

Tulchin's perception is not the product of secret sympathies with a bloodthirsty regime, but the personal, finely tuned intuition of someone who knew the country well at a time in which taxi drivers used stickers on their windshields with the slogan *"los argentinos somos derechos y humanos."*[73] His perception is to some extent verified by the public opinion data of the period. Unfortunately, the only data available are related to public perceptions of the economic situation. I have had access to the Gallup archive, which shows that in March 1980, approximately 64 percent of the population considered that living standards were *stable or rising,* while 62 percent considered that the family economy was in *equal or better* shape than in the previous year. What is more impressive, however, is that, in 1980, 67 percent considered their incomes sufficient for their basic needs. There are no data for the years immediately following 1980, but the question has been taken up on a yearly basis since 1985.[74] Not once during the democratic government did public opinion approve of the economic situation as it did in March 1980, and the only instance in which public approval rose above 50 percent during the later years corresponded to the high expectations generated by the then-recent launching of the Austral plan. This does not, of course, demonstrate political approval (for which we have no data), but on that point Tulchin's perception seems quite correct to me, and these data do not contradict it.

To what extent was this public approval (at least at an economic level) of the human rights–violating regime a consequence of U.S. economic support? It surely cannot be determined, but there is a good probability that U.S. policy had something to do with it. And this surely must have polarized public opinion to a dangerous degree, because while this unpublicized but significant economic support was taking place, a very noisy campaign that publicized the atrocities being committed by the regime was also being carried out by the very same U.S. government. If one makes contact with Argentine society today, one will find that there is a significant segment of the population who hates the military (for obvious reasons). Concomitantly, there is another segment of the population, also significant and permanently influential, who has a widespread hatred of all those who hate the military. This is so partly because they care not a fig about the victims of the so-called dirty war, and they remember the well-being that they enjoyed during the dictatorship, which, as Tulchin says, was for an extended period of time one long shopping spree. The impact of this sort of policy contradiction cannot but be divisive. Just *how* divisive, however, is another question. We can identify the (negative) direction of the impact of these U.S. policy contradictions, firmly asserting that they do not good but harm to the societies affected by them. But this negative impact cannot be quantified. We can assert that the Carter administration helped to make Pinochet popular among the economic beneficiaries of his regime, but we cannot even guess with respect to what part of the 43 percent of favorable votes he got in the referendum is attributable to U.S. policy, or what part of the votes *against* him were the product of the liberal dimension of that very same, contradictory U.S. government policy. If we could, we would know precisely just what segments of Chilean society have been pitted against each other by the U.S. government. *This proportion may not be overwhelming, but that is not the point. The point is that harm is being done.* And if that (unmeasurable) proportion should be greater than, say, 10 percent, it would be a variable that no econometrician would ever reject from his model with contempt: that 10 percent can be crucial to scientific explanation. So the point, once again, is not to suggest that domestic variables are not the main factors in explaining political polarization in societies such as Argentina and Chile, but to show that external variables—and in this case, U.S. policy contradictions—are a factor that should not be excluded from attempts at explanation.

Finally, a comment is due on the widespread belief that the Carter human rights policy contributed to the weakening of the military regime and to the eventual democratization of Argentina. As has already been suggested in Tulchin's citation, it would appear that this policy, rather than weaken the regime, generated a rally-round-the-flag, nationalistic effect that strengthened it momentarily. It was later weakened by its economic failures, and it eventually collapsed because of the Falkland debacle. The 1983 democratization was much more related to defeat in war than to the human rights policy. Nonetheless, one important positive consequence of this otherwise ineffective and oft-betrayed policy lies in the long-term and cannot be ignored: Carter's policy did not *then* weaken the military, but it does *now* retrospectively deter them, to some degree and for the time being, from new authoritarian political adventures. Here, at last, is a positive effect. It is also yet another largely unintended effect, perhaps the ultimate proof that we cannot engineer history.

Conclusions

It is needless to say that there was nothing in Carter's human rights policy to equate it even remotely with Hull's zeal. Hull had directly and successfully discouraged U.S. private investments, and had applied the strongest available economic sanctions. Whatever may have inspired him (his missionary interventionism or his hatred of Argentina), it was truly a Wilsonian policy and not merely the Wilsonian dimension of a juxtaposed contradiction that included U.S. government support side by side with the loud condemnations. Hull had gone all the way: he even modified the South American balance of power in favor of Brazil and against Argentina, for reasons unrelated to World War II.[75] Nevertheless, despite these differences, if we turn not to Hull's subperiod but to the whole of the 1943–55 period, we find a striking similarity of patterns with the 1976–83 period. With the exception of the 1947–49 subperiod, contradictory policies were not juxtaposed, but this is not to say that there were no contradictions, which came in the way of contradictory stages. In fact, the analysis of the 1943–55 years is very complex because of the many subperiods and contradictions involved. U.S. policy toward Argentina was always laden with intense bureaucratic and ideological conflict from 1942 onward. Although (with the important exception of Rockefeller in 1945) the hard line usually won until 1947, the contradictory signals produced served only to divide Argentine society. Sumner Welles catered to moderates, Cordell Hull catered to tough anti-government elements; Nelson Rockefeller catered to moderates, Spruille Braden to recalcitrant anti-Peronists; George Messersmith catered to moderates and to Perón himself. Finally, Braden and Messersmith clashed. Messersmith apparently won, relations were normalized, but the economic boycott continued through ECA at a covert level, finally ending in 1949. This was all the product of the conflict of those who, in the name of democracy, wanted the government overthrown, and those who, in the name of pragmatism, wanted to befriend first the military regime and then Perón, the popular dictator.

By 1950, the crusade had ended. Thereafter, the aim of the U.S. government was to get Perón to cooperate. After 1949, the democratization rhetoric was activated when it seemed that Perón would not cooperate, and deactivated when it appeared that maybe he would come around. During this period, also, human rights and civil liberties issues that were highlighted by the State Department (sometimes only for internal consumption) were basically issues in which the interests of an important U.S. lobby were at stake. When, in 1953, Perón finally did become a friend, the democratization rhetoric was definitely deactivated. By 1955, when he was overthrown, the U.S. government was Perón's best friend. But U.S. policy had shaken the Argentine polity, as a city would be shaken by an earthquake, ever since 1942.

During a great part of this period, men like Hull and Braden had resorted to lies and exaggerations (such as claiming that World War III could eventually come from Argentina if it was not subdued) in order to sell their policies to the White House, and indeed let very personal factors blind them with respect to policy (Sumner Welles's judgment of Hull's "psychopathic" bias against Argentina should here be recalled).[76] One has the feeling that the overthrowal of a dictator had become a sort of sport for them, and that every lie was valid if it helped to convince their superiors, and every measure, no matter how counterproductive in terms of their own professed objectives, was legitimate. And so it is that during the 1942–45 period Argentina was driven, through offensive State Department and U.S. Board of Economic Warfare measures, into an increasingly unfriendly attitude, and this they did not seem to care about: it gave them more opportunities for muscle flexing. After all, although their rhetoric claimed quite the opposite, rationality in policy toward Argentina was far from being vitally important to the interests of the United States.

To these essentially counterproductive but consistent tactics, we must add the comparatively pro-Argentine policies represented by the Rockefellers and the Messersmiths of this tale, which so blatantly contradicted the former policies. Overall, I think that it is clear that, during the 1943–55 period, the U.S. drive to export democracy to Argentina operated in a direction that was contrary to its professed objective, destroying whatever remnants of stability remained in the Argentine political system and polarizing

Argentine society. Although I cannot prove it, it appears to me that, after such a process, making amends with the dictator *also* fed back into instability: we must bear in mind the destructive consequences of the agony of a regime, an agony that is the product of erratic doses of destabilizing measures *and their combination with local political forces*. And there are times (such as the case being treated here) when the regime survives the agony, with a painfully divided society, and then the U.S. government, despairing of overthrowing the dictator or even of reforming him, attempts to become his friend. This was the case of Argentina both after 1950 and after 1980. In the first case the change of heart was produced within the same U.S. administration; in the second, it came with a change of administration. But for all practical purposes, it was the same thing, and it amounted to the application of a sound pragmatic principle: "if you can't beat him, join him." Its effects upon Argentina, however, could not be more perverse: it cannot presume of idealism. I think that it is very clear that those perverse dynamics were allowed to operate unchecked basically because, in both periods and, indeed, always, Argentina was (and still is) a country that is relatively irrelevant to the vital interests of the United States.

Comparisons between such different historical contexts should not, of course, be stressed excessively. The world of the 1940s was very different from that of the 1970s, and although Argentine power was very much exaggerated by Hull and Braden, in the 1940s Argentina was a country to be taken seriously from the point of view of its overall significance (despite its very secondary importance for U.S. interests), whereas in the late 1970s it had already become the petty state it now is. This may go a long way toward explaining why, despite the similarity of patterns I have described, there were such major differences in U.S. economic policy toward Argentina during the two periods under study. In a way, the contradiction seems wilder during the Carter years, a period in which violations of human rights in Argentina were much more serious than during the 1943–55 years: the Carter administration's loud condemnations of human rights abuses not only came together with considerable U.S. government support, but with the most massive influx of private U.S. funds ever received by Argentina. This money, if competently invested, could have laid the bases for a much more sound economy, consolidating the regime. And although the private funds were part of a worldwide phenomenon at a time of overabundance of money supply, there was clearly no government attempt to discourage the flow of private capital; on the contrary, the existence of U.S. government economic support was an incentive for the U.S. private sector to invest in Argentina. That the money was ill-used is another quite independent affair. All things considered, it was a time in which Argentina was economically promoted. This was very different from the 1943–55 period, which were years during which the Argentine economy was never promoted by the U.S. government or by the U.S. private sector; the most the pragmatists could do, when they got the upper hand in shaping government policy, was to interrupt the boycott.

Despite these major differences, when viewed in comparative perspective the similarity of patterns between the 1943–55 and the 1976–83 periods is striking.

1. In both cases we find that during the first stages—while there was a real democratization or human rights drive in U.S. policy—there was intense bureaucratic and ideological competition within the U.S. decision-making process.

2. In both cases, aggressive U.S. pressures generated counterproductive nationalism, encouraging neutralism and, indeed, pushing Argentina closer to the Axis in 1943–44, just as they rallied the opinion of Argentina's dominant elite in support of the junta in 1977–80.

3. In both cases, disappointment with the democratization policy led to U.S. government attempts to seduce the culprits in question—that is, to a counterpolicy that sowed confusion in Argentina.

4. Finally, in both cases, the many contradictions in U.S. government policy had perverse unintended consequences that were basically contrary to the professed objectives of both conflicting sectors of U.S. government and society.

Indeed, in both cases, the *overall* policy of the United States—that is, the aggregate that includes both the democratization drive *and* its pragmatically oriented counterpart—if analyzed as if it came from a rational actor, in which consideration of the bureaucratic and ideological competition known to have taken place is excluded, seems almost designed to generate internal conflict in Argentina.

This statement is more than sensationalistic. It points to a political scientific hypothesis that cannot be demonstrated here, given the data I have presented, but only suggested as possible: given a country that is relatively irrelevant to the vital interests of the United States, is dependent and hence vulnerable to U.S. policy, and is already deeply divided, the bureaucratic and ideological divisions within the U.S. government and society vis-à-vis policy toward that country (which are very minor in terms of their overall significance for U.S. government and society) tend to be projected into the dependent society through contradictory policies whose divisive impact can be far greater than the divisions that originally bred these policy contradictions within the U.S. government. In other words, divisions within the U.S. government that are projected into societies fitting this description tend to be magnified. The measure of this magnification, of course, we cannot know, and will vary from case to case, but it is a divisive force within the society that receives it. This hypothesis is a complement of one previously suggested in this text: that bureaucratic and ideological conflict within the U.S. government tends to be allowed to run wild when policy toward countries that are relatively irrelevant to the vital interests of the United States is being formulated, because the cost of policy errors toward such countries is (relatively) low, and hence contradictions are less costly.[77] These hypotheses appear plausible for both periods under study.

Nevertheless, our conclusion cannot be that the U.S. drive to export democracy must end. On the contrary, another of the similarities between both periods under study lies in the paradoxical fact that in both cases the opportunity was lost to apply, *without contradictions,* an ideologically inspired policy toward a remote country that is relatively irrelevant to the vital interests of the United States. In both cases, the very secondary economic and geopolitical significance of Argentina for the United States generated intense bureaucratic and ideological conflict as well as acute policy contradictions, instead of greater consistency in the application of a policy that, due to the said irrelevance, could have been based exclusively on principle, at little or no cost. From this point of view, both cases were lost opportunities for true Wilsonianism. The problem, then, lies not with the U.S. drive to export democracy itself, but with the contradictions generated in the decision-making process. If these contradictions cannot be checked; if the rules of the game cannot be laid down explicitly, without ambiguities; if the U.S. government will persist on a pattern of intervention, which in actual practice is seldom translated into positive terms but rather consists of only vetoing certain situations deemed undesirable (because of a variety of reasons that include both pragmatic security considerations and the idealistic defense of democracy and human rights); if intervention will thus limit itself to wrecking the existing political system and then, having neutralized the threat or overthrown the tyrant, leaves a sorely divided society to help itself, without an active, positive, and tangibly material support for democracy—if all these conditions hold, then the best thing that will be said for this self-appointed mission, this promotion of democracy which has become such an important dimension of U.S. foreign policy over the last hundred years, is that the United States hurts only those who hurt themselves.

Notes

1. Human rights abuses may have been more prevalent during the 1946–55 period than during the 1943–46 military regime. In the earlier period, for example, there were no massive intimidation campaigns for teachers and state employees to join the official party; also, although violations of human rights and civil liberties are never justifiable, some might argue that the threat of sabotage during World War II was sufficient to restrict civil liberties (one must not forget that during the war, for example, Japanese-Americans were massively interned in the United States and their constitutional rights thus blatantly violated). Wartime hysteria is one excuse that Perón did not have when he became president. Furthermore, to my taste at least, the constitutional facade of the 1946–55 regime made violations of human rights more despicable (although some may feel that "popular" violations of human rights are more palatable than unpopular ones).

Another (connected) point relates to the conceptual links between the exportation of democracy and the castigation of human rights abuses. The techniques, organizations, and policy measures appropriate for the promotion of democracy may at times be very different from those appropriate for the promotion of human rights. However, they share a common Wilsonian substratum, and the need to compare two periods with very different characteristics—in the first there were systematic violations of human rights in the context of what was formally a democratically elected regime, whereas in the second the human rights abuses took place in a military dictatorship—makes a certain imprecision necessary. The same apparent imprecision is present in U.S. policy itself, insofar as it is often difficult to separate these two objectives. Nonetheless, I think it is clear that the main thrust of the Wilsonian dimension of U.S. foreign policy has been, at least historically, more focused on human rights than on the democratic election of leaders. Notice, for instance, that the curtailment of U.S. military aid to Argentina and several other countries in February 1977 was decided explicitly on the grounds of human rights abuses and not because of the absence of democratically elected governments. Naturally, this is related to the problem of what it is we mean by democracy, and it can be argued that human rights are essential to the concept of liberal democracy: hence, in the case of a democratically elected government that systematically (and perhaps even with popular support) violates the rights of the opposition (or of other minorities), we would not in truth have a democracy but a "popular dictatorship," a concept that I would distinctly separate from that of a "restricted democracy" (i.e., governments that were duly respectful of human rights but were the product of elections in which Peronism was proscribed).

2. It must be borne in mind, of course, that there are great methodological differences in the way these periods can be treated. The 1943–55 period offers a wealth of previously classified archival material, and hence decision making and underlying rationales can be studied in much more detail than for the 1976–83 period, for which there has been no such massive declassification.

3. Argentina and the United States had conflictive diplomatic relations since at least 1889, when the first Pan American Conference was held in Washington. See J. S. Tulchin, *Argentina and the United States: A Conflicted Relationship* (Boston: Twayne Publishers, 1990). Also, T. F. McGann, *Argentina, the United States and the Inter-American System, 1880–1914* (Cambridge: Harvard University Press, 1957).

4. J. S. Tulchin, "Argentine Proposal for Non-Belligerency, April 1940," *Journal of Inter-American Studies* 11, no. 4 (1969): 571–605, and S. E. Hilton, "Argentine Neutralism, September 1939–June 1940: A Re-examination," *The Americas* (January 1966): 227–57.

5. For the impact of nationalistic education on foreign policy, see the last chapter of my *Patología del Nacionalismo: el caso argentino* (Buenos Aires: Editorial Tesis, 1987).

6. Works on this subject include: C. Escudé, *Gran Bretaña, Estados Unidos y la Declinación Argentina, 1942–1949* (Buenos Aires: Editorial de Belgrano, 1983); M. L. Francis, *The Limits of Hegemony: United States Relations with Argentina and Chile during World War II* (Notre Dame, Ind.: University of Notre Dame Press, 1977); Gary Frank, *Struggle for Hegemony: Argentina, Brazil and the Second World War* (Coral Gables, Fla.: University of Miami Press, 1979), and *Juan Perón vs. Spruille Braden* (Lanham, Md.: University Press of America, 1980); R. A. Giacalone, "From Bad Neighbors to Reluctant Partners: Argentina and the United States 1946–1950" (Ph.D. dissertation, University of Indiana, 1977); S. E. Hilton, "Brazilian Diplomacy and the Washington-Rio 'Axis' during the World War II Era," *Hispanic American Historical Review* 59 (May 1979): 201–31; R. A. Humphreys, *Latin America and the Second World War*, 2 vol. (London: Athlone Press, 1981–82); C. A. MacDonald, "The Politics of Intervention: The US and Argentina 1941–1946," *Journal of Latin American Studies* 12, no. 2 (1980): 365–96, and "The US, the Cold War and Perón," in C. Abel and C. Lewis, eds., *Latin America, Economic Imperialism and the State: The Political Economy of the External Connection from Independence to the*

Present (London: University of London by the Athlone Press, 1985); R. C. Newton, "The United States, the German-Argentines and the Myth of the Fourth Reich," *Hispanic American Historical Review* 64, no. 1 (1984): 81–103; M. Rapoport, *Gran Bretaña, Estados Unidos y las Clases Dirigentes Argentinas* (Buenos Aires: Editorial de Belgrano, 1980); B. Wood, *The Dismantling of the Good Neighbor Policy* (Austin: University of Texas Press, 1985); and R. B. Woods, *The Roosevelt Foreign-Policy Establishment and the 'Good Neighbor': The United States and Argentina, 1941–1945* (Lawrence: Regents Press of Kansas, 1979). In 1986, a seminar was held at St. Antony's College, Oxford, that considered Argentine relations in general as well as certain aspects of U.S.-U.K. relations during the 1940s. The resulting volume is G. di Tella and D. Cameron Watt, eds., *Argentina between the Great Powers, 1939–1946* (London: Macmillan, 1990).

7. A Foreign Office minute offers very similar concepts to those presented by Sir David Kelly later on in the text: "To be consistent, the US government should apply similar pressure to bear on other backsliders in Latin America . . . but the fact must be faced that their policy to Argentina is a thing apart; their opposition to the present Argentine regime only differs from their opposition to the former constitutional regime in that the dictator form of the present government makes it more open to attack. The military regime only were able to overthrow the constitutional government because the latter had been undermined by 18 months of public and private opposition on the part of Mr. Hull and Mr. Sumner Welles, and the revolution was at first hailed by the US Embassy as their own victory. When disappointed they maintained similar pressure, resulting in the elimination firstly of Admiral Sotrni and other respectable elements in the Argentine Government, then of Generals Ramirez and Gilbert. This pressure, applied on and off, keeps the country in perpetual ferment, making return to normal conditions impossible; and if the United States Government are going to insist that whatever Government succeeds the present regime should toe the line and generally accept United States directives, present difficulties may continue for years." (AS 3412/12/2, FO 371/44687, Public Record Office [PRO], Kew Gardens, London).

8. Dawson to Duggan, June 5, 1943, Memoranda-Argentina, RG 59, Department of State (DOS), National Archives of the United States (NA). For the optimism displayed by the U.S. press at the "good news" of the coup, see the *New York Times,* June 5, 1943.

9. D. Kelly, *The Ruling Few* (London: Hollis & Carter, n.d.), p. 297.

10. R. B. Woods, p. x.

11. Ibid., pp. 97–98.

12. J. M. Blum, *The Price of Vision: The Diary of Henry Wallace, 1942–46* (Boston: Houghton Mifflin, 1973), pp. 67–68, 77, 91, 99–100.

13. *New York Times,* August 18, 1948, and 835.00/2-2645, RG 59, DOS, NA.

14. AS 5361/268/2, FO 371/37764; Halifax to Foreign Office, PRO. Quotation from the *Pacific Shipper,* September 25, 1944, cited by B. Wood, p. 73.

15. *The Foreign Relations of the United States (FRUS) 1945,* vol. 9 (Washington, D.C.: U.S. Government Printing Office, 1969), pp. 526–99.

16. For a fully detailed account of the U.S. economic boycott of Argentina see Escudé, *La Declinación Argentine,* esp. chaps. 5 and 6.

17. Much the same can be said for Nicaragua in the 1980s. In the case of Argentina the gross exaggeration is obvious. Argentina was a very prosperous country in the 1940s, to the point that in 1937 she had a per capita income (in U.S. dollars) of $510, vis-à-vis France's $540, Austria's $370, Italy's $260, and Japan's $185; see A. Maizels, *Industrial Growth and World Trade* (Cambridge: Cambridge University Press, 1963). Nevertheless, the Argentine economy was never more than approximately 5 percent of the U.S. economy. In the very best of cases Argentina could have measured up to Canada or Australia, but its basic endowment of resources was far poorer than that of the United States. One must bear in mind, however, that its promise was such that in 1942, in his *The Economics of 1960* (London: Macmillan,

1942), noted Australian economist Colin Clark predicted that by the date borne in the book's title, Argentina would have the fourth highest per capita income in the world. But of course, to say that it had good chances of having one of the world's best living standards is not to say that it could compete for power on a global scale.

18. 711.35/7-3146, RG 59, DOS, NA.

19. "Inter-American Collaboration," 711.35/1-2447, RG 59, DOS, NA. (This 1946 memo was also sent to Gen. George Marshall somewhat later, on January 25, 1947, and I have found it filed on this date.) Messersmith to Marshall, January 24, 1947, 711.35/1-2447.

20. 711.35/6-2347, RG 59, DOS, NA. Minute corresponding to June 23, 1947 (filed together with previous minutes).

21. 840.50 Recovery 1-2549, RG 59, DOS, NA. This episode is best treated in Escudé, *La Declinación Argentina*. For a treatment of the British and continental European side of the ECA boycott, see my later piece, "US Political Destabilization and Economic Boycott of Argentina during the 1940s," in di Tella and Cameron Watt, *Argentina*.

22. "Comments on our relations with Argentina," memo Ray to Marshall, 711.35/1-548, RG 59, DOS, NA, pp. 4, 8.

23. 711.35/12-948, RG 59, DOS, NA.

24. 711.35/12-1648, RG 59, DOS, NA, and 711.35/2-1049, RG 59, DOS, NA.

25. 611.35/3-215, RG 59, NA, Policy Statement—Argentina, March 21, 1950, p. 1.

26. Ibid., pp. 7-8.

27. C. Escudé, "Crónicas de la Tercera Posición: la ratificación, argentina del TIAR en junio de 1950," *Todo es Historia* 22 (November 1988): 6–26.

28. Frank, *Struggle*.

29. Escudé, "Crónicas."

30. 611.35/5-250, RG 59, DOS, NA.

31. Ibid., Miller to J. S. Potofsky.

32. 611.35/8-2952, RG 59, DOS, NA. To such an extent were they whimsical that one of the most hysterical anti–United States campaigns was unleashed because Eva Perón could not get her book, *La razón de mi vida,* published in the United States.

33. 611.35/2-1351, RG 59, DOS, NA, enclosure 3 to dispatch 1184, memo dated February 10.

34. 735.00/3-652, RG 59, DOS, NA, embassy's *Monthly Summary* of February 1952.

35. *Historical Statistics of the United States, Colonial Times to 1970,* Bicentennial Edition (Washington, D.C.: U.S. Bureau of the Census, 1976), Series U-75-186 on foreign aid. A credit was announced in early 1955, but Perón was overthrown before it was disbursed, and the credit was suspended.

36. CCS 381 Western Hemisphere (3-22-48) (sec. 18 and 19), RG 218, Military Branch NA, Report by the Strategic Plans Committees, May 12, 1954.

37. 611.35/2-1451, RG 59, DOS, NA.

38. 611.35/2-251, RG 59, DOS, NA.

39. 611.35/3-651, RG 59, DOS, NA.

40. 611.35/3-2151, RG 59, DOS, NA, enclosure 1 to dispatch 1438.

41. 735.00/6-750, RG 59, DOS, NA. Closed newspapers included *La Nueva Provincia* (Bahía Blanca), *Trópico* (Tucumán), *Democracia* (Junín), *El Intransigente* (Salta), *Democracia* (Olvarría), and *Veritas* (commercial information, Buenos Aires), plus the Communist periodicals *La Hora, Orientación, Renacimiento, La Protesta, España Independiente, Nuestras Mujeres,* and *Pueblo Unido.*

42. 611.35/5-351, RG 59, DOS, NA, embassy memo on U.S.-Argentine relations.

43. 611.35/3-1953, RG 59, DOS, NA, dispatch 1165 of March 13, "Attitude of the US press toward the Argentine government."

44. 611.35/3-1653, RG 59, DOS, NA. Meeting of Ambassador Nufer with Perón of March 13, enclosure 1, p. 6, to dispatch 1165 of March 16. Nufer admitted the same thing

during a previous conversation with Perón held on February 3, in which it was also stated that in the U.S. press there were no adverse comments on Somoza or Trujillo (611.35/2-553, RG 59, DOS, NA, enclosure 1, p. 12 of dispatch 1003).

45. J. T. Deiner, "ATLAS: A Labor Instrument of Argentine Expansionism under Perón" (Ph.D. dissertation, Rutgers University, 1969).

46. 611.35/5-351, RG 59, DOS, NA, p. 6.

47. During this meeting, a paper prepared March 11 on proposed policy changes toward Argentina was studied. Both in this paper and in the memorandum of conversation referred to in the text there was a mystery point, number nine and last, with respect to policy, which was for verbal presentation to the new ambassador (Nufer) only. It is possible that it may have referred to the possibility of economic sanctions as a last resort, because this is the subject of the question made by the ambassador after point nine was treated. It should be noted that it is not altogether impossible that secret economic sanctions might have been adopted at this time or soon afterward. The odd character of the 1948–49 ECA sanctions should remind us that such things are possible and can remain forever undisclosed. On the other hand, in a mid-1954 dispatch, Nufer stated that "Perón bore the scars, and of recent origin, of US action adverse to his country's economic interests" (611.35/5-1954, RG 59, DOS, NA, dispatch 1077, "Security significance of improved US-Argentine relations"). He might have been referring to something more recent than the 1948–49 ECA boycott (ambassadors rarely have a memory extended to a period previous to their appointment). We probably will never know. The meeting is filed at 611.35/5-1552.

48. 735.00/8-2652, RG 59, DOS, NA, "Propaganda campaign of the Argentine government" sent to U.S. diplomatic officers in the other American republics.

49. See, for example, 611.35/1-2953, RG 59, DOS, NA, memo of conversation with Foreign Minister Remorino, by Nufer, January 27, enclosure 1 to dispatch 970, p. 2.

50. 611.35/3-353, RG 59, DOS, NA, telegram from Dulles to Nufer.

51. 611.35/3-1653,RG 59, DOS,NA, enclosure 1 to dispatch by Nufer with memo of conversation March 13, p. 2.

52. 611.35/7-3153, RG 59, DOS, NA, enclosure 1 to dispatch 93, memo of conversation Nufer-Perón, held July 24.

53. 611.35/3-353, RG 59, DOS NA.

54. 611.35/7-3153, RG 59, DOS, NA, dispatch 103 signed by First Secretary Martindale.

55. 611.35/10-753, RG 59, DOS, NA, "Instructions on US-Argentine relations to all ARA diplomatic and consular posts. . . ."

56. 611.35/5-1954, RG 59, DOS, NA, Nufer's dispatch 1077. Also FO 371/114019, Public Record Office (British archives), British embassy in Buenos Aires to Foreign Office, American Department, August 18, 1955. Contrariwise to the United States, the British seemed happy with Perón's overthrow. One Foreign Office manuscript comment stated: "I cannot understand why the Argentines did not shoot this dangerous man" (British Chancery at Rio de Janeiro to Foreign Office, November 8, 1955, FO 371/114025, PRO).

57. A. A. Borón and G. Selser, "Las relaciones argentino-norteamericanas bajo la administración Carter," in *Cuadernos Semestrales,* no. 6 (Mexico: CIDE, second semester 1979), pp. 235–36.

58. Ibid., p. 329.

59. Ibid., p. 237.

60. J. F. Buncher, ed., *Human Rights and American Diplomacy: 1975–77* (New York: Facts on File, 1977).

61. Tulchin, *Argentina,* chap. 8.

62. L. Schoultz, *Human Rights and United States Policy toward Latin America* (Princeton: Princeton University Press, 1981), p. 311.

63. R. Russell, "Las relaciones Argentina-Estados Unidos: del 'alineamiento heterodoxo'

a la 'recomposición madura,'" in M. Hirst, ed., *Continuidad y Cambio en las Relaciones América Latina-Estados Unidos* (Buenos Aires: GEL, 1987), p. 16; Borón and Selser, pp. 244–47; and Schoultz.

64. "Argentina Today: Coming Apart," *Update* (September 1981): 5.

65. W. Grabendorff, "¿De pais aislado a aliado preferido? Las relaciones entre la Argentina y los Estados Unidos: 1976–1981," in P. Waldmann and E. Garzón Valdés, eds., *El Poder Militar en la Argentina, 1976–1981* (Buenos Aires: Galerna, 1982), p. 158.

66. J. I. Dominguez, "Un valioso desafío para una sabia diplomacia," *A Fondo* 33 (November–December 1983): 32; Russell, p. 26 (Russell relied on Dominguez's authority for his information on this point); and A. Vacs, "Regime Change and International Constraints: Democratization and Foreign Policies in Argentina," paper delivered at the 29th Annual Convention of the International Studies Association, St. Louis, Missouri, March 29–April 2, 1988, p. 7 (Vacs relied on Grabendorff on this point).

67. "Human Rights and US Policy on the Multilateral Development Banks," hearings before the Subcommittee on International Development Institutions and Finance, House of Representatives, 97th Congress, 1st Session, July 21 and 23, 1981, microfiche catalogue 1982 H 241-2.

68. "The Ottawa Summit and US International Economic Policy," hearings before the Joint Economic Committee, 97th Congress, 1st Session, July 14, 1981, microfiche catalogue 1982 J 841-7.1. The State Department report on Argentina is included in this oddly titled publication, which is mostly on Latin America.

69. Department of the Treasury, *Statistical Appendix to the Annual Report of the Secretary of the Treasury on the State of the Finances* (Washington, D.C.: U.S. Government Printing Office, various years); Department of the Treasury, *Status of Active Foreign Credits of the United States Government* (Washington, D.C.: U.S. Government Printing Office, various months and years); and Department of the Treasury, *Contingent Foreign Liabilities of the United States Government* (Washington, D.C.: U.S. Government Printing Office, various months and years). Contingent foreign liabilities figures are available, in published form, from 1979 onward. Through a telephone interview with Mr. Tom Moran of the treasury, Prof. Carlos Miranda of Texas Christian University got the Argentine figures for 1977 and 1978 on my behalf. In a later telephone interview with me, Mr. Moran was unable to inform me with respect to any source with data for the preceding years. When I told him that I would be helpless if the information—in compliance with Section 634(a)(4) of the Foreign Assistance Act of 1961—had been published in a periodical with a title both as precise and obscure as *Contingent Foreign Liabilities,* he laughed and said that this is precisely the sort of title that they had been instructed to create (presumably in 1979). He advised me to get earlier data at the agencies themselves. When I told him that I had been to Eximbank headquarters and had found the information there less helpful than the Treasury's information on Eximbank, he laughed again and implied that this was intentional (August 1989). Whatever the intentions, moreover, the issue of visibility is objective, and the best illustration of its significance is the error committed by such a careful scholar as M. Falcoff in *A Tale of Two Policies: US Relations with the Argentine Junta 1976–83* (Philadelphia: Foreign Policy Research Institute, 1989), 23. Falcoff repeats this mistake when, later on in his text, he says that when the United States decided to side with the United Kingdom in the Falkland war, it "announced that it would withhold certification of Argentine eligibility for . . . Eximbank credits and guarantees. . . . In other words, operating with very different assumptions and in different contexts, both the Reagan and Carter administrations ended up with roughly the same Argentine policy" (p. 53). As will be seen further on in my text, this is way off the mark, especially with respect to guarantees. Reagan, not Carter, applied real economic sanctions, and their policies ended up being nearly opposite: in fact, for different reasons and inspired by different values, Reagan's post–April 1982 economic policy toward Argentina looked like Carter's *should* have looked.

70. S. J. Heginbotham, updated by L. Q. Nowels, *CRS Report for Congress: An overview of US foreign aid* (Washington, D.C.: Congressional Research Service, March 30, 1988).

71. State Department data sheet included in hearing cited on n. 68, and the report cited in the text; House of Representatives, Committee on Ways and Means (transmitted by the president of the United States on April 17, 1980; published April 21).

72. Tulchin, *Argentina,* p. 149.

73. "We the Argentines are righteous and humane"—a play on words that capitalizes on the fact that *derechos* means both "rights" and "righteous" and *humanos* is the plural for both "human" and "humane."

74. In March 1985, 40 percent said that their income sufficed for their basic needs, while 58 percent said it did not suffice. In March 1986 it was 53 percent and 46 percent; in May 1987, 50 and 48 percent, and in March 1988, 36 and 62 percent (i.e., the 1980 results were practically inverted by 1988).

75. Frank, *Struggle.*

76. S. Welles, *Where Are We Heading?* (New York: Harper & Brothers, 1946), p. 186.

77. Escudé, *La Declinación Argentina,* basically chap. 4, which is a theoretical chapter dedicated to these concepts.

2 | Chile: The Limits of "Success"

Heraldo Muñoz

A WIDESPREAD Latin American perception tends to associate the U.S. government with unpopular authoritarian regimes that repress efforts to promote socioeconomic transformations and democracy. Some argue that there is no real interest on the part of the United States to favor democracy building in Latin America. Whatever its subjective aim, the fact is that, alleging "security reasons," Washington repeatedly has ended up on the side of dictatorial regimes, or else has kept silent while "friendly regimes" murdered, tortured, and exiled thousands of dissidents.

True, U.S. foreign policy has often expressed a genuine humanitarian concern for freedom, democracy, and the well-being of Latin American nations, and sometimes it has acted on those concerns. In other words, not always do "hard" or "primary" security-related values prevail in U.S. policy. The weight given to particular interests are relative and fluid, not fixed. The international context or a given historical moment—for example, the post-Watergate period—may lead to an upgrading of democracy or human rights to lend greater credibility or moral weight to foreign policy. One should also consider other explanatory factors, such as geographic location, since the United States may accept Communists in a government coalition in Bolivia, but reject such degree of pluralism in geopolitically sensitive Central America or the Caribbean. In addition—as shall be seen in the Chilean case—the role of key individuals and nongovernmental actors has sometimes affected the level of concern on the part of the U.S. government with reference to democracy in Latin America.

Nevertheless, this essay will suggest that in Chile, from the 1960s onward, the anti-Communist security concern overshadowed other U.S. foreign policy objectives, including the support or promotion of democracy. I shall argue, however, that the Chilean situation also shows that the undisputed primacy of the security purpose is unstable, because the U.S. executive cannot totally dismiss for very long periods the humanitarian values in foreign policy without provoking adverse reactions from various important domestic governmental and nongovernmental sectors.

As Hunt has affirmed, although "the ideas that make up a foreign-policy ideology may be reassembled by different leaders," there is still an ideological inheritance in U.S. policy that includes the "promotion of liberty as a fundamental concept."[1] It would seem that the United States is exceptionally reliant on certain ideological tenets in order to preserve a sense of national identity. Liberalism, both economic and political, constitutes the core of this national ideology and explains why promoting democracy (although the concept is rather elastic) remains sufficiently resilient in the U.S. national consciousness so as to contain policy makers when they stray too far for too long.[2] In other words, ideology has been a powerful mediating or conditioning factor in U.S. policy in general, as well as in U.S. policy toward Chile in particular.

In this same line, I will also try to demonstrate that both Chilean and U.S. nongovernmental actors have played a mediating role in U.S. policy toward Chile, often triggering or stopping actions on the part of the U.S. government, thus contributing to either opening or closing the Chilean political system.

The United States and Democracy in Chile:
The Uneven Historical Record

The emergence and consolidation of Chilean democracy was an indigenous phenomenon, independent of U.S. policies and preferences.[3] Fostering democracy was not a relevant objective of U.S. policy toward Chile prior to the military coup of 1973. Washington worried principally about curbing the growing influence of the left in Chile, obtaining Chilean support to isolate Cuba (after 1960), and protecting U.S. economic interests in the country. Naturally, the broader international concerns of the United States did have an impact on Chilean democracy, as well as on the bilateral relationship.

During the first years after the end of World War II, a major concern in Washington was securing full hemispheric support for its cold war confrontation with the Soviet Union. Chile became incorporated into the Latin American network that emerged in the late forties as it saw no other alternative except to align behind the U.S. anti-Communist policies in a time of rigid bipolarity.

During the conservative regime of President Jorge Alessandri (1958–64), U.S. policy toward Chile and the rest of the region was tainted by the Cuban revolution. The White House sought to obtain Chilean support for its anti-Cuban crusade and to promote substantial internal reforms so as to curtail Cuban-inspired revolutionary insurgencies that might attract popular support because of deep socioeconomic inequalities.

The one aspect that, on the surface, contributed to democracy building in Chile during this period—by stimulating the extension of political democracy into the socioeconomic realm—was Washington's insistence on the need to carry out serious reforms and modernization under the Alliance for Progress. Chile seemed to be the ideal country to implement such reformist transformations since it already enjoyed a system of liberal democracy.

However, one fundamental reason behind U.S. policy in favor of reform was to impede the access of the left to power in Chile, particularly in view of its growing electoral support. Moreover, the shift in U.S. policy toward a greater emphasis on development values was accompanied by a change in inter-American military relations from the classic "defense against an extra-hemispheric threat" approach to the antisubversive perspective—that is, replacing the notion of an external adversary with that of an internal enemy. Hence, Chile during the Alessandri years was one of the largest recipients of U.S. military aid, with a 13 percent share of total assistance to the region. At the same time, counterinsurgency training accelerated and the Carabineros, the national police force, began to be trained and equipped to fight against urban guerrilla warfare.

A clear erosion of Chile's democratic system occurred later as the United States began to intervene in a covert fashion in domestic politics so as to spoil the left's chances of gaining access to presidential power.

After an evaluation conducted by the Goodwin-Moscoso mission in 1962, Washington concluded that reforms in Chile had been insufficient and that the conservative sectors were incapable or unwilling to carry them out. Therefore, also taking into account the increasing political stature of the left, the White House decided to throw its weight behind the Christian Democratic party and Eduardo Frei. A successful reformist government in Chile, in the opinion of U.S. authorities, would seriously damage the future possibilities of the left, and Chile could become a showcase to counter the Cuban revolutionary example. In 1964, Chile received 15.3 percent of all U.S. aid to Latin America and 5.7 percent of all credits from Eximbank to the region, compared with 12.5 and 0.5 percent, respectively, in 1960.[4]

During this time, Washington continued its covert activities in Chile, which reflected an overwhelming concern over security threats. In June 1965, the "Camelot Plan" was publicly unveiled, originating a formal protest by the Chilean government before the State Department. The project, organized by the American University with the support of the Pentagon, sought to identify the factors that could lead to revolutionary uprisings in underdeveloped countries, including Chile. The State Department provided explanations to the Frei government and the project was suspended.

The hostility toward the Chilean left led to additional financing and covert operations to impede a possible victory of Salvador Allende in 1970. Once Allende was elected president, the White House went even further to try to block his accession to office through terrorist actions and then, when that failed, to destabilize Chilean democracy.[5]

U.S. economic interests in Chile were of secondary importance compared with the perceived danger of a successful experience of peaceful transition to socialism in the hemisphere. Also, the demonstration effects for countries like France and Italy, with strong Socialist parties and emerging Eurocommunism, were judged to be extremely negative. So were the implications for the international balance of power. The mere existence of the Allende government was the determining factor behind the U.S. effort to destabilize the constitutional regime. The specific policies pursued by the Popular Unity administration only reinforced a North American strategy of intervention that had been decided beforehand.

The breakdown of democracy in Chile was largely the result of a complex process of domestic polarization and could hardly be blamed on external forces. Without a doubt, however, U.S. intervention contributed to the overthrow of the constitutional government.

After September 11, 1973, the U.S. government played a crucial role in aiding the process of consolidation of the dictatorship in Chile. The CIA collaborated in the preparation of the first economic plan of the military junta, contributed to the publication of a "white book" justifying the coup d'etat, and provided funds to improve the international image of the new regime. At the same time, the Nixon and Ford administrations backed the renegotiation of Chile's debt in the Paris Club and, between 1974 and 1976, provided massive economic assistance to the military government.

However, support for dictatorship on the part of the executive branch began to be partially offset by Congress, which sought to incorporate humanitarian components into the U.S. policy toward Chile. It became increasingly clear that the undisputed primacy of the security purpose in U.S. policy with regard to Chile was indeed unstable, since Congress and various nongovernmental actors reintroduced humanitarian values in official U.S.-Chilean relations. In June 1976 the Senate and House of Representatives voted to suspend military sales to Chile and limited economic assistance to $27.5 million until the Chilean regime made substantial progress on human rights issues. From then on, the Congress and a network of nongovernmental entities in the United States contributed to restrain internal repression in Chile.

During the Carter-Ford presidential race, U.S. policy toward Chile even became an important issue in the presidential debates, as Jimmy Carter effectively denounced the Nixon and Ford administrations' support for Pinochet. The new dominance of moral values in U.S. policy later would lead a high government official of the Carter administration to apologize publicly for U.S. intervention in Chile during the Allende period.

The Carter administration placed humanitarian values like democracy and human rights high in the foreign policy agenda. Such policy provoked confrontation with the Pinochet regime, as well as with other authoritarian governments, but made an important contribution to the Chilean democratization efforts. Although the human rights strategy of President Carter had important flaws and was eroded by an international overabundance of petrodollars from private sources, which severely weakened the effectiveness of economic pressures on Latin American military regimes, it probably saved many lives and shortened many jail sentences of dissidents. It should be remembered, for example, that less than two weeks after Carter's election, Pinochet surprisingly freed 304 political prisoners. Toward the end of his term, Carter applied various diplomatic, economic, and military sanctions on the Pinochet dictatorship for failing to conduct a serious investigation into the Letelier-Moffit assassination case, which became a central issue in U.S.-Chilean relations, and that mobilized important sectors of U.S. society against the Pinochet regime.

When Ronald Reagan took office in early 1981, he immediately lifted all sanctions imposed by his predecessor. The Chilean military government was viewed as an ally in the global strategy of containment of Communism. Thus, violations of human rights and the regime's refusal to allow a transition to democracy were disregarded. Based on the distinction popularized by Jeane Kirkpatrick between authoritarian and totalitarian regimes, the Reagan administration identified Latin American military governments, including Chile's, as "authoritarian"—that is, traditional societies without sufficient development to sustain democracy. Hence, to push them on human rights would open the door to Marxist-Leninist totalitarian regimes. Instead, a policy of "silent diplomacy" was to be implemented with regard to authoritarian governments. Even the Letelier case was downplayed by the Republican administration. The humanitarian concern regarding Chile, however, continued to be expressed in Congress, thus impeding a full rapprochement between Washington and Santiago. The 1976 arms embargo could not be lifted and, instead, the Reagan administration agreed that it could be rescinded only after a presidential certification that human rights had improved in Chile.

Silent diplomacy was perceived in Santiago as a green light for repression. Consequently, systematic violations of human rights continued, and the Pinochet government did not even attempt to introduce cosmetic changes on the Chilean political situation. In such context, the certification could not be granted.

The stage of cordial relations between Reagan and Pinochet gave way to a period of increasing bilateral tensions. In 1983, massive national protests in Chile, following the collapse of the monetarist experiment, activated the classical U.S. security concern over violence and radicalization in a country previously considered to be safe and stable, while the inconsistency between a policy of aggression toward Nicaragua and one of tolerance with regard to right-wing dictators came under heavy domestic fire.

By 1984, silent diplomacy was being abandoned as the State Department openly criticized governmental repression of popular protests in Chile. The Reagan administration restored humanitarian values like democracy and respect for human rights in the foreign policy agenda, although they were subordinated to the principal security goal of fighting Communism.

In addition, the shift toward an explicit concern for human rights and democracy in Chile was favored by the change in the regional context in the direction of democratization in countries like Argentina, Brazil, and Uruguay; by the defeat of the ultraconservatives within the administration as exemplified in the replacement of James Theberge, a political appointee, by career diplomat Harry Barnes as ambassador to Chile; and by the Philippine experience, which showed Washington that in some countries there was a centrist "third-force option" between the friendly but unpopular dictator and the unacceptable radical-leftist opposition.

Thus, the Reagan administration came to favor a smooth transition to democracy in Chile, one without abrupt breaks and in which the basic thrust of the neoconservative, market-oriented economic order could be preserved—for this economic aspect remained an important value in the foreign policy orientation of the Reagan presidency. Moreover, before and after the October 1988 plebiscite that resulted in Pinochet's defeat by a massive "No" vote and that led to the democratic elections of December 1989, the United States played an important role on behalf of redemocratization in Chile.

In sum, the Chilean case supports the thesis that the anti-Communist security interest was more important than other foreign policy purposes, including the promotion of democracy and human rights. However, the Chilean case also suggests that any U.S. administration, even that of Ronald Reagan, faces limits on prolonged and close friendships with unpopular governments that violate human rights and deny widespread demands for democracy, since this eventually provokes adverse reactions from the media, church groups, concerned nongovernment entities, Congress, and sometimes even from policy makers within the administration itself. On the other hand, given the persistent centrality of geopolitical interests and free-market criteria, U.S. policy also faces limits in the opposite direction; in other words, Washington will generally not engage in an open confrontation with a government that shares its anti-Communist strategic world view and has a free-market-oriented economic policy at work.

The Mediating Role of Nongovernmental Actors and the Influence of Ideology

Democracy in U.S.-Chilean relations cannot be separated from the behavior of key Chilean and U.S. individuals and nongovernmental sectors. In fact, as already noted, both Chilean and U.S. nongovernmental actors have played a mediating role in U.S. policy toward Chile, often triggering or stopping actions on the part of the U.S. government, thus contributing to either opening or closing the Chilean political system. Likewise, the influence of ideology has been a powerful conditioning factor in U.S. policy in general, as well as in U.S. policy toward Chile in particular.

The influence of nongovernmental groups has been critical at some moments. It can be hypothesized that the White House will act in favor or against a dictator depending on the opinion of its most trusted local reference groups. These, in turn, realize that they have some power to enlist U.S. support for their efforts to open or close their respective political systems.

Robert Pastor, writing on U.S. policy toward Nicaragua during the Somoza regime, has argued that the U.S. government follows the middle or centrist sectors in Latin America. As Pastor notes, "when the middle delegitimizes a dictator, U.S. officials are compelled to follow the middle. Even a conservative administration cannot sustain a policy of supporting a dictator if the middle groups in that country have rejected him."[6]

The weight that these groups have in affecting U.S. behavior is also conditioned by another key ideological factor indicated by Hunt: a defensive attitude toward revolutionary change.[7] An inordinate fear of revolution and a proclivity to equate revolutionary change with security threats may explain why the United States chose not to destabilize Somoza in Nicaragua, even when the middle forces there fought for democracy.

In any event, it is clear that U.S. government actions are influenced by the views and pressures of valid interlocutors in the country affected, be they centrist or rightist. The attitude of the conservative Reagan administration changed toward Pinochet, among other reasons, because important right-wing sectors in Chile split away from the dictatorship and assumed a "semiopposition" stance, particularly after the minister of the interior, Sergio O. Jarpa, was removed from Pinochet's cabinet in early 1985. The participation of the right, together with political parties of the center and left, in the signing of the National Accord for a Transition to Full Democracy, in August 1985, was a clear demonstration for Washington of the new attitude of Chilean conservatives with regard to the military regime.

However, some Chilean sectors actively lobbied in the United States against a shift in U.S. policy in the direction of a greater emphasis on redemocratization. For example, the U.S. Chilean Chamber of Commerce (AmCham-Chile) and the Sociedad Nacional de Agricultura (SNA), a conservative organization of Chilean landowners, were particularly active supporters of the Pinochet regime and openly criticized the promotion of democracy in Chile. Moreover, the SNA was the host to U.S. Senator Jesse Helms during his polemic private visit to Chile in July 1986, when the ultraconservative politician praised the Pinochet government, strongly reproved President Reagan's policy toward Chile, accused Ambassador Harry

Barnes and Elliott Abrams, assistant secretary for inter-American affairs, of backing the left in Chile, and declared that he was "ashamed" of how U.S. media treated Pinochet's Chile.[8]

The historical record shows an even clearer incident in 1970 when a key local actor triggered actions by the United States that seriously affected the existing democratic system. Although U.S. intervention conceivably could have occurred even without direct request by Chilean citizens due to the "fear-of-revolution factor," evidence suggests that such lobbying heightened White House attention to perceived dangers in Chile, leading to concrete U.S. involvement in the country's internal affairs.

On September 15, 1970, the Chilean owner of the conservative newspaper *El Mercurio,* Agustin Edwards, who had left Chile after the September 4, 1970, elections, met during breakfast with Attorney General John Mitchell, CIA Director Richard Helms, and Pepsi Cola Chairman of the Board Donald Kendall—a business partner who had arranged the breakfast meeting—and prophesied great disasters in Chile if Washington did not act quickly. That same afternoon, President Richard Nixon summoned Helms and, in the presence of Kissinger and Mitchell, instructed the CIA director to "leave no stone unturned . . . to block Allende's confirmation."[9]

As Nathaniel Davis, former U.S. ambassador to Chile, recalls, Helms would testify later before the Senate Select Committee on Intelligence: "If I ever carried a marshal's baton in my knapsack, it was that day."[10] The program developed by Helms, known as "Track II," finally led to the kidnapping attempt and murder of the Chilean army commander-in-chief, Gen. René Schneider, and was a first step in a policy of "destabilization" that contributed to the breakdown of Chilean democracy.

As is widely known, a U.S. multinational enterprise, ITT, developed in 1970 its own strategy of intervention in the internal affairs of Chile and actually pressured the U.S. government into proceeding covertly against the constitutionally elected president of Chile, Salvador Allende. A concern of ITT was that Allende would bring under public ownership service industries such as the national telephone company, at that time a subsidiary of ITT. However, it should also be considered that one important member of ITT's Board of Directors had served in the CIA and was particularly sensitive to the "revolutionary threat" posed by the election of Allende. Thus, both ideology and economic interests were mixed in this case.

John McCone, a former CIA director and member of the board of the multinational corporation, had easy access to CIA Director Helms, with whom he consulted on the Chilean situation. Obviously, this relationship only reinforced the appeal for action made by Chilean actors upon the U.S. government. The CIA apparently did not develop joint operations with ITT to impede Allende's election, although it is clear that there was coordination between them. But, after Allende was actually elected, it was the U.S. government that approached the directors of ITT and other North American businessmen to unleash economic warfare on the democratically elected government in Chile.[11]

During the decade of the sixties, various other Chilean and foreign nongovernmental actors exercised great influence on the contents and direction of Chilean democracy. However, it should be noted that these actors were impelled by an activist U.S. foreign policy that emphasized the need to link democracy with development.

As early as the Dwight D. Eisenhower administration the White House "came to see the lack of democratic governments in Latin America as a serious policy problem," since antidemocratic or nondemocratic regimes, being unsympathetic to the problems of underdevelopment and to the misery of the populations, were potentially unstable regimes.[12] This thesis had been argued, though ignored, in Milton Eisenhower's report on Latin America, and in the 1958 memorandum sent to President Eisenhower by the president of Colombia, Alberto Lleras, and the president of Brazil, Juscelino Kubitschek, who proposed a program known as "Operation Pan America." Interestingly, during this period a number of Latin American leaders, particularly José Figueres of Costa Rica and Rómulo Betancourt of Venezuela, urged U.S. action, jointly with the Organization of American States, "to oust bad governments so that democratically elected popular governments could lead the movement toward development."[13]

The Kennedy era and the Alliance for Progress signaled the triumph of the thesis that linked democracy and development. The Cuban revolution, of course, gave this new approach in U.S. policy toward Latin America a sense of urgency. The national security motive was then added as an explicit component of the programs launched.

In Chile, the "Chicago boys" group, perhaps the most influential nongovernmental sector, which designed and managed the economic policies of the Pinochet regime and contributed to the consolidation of authoritarian rule in the post-1973 context, was born as a by-product of U.S. policy. Under the aegis of the "Point Four" initiative of technical cooperation for development of President Truman, the University of Chicago was given funds to establish a training and research agreement with the Catholic University of Chile. The agreement, signed in March 1956, contemplated visits to Chile by U.S. professors, the creation of a Center for Economic Research at the Catholic University, and scholarships to Chilean students to study economics at the conservative-monetarist Department of Economics at the University of Chicago.[14] Interestingly, when prior to the 1973 military coup U.S. intelligence became involved in the preparation of an economic plan for the new government, the work was allegedly done through a research organization dominated by the Chicago-trained economists.[15]

However, although U.S. policy facilitated the creation of a powerful nongovernmental group as the Chicago boys, it is evident that it did not become a mere reflection of Washington's policies. Thus, although important changes in U.S. policy with regard to Chile occurred during the sixteen years of military rule, the Chicago group lent constant support to the Pinochet regime. In other words, sometimes doctrine outlasts reality; ideas become autonomous of the policies and entities that originated them and often have a lasting and powerful impact on a given political system. In the perspective of the Chicago group, dictatorship in Chile was justified—as Foxley correctly points out—in the following way. Economic freedom achieved through the market is extended to other decisions by reducing the role of political institutions (particularly the state) and taking decisions back to the individual. However, what if voting processes are imperfect and, in addition, individuals are not rational in the ways that market allocation requires? If socialist ideas have crept into the minds of individuals, the argument goes, rational behavior cannot be expected, at least not until the superiority of the new, free-market principles have been widely demonstrated. Hence, authority must be strong and vigilant and democratic decisions must be postponed. "Economic freedom must coexist with authoritarian government for the model to be viable."[16]

A similar lasting negative effect on Chilean democracy stems from the counterinsurgency criteria embodied in the National Security Doctrine espoused by the United States during the sixties and fully assumed and practiced by the Chilean armed forces even when this doctrine was no longer actively promoted by Washington. Although the original intent of counterinsurgency was to fight Communism through a strategy of development and nation building, the purely ideological component prevailed and shaped the views of the Chilean military.

Between 1966 and 1974 nearly fifteen hundred Chilean officers were trained in Panama, and Chile was a privileged recipient of U.S. economic and military aid.[17] Chile was particularly important, as is known, because it could be perceived as a showcase of U.S.-directed reform that could be presented as an alternative to the Cuban model. The report *Covert Action in Chile* describes the relations between the U.S. and Chilean armed forces up to 1973 as "close, personal and professional cooperation."[18] Nevertheless, after Washington imposed military sanctions on the Chilean government in 1976, relations deteriorated noticeably. Efforts under the Reagan administration to influence the Chilean military, through the Pentagon, into promoting political liberalization totally failed, particularly with regard to the Chilean army. Invitations to visit the United States were refused and private exhortations on democracy rejected. New sources of indigenous supply and a growing national military industry only increased the distance between U.S. and Chilean military institutions. Still, the basic tenets of national security and counterinsurgency of the sixties continued to prevail in the orientation of the Chilean armed forces in the late eighties.

Washington's policy of supporting Chile as a "showcase of democracy and reform" or an alternative to Cuba also affected other nongovernmental groups, such as the Church. In this case, however, the impact on the Chilean political system was positive, since the Church was able to discard its questionable public image of being an ally of the privileged classes by strongly advocating agrarian reform—a key point of the Alliance for Progress—and lending support to a more egalitarian development model. Since Vatican II, the Catholic church deepened its commitment to the active defense of human rights and the promotion of democracy in Latin America. Moreover, during the seventies the Church contributed to the elaboration of a human rights doctrine and stimulated the creation of an impressive network of nongovernmental institutions throughout the region oriented toward the protection of human rights.

In Chile the Catholic church played a key role in the protection of human rights. Today, the Catholic church has great influence and credibility among decision makers in Washington, and it acted as a trusted mediator for various U.S. administrations during the military regime. In addition, the Chilean Catholic church developed strong linkages with its counterpart in the United States, with solidarity for human rights as the driving force.

Although not in the category of "nongovernmental actors," U.S. ambassadors can also affect Washington's policy on democracy in Chile, by making an important difference in the execution of a given policy. Throughout the rule of the military government up until 1985, the United States had in Chile representatives who maintained low profiles, had hardly any contacts with the opposition, and thus lent little credibility to Washington's stated policy of supporting a transition to democracy in Chile. The arrival of Ambassador Harry Barnes to Santiago in 1985 turned that situation around. Democracy seemed to be high on the U.S. agenda for Chile; the opposition welcomed the change, while the military regime tried to isolate Barnes. However one may evaluate Barnes's work in Chile, he clearly played a critical role days before the October 1988 plebiscite when, in the face of widespread rumors of a government-induced disruption of the referendum, he urged the U.S. government to express its serious concern about the rumors, forcing the Chilean government to reiterate its commitment to carrying out the plebiscite. An overcautious ambassador may not have acted at that crucial moment.

Political parties have also played an increasingly important role in U.S.-Chilean relations, contributing to either opening or closing Chile's political system. Traditionally, the U.S. government had particularly close relations with the conservative parties in Chile, although maintaining open contacts with the U.S. government was avoided by all Chilean parties, as it created negative images.

During the sixties, Washington assigned priority to developing an active relationship with the Christian Democratic party of President Eduardo Frei, while still keeping close contacts with the right-wing National Party.

The White House covertly provided funds to finance the presidential and parliamentary campaigns of the Christian Democrats and the right, during both the 1964 and 1970 elections.

Under the military government this situation changed. The U.S. government developed linkages with a wide ideological spectrum of parties from right to left, while, under hard dictatorial conditions that required broad external support and solidarity, Chilean political parties in general learned to view contacts with the U.S. government as necessary and convenient. Washington's official policy of favoring democracy in Chile facilitated dialogue with center-left parties that would have been unthinkable during the sixties. Hence, practically all political parties in Chile now have interlocutors in the United States, are better acquainted with the decision-making processes in Washington, and channel their views directly to U.S. officials.

Although U.S. policy toward Chile now benefits, therefore, from a pluralistic range of views on local affairs, it is also subject to a greater variety of political pressures. Right-wing parties lobbied in favor of Pinochet and the Chicago economic model through private U.S. bankers, the Treasury Department, and senators like Jesse Helms. Opposition parties lobbied in favor of democracy through church and human rights groups, the State Department, and senators like Edward Kennedy or Tom Harkin. Since this is a relatively new situation, only very slowly are Chilean political parties learning the limits and disadvantages of enlisting U.S. support for their respective efforts to influence Chilean politics.

Some Final Reflections

The historical record on U.S. policy and democracy in Chile shows an obsessive tendency to halt the ascendancy of the left in Chile at the cost of eroding Chilean democracy, even to the point of destabilizing the constitutional Allende government and contributing to its overthrow, thus revealing the exaggerated role of the anti-Communist motive in foreign policy. However, in specific periods the United States did contribute to the promotion of democracy in Chile, guided by humanitarian motives or libertarian ideals.

The lesson of Chile is that U.S. policy makers should come to realize that relations between Washington and authoritarian regimes are indeed inherently unstable and eventually untenable. The United States has backed military coups and maintained cordial relations with authoritarian regimes. But, inevitably, public opinion and Congress pressure the White House to criticize violations of human rights and to recommend gradual openings of the political systems of dictatorial regimes. The military government affected tends to react by splintering away from Washington, feeling that it is being betrayed.[19] The authoritarian regime, and particularly the new generations of military officers, come to view Washington with great mistrust, and sometimes as a decadent power, so soft on Communism that, in the end, it becomes part of the enemy camp. The only policy that tends to be acceptable to an authoritarian regime is one of unconditional, uncritical support, which, given the U.S. political and value system, is practically impossible.

The frictions registered in the bilateral relationship between the Chilean military government and the United States both under the liberal Carter administration and under the conservative Reagan administration demonstrate the endurance of humanitarian values as an active component of U.S. policy, thus questioning the undisputed primacy of security-related motives. In both instances, nongovernmental actors played a key role, through lobbying and applying pressure, in activating the U.S. concern for humanitarian values such as freedom and respect for human rights.

What instruments should the U.S. government use to promote democracy in the region? Diplomatic pressure is evidently an accepted practice of international relations, as well as certain kinds of economic measures, particularly if they are applied in a multilateral setting and follow the strategies adopted by the local dissident forces. Covert or overt intervention is totally unacceptable as a means of promoting democracy in Latin America and, when used, as in the Chilean case, generally does not lead to the desired outcome.

Also with regard to instruments, some minimal convergence on policy is needed among the decision-making agencies in Washington, so as to place the full weight of the U.S. government on the side of democratization. It should be noticed that at one point, official U.S. policy toward Chile at the State Department was democracy promotion, while the Treasury and the Pentagon were doing everything possible to make life easier for Pinochet.

In the same vein, the Chilean experience shows that relatively autonomous linkages between nongovernmental actors such as business or labor groups can alter policy at the official level. Specifically, Latin Americans have learned to lobby in Washington for their preferred perspectives on democracy and other issues. In sum, nongovernmental actors and ideology must be considered as powerful intervening variables in the relationship between U.S. policy and democracy promotion.

The limited range of instruments that Washington should employ to favor democracy in the region suggests that the United States must understand that its capacity to bring about change and democratization is also very limited. In the end, this further implies that the task of democracy building belongs principally to the citizens of the country involved, and that the United States, although still significant, can play at most a complementary role.

Notes

1. See Michael Hunt, *Ideology and U.S. Foreign Policy* (New Haven: Yale University Press, 1987), pp. 16–17.

2. I owe this additional reflection to Elizabeth Cobbs, who commented on the central thesis of my essay in an exchange of letters following a conference in Los Angeles at which these ideas were presented.

3. On this point see, for example, Arturo and Samuel Valenzuela, *Military Rule in Chile* (Baltimore: Johns Hopkins University Press, 1987), p. 8; and John Peeler, *Latin American Democracies: Colombia, Costa Rica, Venezuela* (Chapel Hill: University of North Carolina Press, 1985), pp. 17–18.

4. Heraldo Muñoz and Carlos Portales, *Amistad Esquiva: las relaciones de Estados Unidos y Chile* (Santiago: Pehuen, 1987), p. 69.

5. The classic text on this subject is the U.S. Senate report *Covert Action in Chile: 1963–1973* (Washington, D.C.: U.S. Government Printing Office, 1975).

6. Robert Pastor, *Condemned to Repetition: The United States and Nicaragua* (Princeton: Princeton University Press, 1988), p. 272.

7. See Hunt, p. 18.

8. See *Los Angeles Times,* July 13, 1986, p. 13, and *El Mercurio,* July 13, pp. A1 and A12.

9. See U.S. Senate, *Covert Action,* pp. 11–12.

10. See Nathaniel Davis, *The Last Two Years of Salvador Allende* (Ithaca: Cornell University Press, 1985), pp. 7–8.

11. See U.S. Senate, *Covert Action,* pp. 11–13.

12. Joseph Tulchin, "The United States and Latin America in the 1960's," mimeograph copy on file at the University of North Carolina, April 1987, p. 13.

13. Ibid., p. 18.

14. An interesting account of the Chicago boys' story can be found in Arturo Fontaine A., *Los Economistas y el Presidente Pinochet* (Santiago: ZigZag, 1988).

15. See U.S. Senate, *Covert Action,* p. 40; also, John Dinges and Saul Landau, *Assassination on Embassy Row* (New York: Pantheon Books, 1980). This book identifies the research organization as the Instituto de Estudios Generales, led in 1973 by Pablo Baraona, a Chicago-trained economist who later became a member of Pinochet's cabinet.

16. Alejandro Foxley provides an excellent analysis of monetarist-Chicago thinking in his *Latin American Experiments in Neoconservative Economics* (Berkeley: University of California Press, 1983), pp. 100–102.

17. See Muñoz and Portales.

18. U.S. Senate, *Covert Action,* p. 36.

19. Not surprisingly, after Batista was overthrown, he wrote his memoirs under the title *Cuba Betrayed* in which he criticized the United States, while Somoza wrote a similar book on the 1979 Nicaraguan experience entitled *Nicaragua Betrayed.*

3 | The Dominican Republic: The Legacy of Intermittent Engagement

Jonathan Hartlyn

> Perhaps in no other country has the influence of the United States been so long and so continuously exerted as in the Dominican Republic, yet in few places have the limits of America's power to transform foreign realities been more evident.
> —Abraham F. Lowenthal, *The Dominican Intervention*

THE Dominican Republic has a long history of U.S. involvement in its internal affairs. Actions by the United States have often been triggered by events on the island republic, although precise policies have usually responded to broader world events, domestic pressures, and the ideological mind-set of central U.S. government actors. The promotion of democracy in the Dominican Republic has rarely been the central, or even a major, goal of U.S. policy, and the consequences of U.S. involvement in the country have sometimes been distinctly counterproductive for that goal.[1]

In some instances, U.S. pressure helped encourage liberalization, while at the same time enmeshing the United States extensively in Dominican affairs in a fashion and with an intensity that could not be sustained. On three different occasions, once in the 1920s and twice in the 1960s, the United States propped up a provisional Dominican government, helped oversee elections, and sought to insure that the winner took office. Yet, military take-overs followed the two elections of 1924 and 1962 (leading eventually in the latter case to a U.S. military invasion). The third election, of 1966, was followed by a set of fraudulent ones. In 1978, employing diplomatic instruments, the United States was helpful in moving forward Dominican democracy, still certainly fragile and uninstitutionalized. Since 1978, the U.S. government has sought to support the integrity of the electoral process while maintaining a low profile. However, each of the subsequent elections has been incident-prone, and in 1990 former president Jimmy Carter, at the head of an international observer team, played an important role supporting the country's Central Electoral Board and mediating among the major candidates.

Some actions taken by the United States appear more positive than others with regard to fostering democratization. Yet, these apparent recurring successes mask a more fundamental failure. Even if the United States had acted solely or primarily to promote democracy over this period, which has not been the case, it cannot simply transform the realities of another country to fit its image of stable, constitutional government. Its efforts to do so, combined with the sometimes abrupt shifts in U.S. policy, have helped distort internal Dominican politics in unintended and occasionally counterproductive ways for the institutionalization of democracy. In the short-term, democratization has sometimes been advanced by U.S. actions, but each of these steps has also helped to reinforce an international dimension to political conflict in the country ultimately inimical to democracy in a sovereign state. The cumulative impact of extensive U.S. involvement in the internal politics of the country itself represents a legacy that will need to be overcome if democracy is ever to be consolidated in the Dominican Republic.

This chapter explores the Dominican political process, U.S. goals and principal policy instruments, and the interaction of major U.S. and Dominican actors in five periods, giving analytical priority to political processes and their relationship to "democracy." Each of these was a critical period in the evolution of Dominican politics; however, the United States was not equally engaged (though it was certainly involved) in all of them. The first period partially overlaps the Wilsonian period and involves the U.S. military occupation of 1916–24. The second is the 1930 accession to power of Rafael Trujillo. Third is the immediate post–World War II period, which was one of relatively brief democratic ferment across the continent. The fourth period covers the complex events from 1959, when the U.S. finally decided it should actively seek the removal of Trujillo, to late 1966, when Joaquín Balaguer was inaugurated president. Major incidents during this period can be subsumed into two subperiods: the first including the assassination of Trujillo and its aftermath, and the victory of Juan Bosch in free elections in 1962 and his overthrow only months after his inauguration; the second, the 1965 U.S. intervention and extensive negotiations leading to elections and Balaguer's victory. Finally, the domestic and international factors related to the democratic transition represented by the 1978 elections will be examined. These elections permitted the first transfer of power by means of elections from one political party to another in the history of the country.

The five periods or "case studies," taken together, suggest that U.S. efforts to promote democracy in Latin America have often occurred in one of three ways: as an ostensible part of military occupation, as part of an extrication effort, and as a means to block a perceived or potential Communist challenge. In each of these cases, democracy forms part of a package of more extensive U.S. goals and intentions, usually involving balancing the felt need to protect certain strategic and economic concerns with the need to gain international or domestic U.S. support for (or blunt opposition to) U.S.

policies, including direct intervention or eventual extrication from such intervention. Extensive involvement in the internal affairs of the target country are often required to insure that basic electoral procedures are followed and constitutional forms obeyed; however, the beneficial long-term impact of such involvement on democracy is questionable. One of the five periods also points to a fourth way that the U.S. promotion of democracy has occurred: it may be a priority goal for a given administration due to ideological reasons, and policies in support of it may be applied particularly when it appears that other perceived national security concerns are not at risk. When security interests are not engaged, military intervention or the threat of its use is unlikely, and the relative success of such policies may depend more clearly and immediately on the nature of internal circumstances in the country. Finally, the Dominican material indicates that at other times the United States has opted not to act in support of democracy or to do so only feebly, as a consequence of a policy of nonintervention in the internal affairs of other countries, conditional on the absence of perceived national security threats. In the Dominican case, these shifts from interventionist policies to a noninterventionist stance had a major impact on internal Dominican politics and were sometimes met with skepticism and confusion by major Dominican figures accustomed to considering the United States as an active participant in their affairs.

Indeed, Dominican actors were not simply passive in the face of U.S. actions. In each of the periods to be examined, Dominican actors sought to enlist U.S. support for their own policies or actions, by employing, manipulating, or subverting U.S. concerns for "democracy," "nonintervention," or "anti-Communism" to their advantage. In that sense, given the weight of U.S. actions in Dominican internal affairs, domestic Dominican political struggles have inevitably incorporated an international dimension as Dominican actors have attempted to build transnational coalitions in support of their particular objectives.

The U.S. Military Occupation, 1916–1924

The U.S. military occupation of the Dominican Republic in 1916 was an outgrowth of a more general policy that led to direct interventions in Cuba, Haiti, Nicaragua, and elsewhere in the same period, as well as the result of specific problems the United States perceived with the management of the Dominican financial debt by its leaders. Yet, serving as a historical backdrop were two conditions: a U.S. strategic concern that no extracontinental power take control of an island so close to its border; and the fact that Dominican leaders, for a combination of reasons related to their own views of national security or for personal advancement, had often actively sought U.S. involvement in Dominican affairs.

The nineteenth-century struggle for independence and for formal sovereignty was a difficult process for the Dominican Republic. Initial independence from Spain, declared in 1821, lasted only a few months in the face of a take-over by neighboring Haiti. In 1844, independence (or secession) was declared anew and successfully withstood some fifteen years of attempts by Haitian governments to reincorporate Dominican territory. Fear of Haiti, which evolved into a strong racist sentiment, led Dominicans to seek protection from powerful third countries, chiefly France, Spain, and the United States. Complex interactions among Dominican governing groups, opposition movements, Haitian authorities, and representatives of these powers ensued.[2] Government revolved largely around a small number of caudillo strongmen and their intrigues involving foreign powers. Spain was persuaded to reannex the country in 1861 (when the United States could do little as it was preoccupied with its own civil war), but internal opposition finally helped restore independence in 1865. An effort to convince the Grant administration to take over the country failed when the U.S. Senate rejected it. Gradually, however, Dominican dependence on its northern neighbor grew.

Financial obligations, political instability, and U.S. involvement in Dominican affairs all expanded from the late nineteenth century and serve as the backdrop for the U.S. intervention in 1916. The assassination of Ulises Heureaux in 1899, ending a seventeen-year reign, led to a period of tremendous upheaval, aggravating the country's serious debt problems. The pressures by European creditors on the Dominican Republic (as well as the Anglo-German blockade of Venezuela in 1902–3) led to President Theodore Roosevelt's "corollary" to the Monroe Doctrine. By 1905, Dominican customs was headed by a U.S. appointee, a relationship that became formalized in a 1907 treaty that also paid off all previous loans with a new one converting the United States into the country's only foreign creditor. The United States took these steps not only to block European actions and insure bond payments, but also because it viewed customs revenue as the main booty in Dominican politics and hoped that U.S. control would promote greater political stability in the country.[3] However, the relatively popular and stable government of Ramón Cáceres established in 1906 ended in 1911 when he, like Heureaux earlier, was assassinated.

The United States unsuccessfully sought the establishment of both a stable and a pliant government in the Dominican Republic from 1911 on, but the two goals worked against each other. Shortly after the inauguration of President Juan Isidro Jiménez in December 1914, the United States demanded the right to appoint U.S. citizens to key financial posts in the Dominican government, even as the U.S. customs officer would also become responsible for collecting and managing internal revenues. Following the U.S. occupation of Haiti in July 1915, demands were added relating to the replacement of the factionalized and politicized Dominican armed forces by a constabulary force controlled by U.S. officers, which the Dominican leader also resisted. Finally, when President Jiménez refused to accept U.S. military troops (he requested only arms) to help put down a rebellion by the head of the armed forces, General Desiderio Arias, U.S. troops were landed anyway to "protect the life and interests" of the American legation and other foreigners.[4] Dominicans expected a brief U.S. military presence that would depart following elections, and even U.S. officials had not planned for a lengthy occupation. Following Jiménez's resignation, "Dominican politicians continued their fratricidal struggles for power, particularly over control of the now vacant presidency."[5]

In the face of Dominican refusal to accept all the financial and military conditions requested, State Department and Navy Department officials implemented a plan for a U.S. military government in the country in November 1916, following its approval by President Wilson. The legal and diplomatic justification for the intervention was built on presumed increases in Dominican debt in violation of the 1907 treaty. What mix of motives lay behind the decision is still a matter of scholarly debate. Some focus on the protection of U.S. economic interests. In a narrow sense, an economic argument is not convincing given the minimal U.S. investments in the country even compared with those in Cuba or Mexico and the fact that Dominican leaders had in fact generally favored foreign economic interests. Understood in a broad sense (sometimes blurring with strategic concerns) of seeking not only guaranteed access to the Dominican market but also control of the sea lanes close to the Panama Canal and to markets throughout the continent, this could be a background motive. Others note growing U.S. strategic or geopolitical concerns, especially with a potential German presence in the Caribbean, given the fact that General Arias and other Dominican politicians were openly pro-German; yet, there is little reference to Germany in U.S. diplomatic and military papers until after the occupation, suggesting this was also a background factor and not an immediate concern.[6] Finally, a third background motive that almost certainly played a role is the Wilson administration's liberal interventionist zeal, which combined self-righteousness, a sense of superiority, and a desire to bring "good government" to Latin American peoples.[7]

As the Dominican case receded from the concerns of top administration officials, day-to-day management of the military occupation fell to Navy Department officials, particularly those in the Dominican Republic who were left largely on their own. The State Department found itself increasingly marginalized until internal problems and political debates within the United States, sparked in part by the efforts of Dominican nationalists, forced greater attention to the issue in 1920–21.

The goals of the occupation forces only gradually began to take shape. Their immediate actions were intended to establish control over the country quickly and seek to insure peace and stability. Military officers were named to major posts in the executive, while press censorship was imposed and steps were taken to disarm the population; the legislature, in turn, was "suspended." Eventually, the military moved to implement what could be characterized as "technocratic Progressive" reforms, under the assumption that certain socioeconomic, financial, and administrative changes would generate the conditions for political and constitutional stability. Programs were enacted in education, health, sanitation, agriculture, and communications; highways were built and other public works were carried out; and a census was taken. The United States was to discover, though, that problems relating to politics, stable government, nationalism, and coalition building could not be resolved so neatly.[8]

Ultimately, the most significant measure was the establishment of a new Dominican constabulary force. In the Dominican Republic as elsewhere in Central America and the Caribbean, U.S. officials hoped that the establishment of new constabulary forces initially under U.S. tutelage would permanently depoliticize the armed forces in these countries, serving to bolster stable, constitutional government. In the Dominican case, the newly formed Guardia Nacional Dominicana suffered from lack of resources, from difficulties in attracting good recruits, and from unclear objectives, as its duties and size made it fall somewhere between a police force and a military force. Only after the mid-1921 announcement of a plan for withdrawal did the U.S. military government focus its attention on creating an effective force.[9]

The U.S. occupation always confronted domestic Dominican opposition. This included peasant guerrilla conflicts in the eastern region of the country (characterized by the occupation government as banditry) for almost five years, from 1917 to 1922. More effective use of local Dominican forces against the guerrillas, a generous amnesty, and the increasingly apparent fact that the United States was seeking to end its occupation facilitated what was essentially a negotiated surrender by the guerrilla groups in early 1922.[10]

A campaign mounted by a variety of Dominican political and economic groups was much more significant in accelerating the U.S. withdrawal. This effort was led by Francisco Henríquez y Carvajal, who had been elected provisional president by the Dominican Congress in 1916 prior to the declaration of the U.S. military government, and many of his close associates. Although not linked to the violent peasant-based conflicts of the country's eastern region, the existence of the latter probably strengthened their case. Nationalist activities began vigorously in 1916 but were suspended as the United States entered World War I. The end of the war, however, quickly revived efforts to force an end to the occupation. Henríquez y Carvajal traveled to the Versailles Peace Conference in early 1919 though the United States successfully blocked his attempt to have the Dominican case considered there. With the end of the war, however, the Dominicans found a greater receptivity among some U.S. groups (especially the American Federation of Labor) and magazines (including *The Nation* and *Current History*). They hired a U.S. lawyer, Horace Knowles, who became an effective advocate for their cause. Dominicans also lobbied in Europe and in Latin America, and increasing protests by Latin American governments began to receive greater attention in the U.S. State Department. Within the Dominican Republic, the impact of the nationalist groups was initially more limited due to military censorship and political infighting.

Tensions between the State Department and the U.S. military governor grew. The latter urged the State Department to announce that the occupation should continue for at least another twenty years, the time deemed necessary to insure Dominicans could govern themselves. In the typically understated words of a U.S. diplomat of that period, this advice "gave the Department of State cause for reflection."[11]

The State Department began to take greater responsibility for managing Dominican affairs. It told the military governor to appoint a local "Junta Consultiva" similar to one recommended by Henríquez y Carvajal. Sensitive to Latin American and international pressure, the State Department cautiously began pursuing withdrawal options. Rejection by the military governor of several of the modest demands of the junta helped mobilize increased domestic support for the nationalists, including more radical, uncompromising positions than those espoused by Henríquez y Carvajal and the exiled Unión Nacional Dominicana organization. At the same time, lobbying efforts by Dominicans within the United States as well as in Latin America and Europe expanded, and the Dominican Republic became a topic of discussion in the 1920 U.S. presidential campaign.

Complex negotiations ensued beginning in 1920 that finally led to a U.S. withdrawal in 1924. Sumner Welles in the State Department drafted a plan made public in December 1920 that declared the U.S. intention to withdraw from the Dominican Republic following the enactment of certain constitutional amendments. Radical nationalists, who increasingly dominated the domestic political scene, rejected it out of hand, calling for immediate withdrawal with no conditions *(evacuación pura y simple)*. Following Harding's inauguration, pressure increased for an end to the occupation. A new, more moderate military governor presented a Harding plan for withdrawal in June 1921, which included measures for a possible extension of U.S. control over internal Dominican revenues, a Guardia Nacional to be led by U.S. officers, and withdrawal to follow several months after elections under U.S. supervision. Dominican nationalists accepted elections under the U.S. occupation but called for all other details to be negotiated following withdrawal. However, their hopes that a U.S. Senate investigation of the Haitian and Dominican occupations in late 1921 would be sharply critical were not realized even as efforts to forge greater political unity among themselves also failed. This opened the door for a compromise agreement worked out between a prominent Dominican, Francisco Peynado, and the

U.S. secretary of state, Charles Evans Hughes, even as a barrage of negative publicity about the continuing occupation continued within the United States.[12] The Hughes-Peynado agreement removed onerous elements of the previous plans, including the presence of U.S. officers in the Guardia, a U.S. financial adviser, and possible control of internal finances. It called for a provisional Dominican government to oversee the elections, maintenance of the 1907 customs treaty until payments on 1918–22 bonds had been completed, and other prewithdrawal measures.[13]

Delicate, skillful diplomacy was required to convince Dominicans to accept the accord. That task fell to Sumner Welles, who managed to curtail demands of the military governor as well as to marginalize remaining nationalist opposition to the agreement, published in final form in September 1922. Nationalist forces that had played such an important role in pressuring for U.S. withdrawal ultimately became marginalized from the political process as the leaders of the traditional parties began to reassert themselves.

The provisional government was appointed in October 1922 and confronted numerous obstacles, particularly revolving around charges of bias and questionable procedures in the upcoming elections. As described by Dominicans and North Americans alike, the electoral campaign involved brutal, nasty tactics, with a willingness by some political leaders to do almost anything for personal political advantage (even at the risk of continuing the occupation) and an unwillingness to compromise among certain nationalists; an assassination plot by nationalist forces against the presidential candidates, Welles, and others was even uncovered. Nevertheless, the elections went off as scheduled in March 1924, with effective measures implemented to insure their fairness. Horacio Vásquez and his party emerged as clear victors, a result almost immediately recognized by his principal opponent, Francisco Peynado. Vásquez was inaugurated president in July 1924 and the last U.S. marine left the country in September of that year.[14] Ultimately, the timing and nature of the withdrawal have to be understood as a result of the effectiveness of Dominican opposition domestically and especially abroad and the perceived increased costs of the Dominican occupation to U.S. interests elsewhere in Latin America.[15]

The promotion of "stable, constitutional government"—the holding of elections and the transfer of power to the duly elected government by the U.S. occupying force—was an essential part of the extrication package carefully put together by the State Department, although the economic agreements and other measures were also of crucial importance. The U.S. military leaders in charge of the occupation had foreseen as necessary a much lengthier stay to achieve constitutional Dominican self-government. At best, they were naive about the likely consequences of their already extended presence in the country, their well-meaning intentions to help the Dominican Republic with good works notwithstanding. Among these consequences was an important current of nationalist resentment coexisting with another ambivalently seeking to continue involving the United States in Dominican affairs. Yet, the most powerful illustration of the tragic consequences of occupation, however unintended, was to be the emergence of the brutal Trujillo dictatorship.

Trujillo's Accession to Power and the Role of the United States

From military occupation—the most complete involvement possible in the affairs of another country short of formal colonization or annexation—the U.S. began to move toward an opposite extreme of "noninterventionism" in the 1920s.[16] This approach emerged in reaction to the growing Latin American and international opposition to U.S. occupations in the Caribbean and Central America. It was facilitated by the absence of any perceived threat to continued U.S. influence in the area from an outside power, as it gradually became transformed into President Roosevelt's Good Neighbor Policy.

Largely unintentional, but somewhat predictable, consequences of the occupation combined with this shift in U.S. policy toward noninterventionism to provide an opportunity for the head of the country's newly established military force to take power. Rafael Leonidas Trujillo Molina began his meteoric rise within the newly established Guardia Nacional Dominicana in 1919. Six years later he became a colonel and head of the renamed Policia Nacional. In May 1928, he was promoted to brigadier general in order to head the national army, which had evolved from the country's police force.[17]

At the same time, the country's political patterns, which predated the U.S. occupation, continued. These were based on personalistic and clientelistic rule, intrigue, and occasional rebellion. President Vásquez, elected for a four year term in 1924, arranged for a constitutional reform to extend his term an additional two years, and subsequently sought reelection. Complex political maneuverings by opposing groups ensued, as discontent grew and the country's economic situation deteriorated. Finally, an uprising against the president occurred in Santiago in February 1930, some three months before the scheduled elections. Through complex negotiations that preserved the form of constitutionalism, the presumed leader of that rebellion, Rafael Estrella Ureña, became provisional president pending the elections. What became increasingly evident was that Trujillo had played a critical, secretive role in insuring the success of the rebellion against Vásquez, in large part because he realized that if Vásquez remained in office he would be replaced.[18]

An elaborate, occasionally bloody, charade then ensured. Two political groups emerged for the elections, one with Trujillo and Estrella Ureña as presidential and vice-presidential candidates respectively. Trujillo employed the army for his own selective purposes of repression, leading the Central Electoral Board to resign some nine days before the elections and then the other party to withdraw the day before. Official results gave Trujillo the victory by a 99 percent margin, with a reported 45 percent abstention rate.[19] Following the election, Trujillo reassured the U.S. legation that he would seeks its guidance and counsel.

What role did the United States play in Trujillo's election? Although the political events that eventually brought Trujillo to power were consistent with past political patterns in the country, several consequences of the U.S. military occupation combined with "lessons" Trujillo may have learned greatly strengthened his capabilities as head of the newly formed military force. The U.S. military occupation had changed the Dominican Republic. The major regions of the country were now linked to Santo Domingo, the capital city, by highways and improved communications. The population was largely disarmed, limiting further the possibilities of armed uprisings as had occurred in the country's past. The intention had been to provide the material bases for constitutional rule whose stability would be assured by a stronger but depoliticized police force. Yet, there were two other alternatives. One was that the new armed force would fractionalize, provoking civil war (a central element of what was to happen years later in April 1965). The other was that the head of this new force, in part because of the changes instituted during the occupation period, could more effectively control the country in dictatorial fashion, as in fact occurred under Trujillo. In addition, the U.S. military had confronted the guerrilla challenge and controlled the population through a variety of repressive measures. It is difficult to determine the particular link between these actions and the repressive steps applied by the head of the newly formed and newly trained centralized police force that was one of the legacies of the intervention, although it is not unreasonable to assume there were some.[20]

Finally, the policy of "nonintervention" espoused by the State Department was to assist Trujillo. Throughout this period, Trujillo was concerned about a potential U.S. veto; he apparently surmised (correctly, as it turned out) that the United States would accept a government he headed if it appeared to come to power through elections, even questionable ones, although an outright coup d'etat would be unacceptable. The United States had accepted the questionable extension of Vásquez's term in office from four to six years as it was accomplished respecting constitutional formalities. And in the negotiations that followed the February 1930 "revolution," the U.S. minister in the country, Charles Curtis, had reluctantly accepted Estrella Ureña's provisional presidency in part because it had complied with constitutional requirements. During the discussions between President Vásquez and Estrella, which took place in the U.S. legation, Curtis indicated that the legation would not under any circumstances recommend U.S. recognition of a Trujillo administration (Trujillo had hoped that he, rather than

Estrella, could become the provisional president). The agreement between Vásquez and Estrella had specified that neither Trujillo nor Vásquez's vice-president could be candidates in the 1930 elections.

Curtis later came to believe that estimates of potential U.S. behavior entered into the calculations of most major Dominican politicians. He argued that Estrella and a coconspirator, Elias Brache, had convinced Trujillo to join them against Vásquez by promising Trujillo that he would be the presidential candidate of a party organized by them for that purpose. But then, in the negotiations with Vásquez, they betrayed Trujillo by eliminating him as a candidate, counting upon the United States to enforce the agreement (Estrella had sought out Curtis's view of Trujillo before reaching agreement with Vásquez). Brache, in turn, was the figure who placed Trujillo's name in nomination, removing Estrella as a rival. He, too, hoped that Trujillo would be blocked by the United States, which would pave the way for his own candidacy.[21]

In the meantime, Trujillo began his practice of reaching out to U.S. government and military officials he felt might be friendly to him. In January 1930, Trujillo sent a group of Dominican officers to speak with his former military commander, Colonel Cutts, stationed in Haiti. They told Cutts that Trujillo felt the army might be forced to take charge of the situation because of the political crisis in the country. Cutts informed the State Department of the meeting, asserted he made no promises, and noted that he did not believe Trujillo was politically ambitious and that, as Trujillo was already wealthy, he would not seek power for that reason either.[22] Crassweller asserts that Cutts visited Trujillo in March 1930. At that time, he informed Trujillo that the United States did not favor his coming to power, although he also assured him that the United States would recognize any government that resulted from regular elections.[23]

In part, Cutts was reflecting State Department policy, which could be characterized as *conditional* nonintervention. Curtis, who distrusted Trujillo, was refused permission by the State Department to declare that a Trujillo government would not be recognized (a step that Estrella Ureña was urging and Curtis supported). The State Department showed no interest in interfering actively in Dominican affairs, *unless* U.S. lives or property or the operation of the customs receivership were at risk.[24] Although the State Department did suggest that the minister try to convince Trujillo not to run, it was prepared to recognize a potential Trujillo victory, noting that "through scrupulously avoiding even the appearances of interfering in the internal affairs of the Dominican Republic our relations with Santo Domingo have been put on a very sound basis in the 6 years since the withdrawal of the military occupation."[25] None of the candidates in the 1930 elections presented a threat to U.S. interests; in fact, the opposition candidates in certain respects may even have been preferable. In essence, as Trujillo's election at least obeyed the formalities of the Dominican constitution, it could be viewed with indifference in the absence of any threat to U.S. interests.[26]

In retrospect, it is unclear if a more forthright U.S. attitude in 1930 short of military intervention or threatened intervention could have prevented Trujillo's accession to power. However, a more vocal protest of the trampling of electoral procedures and of the violence perpetrated by Trujillo's henchmen could at least have put some distance between the United States and Trujillo's government. The United States facilitated Trujillo's coming to power by a variety of conditions, even if mostly unintentional, that resulted from military occupation of the country. That the larger power would then switch to the opposite extreme and refuse to take more aggressive steps to prevent Trujillo's coming to power on the grounds that it would be inappropriately interventionist to do so left many Dominicans confused and doubtful about true U.S. intentions.

In the absence of a serious threat to U.S. lives and property, the State Department did not want the United States to be open to the charge of intervention in the Dominican elections, the views of its representative in the country notwithstanding. Yet, it also appears that in U.S. military circles, Trujillo's take-over of power was not viewed unfavorably. In subsequent years, Trujillo would continue to sidestep U.S. diplomats in Santo Domingo when necessary, assiduously cultivating his U.S. military contacts, even as he provided attention and lavish gifts to U.S. congressmen and hired lobbyists he thought could gain him influence in Washington.

In the case of the Dominican Republic, as in a number of other Central American and Caribbean countries, the United States had an overwhelming presence and a history of intervention. In these situations, a shift to a policy of nonintervention (or, more precisely, of more restricted conditions under which it would actively intervene) can have consequences for the internal affairs of the other country as dramatic as actual intervention. As Dominicans doubted this represented a permanent shift away from intervention in their affairs, they continued their ambiguous attempts to reach out to, seek to identify with, or attempt to employ U.S. power for their purposes while resenting its presence. As we shall see, in subsequent periods when it felt its national security was at greater risk, the United States did not hesitate to attempt once again to micromanage Dominican affairs.

Trujillo and the Post–World War II "Democratic Period"

The final years of World War II and the first postwar years in the Dominican Republic, like in much of the rest of the continent, were years of democratic ferment. Military governments were replaced in El Salvador, Guatemala, and Venezuela, and strongmen throughout the continent felt uneasy. As it turned out, U.S. attention was soon diverted largely to other areas of the world and to concerns about Communism rather than democracy. Yet, during this period in the Dominican Republic, an incipient Dominican labor moment and other democratic elements emerged. Trujillo felt the need for a controlled liberalization, but little else. As in much of the rest of Latin America where liberalization often went further, even this minuscule opening in the Dominican Republic was short-lived. The labor movement and Communist leaders were brutally repressed, and Trujillo was easily able to manage his reelection in 1947.

Through the 1930s, Trujillo began to centralize power in his hands quickly. A number of conspiracies, including at least two major ones, were discovered and brutally put down in his first term in office. At that time, Trujillo also created the Dominican party, which came to monopolize electoral politics, and all elected officials were required to give written but undated resignations to Trujillo, as head of the party. Through ceaseless and imaginative manipulation, Trujillo would continue to maintain the fiction of preserving constitutional forms: constitutions, carefully amended as necessary; elections, with results duly certified; and laws carefully approved according to constitutional requirements. At the same time, he insured his total personal power, while amassing tremendous wealth and demonstrating his resentment of the so-called *gente de primera* (aristocratic elite) in the country. He easily gained reelection for a second four-year term in 1934. However, reaction by the United States and other countries to the brutal massacre of 12,000 to 25,000 Haitians in October 1937 in the border region between the two countries forced him to step aside for the 1938–42 period.[27]

Trujillo proved himself a loyal ally to the United States as war became more imminent. In the 1933–37 period, there is evidence not only of Trujillo's sympathies toward fascism and particularly toward Nazi Germany, but of concrete assistance to them. However, pragmatically recognizing his country's dependence on the United States and President Roosevelt's open hostility to Hitler from early 1938 on, Trujillo began to cooperate actively with the United States against German interests in his own country. U.S. military remained on extremely close terms with Trujillo. On his visit to the United States in 1939 (in fact, his first trip ever outside of the Dominican Republic), Trujillo was accompanied by a U.S. marine officer who had stayed on following the occupation as an adviser. In Washington, his warmest receptions were among the military; for example, General Breckridge, Trujillo's former commanding officer in the Guardia Nacional in 1924, received him with fullest honors as the head of Quantico Military Base. President Roosevelt did agree to see Trujillo, though only in a private meeting, and Trujillo's meeting with Secretary of State Cordell Hull was also quite formal.[28]

During the war, the overriding concern of the United States in the Caribbean was the maintenance of sympathetic, cooperative governments. Never was a doubt expressed about the logic of opposing the Axis powers in the name of democracy while maintaining good relations with dictators such as Trujillo. Under the circumstances, Trujillo was easily able to arrange his election for a five-year term in 1942. Even though he was anti-Trujillo, Under Secretary of State Sumner Welles gave little encouragement to the various Dominican exile groups with whom he maintained informal contact, citing the overriding importance to his country of the war effort.[29] The most important of these exile groups was the Partido Revolucionario Dominicano (PRD—Dominican Revolutionary Party), led by Juan Bosch and formed in exile in Cuba in 1939. In its 1943 Congress, the PRD adopted the phrase "For the Victory of Democracy in the Dominican Republic and in the Whole World." However, though they did not suspend activities as did nationalist Dominicans during World War I, even they recognized that Trujillo was unlikely to fall during the war.[30] Yet, their hopes that Trujillo's fate would change after the war were not to be realized.

The end of the war and changes in State Department personnel did bring new pressures to bear on Trujillo. Spruille Braden was named assistant secretary of state for American Republic Affairs in August 1945, following his vocal opposition against the Peronist government as U.S. ambassador in Argentina (which he continued in an ultimately counterproductive fashion from Washington). His appointment reflected an endorsement of his more activist, "prodemocratic" policies following the victory of "democracy" in the war.[31] This soon became evident in U.S. attitudes toward Trujillo. In December 1945, the State Department rejected a Dominican request for an export license for a large shipment of ammunition; in uncharacteristically blunt language, it was explained that the United States had a "warmer feeling of friendship" with democratic governments and that the U.S. government "has been unable to perceive that democratic principles have been observed there (in the Dominican Republic) in theory or in practice."[32] Trujillo was outraged and focused attacks on Braden. He sponsored the publication of a vitriolic tract that accused Braden of "serving Soviet interests," of viewing as democratic "the flirting of Communist and Communistoid governments with the Kremlin," and of qualifying "resistance to Soviet penetration . . . as fascism." The book also bitterly attacked the Venezuelan political leader, Rómulo Betancourt ("Communist of wide repute"), among others.[33]

Changes and ferment within the Dominican Republic also put pressures upon Trujillo. Inchoate Communist influence within the Dominican Republic expanded with the arrival in 1939 and 1940 of a small number of Communist-inspired Spanish refugees. The constituent congress of the country's first Communist party, which came to be called the Partido Socialista Popular (after Cuba's Communist party, which became a crucial link for the Dominican party), took place in February 1944. Persecution soon drove many of the leaders into exile. However, in January 1946 the first (and only) successful strike during the Trujillo period broke out in the sugar lands of La Romana and San Pedro de Marcorís. It was led by Mauricio Báez, a Communist who was apparently killed on Trujillo's orders four years later while in exile in Cuba.[34]

Trujillo responded to the external and internal pressures through a carefully controlled opening. In 1945, he established diplomatic relations with the Soviet Union. Through emissaries, he convinced Dominican Communists in their Cuban exile to return in order to function openly and legally, which they did in late 1946. They held a labor congress and several rallies around the country. However, the month after Trujillo's reelection in May 1947, he had the party declared illegal. An ensuing wave of repression effectively destroyed the party, as Trujillo swung sharply behind the growing U.S. cold war attitude.

Trujillo also sent letters to leaders of past political parties, encouraging them to reorganize them. Rafael Estrella took up the invitation, reorganizing his Republican party. However, indirect media attacks against the party led the other previous leaders of the party to reaffirm their loyalty to Trujillo and the brief and limited revival ended with Estrella's death in September 1945. Two other parties, the National Labor and National Democratic, were seemingly brought back and participated in the 1947 elections. However, the opposition candidates expressed their adherence to Trujillo in the press, and in 1952 were elected deputies as members of Trujillo's Dominican party.[35] In that year, Trujillo also stepped aside from the formal duties of the presidency; his brother, a pliant individual, was duly elected.

During this period, Trujillo also faced increased challenges from hostile Latin American governments, particularly those of Ramón Grau San Martín in Cuba, Rómulo Betancourt in Venezuela, and Juan José Arévalo in Guatemala, and the Dominican exile groups they supported. As early as January 1945, Bosch in exile was actively seeking weapons and funds for a possible invasion and overthrow of Trujillo. The Dominican legation was attacked in Caracas and the new Venezuelan government broke diplomatic relations with Trujillo (as did the Cuban and Guatemalan governments during this period), as part of its diplomatic offensive in favor of collective intervention in support of democracy. At the same time, Trujillo was involved in conspiracies seeking the overthrow of Betancourt in Venezuela and Grau in Cuba.[36]

Increasing collaboration among figures of the democratic left in the Caribbean area led in 1947 to the first of several attempted invasions to overthrow Trujillo. The United States was aware of these invasion plans as early as November 1946, though it made little effort to stop them and there is no evidence that it passed this information on to Trujillo. However, beginning in March 1947, the United States attitude began to harden. It informed the Cuban, Dominican, and Venezuelan governments of its opposition to the use of U.S. territory in order to organize invasions of other countries.

Yet Cuba continued to give considerable assistance to the formation of an exile military expedition throughout 1947, which gradually organized itself on Cayo Confites, a small key off of Cuba. The United States continually pressured the Cuban government to deter the invasion and took careful measures to track the progress of the invasion. Under this U.S. pressure, the Cuban military largely stopped the operation, though a small group managed to embark and was subsequently captured by the Cubans.[37] A subsequent attempt against Trujillo organized from Guatemala led only to one small group arriving in the coastal Dominican town of Luperón in July 1949, where they were quickly captured.[38]

Ultimately, overriding U.S. policy concerns in Europe combined with a general Latin American preference for noninterventionism help explain U.S. unwillingness to involve itself extensively in efforts to oppose dictatorial though seemingly stable regimes, such as that of Trujillo. By 1947, the United States was expressing opposition to "outside"—that is, Communist—intervention in Europe (especially Greece). Inconsistency by supporting outside intervention in the Caribbean could work against U.S. policy goals in Europe and appeared unnecessary in the absence of any perceived U.S. national security reason to do so. This attitude of opposition to outside intervention found resonance in a general Latin American preference for noninterventionism (as represented in various resolutions of the emerging Organization of American States).[39] Both of these factors came to favor Trujillo, despite the willingness of some Latin governments to assist exile groups opposed to him. Exile groups were largely unsuccessful in encouraging more active U.S. participation against Trujillo, even as the United States came to oppose the exile invasion operations. Perhaps if these invasions had occurred even a year earlier, the attitude of the United States would have been different. Essentially, with the retirement of Braden from the State Department in June 1947 there was a return to correct and cooperative, though not excessively cordial, relations between Trujillo and the United States until the end of the 1950s.

U.S. Intervention and Dominican Democracy, 1959–1966

If the last two sections have highlighted a U.S. policy of relative restraint and nonintervention, in sharp contrast to the period of military occupation, the pendulum swung sharply back again in the late 1950s. From 1959 to 1961, the "United States engaged in its most massive intervention in the internal affairs of a Latin American state since the inauguration of the Good Neighbor Policy."[40] This extensive involvement continued even following the death of Trujillo, culminating with the 1965 intervention and its aftermath. A summary of U.S. policy intentions during this period is provided in President John Kennedy's often-cited dictum that in descending order of preferences the United States would prefer a democratic regime, continuation of a Trujillo regime, or a Castro regime, and that the U.S. should aim for the first, but not renounce the second until it was sure the third could be avoided.

From the perspective of U.S. policy, the weight analysts place on different U.S. policy objectives during this period, as well as the estimate they make of the relative "threat" to U.S. interests, determines the extent to which U.S. activities are characterized as a "success" or a "failure." Unlike Nicaragua, where the family dynasty continued following the assassination of Anastasio Somoza (the father) in 1956, in the Dominican Republic efforts by the Trujillo family to retain power after Trujillo's death failed, and U.S. pressure played a central role in that. The different political trajectories of the Dominican Republic and of Nicaragua may be due, at least in part, to this fact. Similarly, the extent of polarization and of bloody repression that followed in the years after the U.S. intervention in the Dominican Republic in 1965 were certainly less than those that came in the decades after the U.S.-sponsored overthrow of Jacobo Arbenz in Guatemala in 1954. The weight of different domestic circumstances, including the different internal dynamics generated when an established government is overthrown (Guatemala) versus the interruption of an effort to return a government to power (Dominican Republic), probably plays a greater explanatory role here regarding the lesser extent of polarization and repression in the Dominican Republic, though U.S. policies must also be factored in.

Ultimately, though, the events of this period must be viewed as representing a failure of U.S. policy, particularly as related to the ambivalent U.S. commitment to the promotion of democracy. Although the United States helped prevent a direct continuation of Trujillismo by its actions in 1961–62, and played a key role in the democratic 1962 elections, its extensive involvement in Dominican affairs did not translate into successful democracy as Bosch was overthrown a few months after his inauguration. Multiple internal causes may be cited to explain Bosch's overthrow, but his overthrow and the civil-military conspiracies it eventually spawned, combined with the U.S. fear of a "second Cuba," set the stage for the 1965 U.S. military intervention. Although some have viewed that intervention as a key factor in generating Dominican democracy (an argument explored later), in my view, in addition to its cost in human lives, it once again drew the United States into Dominican politics as a central actor, reinforcing conspiratorial and cynical attitudes toward politics that have been so inimical to Dominican democracy. During this period of extensive, complex, and oscillating U.S. involvement in Dominican affairs, democracy promotion was associated primarily with issues of anti-Communism and of extrication.

Several factors contributed to the massive change in U.S. policy toward the Dominican Republic in 1959. Of these the most important was the startling collapse of Batista in Cuba to the forces of Fidel Castro. Suddenly, support for Trujillo appeared to carry greater risks than it had in the past. This fear was itself augmented by a turn toward more erratic and repressive rule by Trujillo in the late 1950s, including abductions and assassination plots outside of the Dominican Republic. Trujillo also faced growing domestic opposition, exile activism, and international pressure, particularly from Latin American governments, several of which had historic enmities with Trujillo. Costa Rica, and particularly Venezuela with the return to power of Betancourt, pursued strongly anti-Trujillo policies and urged the same on the United States, particularly as a useful strategy prior to any U.S. request for hemispheric solidarity against Cuba.

In contrast to 1947, arguments revolving around national security concerns and consistency in foreign policy now impelled the United States toward a more, rather than a less, interventionist course in the Dominican Republic. The United States moved against Trujillo, then, for two major reasons. On the one hand, the Eisenhower and then the Kennedy administrations wished to embark on a more interventionist policy against the perceived growing threat in Cuba, and Latin American support for a shift away from noninterventionism against Cuba required a willingness for the United States to act against rightist dictators as well. On the other hand, after the fall of Batista, the United States also began to believe that political democracy and social reform might serve as stronger bulwarks against Communism than dictators such as Trujillo. This, too, called for a more active, interventionist strategy. The promotion of liberalization (and, eventually, perhaps democracy) as a strategy, then, appeared subsumed to other objectives related to the struggle against Communism, in Cuba specifically, and against its spread elsewhere in the hemisphere. Yet, regardless of their motives, the pressures placed upon the Trujillo regime were very real, and several of the actions taken against it have now generally been recognized as acceptable, though more due to their link to the preservation of human rights than to their promotion of democracy per se.

The U.S. shift did not occur immediately following the fall of Batista. At a meeting of OAS foreign ministers in August 1959, the U.S. secretary of state Christian Herter opposed Cuban and Venezuelan calls to relax the principal of nonintervention. Yet, activities against Trujillo were picking up force. In June of that year, with assistance from Castro and moral and probably more substantial support as well from Betancourt, Dominican exiles had launched another failed attack against the hated dictator. An underground movement inspired by that attack and by the Cuban example sprung up and massive human rights violations followed its destruction in January 1960. Many of those now resisting Trujillo espoused far more radical objectives than did the exiles of the 1940s and early 1950s.[41]

And, in the United States the PRD worked hard to mobilize U.S. public opinion against Trujillo. In their view, one of their greatest triumphs was a letter sent to the U.S. ambassador to the OAS in March 1960, signed by

Norman Thomas and some 250 others, including Sidney Hook, Arthur Schlesinger, Hubert Humphrey, Paul Douglas, and Henry Kissinger, which also appeared as a paid advertisement in the press. The letter called on the OAS to appoint an ad hoc committee to protect human rights in the Dominican Republic, as the situation in the country threatened not only innocent lives but also hemispheric peace. Trujillo's response, by means of a declaration of the Dominican Congress also published in the U.S. press, attacked racism in the United States and persecution of Puerto Rican nationalists, serving to strain relations with several of Trujillo's supporters among conservative southern Democrats.[42]

By the spring 1960, a new orientation was emerging. The first report of the Inter-American Peace Committee chaired by the United States, released in April 1960, expressed tremendous sympathy for antidictatorial exiles, who "taking refuge in other American States . . . find sympathy and moral support," sometimes even for violent action. The report came close to suggesting that the dictatorial regime was at fault, regardless of who started the hostilities. Collective action against dictatorships could be possible, then, as these governments represented a threat to international peace.[43] A second Peace Committee report, released in June, confirmed Venezuelan charges of gross human rights violations in the Dominican Republic, and blamed these for aggravating international tensions in the Caribbean area. For the first time, an OAS body had ignored the principle of nonintervention and had condemned the internal policies of a non-Communist American state.[44]

Further steps against Trujillo soon followed, though Latin American states remained divided on how to balance concerns over human rights violations and dictatorship in the Dominican Republic with the principle of nonintervention. These steps were facilitated by the convincing evidence linking Trujillo to a failed assassination attempt against Betancourt in June 1960. At the next meeting of the OAS foreign ministers in August 1960, Venezuela sought an economic embargo and collective suspension of diplomatic relations with the Dominican Republic. The United States, in turn, desired the establishment of an OAS committee to travel to the Dominican Republic to negotiate for free elections; if this effort failed, then sanctions should be imposed. In this way, the United States hoped to control leadership succession in the Dominican Republic, but its interventionist tone went too far for most Latin American states. Instead, OAS members agreed to interrupt diplomatic relations and to end arms shipments to the island republic, with additional sanctions to come if deemed necessary. The United States, in any event Trujillo's only arms supplier, had already suspended shipments, but this was the first time since the OAS was founded that sanctions were imposed.[45]

Trujillo attempted again a controlled "liberalization" but the United States and other international actors were now openly skeptical. Prior to the OAS meeting, Trujillo resigned as head of the Dominican party and in

August his brother resigned from the presidency, to be replaced by the vice-president Joaquín Balaguer. Free elections were promised and opposition parties were asked to organize. Out of desperation, Trujillo began to turn to the Soviet bloc. The Communist party was legalized in June 1960 but emissaries to the Soviet Union met with no success. And, according to evidence uncovered by the Church committee in 1975, in the spring 1960 the U.S. ambassador had made contact with a conspiratorial group in the Dominican Republic who he knew intended to assassinate Trujillo. In July 1960, the delivery of "sterile" rifles to the conspirators was authorized by CIA and State Department officials, though the delivery was postponed upon their request—the conspirators were seeking a support figure within the armed forces whom they did not find until the spring 1961.[46]

The Eisenhower administration took an additional step against Trujillo by insuring the Dominican Republic would not experience a bonanza due to the cancellation of Cuba's sugar quota in July 1960. Members of the southern agricultural leadership in Congress, many still supportive of Trujillo, prevented legislation authorizing the president to limit the Dominican quota. The problem was circumvented, however, by placing an additional tax on all imported Dominican sugar. Toward the end of the year, under the urging of the United States and of Venezuela, OAS economic sanctions were extended to include petroleum, trucks, and spare parts.[47] The country's economic situation declined, capital flight—notably by Trujillo family members—increased, and blundering repression continued.

In that context, conspirators who had largely been former supporters of the regime successfully assassinated Trujillo on May 30, 1961.[48] However, their plot was discovered before they could move against other major members of the Trujillo clan. Attention immediately focused on what kind of regime would replace Trujillo. Members of the Trujillo family sought to retain power, Balaguer fought for an independent power base, multiple underground movements began to function more openly, and exile groups, including Juan Bosch's PRD, soon returned to the island. In the days after Trujillo's assassination, a U.S. Navy task force patrolled off shore, prepared to implement previously approved plans for armed intervention. Its purpose was to block any possible Cuban involvement and prevent the success of any pro-Communist movement in the country.[49]

The United States now sought both directly and through the OAS to insulate the country from "Castro Communism" while hopefully moving it away from Trujillismo. All available policy instruments—diplomatic, economic, military, covert—were employed, a fact that was feasible given U.S. strategic dominance of the Caribbean and that came at relatively low cost both domestically and internationally, given the hatred that the Trujillo name evoked. A special OAS committee was sent to the Dominican Republic in June. But United States' desires that it remain for an indefinite stay and play a central role in a process of democratization were disappointed, as it left after one week. The representatives from Panama, Colombia, and Uruguay may have been sympathetic to U.S. objectives, but they feared a split within the OAS. Argentina and Mexico had both refused to serve on the committee. Nevertheless, OAS sanctions were retained on the grounds that the extent of change represented by the new Balaguer regime was uncertain. The United States imposed additional pressure by means of an informal boycott of Dominican sugar. Both Balaguer from the presidency and Trujillo's son Ramfis, as commander of the armed forces, began to implement "democratization" measures, exiling some of the most visible symbols of repression and promising free elections for May 1962.

The United States, fearing a potential breakdown of order that could favor Communist groups, opted to work with Balaguer and the army while putting pressure on them to move the country toward liberalization. But this controlled liberalization confronted growing domestic opposition, fueled by the return of political exiles, as well as opposition from Venezuela. By mid-1961, the government faced serious domestic opposition from three primary sources: the PRD returned from exile; the Unión Cívica Nacional (UCN—National Civic Union), formed by some of the most prominent Dominican businessmen and which was to become a conservative but anti-Trujillista movement; and the Agrupación Política 14 de Junio (1J4—Political Group 14th of June), which would become a leftist, Castro-influenced party. In spite of bitter differences, all three were united in their desire to rid the country completely of the Trujillos.

Events gradually drove the United States to show a more forceful card, a stance the UCN had been seeking. As part of the liberalization strategy, the United States encouraged Balaguer to incorporate the opposition groups into a coalition government, but these continued to resist Balaguer's overtures. Nevertheless, following the exit of Trujillo's hated brothers, the "Wicked Uncles," in late October, the United States called for a partial lifting of OAS sanctions against the country. Then, Trujillo's son Ramfis, still head of the armed forces, suddenly decided the pressures of office were too much for him and opted to go into gilded exile.[50] He urged his uncles, Trujillo's brothers, to return to the island and to power if they could, which they did on November 15. However, the United States was determined not to allow them to assume power. U.S. policy makers feared that the violence and instability that would be provoked by their dictatorial rule would favor Communism, as Batista's rule was perceived to have done in Cuba. Balaguer, opting to break with the Trujillos and side with the United States, refused to step aside from power.

U.S. diplomatic and military steps soon followed. Secretary of State Dean Rusk came out with a sharply worded statement that the United States would not "remain idle" if the Trujillos tried to "reassert dictatorial domination" and that "further measures" would be considered, if necessary. A U.S. naval group was ordered to move to a position just outside Dominican territorial waters near the capital (still called Ciudad Trujillo), Navy jets flew along the shore near the capital city, and U.S. officials suggested that marines were prepared to land if necessary. Four days after they returned, Héctor and José Arismendi Trujillo and a number of their close collaborators fled into exile. The country celebrated as the Trujillo period finally came to an end, ripping down statues, destroying busts, and attacking other symbols of the dictatorship.[51] It should be emphasized that most Dominicans supported the U.S. show of force as it helped rid the country of the Trujillos. But, as the warships lingered offshore, elements of the left began to attack the United States for its presumed support of Balaguer.[52]

The United States remained deeply enmeshed in Dominican affairs, and eventually successful democratic elections were held. The new leader of the armed forces, Gen. Pedro Rafael Rodríguez, began to show political ambitions even as he now served as a critical support for the Balaguer government. The UCN declared a general strike in an effort to force Balaguer to step down. As it had in the past, and as it would again in the near future, U.S. officials interposed themselves as intermediaries between government and opposition forces in the country, seeking to help forge a compromise that would insure stability and move the country toward elections. On January 1, 1962, a power-sharing Council of State was established, formed by Balaguer at its head, three leading members of the UCN, an anti-Trujillo priest, and the two survivors of the group that had carried out Trujillo's assassination. The OAS agreed unanimously to lift all sanctions (Cuba abstained), and the United States resumed normal diplomatic relations and purchases of Dominican sugar, and promised economic aid. But Balaguer had promised to step down once sanctions were lifted, and the UCN continued to pressure for it. General Rodríguez made a grab for power, but that failed in forty-eight hours due to domestic opposition and U.S. pressure, including denial of diplomatic recognition and a threat to withdraw economic aid. Both Rodríguez and Balaguer eventually left to go into exile, and the Council of State was reconstituted with Rafael Bonnelly at its head on January 18, 1962. This Council managed to hold elections in December 1962, and hand power over to the winner, Juan Bosch, in February 1963.

Yet, this electoral process also demonstrated a major problem with apparent successive U.S. triumphs in promoting democracy in the Dominican Republic, as illustrated in a comment by the U.S. ambassador during this period, John Bartlow Martin. Martin wrote a remarkable book providing historical background on the country and a detailed analysis of the events he witnessed and helped to shape. In discussing the role of Sumner Welles at the end of the U.S. military occupation in the 1920s, Martin wrote unself-consciously: "His task foreshadowed mine forty years later—to keep the provisional government in office, help it hold elections, and help get the winner into the Palace alive. He succeeded and so did I. But before he succeeded, he encountered nearly every obstacle I encountered."[53]

These diplomatic achievements were significant, reflecting considerable intelligence, skill, and effort. Yet, success at this level covered up the fundamental fact that the United States could not simply establish the Dominican Republic as a consolidated democracy. If it could, then Martin would not have needed to carry out decades later the same tasks as Welles. Nor would a military coup have put an end to constitutional government only months later and a few short years before a U.S. military intervention would require yet another U.S. diplomat, Ellsworth Bunker, to seek to achieve the same three goals of supporting a provisional government, helping it hold elections, and insuring a transfer of power.

Although Ambassador Martin in 1962 shared these three goals with Sumner Welles, the background strategic issue of desiring a stable, aligned regime—defined in the 1960s as anti-Communist—was viewed as much more important given the Cuban Revolution than it had been in the post–World War I 1920s. The promotion of democracy, rather than part of an extrication strategy as it was in the 1920s and as it was to be again in 1965–66, was the central component of a highly interventionistic strategy to prevent a "second Cuba" in the Dominican Republic. The Council of State was supported with extensive economic aid for short-term needs, and assistance was provided to train the police in riot control and to prepare a military counterinsurgency unit, as well as more directly to assist the elections themselves. However, what could have been the most useful democratic measure, purging the Dominican armed forces of Trujillista officers, largely did not meet with U.S. support because of its concern with Communism and was only minimally carried out.[54]

The inauguration of Juan Bosch as president in February 1963 brought an honest man and a democrat to the country's highest office. However, Bosch confronted enormous opposition from a variety of business and military groups. And U.S. officials grew increasingly frustrated by his nationalism, his lack of enthusiasm over opposing "Castro Communism," and his passive and somewhat pessimistic administrative style. Although Ambassador Martin worked hard to sustain Bosch in office, his military attachés were concerned about Communism in the country and Bosch's attitude with regard to it. There is no evidence that they actively promoted a coup, but at a minimum their defense of constitutional government was weakened by their concerns. Additionally, the U.S. labor attaché appeared to support a Bosch overthrow.[55]

United States reaction to Bosch's overthrow in September illustrates the fact that the promotion of democracy and of Bosch's government was subsumed to a strategy to prevent a "second Cuba." When the coup threat finally came and Ambassador Martin requested an aircraft carrier to block it in a fashion similar to the events of November 1961, he was informed by the State Department that unless there was a threat of a Communist takeover, which there did not appear to be, there would be no military intervention or show of force.[56] An effort to make the coup conform to constitutional provisions failed, but the UCN-dominated "Triumvirate" vaguely promised elections. The United States strongly condemned the coup and withheld recognition and aid until December, but a determination was made early on that the United States did not want Bosch back because, in Martin's words, "he isn't a President."[57]

Involvement in the country declined somewhat from the feverish U.S. activity of the 1961–63 period, and the central focus remained squarely on the question of Communism rather than democracy. The Triumvirate that eventually replaced Bosch was increasingly dominated by the conservative businessman Donald Reid Cabral. Reid Cabral sought to prolong his stay in office by means of elections scheduled for September 1965 that would exclude the participation of his two potentially most significant opponents who remained in exile, Bosch and Balaguer. As a result, numerous civil-military conspiracies emerged. It was Reid Cabral's efforts on April 25, 1965, to prevent one of these conspiracies that helped provoke a series of events leading to the "constitutionalist" uprising that sought to bring Bosch and the PRD back to power and then resulted in the U.S. intervention three days later as the "loyalist" Dominican military was unable to control the civil-military rebellion.

Most analysts concur that the U.S. intervention, in which as many as 23,000 troops were ultimately involved, was the result of an exaggerated fear regarding a potential "second Cuba."[58] As such, the intervention itself was unrelated to democracy promotion. An effort was made to legitimate the intervention by adding a Latin American military presence. This was accomplished through an OAS-established Inter-American Peace Force on May 6 (the last necessary vote in the OAS came from Reid Cabral's representative, despite questions about which was the legitimate Dominican government at the time). As it became clear that the costs of a purely military solution to the continuing presence of constitutionalist forces in downtown Santo Domingo were too high, the United States sought political solutions. Initially, it considered "constitutionalism without Bosch" as a possible solution, with PRD leader S. Antonio Guzmán to be named president. But negotiations ultimately broke down between Guzmán and U.S. government leaders, as the United States increasingly came to prefer the naming of a provisional government and the holding of elections—as specified by an OAS resolution—as the best extrication strategy.

This extrication strategy involved the naming of Héctor García Godoy as provisional president in September 1965 and then another U.S. effort "to keep the provisional government in office, help it hold elections, and help get the winner into the Palace alive" (in Martin's words). Ultimately, negotiations to arrange a peaceful surrender of the constitutionalist forces surrounded by foreign troops in downtown Santo Domingo, to prevent a new outbreak of hostilities, and to provide for elections were successful. Bosch and Balaguer were the two main candidates. Bosch, understandably, felt betrayed by the United States, which had blocked his possible return to power and turned on his militant supporters. Although he returned to the Dominican Republic in September 1965, fearing for his life he ventured out to campaign for the June 1966 elections only three times. Balaguer, in turn, ran a skillful and energetic campaign, promising peace and stability. It was clear that Balaguer was the candidate favored by most conservative business interests and by the officer corps that retained control of the armed forces and now felt hatred toward Bosch, the PRD, and elements of the left. Furthermore, many Dominicans were convinced that Balaguer was also the candidate strongly favored by the United States. At the same time, U.S. policy makers did not view a victory by Bosch as a serious security threat to the United States.[59]

The 1966 elections were in part for international and domestic U.S. consumption, providing legitimation for the U.S. intervention and a basis for the withdrawal of U.S. forces. But, they also had extensive consequences within the Dominican Republic. Technically, the elections were probably free. Certainly the United States sought to make them so and the numerous international observers who attended, ranging from a U.N. mission, the Inter-American Commission on Human Rights, an OAS Electoral Assistance Mission, a forty-two person OAS Electoral Observation Mission, and some seventy generally pro-Bosch U.S. liberals headed by Norman Thomas and Bayard Rustin, reported that they were.[60] Yet, for most Dominicans, unaccustomed in any event to free and fair elections, the situation was hardly propitious. In 1965, the United States had not helped rid the country of the family of a hated dictator as it had in 1961. Rather, it had prevented a constitutionally elected president who had been deposed from returning to power, thus casting a cloud over his candidacy by its continuing military presence in the country. Although the civil war had been contained largely to urban areas, it left some three thousand dead and a more polarized country even more committed to conspiratorial politics. Many in the country viewed Balaguer's electoral victory as tainted and his administration as lacking in moral legitimacy.

Ultimately, how should the U.S. efforts of this period, and particularly the 1965 intervention, be judged from the perspective of democratization? At the time, some argued that the Dominican intervention was a success: the lives of foreign citizens were protected, violence was halted, a Communist takeover was prevented, and constitutional processes were restored. Yet, critics charged, the cost was high even in a situation "relatively favorable for the exercise of U.S. power." Indeed, one probable cost was that the intervention encouraged right-wing forces around Latin America in the belief that they did not need to accommodate to the demands of nationalist reform movements, even as it drove previously committed democrats, such as Juan Bosch, to reject democratic procedures (though he has moved back to them).[61]

More recently, as the country has evolved into a political democracy, the argument has been made that "it appears that the United States may have helped effect a structural transformation in the Dominican Republic which could not have happened without something like the 1965 intervention occurring."[62] This latter argument rests on two main points. The first is that in the late 1960s the United States provided generous economic assistance to the island republic, at levels that would not have been forthcoming in the absence of the intervention. The second is that this economic aid assisted in the country's structural transformation that helped move Dominican democracy forward.

Yet, there are at least three problems with this view. One is that the structural transformation that took place in the country was an unintentional by-product of the initial U.S. decision to intervene; the intervention itself was not related to seeking either democracy or economic development in the Dominican Republic, but to perceived U.S. security concerns. In the same way that one cannot directly "blame" the U.S. military occupation for Trujillo's rise, one cannot "praise" the intervention for the subsequent economic changes that resulted in part from the generous economic aid the U.S. provided the country to help support the Balaguer regime. Another problem is that there are many possible paths to democratization and it is not at all clear that the structural transformation that did take place was the only one potentially supportive of democratization. One might well imagine other transformations, potentially even more favorable to Dominican democratization, realized without a U.S. intervention. Finally, the mix of motives and actions by the United States during this period reinforced the reality of the overwhelming presence, and often critical role, that it has played in the internal affairs of the Dominican Republic. Although that reality may occasionally promote democratization, it inhibits its consolidation.

The 1978 Elections

Today, the Dominican Republic is considered a political democracy, albeit one that remains uninstitutionalized and unconsolidated.[63] Although some politicians and diplomats may wish to date the current democratic regime in the country from Balaguer's election in 1966, most academics would consider the twelve years of Balaguer's rule from 1966–78 as a form of authoritarianism. But in 1978, in what may be considered a democratic transition, Balaguer lost elections and after complex maneuverings handed power over to S. Antonio Guzmán of the PRD. The Dominican case is distinct from other Latin American cases of democratization in that the transition was from one civilian ruler to another and occurred as part of an electoral process without a formal constitutional break. Both international and domestic pressure were important to insure that the electoral results, at least at the presidential level, would be respected, and that the devolution of power would occur. Contested, though also incident-prone, elections followed in 1982, 1986, and 1990. In contrast to the full range of policy actions deployed by the United States in the 1959–66 period, only limited policy instruments were employed in the period surrounding the elections, in circumstances in which broader national security questions for the United States were not an issue.

The initial Balaguer years were a period of relative polarization, with repression from government and sporadic terrorist activities by opposition groups. Yet, Balaguer's treatment of economic, military, and political power differed substantially from that of Trujillo, in part due to changes in Dominican society and international circumstances.

Economically, the period from 1966 to 1978 was one of high economic growth, averaging a 7.6 percent increase in real gross domestic product over the whole period, and an 11 percent in the years from 1968 to 1974. Growth was based upon increased export earnings, import substitution in consumer goods, and public investment projects. It was facilitated by the U.S. sugar quota and generous economic assistance, particularly in the early Balaguer years. Balaguer sought to maintain a predominant political role by insuring he was the central axis around which other major political and economic forces revolved. At the same time, he eventually undermined his position by promoting the development of business groups separate from, even if dependent upon, the state. Organized labor remained extremely weak, a combination of repression, co-optation, and extremely restrictive labor legislation.[64]

Relations between business and Balaguer were complicated by the growing incursions of the armed forces into business and into politics. Balaguer had a commanding presence within the military as a result of his ties to the Trujillo period, his anti-Communism, his statesmanlike caudillo figure, and his acceptance of military repression as well as large-scale corruption. He sought to manage the military by playing off the ambitions of the leading generals and shifting their assigned posts. Yet, he occasionally confronted serious challenges. In 1971, he successfully dismantled a coup effort led by Gen. Wessin y Wessin, who was sent into exile. Through the 1970s, however, the economic and political ambitions of the military increased.

Balaguer assiduously practiced a policy of co-optation. PRD and other party figures were brought into his government or offered diplomatic posts following the 1966 elections, and following subsequent elections. Similarly, several radical opponents were given posts at the public university and given a degree of autonomy to act within that sphere. By the 1978 elections, though, Balaguer had alienated a number of his former supporters due to his drive for power, reelection aspirations, and policy decisions.

In a number of respects, Balaguer was approaching the 1978 elections from an unfavorable perspective. An economic downturn finally affected the country around 1976, when the sugar boom that had offset oil price increases faded. The immediate problems for the regime created by the economic slowdown were exacerbated by the country's structural transformation under Balaguer. The country's substantial growth, industrialization, and urbanization had expanded middle-sector and professional groups disgruntled by Balaguer's patrimonial politics that appeared to discriminate against newer and regional groups. In the absence of any "threat" from below, they were supportive of democratization, and a few of the PRD directly. Another problematic feature was Balaguer's own physical decline, particularly his failing eyesight, which became public knowledge in January 1977.

Yet, without the changes that had occurred within the PRD between 1974 and 1978 it is difficult to conceive that an electoral victory and a successful democratic transition would have occurred in 1978. Following the bitter experience of 1965–66, the PRD went through a divisive phase of radicalization, even as it confronted military repression, which ended with the startling decision of Juan Bosch to leave the party in November 1973. Bosch founded the Partido de la Liberación Dominicana (PLD—Party of the Dominican Liberation), intended to be a more radical, smaller, better-disciplined, and more tightly organized party than the PRD.[65] Bosch's exit and the frustrations generated by a last-minute decision to abstain from the 1974 elections due to a lack of guarantees facilitated the generation of a conscious strategy to gain electoral victory within the PRD. This strategy involved not only organizational work and a "deradicalization" in a programmatic sense, but also a conscious policy to renew and strengthen international ties out of the conviction that an electoral victory, alone, could well not be sufficient to reach power.

Because of the predominant U.S. role in the country, the PRD viewed a "counterlobby" to Balaguer's strong diplomatic and corporate ties within the United States as important. In a series of speeches between May and December 1973, as the PRD-Bosch crisis unfolded, the PRD leader Peña Gómez defended the importance of PRD ties with U.S. liberal politicians. He associated the curtailment of the actions of a major paramilitary group (known as La Banda), linked to the then national police chief, to the PRD's campaign against it in the United States and efforts by concerned U.S. politicians. PRD leaders also reestablished and strengthened ties to the Socialist International, fortuitously at the precise moment when that organization was becoming more interested in expanding its programs in Latin America. From 1975 on, Peña Gómez and other PRD leaders traveled abroad to strengthen international ties, while emphasizing that the PRD rejected violence and foresaw the next (PRD) government as a gradualist and transitory one.

The PRD candidate for the 1978 elections, Antonio Guzmán, was an excellent choice both domestically and internationally. His PRD and anti-Trujillo credentials were intact. Yet, Guzmán was also a conservative landowner widely known to businessmen in Santiago, the country's second largest city. (As charges of "Communist" could not be made against Guzmán, an attempt was made to argue that he would be "controlled" by "Communist elements" within the PRD). In 1965, Guzmán had been the favored candidate of a number of liberal U.S. policy makers to serve as provisional president following the U.S. invasion, though in the end top policy makers rejected him, at least in part because of his perceived closeness to Bosch.[66] At the same time, he became known to a wide number of U.S. policy makers, including Cyrus Vance, then deputy secretary of defense, who was the secretary of state during the 1978 Dominican elections.

The PRD carried out an effective campaign, with financial support and technical campaign services provided by the parties of the Socialist International, particularly Acción Democrática of Venezuela (where Carlos Andrés Pérez, a former aide to Betancourt, was now president). Portugal's prime minister Mario Soares visited the country and lent his support to the PRD. In contrast to 1974, the military harassment of the PRD was not as intense.

All Dominican actors followed the position of the United States with intense interest. Balaguer's effort to take advantage of flattering statements regarding his administration by President Carter at the signing of the Panama Canal Treaty in September 1977 led PRD supporters in Congress to demand greater U.S. government impartiality. As it turned out, with Guzmán as the PRD candidate, the U.S. government was strictly impartial. In addition, major U.S. multinationals, including Gulf & Western, which owned sprawling sugar lands, a major sugar mill, and tourist facilities, also opted for neutrality unlike the past elections. The sudden replacement of U.S. Ambassador Robert Hurwitch by Robert Yost just before the elections was interpreted as a U.S. tilt toward the PRD, as Hurwitch was viewed as pro-Balaguer.[67] Statements by the incoming ambassador regarding his country's support for free and open elections were given extensive publicity, as if they were a repudiation of past policies. In fact, under Hurwitch's supervision the embassy had prepared a contingency plan if there was an attempt to subvert the elections, and it is unlikely U.S. policy would have been different if there had been no change of ambassador. Balaguer delayed the presentation of Yost's credentials until just before the elections, so a picture of the two of them together would appear in the newspapers on election day. Ironically, since the new ambassador was now officially recognized by the Dominican government, he was able to act far more effectively in the postelectoral crisis.[68]

Foreign observers, some invited by the government and many not, flocked to the election. In response to Balaguer's invitation, the OAS sent a team of three former Latin American presidents under the leadership of Ecuadorean Galo Plaza. The Democratic Conference, a coalition of liberal organizations with strong ties to the Democratic party with whom the PRD had developed solid links, also sent an official observer. He formed part of a group of Socialist International observers, including individuals sent by Acción Democrática of Venezuela, the Socialist party of Japan, and the Socialist Worker's party of Spain. These observer teams, encouraged by the PRD, played a central role in mobilizing international opinion.

Balaguer and his closest advisers were convinced he would win the elections. As the results were tabulated, however, it became evident that the PRD was gaining a wide margin of victory. In an uncoordinated action that had only the tacit blessing of Balaguer, a group of military stopped the vote count at the Central Electoral Board at four o'clock in the morning on May 17, as the military around the country harassed PRD candidates and poll watchers.

Intense domestic and international protest ensued, as the PRD pursued a cautious, prudent strategy urging its followers to stay off the streets. The domestic protest began as a prominent and powerful group of Santiago businessmen who knew Guzmán, urged by certain church officials, placed an advertisement calling for the electoral results to be fairly counted and respected. Soon, newspapers were filled with advertisements from professional, educational, labor, and other organizations.

International protest was also massive and important. The OAS observers were in constant contact with U.S. officials and various Latin American presidents. The Socialist International generated a barrage of letters, telegrams, and protests. But, the most important actions came from the United States. This included visits by embassy staff and military attachés, strong statements by Secretary of State Vance and President Carter, and, upon the request of the State Department and the National Security Council, a phone call to the Dominican military from General McAuliffe, the commander in chief of the Southern Command in Panama. Indeed, the U.S. military in the country and through phone calls gave a consistent message that there was no "dual-track" policy, and that the Dominican military intervention was clearly repudiated. In a rare step, both Carter and Vance actually strengthened the language of their diplomatic protests; here, Vance's personal acquaintance of Guzmán was probably important.

The postelection, preinauguration period was tense, and electoral results were "adjusted" to provide Balaguer with some "guarantees," namely a majority in the Senate (which appoints judges). Yet, the succession went through. Just as critically, from the point of view of referring to this as a democratic transition and in contrast to some Central American cases in the 1980s, Guzmán took advantage of the presence of a high-level U.S. delegation at his inauguration to purge the Dominican military of some of its most Trujillista generals.

Subsequent Dominican history has been an unhappy one of political fragmentation and economic crisis. The eight years of PRD rule from 1978 to 1986 were marked by policy errors, excessive ambitions, divisive behavior, and questionable activities. The party emerged from the administration of Salvador Jorge Blanco (1982–86) bitterly divided, with its image badly tarnished due to a difficult process of economic stabilization, charges of corruption, and its inability to transact even basic promised political reforms such as no immediate presidential reelection.[69] In 1986, Balaguer, seventy-nine years old and virtually sightless, defeated Jacobo Majluta, the PRD candidate, by a narrow margin. Juan Bosch, who had moderated his views, came in third, receiving a respectable 18 percent of the vote.

Balaguer's presidency that began in 1986 has been marked by ambitious government public works programs, which initially helped to reactivate the economy but also fueled record inflation by Dominican standards. Although Balaguer began his administration on an anticorruption campaign that first drove Jorge Blanco, the past president, to flee to the United States and then to return to face trial (still ongoing in mid-1990), accusations of corruption against members of Balaguer's own administration have been raised.

The 1990 elections pitted the wily eighty-three-year-old Balaguer, again seeking reelection, against the eighty-year-old Bosch, who continued to move toward the center, and two candidates of the PRD, now apparently irremediably divided. Bosch, ahead in the polls, feared that Balaguer or close associates of his would be unwilling to recognize an electoral victory by the PLD. Reflecting this fear and the continuing weight of the United States on internal Dominican politics, Bosch asked Carter to head a delegation to observe the Dominican elections. Carter appeared to be a particularly propitious choice given the vigorous role he had played as an observer in both the Panamanian (May 1989) and Nicaraguan (February 1990) elections, as well as the role of his administration in the 1978 Dominican electoral crisis. Carter, anxious to avoid any appearance of partiality to a particular candidate, finally accepted the invitation once it was extended by the Central Electoral Board, responsible for administering the elections.

As in previous elections, the Central Electoral Board was perceived with distrust by the major candidates and charges of fraud during the campaign were common. The elections were marred by numerous irregularities (though no obvious pattern of significant fraud) and by a slow vote count, which gradually gave Balaguer a very narrow plurality victory. In the days following the election Carter was called upon to provide legitimacy to the Central Electoral Board's count and to reassure the opposition candidates, particularly Bosch, that Carter would not countenance a fraud. By the end of June 1990, both in the Dominican Republic as well as in the United States, the PLD was continuing to allege fraud, but Carter had withdrawn himself from further active participation. Processes of political protest, legal challenges, and behind-the-scenes negotiations among the major actors continued in the country.

Since the 1978 elections, the United States government has remained deeply involved in efforts to insure that each electoral process in the country would proceed as smoothly as possible. It has purposely sought to act in a quiet, low-profile fashion and to appear completely neutral with regard to major candidates, a position facilitated by the fact that none appeared to represent a threat to U.S. interests. Thus, in 1990, Carter's visit was neither sought nor promoted by the U.S. government, though it was ultimately endorsed by it.[70]

The United States has also been a major actor in Dominican democracy in another critical sense. In part due to constraints of length, this chapter has not considered questions of economic policy and economic aid in the period since the late 1970s. However, at this point it is necessary to point out that like much of the rest of Latin America, the country's serious economic problems have been an incredible strain on democracy. The country's economic crisis—which has led to low growth, high inflation, declining living standards, and deterioration in state services—has been exacerbated by domestic policy errors and resistance to reform from business elites. Yet, it was "overdetermined" by international market forces, including in particular the debt crisis and changes in the world sugar market. Low world-market sugar prices for many years combined with the gradual (albeit uneven) reduction of the U.S. sugar quota, though announced for several years, have been a bitter blow for the Dominican economy and have been far from offset by the economic aid provided to the country. The country has grown increasingly dependent on the remittances of overseas Dominicans (some 10 percent of the population lives overseas), and on economic diversification into tourism, agro-exports, and industrial-free zones. The country's bleak economic picture continues to heighten political tensions. And democratic consolidation in the Dominican Republic is difficult to conceive without significant socioeconomic changes toward a more vigorous and participatory society.

Conclusions

As a set, these case studies reflect four ways that the promotion of "democracy"—of elections and of stable, constitutional government—has formed part of U.S. policies toward the Dominican Republic: democracy by military occupation, as extrication, as anti-Communism, and in the absence of threat. Some of the cases illustrate primarily a single orientation, though others are more properly considered a mix.

The most indirect of these four is democracy by military occupation. U.S. military officials envisioned in the 1916–20 period (before the State Department took back control of the occupation) a long-term strategy by the United States that would eventually reshape the Dominican society and polity so that constitutional government might then be possible. Despite the undemocratic form of governance they practiced, the U.S. military believed their material accomplishments would move Dominican democracy forward. Instead, the occupation generated nationalist resentment while various measures had the unintentional effect of facilitating both the rise of Trujillo and his consolidation of power. The local institutions, customs, and structures in the Dominican context were largely inimical to democracy, and U.S. occupiers were often ignorant or insensitive to cultural differences.

Elections were most clearly a cornerstone of a U.S. policy of extrication in 1924. The United States sought the removal of its troops in the face of Dominican, international (including other Latin American countries), and domestic opposition. Subsequently, it desired stable government that preserved constitutional forms, but in the absence of any security threat, "noninterventionism" became the preferred policy as it was generally well received by Latin American opinion. This helps explain the U.S. attitude toward Trujillo's accession to power in 1930. The fact that as U.S. security concerns changed such a policy could be reversed, as it subsequently was, has left Dominican actors alternatively ambivalent and resentful about the involvement of the United States in their internal struggles.

U.S. actions in the period from 1959 to 1961 reflect a commitment to the promotion of democracy as part of an anti-Communist strategy. The United States showed a determination to use extreme measures to pressure for liberalization—such as involvement in assassination plots against Trujillo and a military show of force to insure the flight of his brothers in November 1961. Pressures for liberalization and democratization were genuine. However, the willingness of the United States to press for these goals was subordinated to its primary anti-Communist goal. This was reflected in its initial willingness to work with Balaguer for further liberalization and its subsequent unwillingness under the Council of State to assist in the purging of Trujillista influence from the Dominican army. It was also evident in 1963 when, in the absence of an apparent Communist threat, the State Department rejected the possibility of employing a military show of force to try to prevent Bosch's overthrow.

Like the initial military occupation in 1916, the U.S. intervention in 1965 responded to issues totally unrelated to democracy. Ultimately, however, the negotiations that followed the 1965 intervention and the 1966 elections revolved primarily around a strategy of extrication, with some elements of anti-Communism. The holding of elections was vital in the face of international and domestic U.S. criticism of the intervention, as they permitted the United States to complete the removal of its troops from Dominican soil. However, they were also seen as the best mechanism to bring a stable, anti-Communist government into power.

When U.S. national security interests are not perceived to be at stake, the United States may engage in a policy of nonintervention. This occurred in the Dominican Republic in 1930 and, with some initial inclinations to a more overtly democratic posture immediately following World War II, in the late 1940s until 1959–60. In the absence of perceived security concerns, nonintervention may be practiced because of its general support within the Latin American community, or because of a desire for consistency with other, perhaps overriding, U.S. national security goals. Both of these played a role in the late 1940s as the cold war began and the United States criticized Soviet interventionism in Europe.

However, when national security interests are not directly engaged, the U.S. government may also pressure for democracy because it is a policy goal of a particular administration and it appears safe to do so. In this situation, the arguments of pragmatic "democracy promoters" regarding the risks of sustaining authoritarian governments are usually not superseded by the claims of those seeking anti-Communist stability, particularly if the likely electoral outcome would appear to favor (or at least not do more harm to) U.S. interests. Depending on how U.S. policy is carried out and the nature of local circumstances and forces, real assistance to democratization may result.

U.S. actions surrounding the 1978 elections remain as controversial as previous U.S. involvement in Dominican affairs. Balagueristas protested what they complained was "intervention" in the affairs of their country. At least one academic has asserted the elections provided the United States with an "opportunity to direct that country's internal political situation."[71] Yet, such a view places military intervention or the threat of such intervention to change governments or regimes on the same conceptual plane of "interventionism" as pressuring a dependent government that claims to be democratic to respect the results of its elections.

At a general level, steps taken by the United States in 1978 can be perceived as appropriate because of the policy instruments employed, the nature of the intervention in relationship to the country's internal processes, and its linkage to the actions of other interested states in the region. The U.S. action did not provoke protest internationally, but support. In this case, the United States operated in conjunction with Venezuela and other regional allies (and not alone with a subsequent effort to involve them, or against them), even as several Western European countries also protested the effort to stop the vote count. The presence of the OAS team was clearly helpful.

But, in contrast to the events of 1959–61 or 1966, the action in 1978 could also be perceived as effective promotion of democracy because of its constrained nature, urging honest elections and then pressing for acknowledgment of their results by the incumbent government. The electoral results themselves, however, were a consequence of a variety of dynamic internal processes and decisions made by local actors. The steps taken by the United States, though crucial, were essentially supportive, particularly at a critical moment. The United States was "interventionist," but using standard diplomatic instruments in urging a government to do what it had already promised that it would do (carry out fair elections). At the same time, the steps taken by the United States were easy to implement because its "strategic objective" (in the words of a State Department official of the time) were open elections. The Dominican Republic was not high on the national security agenda,[72] and the likely winner was acceptable, if not actually preferred. Yet, as occurred again with the 1990 elections, it must be recognized that all major political actors in the country felt it necessary to develop a strategy with regard to the United States and sought to involve major U.S. actors on their respective side. It is difficult to conceive of democratic consolidation in this context.

In the end, then, what may be true about appropriate strategies for the promotion of democracy at a general level becomes more problematic when applied to the case of the Dominican Republic. U.S. pressure could be enacted so effectively and almost instinctually because of its historic role in the Dominican Republic. These case studies have been employed to compare differing U.S. approaches and their relative causes and effectiveness; both positive and negative consequences, some unintended, have been presented and analyzed. Examining the case studies as a whole, however, points to a cumulative impact, a legacy of involvement of the United States in Dominican affairs, that will itself need to be overcome if democracy is ever to be institutionalized in the Dominican Republic.

Notes

I gratefully acknowledge the comments of Abraham Lowenthal, Ambassador John Crimmins, and Bernardo Vega on an earlier version of this paper, as well as the numerous points brought up by conference participants. As I have not always followed their valuable suggestions, I need to reiterate that responsibility for this chapter remains mine alone. Financial support for research in the Dominican Republic from the Tinker Foundation, the Vanderbilt University Research Council, and the University of North Carolina Research Council is also deeply appreciated.

1. For the purposes of this chapter, *democracy* will be defined along procedural lines involving political freedom, broad participation, regular and free elections, constitutional guarantees, and the effective control of government by elected civilians. Even within this definition, democracy may be conceptualized quite differently through time, as the standards and the basic requirements necessary for each of these characteristics evolve as societies and views in the international arena change.

2. See H. Hoetink, "The Dominican Republic, c. 1870–1930," in Leslie Bethell, ed., *The Cambridge History of Latin America,* vol. 5, *c. 1870 to 1930* (Cambridge: Cambridge University Press, 1986), pp. 287–98; see also Frank Moya Pons, *Manual de historia dominicana,* 7th ed. (Santo Domingo: Universidad Católica Madre y Maestra, 1983), pp. 281–426.

3. See Bruce Calder, *The Impact of Intervention: The Dominican Republic during the U.S. Occupation of 1916–1924* (Austin: University of Texas Press, 1984), p. 4; and Abraham F. Lowenthal, *The Dominican Intervention* (Cambridge: Harvard University Press, 1972),

p. 21. For the text of the 1907 convention, see Sumner Welles, *Naboth's Vineyard: The Dominican Republic 1844–1924*, vol. 2 (Mamaroneck, N.Y.: Paul P. Appel, Publisher, 1966), pp. 1005–11.

4. Moya Pons, pp. 468–70.

5. Calder, p. 10.

6. Moya Pons, p. 472, describes the potential strategic issue; Calder, pp. 259–60, n. 69, notes the lack of reference to the German question until after the occupation.

7. See Calder, pp. 22–23; see also Michael H. Hunt, *Ideology and U.S. Foreign Policy* (New Haven: Yale University Press, 1987), pp. 125–35, for a discussion of the common roots, differences, and "strikingly similar direction" of the Latin American policies (p. 131) of Theodore Roosevelt and Woodrow Wilson.

8. See Calder, p. xix; also Hans Schmidt, *The United States Occupation of Haiti, 1915–1934* (New Brunswick, N.J.: Rutgers University Press, 1971), esp. pp. 13–16. Schmidt notes the "American policy of pragmatic, materialistic uplift in Haiti was conceptually rooted" both in the Progressive reform movement in the United States as well as in "enlightened British colonial experience" (p. 13). Yet, he also notes this "materialistic approach fit the methods and priorities dictated by selfish American purposes, and also conformed to American prejudices, which held that Haitians were incapable of political and intellectual achievements" (p. 13). The hope was that progress in terms of self-government would follow eventually once the necessary material bases for civilization had been established.

9. Stephen M. Fuller and Graham A. Cosmas, *Marines in the Dominican Republic 1916–1924* (Washington, D.C.: History and Museums Division, Headquarters, U.S. Marine Corps, 1974), pp. 45–52; Calder, pp. 54–60; Moya Pons, pp. 477–78.

10. For an extensive analysis of the guerrilla war, see Calder, pp.115–82; see also Fuller and Cosmas, pp. 33–45.

11. Welles, pp. 822–23.

12. This was orchestrated in particular by Knowles; for example, a speech by Senator William E. Borah in Carnegie Hall against the occupation and legislation sponsored by Senator King calling for immediate U.S. withdrawal were both arranged by Knowles. See Calder, pp. 223–24.

13. Calder, pp. 213–37, esp. 222; Welles, pp. 836–99.

14. Julio G. Campillo Pérez, *Elecciones dominicanas (contribución a su estudio)*, 3d ed. (Santo Domingo: Academia Dominicana de la Historia vol. XLIX, 1982), pp. 165–72; Calder, pp. 232–37; Moya Pons, pp. 488–91.

15. A comparison with neighboring Haiti, which was occupied far longer, from 1915 to 1934, may be instructive. In Haiti, a guerrilla resistance also emerged, though it had less success even than the Dominican one. A political resistance also emerged but it was weakened by at least two factors. One was that some traditional politicians had agreed to form a regime under U.S. military tutelage, obviating the need for direct U.S. military government, as in the Dominican Republic. The other was that Haitian nationalists could not hope to generate the kind of support Dominicans did in Latin America, because of differences in colonial experiences, language, and historic ties. See Calder, pp. 248–50.

16. For a valuable discussion, see Joseph Tulchin, *The Aftermath of War: World War I and U.S. Policy toward Latin America* (New York: New York University Press, 1971).

17. See Robert Crassweller, *Trujillo: The Life and Times of a Caribbean Dictator* (New York: Macmillan, 1966), pp. 39–51.

18. See the valuable analysis by the editor and the documents collected in Bernardo Vega, ed., *Los Estados Unidos y Trujillo: año 1930*, vols. 1 and 2 (Santo Domingo: Fundación Cultural Dominicana, 1986), esp. pp. 27–101 (Trujillo's likely removal is discussed in pp. 39–43).

19. Crassweller, pp. 69–70; electoral figures from Jesús de Galíndez, in Russell H.

Fitzgibbon, ed., *The Era of Trujillo: Dominican Dictator* (Tucson: University of Arizona Press, 1973), p. 19. As mentioned in Crassweller and cited in Galíndez, the U.S. minister in the country asserted Trujillo's vote total exceeded the number of voters in the country at the time. In fact, subsequent elections under Trujillo would never admit to the abstention rate reported for these elections.

20. See Piero Gleijeses, *The Dominican Crisis: The 1965 Constitutionalist Revolt and American Intervention* (Baltimore: Johns Hopkins University Press, 1978), p. 20; Moya Pons, p. 491.

Sumner Welles was well aware of the risk. He wrote (ca. 1928): "Because of its efficiency the Policía Nacional is a body far more potent than the old army ever was" (p. 908). Yet, he saw that risk more from the civilian side: "It is only through the settled conviction of the governors of the country that their own interest as well as the safety of the nation lies in the maintenance of this branch of the service completely apart from politics, that the national security of the Dominican Republic may be assured" (pp. 908–9).

See also the discussions in Vega, *Los Estados Unidos y Trujillo: año 1930,* vol. 1; Marvin Goldwert, *The Constabulary in the Dominican Republic and Nicaragua: Progeny and Legacy of United States Intervention* (Gainesville: University of Florida Press, 1962); and G. Pope Atkins and Larman C. Wilson, *The United States and the Trujillo Regime* (New Brunswick, N.J.: Rutgers University Press, 1972), pp. 44–46.

21. Curtis's views, taken from his dispatches, cited in E. R. Curry, *Hoover's Dominican Diplomacy and the Origins of the Good Neighbor Policy* (New York: Garland Publications, 1979), pp. 154–56.

22. Citations to Colonel Cutts's report, in Curry, pp. 118–20. As Curry notes, Cutts did not have the advantage of hindsight, yet his views on Trujillo's motives "seem naive." The State Department, however, appeared to discount Cutts's views as based in part on his friendship with Trujillo (Curry, p. 120). Vega notes there is written evidence that Trujillo wrote Cutts in March 1929 that friends were encouraging him to be president, of which Cutts never informed the State Department; in Vega, *Los Estados Unidos y Trujillo: año 1930,* 1:89–90.

23. Crassweller, p. 68.

24. Vega, *Los Estados Unidos y Trujillo: año 1930,* 1:83–85; Curry, p. 142.

25. State Department telegram cited in Atkins and Wilson, p. 39.

26. See Curry, pp. 162–66; asked to comment on one of Curtis's dispatches regarding the fraud and violence surrounding the 1930 elections, Dana Munro wrote, "events like this are not uncommon in Caribbean elections" (cited in Curry, p. 162).

27. Tensions also emerged between the United States and Trujillo over the treatment of an Italian citizen and of U.S. investment in a tobacco company that competed with one owned by Trujillo.

Jacinto Peynado, elected president in 1938, governed in name only until he died in office in 1940, to be replaced by the vice-president, Manuel de Jesús Troncoso de la Concha. Upon leaving office in 1938, Trujillo became a five-star generalísimo and was granted all the privileges of the presidency. See Crassweller, pp. 165–70.

28. Bernardo Vega, *Nazismo, Fascismo y Falangismo en la República Dominicana* (Santo Domingo: Fundación Cultural Dominicana, 1985), pp. 159–60; Crassweller, pp. 172–75.

29. Vega, *Nazismo,* pp. 384–86. See also Crassweller, p. 213; Crassweller identified Cordell Hull, secretary of state, as the main architect of a U.S. policy of "tolerance and cooperation" with Trujillo, "believing as he did that although Trujillo was an SOB, he was at least *our* SOB." Whether Cordell Hull or President Roosevelt ever made such a reference (with regard to Trujillo, or Somoza as is usually claimed) is challenged by Robert Pastor, *Condemned to Repetition: The United States and Nicaragua* (Princeton: Princeton University Press, 1987), pp. 3–4. Regardless of the differences between Hull and Welles in the 1930s, however, during the war these were submerged.

In 1940, Hull and Trujillo signed an agreement ratified the following year abrogating the 1924 convention and returning the administration of Dominican customs back to the country. And in 1947, Trujillo paid off the rest of the debt owed in 1930. Both of these were the source of tremendous propaganda within the country.

30. Vega, *Nazismo,* pp. 388–90.

31. On Braden's appointment, see Gordon Connell-Smith, *The United States and Latin America: An Historical Analysis of Inter-American Relations* (New York: John Wiley & Sons, 1974), pp. 194–96.

32. Cited in Crassweller, p. 216; for the full text, related documents, and a valuable analysis by the editor, see Bernardo Vega, ed., *Los Estados Unidos y Trujillo: año 1945* (Santo Domingo: Fundación Cultural Dominicana, 1982). Trujillo was eventually able to purchase weapons from Brazil and acquire warships from Canada, in spite of U.S. State Department opposition.

33. José Vicente Pepper, *I accuse Braden yo acuso a Braden* (Trujillo City: Editora Montalvo, 1947). Quotations from pp. 13, 14, 69. Braden was weakened by the fact his anti-Peronist rhetoric and actions probably helped Perón get elected in 1946, and the State Department never publicly condemned Trujillo during this period.

U.S. ambassadors had few illusions about Trujillo during this period. In a report to the State Department in November 1946, then U.S. Ambassador George Butler noted that Trujillo employed all means possible to demonstrate he and his government had official support from the United States, and that all actions by U.S. diplomats were exploited for political purposes. He also noted he did not believe that Trujillo could make substantial concessions to "our concept of democracy" and remain in power, while there was little evidence that Trujillo was willing to step down (reprinted in Bernado Vega, ed., *Los Estados Unidos y Trujillo: año 1946* [Santo Domingo: Fundación Cultural Dominicana, 1982], 1:419–22).

34. Gleijeses, pp. 308–10.

35. Galíndez, pp. 144–48.

36. See Charles Ameringer, *The Democratic Left in Exile: The Antidictatorial Struggle in the Caribbean, 1945–1959* (Coral Gables: University of Miami Press, 1974), pp. 52–54; and Vega, *Los Estados Unidos y Trujillo: año 1945,* esp. p. 16; and Vega, *Los Estados Unidos y Trujillo: año 1946,* 1:11.

37. See Bernardo Vega, ed., *Los Estados Unidos y Trujillo: año 1947,* vols. 1 and 2 (Santo Domingo: Fundación Cultural Dominican, 1984), especially the analysis by the editor, Bernardo Vega, "Análisis de la política norteamericana para América Latina y la República Dominicana en 1947"; see also Ameringer, pp. 64–72.

38. Ameringer, pp. 88–98. For this operation, the exiles called themselves the "Liberation Army of America," though Trujillo and the other dictators that were targets of their actions referred to the various exile military operations and plots of this period as if they comprised part of a single exile army called the "Caribbean Legion."

39. See Vega, "Análisis de la política norteamericana," pp. 93–96.

40. Jerome Slater, *Intervention and Negotiation: The United States and the Dominican Revolution* (New York: Harper & Row, 1970), p. 7.

41. See Gleijeses, pp. 313–27.

42. See José Francisco Peña Gómez, "La campaña de denuncia al regimen Trujillista," *IV Construcción de la democracia* (Santo Domingo: Editora Alfa y Omega, 1986), 5:1–9.

43. Committee report cited in Jerome Slater, *The OAS and United States Foreign Policy* (Columbus: Ohio State University Press, 1967), p. 186; see pp. 186–88.

44. Ibid., p. 189.

45. Ibid., pp. 190–92.

46. U.S. Congress, Senate, Select Committee to Study Governmental Operations with Respect to Intelligence Activities, *Alleged Assassination Plots Involving Foreign Leaders: An*

Interim Report (Washington, D.C.: U.S. Government Printing Office, 1975). This report also details U.S. involvement in plots to assassinate Patrice Lumumba and Fidel Castro; although the facts in the text are stated authoritatively, the report is more ambiguous about precisely who authorized these actions and who knew about them.

47. Slater, *The OAS,* pp. 193–94; the measure barely passed, as Argentina, Brazil, Guatemala, Haiti, Paraguay, and Uruguay abstained.

48. According to the Church Committee report, already cited, machine guns delivered by the CIA to the Dominican Republic for the use of the conspirators were never handed over to them because of sudden fears raised by the Bay of Pigs debacle in April. Following the boost to Castro's reputation, U.S. officials feared that a power vacuum in the Dominican Republic if Trujillo were suddenly to exit could be taken advantage of by Dominican radicals with close ties to Fidel Castro. Nevertheless, the conspirators went ahead with their plans. The full details regarding the extent of U.S. involvement in and prior knowledge of this conspiracy have yet to be disclosed.

49. Lowenthal, *Dominican Intervention,* pp. 11, 26.

50. Following his resignation, Ramfis Trujillo went on a three-day drinking orgy, personally killed the six remaining imprisoned assassins of his father (two were never captured) who had been brutally tortured, and then left on the family yacht, with his father's body and reportedly $90 million. See Gleijeses, pp. 44–46.

51. Lowenthal, *Dominican Intervention,* p. 11; Gleijeses, pp. 46–74; Slater, *The OAS,* pp. 198–200.

52. Gleijeses, p. 55; Howard J. Wiarda, *The Dominican Republic: Nation in Transition* (New York: Praeger, 1969), pp. 50–55.

53. John Bartlow Martin, *Overtaken by Events: The Dominican Crisis from the Fall of Trujillo to the Civil War* (Garden City, N.Y.: Doubleday, 1966), p. 30.

54. Martin, p. 115.

55. Gleijeses, pp. 97–99.

56. Lowenthal, *Dominican Intervention,* pp. 28–29; Martin, p. 570. Martin writes that he told Bosch as the coup was imminent: "I don't think the military really want to do this. . . . The *cívicos* have convinced them you're handing the country over to the Communists. I know it isn't true, you know it isn't true, but you've got to prove it isn't true. You can do it now. . . . Call a special session of Congress. Tell them first, to enact something like our Smith Act. Second, tell Congress to stop travel to Cuba—pass a law making it a crime to violate passport restrictions. Third, tell them to enact a law permitting deportations" (p. 562). For a variety of reasons, and in a passive manner, Martin writes ("[Bosch] kept saying, 'The revolution is frustrated,' and 'I can do nothing'" p. 564), Bosch rejected the advice.

57. Martin, p. 601.

58. In addition to Gleijeses, Lowenthal, and Wiarda, see Slater, *Intervention and Negotiation;* and Theodore Draper, *The Dominican Revolt* (New York: Commentary, 1968).

59. As Slater notes, many Dominicans viewed their armed forces as "really controlled by 'the Pentagon,'" and others probably believed that U.S. economic assistance would be more forthcoming for Balaguer than for Bosch; thus those who desired "peace and stability" would vote for Balaguer. Naturally, by provoking nationalism, the intervention should have encouraged some voters to turn to Bosch. Yet, given the negotiated surrender of the pro-Bosch forces and Balaguer's active campaigning in contrast to Bosch, this effect may well have been muted. See Slater, pp. 180–81; also interviews with U.S. policy makers.

60. Slater, pp. 171–82; Gleijeses, p. 281; some feel fraud, particularly in more remote rural areas, may have inflated Balaguer's total somewhat, though not enough to change the overall results: Edward S. Herman and Frank Brodhead, *Demonstration Elections: U.S.-Staged Elections in the Dominican Republic, Vietnam and El Salvador* (Boston: South End Press, 1984), p. 40, citing Howard Wiarda, *Dictatorship, Development and Disintegration:*

92 • *Jonathan Hartlyn*

Politics and Social Change in the Dominican Republic, vols. I, II and III (Ann Arbor, Mich.: Xerox University Microfilm, 1975), p. 1799.

61. These arguments are considered in Abraham F. Lowenthal, "The Dominican Intervention in Retrospect," *Public Policy* 18 (Fall 1969): 134; the quotation is from p. 148.

62. James W. Nash, "What Hath Intervention Wrought: Reflections on the Dominican Republic," *Caribbean Review* 14, no. 4 (Fall 1985): 10.

63. Much of the material for this section comes from Jonathan Hartlyn, "Democratization and 'Political Learning': The Case of the Dominican Republic," paper presented to the Latin American Studies Association Convention, Boston, October 1986.

64. See also Rosario Espinal, "An Interpretation of the Democratic Transition in the Dominican Republic," in Giuseppe Di Palma and Laurence Whitehead, ed., *The Central American Impasse* (New York: St. Martin's Press, 1986).

65. See José del Castillo, *Ensayos de sociología dominicana* (Santo Domingo: Ediciones Siboney, 1981).

66. Gleijeses, pp. 266–68; Slater, pp. 85–95.

67. In fact, the replacement was a result of a U.S. Justice Department investigation of Hurwitch involving misuse of embassy funds.

68. G. Pope Atkins, *Arms and Politics in the Dominican Republic* (Boulder, Colo.: Westview Press, 1981), p. 94.

69. Given Trujillo's series of reelections, the PRD had always been strongly opposed to presidential reelection, a measure incorporated into the constitution written during Bosch's presidency. However, in a new constitution written during Balaguer's 1966–70 term in office, that measure was removed, paving the way for Balaguer's subsequent reelections.

70. These paragraphs are based on personal observation of the 1990 Dominican elections. This chapter was revised in June 1990.

71. Michael Kryzanek, "The 1978 Elections in the Dominican Republic: Opposition Politics, Intervention and the Carter Administration," *Caribbean Studies* 19 (April–July, 1979): 51.

72. One indicator is that the Dominican Republic is not even mentioned *once* in the memoirs of President Jimmy Carter, his secretary of state Cyrus Vance, or his national security adviser, Zbigniew Brzezinski.

4 | Mexico: The Exception and the Rule

Lorenzo Meyer

WITH ITS successful revolution for independence, its republican and federal constitution, its political theory based on popular sovereignty, and its economic success resting on one of the closest practices to the theory of pure liberalism, the United States became one of main models of modernity at the end of the eighteenth century and beginning of the nineteenth century. The American experience showed the liberal creoles of Hispanic America the political formula that would permit them to fashion out of the colonies a set of modern nations—that is to say, independent, democratic, prosperous, just societies, which would be respected in the international concert of nations.[1]

In the particular case of Mexico, the U.S. model presented almost from the start of independent life certain contradictions that, essentially, still subsist. From the time of Mexico's conflict with the North American settlers of Texas in 1836, which eventually resulted in a war between Mexico and the United States, the positive part of the American political experiment—democracy, federalism, economic growth, and stability—could not be entirely disassociated by Mexico's elites from the aggressive, arrogant, and imperialistic action of the country of "Manifest Destiny" against Mexico. After the forces of Zachary Taylor and Winfield Scott defeated the improvised and poorly led Mexican armies in 1847, and the peace treaties of Guadalupe Hidalgo of 1848 and La Mesilla of 1853 were signed, causing Mexico to lose the northern half of its territory, the contradictory vision held by Mexican progressives as regards the United States became more apparent: on the one hand, the U.S. represented a danger to Mexican sovereignty and, on the other, it was the embodiment of the future to which Mexican liberals aspired for their own country.[2] For pure liberals of the mid-nineteenth century, the best defense that Mexico could put forth against new American or

93

European aggressions was to imitate the political and economic developments that had permitted the United States to consolidate a system capable
of liberating the productive energies of society in an extraordinarily effective
manner.

In the latter half of the nineteenth century, the Mexican liberal faction
was endeavoring to construct by fire and sword a modern nation having as a
model the neighboring country to the north. The support that the U.S.
government finally gave to these efforts was motivated less by an ideological
solidarity with the Mexican standard-bearers of political democracy than
by reasons of U.S. national interest. Indeed, Washington's diplomatic recognition of the liberal group headed by Benito Juárez was largely undertaken
with a view to extracting territorial concessions and taking advantage of the
desperate military situation of the liberals vis-à-vis their conservative enemies; and, had it not been for the opposition of northern U.S. senators, the
McLane-Ocampo treaty of late 1858, signed between the U.S. government
and the Juarista group, would have come into force and wrested from Mexico perpetual transit rights in the northern part of the country and in Te-
huantepec. The continuing U.S. support of the liberals in subsequent years,
despite the latter finding themselves unable to control the bulk of the territory, is explained less as support for those claiming to defend republican
and democratic values and more as a measure aimed at preventing the transformation of Mexico—through the creation of an empire with a European
monarch at the head—into a client state of France.[3]

Stability as a Central Objective of the United States in Mexico

In fact, the Mexican political process became important for the United
States after the completion of the territorial expansion of the United States
in the latter half of the nineteenth century—achieved, basically, at the expense of Mexico's interests—when American direct investment in the neighboring country to the south became attractive. The main element that the
U.S. government and American investors sought to support in Mexico
thereafter was stability, even if and when stability was opposed to democracy, as was often the case. The existence of a strong central government in
Mexico was acceptable to American interests because with the end of civil
war in both countries, strong authorities were required to insure the prosperity of American interests in Mexico—including mining, railroads, plan-
tations, electricity, commerce, and oil. Predictable political and administrative processes were needed not only for the security and productivity of
these interests but also to prevent a repetition of the chaotic conditions that
in the past had given rise to the involvement of European powers in Mexico.
From now on, Washington wanted to be the dominant influence.

This concern with the stability and viability of the Mexican political model for American economic interests and national security reasons explains the close relationship between the U.S. government and the long dictatorship of Porfirio Díaz, despite an initial relative hostility and, toward the end of the regime, a certain irritation on account of the closeness of Mexico's economic relationships with Europe.[4] Likewise, the desire to reestablish Mexican political stability and ward off European involvement led the United States to attempt a systematic intervention, however contradictory, in the dramatic and violent Mexican political process during the years of its revolution (1910–20). The search for stability motivated Washington's open support of Mexico's postrevolutionary governments in the difficult political conditions of 1923–24, 1929, and 1938–40. On those three occasions, especially the last one, the government of Mexico even acted against certain U.S. economic interests, but U.S. leaders considered that the instability that a change of government in Mexico could bring about could entail even worse consequences.[5]

Long-term stability in Mexico from World War II onward led to a reduction in U.S. intervention. Eventually U.S. involvement in Mexican internal affairs became nearly undetectable. Relations between both countries entered into a period of great normality, which did not prevent the establishment in Mexico of a benignly authoritarian political system based on one-party monopoly.[6]

When, after more than forty years of systematic economic growth, the Mexican economic model entered into a crisis in 1982—a structural crisis, which resulted in seven years of economic depression—Mexican normality came to an end. The initial U.S. reaction was ambiguous. At the beginning, according to the dominant ideological motivations in the United States under the Reagan administration, the weakness of the Mexican regime provided an opportunity to encourage its definite transformation—specifically, by favoring the principal force of the opposition, the Partido Acción Nacional (National Action Party or PAN), a center-right political party. By supporting political reforms that favored the PAN, Washington could serve its own interests directly, for the PAN's views coincided with the Reagan line regarding economic policy as well as on Central America.[7] In 1988, when, much to the surprise of many, the centrist left-wing opposition became the most important rival of the ruling Mexican party, U.S. authorities radically modified their position, giving all their support to maintain the forces of authoritarian rule, despite evidence of systematic electoral fraud since 1983 and particularly in the 1988 presidential elections.[8]

Its concern for Mexican political stability—establishing or preserving it—largely explains the nature of the U.S. government's relationship with the Mexican government from the end of the last century up to the present day. In light of the problems of legitimacy and legality entailed by the interventions of one nation in the domestic affairs of another, U.S. actions aiming to influence Mexico's internal political processes have had to be justified—when they have been obvious and have met with resistance—on the grounds of a defense of the security of American life and property in Mexico or on the grounds of a defense of non-self-serving, altruistic interests, specifically as a support of unquestionably legitimate values in the Western world dating from the triumph of the French Revolution: the sovereignty of the people and its correlate, political democracy.

U.S. support of Mexican efforts to create and maintain a democratic political system appears time and again in the stream of public discourse, yet there only is evidence—and even that is not entirely free from contradictions—to substantiate such a pretension in a relatively short but important period during the Mexican Revolution of 1910–20. In contrast to that period of crisis at the beginning of the century is the current one, which has not resulted in violence but which, with the onset of economic depression starting in 1982, is profoundly changing Mexico's economic, social, and political status quo. In Mexico's contemporary efforts to build toward democratic politics, the United States has been conspicuous by its absence.

Before proceeding to the examination of U.S. policies toward Mexico and its democracy in the present century, it is important to underline one fact: the U.S. government was the most important actor on the North American side but not the only one. In the U.S. efforts to shape Mexican political developments, there were many nongovernmental actors—bankers, oil companies, chambers of commerce, associations of landowners, churches, labor unions, anti-imperialist organizations, academics, journalists, and individual citizens. The pressures exerted by these groups and individuals upon U.S. and Mexican officials and the public were often contradictory and vary a great deal, going from significant in the case of oil companies or bankers, to meaningless. However, I think that it is fair to say that in regard to the subject matter of this essay—the U.S. role in the constructions of Mexican democracy—the more important actor has been the U.S. government. This situation is changing now and rapidly, but up to now the primary roots and explanations of U.S. responses toward Mexico's political development are certainly located in Washington.

The Democratic Revolution of 1910 and the United States: From Tolerance to Siege

The Mexican Revolution was started on November 20, 1910, with the call to revolt made by Francisco I. Madero in his capacity as presidential candidate of the opposing Anti–Re-Electionist party, which did not accept the validity of the results of the July elections of that year giving a new victory to Gen. Porfirio Díaz, who had kept control without interruption of the presidency since 1884. On May 21, 1911, following a defeat that was more political than military, the old liberal dictator agreed to resign, go into exile, and leave power in the hands of a provisional government whose main task would be to prepare new presidential elections in which Madero would once again be a candidate. Given Madero's vast popularity at that moment, few observers doubted then that the young, generous, and audacious landholder from Coahuila would receive the backing of the popular vote in the country's first broadly participatory free elections. In effect, Madero's victory was overwhelming, although the opposition managed to secure a few important places in Congress. Mexico seemed to be on the road, at last, to the establishment of a politically plural and democratic system, but it was not to be.

The causes of the fall of the Madero government that assumed power in November 1911, and which after fifteen turbulent months was destroyed by a bloody military coup that took the life of the revolutionary leader, have been well examined in the existing historiography.[9] In concentrating on the relationship of the United States with Mexican democracy during this period, however, the following points should be highlighted. First, the victory of Madero and his group was not sponsored by the U.S. government, but took responsible American politicians by surprise; still, without the refuge that the U.S. border offered to Madero and his followers in 1910, and without the sympathies of a goodly number of inhabitants in that region, both Americans and Mexicans, the antidictatorial movement of the Maderistas would have had little chance of victory. At any rate, it is clear that the administration under President William H. Taft was not prepared to face the fall of the Díaz regime, in whose shadow American investment had taken first place among all foreign investment. By 1910 American expenditures amounted to, according to different calculations, $650 million at minimum or $1.5 billion at the most.[10]

Second, for the "dollar diplomacy" of which Taft was a conspicuous exponent, the absence of political democracy prior to 1911 was an irrelevant subject. For Taft and his group, the touchstone in judging the political systems of Latin American countries was simply whether they had aided the expansion of American capital. Díaz had created the appropriate conditions for this expansion and, therefore, his methods and continuance in power were fully compatible with U.S. national interest. Hence after the fall of the dictator, President Taft, having full knowledge of the nature of the Díaz dictatorship, deemed it pertinent, instead of congratulating the winner, to send a personal missive to the old dictator in order to "express my warm feelings of friendship and admiration for you as a man, statesman, and patriot."[11]

The deposed dictator must have received Taft's regards with mixed feelings, for in the last months of his government time and again he had demanded from the U.S. authorities a more active support against the democratic revolutionaries who were using the territory north of the Rio Grande—particularly that of Texas—as a sanctuary to organize themselves politically and to prepare surreptitiously their military action against the government of the dictator. To the very end, Díaz suspected that the United States had been deliberately lax in its application of the laws of neutrality and that it secretly favored the revolutionaries, perhaps to chasten the dictator for his sympathies for European capital. Moreover, the mobilization of troops toward the border with Mexico and of naval vessels toward the Mexican coasts that Taft had ordered in early 1911 was interpreted by Díaz not as the product of the need of the American president to demonstrate to public opinion in his country that his government was not idle while the neighbor's house was on fire, but rather as the prelude of an invasion. Despite Taft's assurances that it was not his intention to threaten Mexican territorial integrity, the dictator remained suspicious.[12]

In sum, the Taft administration was indifferent to the dictatorial character of the Porfirio Díaz government. There is no substantial evidence that U.S. authorities supported the action of Maderista insurgents in order to chasten Díaz for his sympathies for European investors,[13] and it is equally true that Washington made no extraordinary efforts to hinder the activity of the revolutionaries and the eventual victory of the democratic project. Although the turn of events might have been different without the refuge that the U.S. border gave to the revolutionaries, the Taft administration's influence in connection to the fall of Díaz was marginal. The chief explanatory elements were of a domestic character.[14]

The relative neutrality that the U.S. government observed during the initial clash between the dictatorship and the revolutionaries quickly turned into overt hostility against the new government once Madero was overwhelmingly elected constitutional president at the end of 1911. The fundamental reason for the change was the American view—to a great extent the product of the reports of Ambassador Henry Lane Wilson, who had arrived in Mexico from Belgium precisely in 1910—that democracy was not adequate for guaranteeing the social and political discipline of a people as backward economically, socially, and culturally as the Mexicans.[15] From this point of view, Madero's attempt to give life to a basically democratic government was fruitless. Indeed, the process was leading to anarchy—Pascual Orozco's rebellion in the north and that of Emiliano Zapata in the south, plus the existence of bands and brigandage, were, in the eyes of the U.S. ambassador, examples of political breakdown—and in that environment the economic interests of U.S. citizens in Mexico were threatened.[16]

The idea that democracy as a system of government was reserved only to a few peoples and cultures, among which Mexico or Latin America as a whole was not included, was not just a peculiar idea of the U.S. ambassador to the Madero government; it was a view shared by many others in the United States and Europe. From this perspective, authoritarianism was the unavoidable destiny of backward peoples, especially those of color.[17]

Faced with continuing instability in Mexico—the failed attempt of

Gen. Bernardo Reyes's rebellion, the uprising in Veracruz of Gen. Félix Díaz, the persistence of the Zapatista movement in Morelos, and the dangerous rebellion of the former Maderista Pascual Orozco in Chihuahua— the U.S. ambassador became impatient and recommended on various occasions to his government that it should avail itself of diplomatic pressure, of troop mobilization along the border, and of the constant presence of naval vessels in Mexican ports in order to force the new government to impose an order, as if the lack of it were a mere product of the authorities' negligence. Obviously, this pressure did not at all contribute to the waters returning to the level they had been at the beginning of 1910. On the contrary, a vicious circle resulted: the more prolonged Madero's difficulties to impose his authority vis-à-vis reactionary or revolutionary rebels, the more the U.S. ambassador stuck to the idea that the only real solution to the Mexican problem was the fall of Madero and the return to an authoritarian system.[18]

Nothing indicates whether the desire of the U.S. Embassy in Mexico or of the State Department in Washington to see Madero replaced by a more effective president was one of the direct causes of the outbreak of a new rebellion by a group of reactionary military officers in the country's capital in February 1913. What is a fact is the demand—and threat—made to Madero by Ambassador Wilson in the middle of the rebellion urging him to restore order immediately or resign from the presidency, lest the United States decide to intervene directly in the Mexican process in order to safeguard the security of its nationals and their property. It is equally a fact that a secret interview was held in the U.S. Embassy between the leader of the military rebels, Félix Díaz, and the leader of the supposedly loyal forces, Victoriano Huerta, which climaxed with the latter's betrayal and the overthrow of Madero. Both situations suggest that the U.S. government shoulders a very important part of the responsibility for the failure of the effort of Maderism to transform the Mexican authoritarian tradition into a democratic one.[19]

After that failure, the subject of democracy only reappeared sporadically and for brief periods on the Mexican political agenda: 1929, 1940, 1946, 1952, 1968, and then, with greater force, from 1983 onward. In none of these instances did the United States take any substantial action in support of those forces claiming to strive for the establishment of a democratic political system in Mexico, although in 1983 and 1988 the struggle of the democratic opposition was viewed with some sympathy, as previously noted, because it was conservative and sympathetic to U.S. political positions.

Woodrow Wilson's Moral Imperialism and the Search for Mexican Stability through Democracy

All modern revolutions have been harassed by the external world, with the great powers being supporters of the status quo. What happened in Mexico between 1912 and 1913 corresponded to the general pattern, but between 1913 and 1914 the situation radically changed and the Mexican Revolution was more supported than fought against by the area's dominant power: the United States. The key to the change is twofold: on the one hand, the rise to power of the Democratic party's reformist wing and, on the other, the non-existence of the militant anti-communism that would dominate the ruling elites beginning in 1917.

The victory in 1912 in the United States of the Democratic party headed by Woodrow Wilson signified not just a change of team and party in the U.S. government, but also a change in approach as regards the role that country's government should play in the social development of the United States and in the international system. The Wilsonian "new liberty" program was the answer to and the result of the populist and progressive movements that had shaken the United States at the close of the nineteenth century and beginning of the twentieth century. For that reason the "new liberty" stressed the advisability of putting a relative distance between government and "big business" with its "special privileges," while seeking a rapprochement between that same government and the concerns and interests of the ordinary citizen. The aim was to recover the lost balance between society and the proper government of democracy.[20]

Wilson assumed power convinced that it was necessary to effect a better redistribution of wealth following the brutal concentration of resources provoked by the monopolization of economic activity, to deal with the problems of urban life, to introduce technique and rationality in the administration of public affairs, and even and despite his southern origin to moderate the distance between the races. Concerning his foreign policy, from the outset he made clear his rejection of the Republicans' "dollar diplomacy," and his determination to cultivate a new relationship between strong and weak countries, one based on a new international morality.[21]

The coup d'etat that did away with the Madero government took place in February 1913, one month before the inauguration of Woodrow Wilson as president of the United States. For this somewhat fortuitous reason, the reformism promoted by Wilson had in Mexico's crisis its first international problem and its first opportunity to put into practice the creed of the Democratic party's progressives on the international stage. In the struggle that then began in Mexico between the Huertista military dictatorship and the supporters of constitutionality headed by Venustiano Carranza (the so-called Constitutionalists), Wilson saw two fields rich in possibilities. The first would permit him to demonstrate to the world that American political action abroad was directed basically by moral rather than economic considerations and that, consequently, he would not support a government like Victoriano Huerta's, born of a military coup followed by a capital murder. The other was to put into practice an intervention different from the kind practiced until then by the European imperial powers. It was to be a beneficial intervention, non-self-serving, that would seek to direct "backward" countries like Mexico or China toward democratic ways, and thus promote greater social justice.

In Wilson's opinion, democracy was a system of government valid for all societies. In principle, nobody was banned from attaining the benefits that such a system could provide. Besides, only democratic and progressive change—and not the counterrevolution that the large vested interests and European powers were urging—could give to Mexico and to all countries in similar situations the long-term stability that suited both the true interests of the backward country itself as well as those of the United States and of the international community as a whole, for only a stable and predictable country could guarantee permanent returns on American investments and commerce.[22] From this point of view, morality and commercial interests were not incompatible; democracy was economically profitable in the long run, as Wilson noted in a public speech he delivered at Mobile, Alabama, on October 27, 1913.[23]

It is clear that President Wilson had a project in relation to the U.S. spheres of influence, but whose results would not be immediate. Unfortunately for the Wilsonian view, the long term was not particularly interesting for American and European miners, landholders, oilmen, or merchants with interests in Mexico. For these practical men, the task facing the U.S. government in a sphere that was already a part of its "international responsibility" was to follow the lines set forth by Taft and his ambassador, and to support the military dictatorship in its effort to restore law and order, and to leave for later the discussion about the best way to preserve a stability that for the time being should be recovered by fire and sword.[24] That too was the position of State Department career diplomats, who insisted that it was American practice to recognize de facto governments. Thus, in its early stage, Wilson's diplomacy in Mexico had to rely less on those diplomats and more on the special agents that the president sent to Mexico.[25]

Faced with the opposition of representatives of large American investors in Mexico, of the bureaucracy in the State Department, of European foreign offices, of a good part of the American and international press, and of some influential Republican congressmen, Wilson refused to recognize Huerta and he demanded from the Europeans that they suspend economic aid to his military dictatorship. Finally, in 1914, he ordered the occupation of Veracruz to show Huerta and his group that it was not possible for them to continue governing against the will of the United States.

Huerta's defeat was basically the product of the military efforts of the Constitutionalist armies. However, Mexican (and, to a lesser degree, foreign) historiography has minimized President Wilson's contribution to the defeat of Huertism; also, the legitimacy of the interventionist actions of the Wilsonian "moral imperialism" has been systematically denied, even by the main beneficiaries of Wilson's action, the Constitutionalists. There are plenty of reasons to explain the negative attitude of Mexican historians in the face of any American intervention. However, and all things considered, it is difficult, not to say impossible, to deny that between 1913 and 1914 American policy contributed in an important way to shortening the life of the Victoriano Huerta government, to making it unviable, and to enabling Madero's successors to impose themselves finally over the supporters of the Porfirista order.[26]

Mexican nationalism and patriotism and its inevitable anti-American reference, resulting from the clash between the two countries since the nineteenth century, allowed Carranza to benefit from the Wilsonian policy without giving it any credit. Carranza's and the revolutionaries' systematic rejection of the Wilsonian "moral imperialism" and interventionism, the tremendous complexity of the Mexican panorama during the war between the revolutionary factions, particularly between 1915 and 1916, and the concentration of American attention on World War I were some of the factors that led to a disenchantment of the Wilsonians regarding the Mexican Revolution. Thus, the space that had been wrested away between 1913 and 1915 was once again yielded to the bureaucracy in the State Department and to U.S. interest and pressure groups.

From 1915 onward President Wilson's insistence on exercising a moral tutelage over Mexico in order to guide it into the path of democracy began to lose force, while the European war demanded ever more attention and energy from Wilson and his group. The protection of American life and property in Mexico gradually caused American influence to turn against the revolutionaries. Beginning with the promulgation of the constitution of 1917, the protection of the rights acquired under the Díaz dictatorship regarding rural and petroleum properties became the central issue in U.S.-Mexican relations.[27] The tensions between the governments of Mexico and the United States between 1917 and 1940 had a great deal to do with U.S. capital's vested interests in Mexico before the revolution, and little or nothing to do with democracy or the lack of it in postrevolutionary Mexico.[28]

Stability, Authoritarianism, and Normality in Mexican-U.S. Relations

The victorious revolution, after settling its internal differences, created a dominant party system that resulted in a new authoritarianism, which was very careful to preserve the democratic forms while emptying them of content.[29] However, unlike the old regime, the new one achieved the creation and preservation of a broad social base through redistributive policies— including agrarian reform, labor legislation, social security systems, and massive education—and with it attained one of the original objectives sought by Wilson when he denied providing support to the counterrevolution: long-term stability.

In 1940 Gen. Lázaro Cárdenas's presidential period ended—the six-year term of government characterized by the institutional incorporation of the masses into the political process—and the postrevolutionary period got started.[30] Thenceforward, all the key pieces of the Mexican political system stayed in place. It was a system that was formally democratic, but in actual fact it was a state-party system, where the exercise of power has remained uninterruptedly in the hands of the official party's leaders (PNR in 1929, PRM in 1938, and PRI since 1946). It likewise involved an inclusionary authoritarianism, based more on co-optation than on repression, and which holds the presidency of the republic as the fundamental institution, ruling over a limited pluralism.[31]

This system's legitimacy derived, basically, from its capacity to satisfy the minimal demands of all the political actors grouped in the grand coalition directed by the president: entrepreneurs, bureaucrats, unionized workers, peasants, and middle-class organizations. The resources to meet that plurality of demands came from a steadily expanding economy based on import-substituting industrialization and on a growing role of state intervention.[32] In this environment of political stability based on a benign authoritarianism and economic growth, Mexican-U.S. relations entered into a long period of somnolence, to use Alan Knight's phrase; only from time to time did incidents arise that altered the routine.[33]

The secure and predictable setting that routinized the Mexican-U.S. relationship began to change, and in a negative way, from the 1960s onward. The economic system gave evidence then of structural faults, as its industrial base could not overcome its inefficiency and was unable to export and, consequently, to generate the foreign exchange that it needed in order to sustain the pace of imports that its normal functioning demanded. By the 1970s, the chronic deficit in Mexico's foreign trade increased and it could only be met with an excessive increase in foreign indebtedness. From 1976 onward, devaluation and inflation became chronic. For a brief period (1978–80), the massive export of oil in a market of rising prices allowed it to be assumed that it would be possible to return to normalcy. When oil prices collapsed in 1981, however, the entire economic system went back into crisis, but with greater severity. Total foreign debt went from $77 billion in 1981 to $105 billion in 1988—which was equivalent to more than 70 percent of gross national product—but the Mexican per capita product decreased by 10.5 percent and the salary's average purchasing power declined by more than 50 percent.[34]

In these conditions of structural crisis, the Miguel de la Madrid government (1982–88) decided to abandon the economic growth model based on import substitution and to start a painful opening up of the economy to the outside world, in order to create a new model based on manufactured exports.[35] The bulk of society resented the cost, and the state-party's political legitimacy dropped. The electoral process, which in the past had played an irrelevant role, gained importance, for it was precisely through elections that the rejection of the government and the system as a whole, by some of the more active and disaffected social sectors, began to let itself be felt.[36]

The first to react was the center-right party (PAN), which obtained various victories as unexpected as they were conclusive in local elections in the state of Chihuahua in 1983; in that same state in 1986 the PRI had to contain the PAN through manifest electoral fraud amid an atmosphere of widespread social irritation that threatened to burst forth. However, the most significant change was the surge of the left as the principal electoral force of opposition in the 1988 presidential elections. Once again, under the shadow of a strong suspicion of electoral fraud, the PRI imposed the victory of its candidate to the presidency—Carlos Salinas—with the lowest percentage of state-party votes in its sixty years of history: 51 percent.[37]

By the second half of the 1980s, it was clear that the economic crisis was becoming transformed into a political crisis. The Mexican political system's vulnerability had no precedent since the crisis at the end of the 1920s. Due to this internal weakness of Mexico, the U.S. government found itself, once again, with the possibility of intervening in the Mexican political process, although not as overtly as it had done during the revolutionary stage, for the traditional Mexican political system, though clearly weakened, was far from having been liquidated.

The discreet American intervention in Mexico had then a double character that, for a moment, was openly contradictory. On the one hand, from 1981, U.S. economic authorities openly cooperated with their Mexican counterparts in order to maintain the minimum necessary resources to prevent Mexico from being compelled to declare an involuntary moratorium on its foreign debt—the second largest in the less-developed world—inasmuch as it would gravely affect the international banking system as a whole and would set Mexico off on unknown and unpredictable roads, a situation certainly contrary to U.S. national interest.[38]

But, on the other hand, not all was aid, for the U.S. government also decided to use the current situation—the relative Mexican weakness—to attempt to solve old disputes with its neighbor to the south and encourage a change in its economic and political systems. In effect, in exchange for the Treasury Department's support in the short-term solution of the foreign-debt problem, U.S. authorities informed the Mexican authorities of the necessity for the economy to open up outwardly, to privatize state-owned enterprises, to reduce government interference with market forces, to liberalize the policy on foreign investment and all other characteristic policies of the dominant neoliberalism in the United States. An attempt was also made to use the Mexican crisis in order to force the government of that country to desist from its opposition to U.S. policies of open intervention in the political processes of Central American countries, and to restructure its police and justice apparatus profoundly with a view to making it a less corrupt and more effective instrument in the U.S. war against the drug trade.[39]

Here U.S. policy toward Mexico meets again with democracy. From the local elections of Chihuahua and up to the 1988 national elections, the American press and the mass media in general devoted themselves to covering the Mexican electoral front as they had never done so before. The result was international publicity about a government that was incapable of meeting its commitment to electoral transparency and about the necessity of doing so in order to proceed with the "Mexican transition." This transition was seen as a prerequisite to prevent the economic crisis from resulting in something much more serious: a loss of legitimacy and stability in a country of 85 million people and with which the United States shared a border of 3,300 kilometers. Such a supposed transition to a democracy was to benefit, in the first place, the party with the longest tradition of democratic opposition, the PAN, whose political platform coincided in many points with the position of the U.S. government on economic matters and on international politics.[40]

These U.S. pressures to force the Mexican authoritarian regime to open up to party competition came from various sources—the mass media, academics, the U.S. Congress, and federal government officials—and was mostly indirect. Still, and in the final analysis, that pressure generated an environment of great tension between the governments of both countries, which was well reflected in the difficult relations between American Ambassador John Gavin and Mexican government officials, in particular with Foreign Minister Bernardo Sepúlveda.

U.S. pressure to broaden Mexican pluralism abated as suddenly as it had arisen. The reason is obvious; from 1988 onward, the possibility emerged that it would not be the PAN but rather the centrist left-wing forces that would most benefit from the existence of a real democratic contest in Mexico. Indeed, when on the Mexican political scene there appeared a centrist left-wing heterogeneous coalition headed by Cuauhtémoc Cárdenas and the National Democratic Front (FDN), the enthusiasm shown by many American groups over the possibility of democracy progressing in Mexico almost died.

After the July 1988 elections, in which the opposing leftist and rightist forces complained on being the victims of a massive fraud, the parties constituting the FDN received officially more than 30 percent of the valid votes. Notwithstanding that the national and foreign press reported evidence of specific examples of widespread electoral fraud, the U.S. government hastened to congratulate the official candidate, Carlos Salinas, for his indisputable victory. The American ambassador, Charles Pilliod, repeatedly declared that his government considered Mexico a true democracy. Once in the presidency, and after reasserting his neoliberal economic project, Carlos Salinas was declared by the government and the mass media of that country as a model leader in the third world.[41] The new Mexican president was quite soon received by George Bush and U.S. authorities, thus reaffirming the support that had already been expressed to him as president-elect. In reciprocity, the Mexican government redoubled its efforts in the struggle against drug trafficking and dismantled what was left of its independent policy in Central America. By the end of 1989 there was, in fact, a "special relationship" policy between Mexico and the United States, directed at underlining all points of coincidence and minimizing to the maximum the differences so as to facilitate an accelerated process of integration of its two economies. The persistence of authoritarian features of the Mexican political system did not signify any problem in this process.

Concluding Remarks

Historically, the nondemocratic nature of the Mexican political system has not been a significant factor in Mexican-U.S. relations, with the sole exception of the period in which the Mexican Revolution as an antiauthoritarian revolt coincided with the American reformism headed by President Wilson, and then only for a very short period. In effect, in the latter half of the Wilsonian period, the "Mexican problem" ceased to be a significant topic in the agenda of U.S. foreign policy, and even less important was the subject of Mexican democracy. In these conditions, U.S. policy toward Mexico went back to being traditional: the protection of interests and rights acquired by Americans in a Mexico where nationalism was on the rise and the bloody civil war did not cease altogether. By the late 1920s, in Washington all interest in fostering democratic change in Mexico disappeared—on account of its irrelevancy.

Once the Mexican Revolution and its system of inclusionary authoritarianism was consolidated, the U.S. government accepted the definition of democratic that the new Mexican regime had made for itself, and the subject disappeared completely from the Mexican-U.S. official agenda. Events such as the government's bloody repression in October 1968 of an urban and middle-class movement that called for a democratic opening up (apertura) did not provoke any alteration whatsoever in the normality of relations between the Mexican and U.S. governments, for the repression did not affect the central elements of that relationship; quite the contrary, it affirmed them.

All this began to change with the onset of the economic and political crisis of Mexico's postrevolutionary regime in the 1980s. Washington's irritation over Mexican interference with its policy in Central America (Mexico's insistence on the validity of the principle of nonintervention in the face of the Reagan government's effort to topple Nicaragua's Sandinista regime), the threats to Mexican stability, and the possibility of achieving a permanent increase in the influence of the centrist right-wing forces in Mexican politics led U.S. governmental circles to consider the convenience of encouraging a change in Mexico's old political system via an opening up toward democracy and pluralism. However, such an idea was discarded the moment a centrist left-wing opposition led by Cuauhtémoc Cárdenas began to gather strength. Faced with the leftist challenge, the government of the United States—just as all others with whom Mexico maintains relations—decided to accept the 1988 elections without any hesitation as legitimate, despite a well-grounded suspicion of a great electoral fraud against the centrist left-wing coalition. With this decision there was a going back to the erstwhile tradition of relations between Mexico and the United States in the postrevolutionary period, which implies accepting as a central premise that Mexico's formally democratic system is also the real system, regardless of abundant evidences to the contrary.[42] This traditional policy of Washington fully coincides with the Mexican traditional position—accepted both by the government and the bulk of its opponents—in the sense that the principle of nonintervention of the U.S. government in Mexican internal affairs should be the basis of the relationship between both neighbors.

Lastly, it may be noted that when Mexican authoritarianism has been efficient in its task of control and has not sought confrontation with the United States, American pressure, in democratic matters and in many other matters more related to Mexico's internal political arrangements, has been insignificant or nonexistent. The opposite is equally true. The pressure of the north on Mexican political elites has increased when the Mexican internal arrangement has weakened. So then, provided that there is control of internal Mexican political processes, and that direct conflicts are avoided in international areas considered critical by the United States, the nature of the power structure in Mexico is an irrelevant factor in the formulation of U.S. policy toward that country. In view of the foregoing, it is clear, even for those who wish that Mexico may move forward from authoritarianism to democracy, that such movement has to be fundamentally the work of internal political forces. Moral imperialism of the Woodrow Wilson style, however democratic it may be, does not lose its imperialistic character, and in practice it is very fickle; it is not, nor is it convenient that it should be so, a substitute for the will and capacity of national political actors to attain democracy.

Notes

1. Jesús Reyes Heroles, *El liberalismo mexicano en pocas páginas (selección de Adolfo Castañón y Otto Granados)* (Mexico: Fondo de Cultura Económica, 1985), pp. 28–29, 32–34, 52, 55; Javier Ocampo, *Las ideas de un día. El pueblo mexicano ante la consumación de su independencia* (Mexico: El Colegio de México, 1969), pp. 223, 307; Ernesto De la Torre Villar, *La constitución de Apatzingán y los creadores del estado mexicano* (Mexico: Universidad Nacional Autónoma de México, 1978), pp. 18, 48.

2. From 1824 onward, the importance of the political model in Mexico's internal discussion increased notably; see De la Torre Villar, p. 83; Nettie Lee Benson, *La diputación provincial y el federalismo mexicano* (Mexico: Cámara de Diputados, LI Legislature, 1980), pp. 85–86, 167. On the reaction following the Mexico-U.S. war, see Josefina Zoraida Vázquez, *Mexicanos y norteamericanos ante la guerra del 47* (Mexico: Ateneo, 1978).

3. Concerning this topic of the relationship between the U.S. government and the Mexican liberal group, one can see Agustín Cue Cánovas, *Júarez, los Estados Unidos y Europa: el tratado de McLane-Ocampo* (Mexico: Editorial Grijalbo, 1970); José Fuentes Mares, *Juárez y los Estados Unidos* (Mexico: LibroMex, 1960).

4. Some authors have insisted that the good relationship between Gen. Porfirio Díaz and the European interests led the U.S. government to favor the enemies of the old dictator. However, Daniel Cosío Villegas's thorough research in this regard does not show any indicators of this conspiracy, but rather to the contrary; see *Historia moderna de México. El Porfiriato. Vida política exterior, segunda parte* (Mexico: Editorial Hermes, 1963), pp. 3–475.

5. Josefina Zoraida Vázquez and Lorenzo Meyer, *México frente a los Estados Unidos. Un esayo histórico, 1776–1980* (Mexico: El Colegio de México, 1982), pp. 143–73; Alan Knight, *U.S.-Mexican Relations, 1910–1940: An Interpretation* (San Diego, Calif.: Center for U.S.-Mexican Studies, University of California, 1987), pp. 3–14, 91–101, 130–42.

6. Olga Pellicer and Esteban Mancilla, *Historia de la Revolución Mexicana. Periodo 1952–1960. El entendimiento con los Estados Unidos y el desarrollo estabilizador* (Mexico: El Colegio de México, 1978).

7. See Soledad Loaeza, "El factor americano," in *El llamado de las urnas* (Mexico: Cal y Arena, 1989), pp. 81–88. The reasons for tension between the Mexican government and Washington following the victory of the revolutionary Sandinistas in Nicaragua are well presented by one of the most notable critics in the United States of Mexican policy in Central America, Constantine C. Menges, in his book, *Inside the National Security Council* (New York: Simon & Schuster, 1988), pp. 56–57, 243, 280–91, 300–305. The Mexican view of the problem is set forth in Claude Heller, "La política exterior de México y Estados Unidos hacia Centroamérica," in Rosario Green and Peter H. Smith, coords., *La política exterior y la agenda México–Estados Unidos* (Mexico: Fondo de Cultera Económica, 1989), pp. 187–230.

8. Concerning this point—U.S. support of the Mexican government stemming from the possibility of an electoral victory of the left-wing opposition—see several articles published by Jorge G. Castañeda in the Mexican weekly newsmagazine *Proceso* in 1988 and 1989, as well as those by Adolfo Aguilar Zínser, published over the same period, in the daily newspaper *Excélsior.*

9. The reader can consult the general interpretations contained in Francois-Xavier Guerra, *México: del antiguo régimen a la revolución,* 2 vols. (Mexico: Fondo de Cultura Económica, 1988); Alan Knight, *The Mexican Revolution,* 2 vols. (Cambridge: Cambridge University Press, 1986); Enrique Krauze, *Místico de la libertad. Francisco I. Madero* (Mexico: Fondo de Cultura Económica, 1987), pp. 21ff.; Stanley R. Ross, *Franciso I. Madero: Apostle of Mexican Democracy* (New York: Columbia University Press, 1955); Charles C. Cumberland, *Madero y la Revolución Mexicana* (Mexico: Siglo XXI, 1981).

10. Luis Nicolau D'Olwer, "Las inversiones extrajeras," in Daniel Cosío Villegas, ed., *Historia moderna de México. El Porfiriato. Vida económica,* vol. 2 (Mexico: Editorial Hermes, 1965), pp. 1130–37.

11. P. Edward Haley, *Revolution and Intervention: The Diplomacy of Taft and Wilson with Mexico, 1910–1917* (Cambridge: MIT Press, 1970), p. 14.

12. Daniel Cosío Villegas, *Historia moderna de México. El Porfiriato. La vida pólitica exterior. Parte Segunda* (Mexico: Editorial Hermes, 1963), pp. 321–75.

13. Knight, *Mexican Revolution,* 1: 184–88.

14. Ibid., p. 184. A different point of view, which gives more weight to American action in the fall of Díaz, is found in Friedrich Katz, *The Secret War in Mexico: Europe, the United States and the Mexican Revolution* (Chicago: University of Chicago Press, 1981), pp. 20–21.

15. Karl M. Schmitt, *Mexico and the United States, 1821–1973: Conflict and Coexistence* (New York: John Wiley & Sons, 1974), pp. 119–20.

16. Haley, pp. 15–20.

17. Victor Gordon Kiernan, *The Lords of Human Kind: Black Man, Yellow Man, and White Man in an Age of Empire* (New York: Columbia University Press, 1986), pp. 299–306.

18. Cumberland, pp. 200ff.; Henry Lane Wilson, *Diplomatic Episodes in Mexico, Belgium and Chile* (New York: Doubleday, Page & Company, 1927), p. 240.

19. Berta Ulloa, *La revolución intervenida. Relaciones diplomáticas México-Estados Unidos (1910–1914)* (Mexico: El Colegio de México, 1971), pp. 48–55; Cumberland, pp. 229, 238–43; Katz, pp. 95–115; Knight, *Mexican Revolution,* pp. 483–86.

20. Bernard Bailyn, et al., *The Great Republic: A History of the American People* (Boston: Little, Brown & Co., 1977), pp. 938–48.

21. Samuel E. Morison, Henry Steele Commager, and William E. Leuchtenburg, *The Growth of the American Republic,* 7th ed. (New York: Oxford University Press, 1980), 2: 268–75.

22. Haley, pp. 6–7, 121; Robert Freeman Smith, *The United States and Revolutionary Nationalism in Mexico, 1916–1932* (Chicago: University of Chicago Press, 1972), pp. 31–34; Josephus Daniels, *The Wilson Era* (Chapel Hill: University of North Carolina Press, 1944), pp. 184–85.

23. Arthur S. Link, ed., *The Papers of Woodrow Wilson* (Princeton: Princeton University Press, 1978), 28: 458–63.

24. Knight, *U.S.-Mexican Relations,* pp. 103–4.

25. On this subject see the work of Larry D. Hill, *Emissaries to a Revolution: Woodrow Wilson's Executive Agents in Mexico* (Baton Rouge: Louisiana State University Press, 1973).

26. A detailed account of the actions of the Wilson administration against the Victoriano Huerta, as well as an expression of the prevailing position among Mexican historians as regards the American intervention in the Mexican revolutionary process, is to be found in the previously cited work by Berta Ulloa, pp. 100–259; for a more positive view of President Wilson's Mexican policy, and for a historiographic appraisal, see Knight, *U.S.-Mexican Relations,* pp. 103–25.

27. For an illustration of the central role that the protection of acquired rights was to occupy in U.S.-Mexican relations from 1914 onward, see Lorenzo Meyer, *México y los Estados Unidos en el conflicto petrolero, 1917–1942,* 2d ed. (Mexico: El Colegio de México, 1972), pp. 83ff.

28. For a very concise account of these conflicts, see Vázquez and Meyer, pp. 138–73.

29. The bibliography dealing with the nature of the political system that emerged from the Mexican revolution is very broad; among the most important general works, the following may be consulted: Pablo González Casanova, *La democracia en México* (Mexico: Ediciones Era, 1965); Peter H. Smith, *Labyrinths of Power: Political Recruitment in Twentieth-Century Mexico* (Princeton: Princeton University Press, 1979); Roger D. Hansen, *The Politics of Mexican Development* (Baltimore: Johns Hopkins University Press, 1971); Arnaldo Cordova, *La ideología de la Revolución Mexicana* (Mexico: Editorial Era, 1973); Luis Javier Garrido, *El partido de la revolución institucionalizada. La formación del nuevo Estado (1928–1952)* (Mexico: Siglo XXI, 1982).

30. Arnaldo Córdova, *La política de masas del cardenismo* (Mexico: Editorial Era,

1974); Nora Hamilton, *The Limits of State Autonomy: Post-Revolutionary Mexico* (Princeton: Princeton University Press, 1982).

31. In addition to the works cited in nn. 39 and 40, see José Luis Reyna and Richard S. Weinert, eds., *Authoritarianism in Mexico* (Philadelphia: Institute for the Study of Human Issues, 1977); Lorenzo Meyer, "El estado mexicano contemporaneo," *Historia Mexicana* 23, no. 4 (October–December 1974): 722–52.

32. For a description and analysis of the basic characteristics of the postwar Mexican economy, see Clark W. Reynolds, *The Mexican Economy: Twentieth Century Structure and Growth* (New Haven: Yale University Press, 1970).

33. Knight, *U.S.-Mexican Relations*, p. 13.

34. Data taken from Comisión Sobre el Futuro de las Relaciones México–Estados Unidos, *El desafío de la interdependencia: México y Estados Unidos* (Mexico: Fondo de Cultura Económica, 1988), pp. 36–43.

35. The nature of the change is described and analyzed by Wayne A. Cornelius, *The Political Economy of Mexico under de la Madrid: The Crisis Deepens, 1985–1986* (San Diego, Calif.: Center for U.S.-Mexican Studies, University of California, 1986); Roberto Newell and Luis Rubio, *Mexico's Dilemma: The Political Origins of Economic Crisis* (Boulder, Colo.: Westview Press, 1984).

36. For a plural discussion dealing with the importance that the electoral process and political democracy have today in Mexico, see Rolando Cordera Campos, Raúl Trejo Delarbre, and Juan Enrique Vega, coords., *México: el reclamo democrático* (Mexico: Siglo XXI, 1988); the work by Soledad Loaeza, pp. 225–319, may also be consulted.

37. The suspicion of massive electoral fraud in July 1988 is documented in José Berberán, et al., *Radiografía del fraude: análisis de los datos oficiales del 6 de julio* (Mexico: Editorial Nuestro Tiempo, 1988).

38. Comisión Sobre el Futuro de las Relaciones México–Estados Unidos, pp. 48–57; Leon Bendesky and Victor M. Godinez, "The Mexican Foreign Debt: A Case of Conflictual Cooperation," in Riordan Roett, ed., *Mexico and the United States: Managing the Relationship* (Boulder, Colo.: Westview Press, 1988), pp. 51–70.

39. The dissatisfaction of the U.S. administration's most conservative wing with Mexico and its policy of putting pressure so as to modify Mexican policy is very well reflected in the work, cited previously, of one of its architects: Constantine C. Menges, pp. 117–19; on this point, see also Jorge G. Castaneda's analysis in his work jointly coauthored with Robert Pastor, *Limits to Friendship* (New York: Alfred A. Knopf, 1988), pp. 159–64, 177–90; likewise, see Bruce Michael Bagley, "Interdependence and U.S. Policy toward Mexico in the 1980s," in Roett, pp. 223–39.

40. William E. Buzenberg, "The 1985 Mexican Elections and the North American Press," in Arturo Alvarado, comp., *Electoral Patterns and Perspectives in Mexico* (San Diego, Calif.: Center for U.S.-Mexican Studies, University of California, 1987), pp. 253–64; Susan Kaufman Purcell, "Mexico in Transition," in Susan Kaufman Purcell, ed., *Mexico in Transition: Implications for U.S. Policy* (New York: Council on Foreign Relations, 1988), pp. 3–17; Blanca Torres, "La visión estadounidense de las elecciones de 1985: presión de coyuntura o preocupación de largo plazo?" in Gabriel Székely, comp., *México–Estados Unidos, 1985* (Mexico: El Colegio de México, 1986), pp. 45–62; Soledad Loaeza, "Nacionalismo y democracia en México: tensión entre dos ficciones," in Cordera et al., comps., pp. 99–105.

41. Andrew Reding, "Mexico under Salinas: A Facade of Reform," *World Policy Journal* (Autumn 1989): 724.

42. It must be said that if the official position of Washington is to consider Mexico as a bona fide democracy, that has not been the case of the academic and the media communities, who repeatedly have questioned the nature of Mexico's political system.

5 | Nicaragua: The Limits of Intervention

Joseph S. Tulchin and Knut Walter

THE ELECTION of Señora Violeta Chamorro in February 1990 as the president of Nicaragua has been understood as part of the alluvial tide running in favor of democracy throughout the world. In Washington, the administration of George Bush, as surprised by the results as most observers, welcomed the outcome as the final vindication of the policy of Ronald Reagan in Central America. To many observers in the United States and in Latin America, that posture appeared disingenuous because for the better part of a decade, the U.S. government had appeared much more concerned with the presence of Cuban and Soviet influence in Nicaragua than with the possibilities for democracy there. Certainly, the manner in which democracy as a policy goal was subordinated to other goals in El Salvador, Guatemala, and Honduras, and the manner in which an armed insurgency against the government of Nicaragua was provided overt and covert support under the justification of anti-Communism, suggested that "democracy" was nothing more than a club or weapon that the United States would use whenever convenient against regimes it considered hostile, in its ongoing struggle with the Soviet Union. In Central America, it was a device to counter what the United States decried as the threat of external intervention in the region.

Given the experience of the past ten years, it is hard to imagine that the U.S. government on several occasions in the twentieth century fervently supported the cause of democracy in Nicaragua and, by explicitly supporting the government there, played a constructive though paternalistic role in the effort to extend the reach and deepen the substance of democracy. That was the case during the first administration of Woodrow Wilson (1913–17) and the administration of Warren G. Harding (1921–23). Indeed, it is harder, still, to imagine the time when the U.S. government did not play any significant role in the internal affairs of Nicaragua. And, yet, such was the case during most of the nineteenth century. Perhaps it is hardest to realize that the policy of the United States toward Nicaragua has gone through a number of important changes and that the government in Washington, when it first turned its attention to events in Nicaragua during the administration of William Howard Taft (1909–13), was uncertain how to act and uncertain how to achieve its goals. A review of the history of U.S. relations with Nicaragua in the twentieth century prior to the Sandinista accession to power in 1979 is extremely useful in understanding the evolution of the concept of democracy in U.S. foreign policy thinking and how changes in that concept affected relations between the two countries. It is useful also in enabling us to see more clearly how U.S. policy makers have viewed democracy as an export commodity and how the defense of democracy may be used to this day as the rationalization for armed intervention in the affairs of another state, as in the invasion of Panama in December 1989.

Recounting the history of U.S. intervention becomes a morality play that suggests compellingly that democracy as an export commodity tends to be long on form and short on substance; that in attempting to impose the trappings of democratic government on Nicaragua over the years, the U.S. government has made little attempt to consider the needs, concerns, or interests of the Nicaraguan people; and that efforts to impose democracy, even when limited to constitutional form and elections, never succeeded in establishing stable democratic conditions in the country. The history of U.S. efforts to impose democratic government on Nicaragua suggests also that there has operated an iron law of intervention under which a little intervention in the domestic affairs of another nation, for the purpose of imposing a certain kind of government or a certain pattern of political behavior, leads inexorably to more intervention. The iron law operates until and unless the U.S. government explicitly decides to limit its intervention and to give up the policy objective of forcing democracy on the intervened people. At that moment, the political forces in Nicaragua return to their traditional patterns of behavior in which governance is organized by personalistic dealings rather than by free expression of the popular will and in which power is considered a zero-sum game, not to be shared or given up except under force. Nicaragua is a penetrated political system in which the U.S. government is a vital actor, passive or active, to be appealed to by Nicaraguan actors for the purpose of achieving or maintaining control over the government. In the current cycle, the Nicaraguan actors appear to know their roles very well. At this writing, it remains to be seen how the United States will respond and whether the Nicaraguans will be capable of sustaining a pluralistic democratic polity that is responsive to the needs of the Nicaraguan people without the suffocating tutelage of the United States.

Historical Background

Those in the United States given to saber rattling south of the border and those in Latin America given to U.S. bashing tend to forget or deny that the United States was not always paramount in Nicaraguan affairs. The United States had attempted to project its power in the region in the nineteenth century, but to little effect. The filibustering of William Walker in the 1850s was the only exception and the U.S. government played little or no role in the episode. Great Britain had been the dominant power in the region throughout the nineteenth century, and by the end of the century, the United States had succeeded barely in neutralizing British power, not in eliminating it. Nicaragua had figured in U.S. policy as the site of a potential isthmian canal. As early as the 1880s, Capt. Alfred Thayer Mahan had referred to the isthmus as critical to United States national security. In the early years of the 1890s, the best route for the canal and the role of the U.S. government in its construction were subjects of political debate in the Congress and among those concerned with U.S. foreign policy. For several years, the route through Nicaragua was preferred by a majority in Congress and it was only through concerted effort by the lobby favoring a route through the Colombian province of Panama and by the separatist movement there that attention turned in the United States away from Nicaragua.[1]

The United States achieved its hegemonic dominance in the Caribbean basin in the years between the war with Spain and World War I. The key to understanding U.S. policy in the area during this period is the nature of its policy objectives—eliminating the conditions that prompted external intervention by European powers, such as fiscal irresponsibility and political instability—and the evolving debate within the government over the appropriate means by which it would accomplish its goals in each intervention in Mexico, Central America, and the Caribbean.

In this early period, the United States shifted from a reactive policy toward European intervention in the Caribbean Basin to a proactive or preemptive interventionist policy. The first step in this process came during the so-called Venezuelan debt crisis of 1902, in which the government of Theodore Roosevelt explicitly gave permission to the other "civilized" nations, as they were called in those days, and the governments representing the holders of the bonds on which the Venezuelan government had defaulted, to "police" the area by using force to extract payment from the Venezuelan government. Public opinion and Congress reacted immediately with a passion that surprised Roosevelt, forcing him to ask the Germans, who had dispatched a naval force to the coast of Venezuela, to speed up their civilizing mission and get out of the Caribbean. Worse, an international tribunal in The Hague, seized with a dispute among Venezuela's creditors regarding how the debts should be repaid, found in favor of the creditors who had taken the trouble to send ships to the region to force resumption of payments.

When a similar episode occurred in 1904, in the Dominican Republic, President Roosevelt knew he could not allow the European creditors to step in. The United States would have to assume the responsibility of the policeman of civilized nations in order to keep the Europeans out. As he told his son in February 1904, "The United States should assume an attitude of protection and regulation in regard to all those little states in the neighborhood of the Caribbean." Later the same month, he told a friend, "It is our duty, when it becomes absolutely inevitable, to police these countries in the interests of order and civilization."[2]

The Congress was not certain it wanted to assume an imperial role in the sense that such roles had been assumed by the European nations. When the executive proposed a formal treaty in 1905 to certify the U.S. activity in the Dominican Republic, the Congress balked. Roosevelt was uncertain as to how to proceed. On one thing, however, he was clear. At the end of the year, as the government discussed its options in the Dominican Republic, he told Secretary of State Elihu Root, "I have about as much desire to take over more territory as does a gorged boa constrictor to swallow a porcupine hind end to."[3]

Thus, the United States approached its first military intervention in Nicaragua in the context of defining its role as a great power. The nation's leaders were confident that they could and should assume such a role but, aside from rejecting the territorial implications of empire, they had not defined carefully what their responsibilities as a hegemonic power might entail. They knew that their basic objective had to be to prevent European intervention in the Caribbean. There was a sense that lapses in international behavior by nations in the region, especially those involving international debts, created the conditions for intervention and that such intervention was justified under international law. In order to prevent intervention by the European powers, the United States would have to act to teach the lessons of civilized international behavior to their client states. What this might mean was anything but clear in the thinking of U.S. policy makers.[4]

Enter Nicaragua

Nicaragua had made little progress in nation building in the seventy-five years since Spanish authority had been overthrown. During most of the nineteenth century, the central government was in the hands of one or another of the regional barons who, calling themselves Liberals or Conservatives, dominated society and economics around León, in the north, or Granada, in the central south. These bosses, cattle barons and merchants, were caudillos in the classical mold of nineteenth-century Latin America. Their power was regional but within their region, it was virtually without significant limitations. No formal institutions, local or national, curbed the power of these caudillos.[5]

In truth, the central government had very little authority over a national territory that was defined only in the most imprecise manner. National boundaries had not been fixed at the time of independence and their location was a question of elite politics, something for the regional bosses to fight over but with little or no symbolic meaning for the nation. To make matters worse, the east coast was virtually cut off from the central plateau and the west coast. There, the British were all but sovereign, English was the dominant language, and the population was Afro-Caribbean and Indian, not mestizo or Indian of the highland tribes. As a consequence of this legacy, there was a marked lack of national cohesion throughout the century characterized by remarkably primitive communications. There was very little state formation and no attempt to make of the central government anything more than the symbolic prize of warfare among the regional caudillos. At the same time, the lack of state formation and lack of definition of the national territory led to a pattern of meddling across international boundaries throughout the region. It was common for caudillos to meddle in the affairs of their allies or enemies even though they might be in a land called Guatemala, or Costa Rica, or Honduras.

So weak was the national state, that a filibuster from the United States, William Walker, invaded Nicaragua in 1855 with an army of mercenaries, under contract with the Liberals, to help them oust the Conservatives. First, he was military chief under a puppet regime and then, in 1856, he declared himself president of the republic. The British provided financial support for a coalition of Conservative forces in the region who managed to oust Walker in 1857. The Liberals were so discredited by their alliance with Walker that the Conservatives held power until 1893, when the Liberals managed to install their leader, José Santos Zelaya, as head of the national government.

Zelaya's subsequent anticlerical policies and persecution of the Conservative faction subjected his government to constant insurrections by his opponents. The Conservative revolt against Zelaya in 1909 was the fourteenth during his rule. In this case, however, it upset the U.S. Department of State because it threatened the property and lives of foreigners and contained the potential to provoke foreign intervention, which the United States was determined to forestall. To alleviate his financial difficulties, Zelaya previously had tried to sell the rights to a canal route across Nicaraguan territory to interests in Europe and Japan. This did not sit well in Washington either, and the agents of the U.S. government in Nicaragua exerted their best efforts to eliminate Zelaya and install in his place General Juan Estrada, a dissident Liberal leader who had thrown his lot in with the Conservatives.

In intervening to tip the scales in favor of the Conservatives, the Department of State expected to repeat what they considered to be their success in preventing European intervention in the Dominican Republic by restoring the conditions of fiscal responsibility. At this point, little mention of politics was made in setting the terms of U.S. intervention in Nicaragua. After the fall of the Zelaya faction in 1910, the U.S. government sent financial advisers to Managua to help President Estrada straighten out his government's budget. This action was consistent with the U.S. policy of dollar diplomacy elsewhere in the world, under which U.S. capital was expected to become "the instrumentality to secure financial stability and hence prosperity and peace in the region."[6]

To accomplish its limited objectives, the State Department solicited support from investment banking houses in New York to consolidate Nicaragua's foreign debt and pay off the European bondholders, thereby eliminating the threat of European intervention. At the same time, the department presented a treaty to Congress under which the United States would guarantee loans to Nicaragua and help end the fiscal irresponsibility that had become an international embarrassment. Much to the consternation of the Taft administration, Congress rejected the treaty in 1910.

At this point, the bankers already were committed to proceed with the consolidation loan and the State Department gave them informal assurances that they could expect government support for their activities. But in 1911, Estrada was replaced in a bloodless coup by Adolfo Díaz, a Conservative. Tension increased until the political situation collapsed completely the following year. Fearing that they could not get a fair deal in the upcoming congressional elections, both Liberals and Conservatives prepared for an armed conflict, as they had so many times in the past. This time it would be different because the U.S. government was committed to maintaining stability in the region and was unwilling to accept the traditional pattern of interelite conflict in Nicaragua.

At Díaz's request, marines landed in August 1912 to protect U.S. lives and property and restore order. When they departed in November, they left behind a legation guard of one hundred soldiers. This was the first time the U.S. government had used troops to restore order and bolster the established government of a Latin American nation. It would not be the last.

The nature of U.S. imperial responsibilities in the Western Hemisphere changed as a result of this episode. Now, there was a presence of U.S. marines to support the constituted government and prevent the usual play of violence in the change of national authorities. The man who directed the legation guard, the U.S. minister, became the arbiter and mediator of Nicaraguan politics, consulted by leaders of both major factions, by ministers of the national government, and by leaders of the national congress concerned about pending legislation. The role of this proconsul was expanded as a consequence of the world economic downturn that cut back on revenues earned by the Nicaraguan government through customs receipts, now collected by an agent of the U.S. government. At the end of 1912, the Ferrocarril del Pacífico de Nicaragua, the national railway, became collateral for the consolidated loan held in New York. In 1913, the same fate befell the National Bank. Both became U.S. corporations administered by boards that met in New York City.

In many ways, some of them totally unanticipated by Washington when it first posed the option of intervention in Nicaraguan affairs, the U.S. government had become an actor in Nicaraguan politics in a manner that would make it difficult to distinguish between internal and external influences. Factions in Nicaragua and the Nicaraguan government itself began to play to the U.S. government in an effort to increase their leverage within the Nicaraguan political system. Still, in 1909, the nature of the government in Nicaragua had not become an issue of U.S. policy; stability, not democracy, was the issue.

When Wilson became president in March 1913, he began immediately to fulfill one of his campaign promises to end dollar diplomacy. His first target was the consortium of bankers intent on using U.S. government influence to make major loans to China. His secretary of state, William Jennings Bryan, was a long-standing critic of Wall Street and greedy capitalism. Yet neither man for a moment questioned the basic goal of avoiding European intervention in the Caribbean, or the assumptions underlying the need to protect U.S. strategic interests in the Caribbean by avoiding the conditions that might precipitate foreign intervention.

Confronted with the critical Nicaraguan situation of 1913, Bryan first tried to get the Senate to ratify the Knox-Castrillo Convention, which contained an option for the United States to build a canal across Nicaraguan territory and a clause similar to the Platt amendment giving the U.S. government authority to maintain order and fiscal equilibrium in Nicaragua. To his dismay, the Senate rejected the convention because it was unwilling to assume the imperial responsibilities it implied.

Bryan then renegotiated the agreement, now called the Bryan-Chamorro Treaty. In place of the explicit assumption of imperial responsibility, Bryan proposed a scheme that anticipated the multilateral lending agencies after World War II. He suggested that the U.S. Treasury float loans on the domestic market at 3 to 4 percent and then lend Nicaragua the money it needed at 5 to 6 percent, significantly under the market rate of 9 to 10 percent for such poor risks as the Nicaraguan government. The U.S. government would use the difference to amortize the loan. Agents appointed by the U.S. government would advise the Nicaraguan government on the disposition of the loan funds and help in the collection of revenues in Nicaragua.

Now, it was Wilson who rejected the scheme, on the grounds that it would commit the United States to unnecessary involvement in Nicaraguan domestic affairs. Yet, just one month later, to keep Nicaragua solvent, Bryan was forced to approve the loan contract negotiated by Brown Brothers in October 1913 under which the U.S. government appointed two members of the board of the National Bank. As a result, all disputes with the Nicaraguan government automatically became diplomatic disputes involving the government of the United States. The involvement of the U.S. government in Nicaraguan domestic affairs had become complete. This financially induced involvement was broken only by the export boom after World War I, which enabled Nicaragua to pay off its long-standing loans and get rid of the offensive U.S. agents. In the period from 1917 to 1929, 43 percent of total government outlays went to cover public debt commitments. The debt crisis of the 1980s was trifling by comparison.

Wilson was not content to be drawn into the domestic affairs of Nicaragua as the satrapy of New York bankers. At the time he was discussing events in Managua with Bryan, the two men were deeply involved in the unfolding drama of the Mexican Revolution. There, as well as in the Dominican Republic, Wilson was convinced that the U.S. government had a constructive role to play in exporting democracy to countries that wanted it but were somehow unable to establish democratic governments without the assistance of the U.S. government. In the case of Nicaragua, Wilson undertook to revise the constitution and take steps to insure the fairness of the coming elections in 1916. For the first time, the achievement of democratic government and the projection of democratic process became an explicit feature of U.S. policy toward Nicaragua, always as a means to secure the basic policy goal: to prevent European intervention by eliminating the conditions that made it possible.

Although it is fruitless to debate Wilson's motives in attempting to export democracy to Nicaragua—it seems clear, as Arthur Link has argued, that Wilson believed a democratic form of government would enhance the quality of life for all Nicaraguans, and it is just as clear that Wilson understood that the imposition of democracy on Nicaragua would enhance U.S. security and expand its influence in the region—it is remarkable that he adopted so limited a conception of democracy in its export version and that he never for a moment questioned whether the governmental institutions and procedures he was prepared to export would have to be adapted in any way, shape, or form to fit the local milieu.[7] It was as if he believed that democracy was democracy, and that it could be exported to another country without any alteration whatsoever, without reference to the historical or cultural context in which it had evolved, and that honest local politicians would behave in a fully democratic manner if only they could be taught what it was. This cultural ethnocentrism and the certitude that accompanied it are the very essence of what we mean today by a "Wilsonian attitude."[8]

As it turned out, the Nicaraguans adapted the mechanisms of democracy to their own political culture with amazing virtuosity. In the run-up to the election of 1916, both factions, the Liberals and the Conservatives, complained to the U.S. minister that their opponents were violating certain laws and using illegal campaign methods and that their control of the press in their regional bailiwicks violated the letter and the spirit of the constitution. Emiliano Chamorro, the Conservative caudillo and presidential candidate, proved more adept than his opponent in manipulating the new instruments of democracy in building a coalition that looked remarkably like the old-fashioned alliances based on regional loyalties. Chamorro mastered the new procedures by adapting them to traditional Nicaraguan political culture. He manipulated the situation with such skill that the electoral agents sent to Nicaragua by the State Department virtually guaranteed his election. As further demonstration that he understood U.S. political culture much better than any North American understood Nicaragua's, he created the first institutional, legally recognized lobby of a Latin American nation in Washington, hiring Chandler P. Anderson to represent the interests of the Nicaraguan government. Time would prove Anderson a very effective lobbyist.[9]

After the war, Wilson was convinced that the threat of European intervention in the hemisphere had all but disappeared. He also was disillusioned with his efforts to implant democracy in Mexico, Haiti, the Dominican Republic, and Nicaragua. As a consequence, he was determined to reduce the intervention by the United States in the domestic affairs of nations in the Western Hemisphere. In Nicaragua, that meant accepting the form of democracy while conscious that its substance was being violated. In the elections of 1920, Chamorro manipulated the rules to insure the election of his uncle, Diego Chamorro, while he remained the power behind the president. The State Department held its collective nose and publicly accepted the hollow shell of electoralism in order to avoid deeper intervention in Nicaraguan affairs.

The succeeding Republican administration adopted and extended Wilson's postwar reluctance to intervene in the domestic affairs of the Latin American nations. So long as the form of democracy was maintained, the State Department sought to remain above the local fray, no matter how dirty it might become.[10] As Paul Drake explains clearly in another chapter in this volume, the political factions in Nicaragua continued to use the U.S. government as a player in domestic politics as they had for years.[11] Each was prepared to do whatever was necessary to precipitate U.S. intervention on their behalf because that was the only way they could have access to power. Without such intervention, either in the form of suasion and pressure by the local representative of the U.S. government or by the threat of force from officials in Washington, it was impossible to effect a peaceful change in control of the central government. Even Augusto C. Sandino, a Liberal who opposed Chamorro and would become the father of Nicaraguan anti-American nationalism, started out wanting elections, supervised elections. His innovation was to request supervision by Latin America observers, not by gringos.

The State Department tried to counter the idiosyncracies of Nicaraguan political culture by imposing additional reforms, correcting the abuses of democracy's substance or spirit with more procedures. The Nicaraguans adapted to them. In 1923, the so-called Dodds Law was imposed on the Nicaraguan government, creating for the first time an explicit requirement for bipartisan politics. This law was drawn up initially by a U.S. professor of political science, Harold Dodds, under contract by the State Department. After some discreet pressure on the Nicaraguan government by the U.S. ambassador and some minor changes in the draft version, the electoral law went into effect in 1923 and remained on the books with some amendments until the 1960s. While the law allowed any political grouping to become a party by submitting a petition signed by a number of citizens equivalent to 5 percent of the total number of votes cast in the previous election, in fact the law institutionalized the two-party system by reserving all appointments to electoral posts to members of the majority parties (the Liberals and the Conservatives). Not only that, but the majority of officials at the various levels of the electoral machinery would be chosen from the ranks of the party in power at the time. With this control of the electoral process, the party in power could proceed easily to disqualify voters from the other parties, count the ballots to its advantage, and in general make it impossible for a contender to mount a successful electoral challenge.[12]

It should come as no surprise that after 1923, with but two exceptions, no opposition party ever came to occupy the executive office of government by means of an electoral process. The first exception took place in 1928 when the U.S. Marines supervised the registration and voting procedures that enabled José María Moncada, the Liberal presidential candidate, to defeat Adolfo Díaz, the Conservative politician who owed the United States his entire political career. The second was in 1990, when an army of civilian observers patrolled the polling places and an opposition force, armed by the United States, camped in the countryside and across the border in Honduras. Moncada's victory was assured by the settlement imposed by President Coolidge's special emissary Henry Stimson to end the brief civil war between Conservatives and Liberals in 1927. Frustrated by their inability to win power through elections, the Liberals had resorted to the traditional device of an armed rebellion, hoping to drag the United States into the fray. Reluctantly, Coolidge intervened, but he ordered Stimson to do the job as quickly as possible and get out. Only Sandino objected to the terms of the arrangement Stimson negotiated and proceeded to fight the Marines from his strongholds in the north of the country. The U.S. government would not withdraw the Marines until the country was pacified. To accomplish its purpose, it adopted the advice of the Marine commander and created a local "professional police force" to keep order. Thus was born the Guardia Nacional.

The international environment in which the United States dispatched the Marines to Nicaragua in 1927 had changed in several important ways after World War I, affecting the manner in which democracy was used as an instrument of policy. While the decline in European capacity to intervene in the Caribbean as a result of the war certainly enhanced United States power and security, thereby diminishing the need for intervention, the nationalism characteristic of European politics of the era began to permeate Latin America as well. U.S. meddling in Nicaragua exacerbated the ongoing crisis in U.S. relations with Mexico.[13] The new revolutionary government in Mexico was determined to counter U.S. influence in the region and made its voice heard with increasing effect during the decade. The U.S. intervention in Nicaragua and the subsequent war between the Sandinistas and the Marines prompted the first concerted effort by Latin American nations to denounce and curtail U.S. hegemony when they met at the 1928 Pan American Conference in Havana. The fact that the intervention was justified by Washington in terms of protecting democracy did not move the critics at Havana. Nevertheless, the need to appear as the defender of democracy became even more useful to U.S. policy makers at the end of the decade, when then Secretary of State Stimson tried to emphasize the distinction between Japanese actions in Manchuria and the way in which the United States operated in Latin America. Democracy was an instrument of foreign policy, to be used against rival powers outside the hemisphere. It was no longer an objective in its own right, as it had been for Woodrow Wilson.[14]

The Somoza Years

When Franklin D. Roosevelt became president of the United States in March 1933, there were indications that his administration would return to the interventionism in Latin American affairs that had characterized the first administration of Woodrow Wilson. Roosevelt himself as assistant secretary of the navy had been involved in the occupation of Haiti. The secretary of state, Cordell Hull, was an avowed Wilsonian in his belief in the universal applicability of democratic norms, and the administration's chief Latin American expert and under secretary of state, Sumner Welles, had been deeply involved in the efforts during the Harding and Coolidge administrations to implant democracy in the Dominican Republic.

Soon after Roosevelt's inauguration, in which the president had declared his special interest in Latin America by promising a policy of the Good Neighbor, Welles went to Cuba to insure a smooth transition to democracy following the overthrow of the cruel dictator Gerardo Machado. Caught up in the factional infighting, Welles soon found himself forced to escalate his threats of intervention in order to encourage the various players to follow the straight and narrow path to democracy. Increasingly frustrated, Welles finally called for military intervention to bring order to Havana. Roosevelt and Hull refused and Welles was forced to retract his threats and swallow Batista as the strongman who would impose order. The U.S.

Government had resisted the temptation to get caught in the quicksand of intervention in the internal affairs of a client state in the Caribbean Basin, although with dubious benefit for the client. A few months later, at the Inter-American Meeting at Montevideo, Hull could accept a motion condemning intervention with only a mild reservation that international law might permit intervention under certain circumstances. Three years later, at the special meeting in Buenos Aires, Hull would accept a similar motion without reservations. The Latin American pressure against intervention of any kind was growing more insistent, to the point that the Roosevelt administration considered it a logical feature of the evolving Good Neighbor Policy.[15]

The effects of the Good Neighbor Policy on U.S. relations with Nicaragua are clear in the episode in which Anastasio Somoza García took power in Nicaragua. Somoza García never hid his presidential ambitions from the moment the commanding U.S. general turned over the control of the Guardia Nacional to him. But he was very careful to respect the democratic and legal guidelines set down in the Dodds Law and the Nicaraguan constitution. By gradually winning over the national legislature and putting his own followers into key positions in the Guardia Nacional, he was ready in 1936 to force the resignation of President Juan Bautista Sacasa, his wife's uncle, and capture the leadership of the Liberal party.[16] The entire procedure allowed Somoza to reach his goal at the beginning of 1937 with a minimum of bloodshed and just a little bending of the law. Somoza García emerged, thus, as a president elected with apparent bipartisan support, the first of a series of similar arrangements that the Somozas would organize in the future. Strictly speaking, no law had been broken openly but the pressure and intimidation exercised by Somoza and his Guardia Nacional, together with his control of the state bank and guardia funds, enabled him to persuade and threaten his way into the office of the presidency.

The cables from the U.S. legation in Managua indicate that the State Department was aware of what was going on. Moreover, in tried and true Nicaraguan tradition, the Conservatives who had refused to participate in the election and the Liberals who had been turned out of office after Sacasa's forced resignation organized a delegation that went straight to Washington to complain to the State Department about the disguised coup d'etat that had taken place and the phony elections that were coming up. To their surprise and dismay, the State Department officials told the unhappy politicians that the internal affairs of Nicaragua were the responsibility of the Nicaraguans themselves and that the United States would do nothing.[17]

In retrospect, it is clear that the United States could have threatened to act under the treaty signed in 1923 that forbade the recognition of governments that came to power by force, or it could have frozen the assets of the National Bank of Nicaragua held in U.S. accounts, or that it even could have invoked the treaty of 1928 that created the Guardia Nacional as an apolitical, nonpartisan body. It is not clear, however, that any of those efforts would have had the desired result. Welles, who had learned a bitter lesson in Havana, was convinced that getting Somoza to behave in a genuinely democratic fashion would have required more than idle threats. It would have sucked the United States deep into the vortex of Nicaraguan politics. U.S. public opinion would not stand for military adventures in the Caribbean basin. Besides, few policy makers in Washington were persuaded that even massive, prolonged intervention would have the desired democratic effect. Not even Secretary Hull, the most Wilsonian of the senior State Department officials, thought imposing democracy on Nicaragua was feasible or that it was worth the political risks to other New Deal programs in Congress. Hull, too, had learned his lesson from the experience in Cuba. He was more interested in what was happening in Europe and in getting the Congress to cooperate with his broad policy goals such as freer trade and cooperation with Great Britain in an effort to preserve peace in Europe, than he was in getting bogged down in the difficult task of exporting democracy to a nation whose leaders seemed uninterested in living by its rules and immune to its spirit.

There were external forces working against a policy of intervention to impose democracy on Nicaragua, or on any nation in Latin America. Escalating intervention by the United States in Nicaragua, even in the name of democracy, would alienate governments from Mexico to Argentina. The gathering storm clouds in Europe made running the risk of alienating potential allies in Latin America much too costly. Consolidating those ties became the top policy priority by the end of the decade. The U.S. government even had adhered without reservations to a resolution at the Inter-American Peace Conference held in Buenos Aires in 1936 to the effect that no state had the right to intervene in the domestic affairs of another. As further elaboration of this Good Neighbor Policy, the United States had sought to insure friendly relations with Mexico, imposing a settlement of the oil expropriation negotiations that the oil companies considered grossly unfair.[18] Consistent with the emerging policy, the Roosevelt administration sought to bolster Somoza, not undermine his rule by insisting on closer adherence to democratic norms. It invited President Somoza García to Washington in 1939 as the official guest of President Roosevelt, including a parade down Pennsylvania Avenue and a speech before the Congress. An initial policy of nonintervention combined with official recognition and public apotheosis in the U.S. capital provided Somoza García with the key elements to consolidate his government within and without Nicaragua.

The United States would do much the same with other dictators in the region. In the face of a perceived threat from outside the hemisphere, the U.S. government would sacrifice democracy and embrace dictators to insure their support. This same policy would be employed during the cold war, on the grounds that any form of government was acceptable so long as it was supportive of the United States in its struggle against hostile forces outside the hemisphere. But democracy did not disappear as a goal of U.S. policy in Nicaragua, or in other countries of the region for that matter, either in the struggle against the Axis or in the cold war. There were leaders in Washington for whom the content of the concept was as vital as the form of the procedures. The U.S. government continued to be concerned about the nature of democracy during the government of the first Somoza and expressed that concern publicly on some occasions. Even in those moments, however, it is clear that concern for the purity of democracy in Nicaragua was subordinate to other national concerns.

Somoza García understood the priorities of U.S. policy and the dynamics of its domestic politics and manipulated them in a brazen and shrewd manner. During World War II, he was quick to declare his participation in the crusade against the Axis. He declared war on Japan and Germany, confiscated the property of Axis nationals, and moved (with help from the FBI) to stem the activity of German agents in Nicaragua. But even he was caught in the postwar concern for democracy that forced Vargas from power in Brazil and made Perón's life so difficult in Argentina. The wartime crusade against the Axis and the anti-Communist crusade of the cold war reduced foreign policy to a zero-sum game. "You are either with us or against us," as John Foster Dulles put it during the 1950s. Within such a scheme, if the U.S. government feared subversion or intervention by the "enemy," then stability and the ability and disposition to oppose that subversion were more important than the quality or nature of the regime. It was the purpose of Somoza and his allies in Washington to make sure that the State Department understood Somoza's support of U.S. policies within the context of that zero-sum game.

The one time he failed, in the "soft" period after the war, clarifies the nature of this mechanistic calculation of policy priorities within the U.S. government. When Somoza made clear his intentions to remain in office past 1947, his relations with the State Department soured noticeably. Spruille Braden, a fervent Wilsonian known best for his public campaign against Juan Perón in the Argentine presidential elections of 1946, tried while he was assistant secretary of state for Latin America to persuade Somoza to relinquish the presidency once his term expired in 1947.[19] In fact, Somoza dropped his reelection plans and put forth the candidacy of Leonardo Argüello, an old Liberal whom Somoza thought he might control easily. Braden wanted Somoza out of the picture entirely to the point of even relinquishing his post as commander of the Guardia Nacional. When Argüello, already inaugurated as president, demanded Somoza's resignation from the guardia, he had reason to expect the United States would back him up.

Somoza moved fast. He had the Nicaraguan congress declare Argüello unfit to occupy the presidency, appointed a new interim president, and chased Argüello into exile in Mexico. The United States responded with the withdrawal of its ambassador and the commandant of the military academy, and, altogether with the other nations assembled in Bogotá in 1948, declared its unwillingness to recognize the puppet regime in Managua. For a brief while, Leonidas Trujillo of the Dominican Republic was the only Latin American head of state to recognize the Nicaraguan government. Through it all, Somoza managed to retain his undisputed control over the Guardia Nacional, the bottom line of his hold on political power in Nicaragua and the one institution that the United States would not risk alienating. By this time, Braden was gone from the government, and the iron zero-sum logic of anti-Communism ruled in the State Department.

Somoza's hold on power was strengthened by a number of social and economic changes that took place in Nicaragua after 1945.[20] These changes also contributed to an evolution in the practice of democracy in Nicaragua. Together, these changes, more than the passive acceptance of the U.S. government, help to explain the extraordinary longevity of the Somoza dynasty. First, there were fundamental economic changes that shifted power among elements of the national elite, thereby ending forever the regional factional politics that had characterized Nicaragua for a century. Part and parcel of these changes were a dramatic expansion of the state, traditionally feeble in Nicaragua, and a significant mobilization of popular forces, mainly through corporatist organizations manipulated by the state, but in some measure through unions with class consciousness and through a number of new political groups that began to address specific social questions.

These changes made Nicaragua appear a more open political system compared with the regimes in El Salvador, Honduras, or Guatemala until the fall of the Ubico dictatorship. And, if we keep in mind the Wilsonian concern for elections and constitutional forms and procedures that characterized the democracy-for-export imposed on Nicaragua by the United States in the decades prior to and following World War I, then we can understand the Somocista system as consistent with that model. The infrastructure of democracy was in place, elections were held, constitutional norms were followed. Of course, they were manipulated shamelessly to keep Somoza in power and to allow the opposition approved by the regime some room for maneuver. For example, Somoza's overthrow of Argüello in 1947 was followed by a heavy-handed persecution of Conservatives and dissident Liberals, but in anticipation of the 1950 elections, Somoza made sure to woo the Conservatives and have them participate in the election. The pre-electoral agreements reached were so explicit that the distribution of elected positions was mostly decided even before the polling took place: the Liberals and the Conservatives would be the only parties running and the Conservatives would get seventeen of the sixty seats in the legislature and representation in all town councils. They also would get a certain number of judgeships, all in exchange for participation and acceptance of the results. General Chamorro, who had been expelled from the country in 1947 for plotting a coup against Somoza, was persuaded to return and sign, with

Somoza, the so-called Pact of the Generals, which set the stage for the electoral charades of the following decades.[21]

Factors outside Nicaragua continued to have a determining impact upon the perception of and concern for democracy in Nicaragua by the U.S. government and upon its policy toward the regime in Managua. First, the establishment of pluralist democracy in Costa Rica after 1948 altered the calculation of priorities within U.S. policy to the detriment of Somoza; and, then, the radicalization of the Castro regime in Cuba after 1959 served to restore the delicate balance of the zero-sum game to forestall any moves in Washington to bring the Somoza dynasty to an end.

Somoza García had been close to the deposed Costa Rican president, Angel Calderón Guardía, and relied on him to provide a measure of international support for his regime. Costa Rica was one of the first to recognize Somoza's puppet president after the overthrow of Argüello in 1947. But as the democratic regime in San José was consolidated, it began to use the machinery of the Organization of American States (OAS) and the rhetoric of the cold war to ostracize Somoza and to try to push him from power. José Figueres made his attacks on Somoza part of a crusade for democracy and freedom. He joined together with other democratic colleagues in the region to form the Caribbean Legion with the avowed purpose of ousting all of the dictators in the Caribbean Basin. The OAS provided the military hardware necessary to defeat the Costa Rican rebels armed by Somoza and coming from Nicaragua.

The U.S. government was happy to have the OAS intervene and apply pressure on Somoza to cease trying to overthrow the Figueres government. It was embarrassed by the conflict and uncomfortable under the pressure from the democratic forces in the area, coming as it did so soon after the military intervention in Guatemala to overthrow a democratic regime whose reformist policies were seen by the U.S. government as discriminating against U.S. capital, dangerously destabilizing, and subject to subversion from outside the hemisphere. The issue was raised whether supporting the Somoza dynasty was more destabilizing than attempting to remove it. It was a delicate balance in which the more conservative posture in Washington was to do nothing unless concerted Latin American pressure made intervention a popular and necessary alternative. As ever, the global concerns of U.S. policy would determine the relative weight accorded to democracy and stability as policy goals in any given episode.

Aside from the conflict with Costa Rica, Somoza earned high marks in Washington during the first Eisenhower administration. He protested his anti-Communism loudly and often. And, thanks in large measure to the strong prices for the country's principal export crops, cotton and coffee, the economy enjoyed a prolonged period of expansion so that Somoza never asked for U.S. aid, only trade and private investment—the perfect model for a conservative business-oriented administration that told Latin American leaders that the best way to end their region's backwardness and poverty was to open their economies to the magic of private entrepreneurship and foreign private investment.[22]

The conflict with Costa Rica came to a halt temporarily with the assassination of Anastasio Somoza in September 1956. Somoza García was running for reelection when he was shot. There is no doubt that he would have won the 1957 elections given the control his government exercised over the electoral machinery. Thus, when Luis Somoza, the elder son of Somoza García, was chosen by the Nicaraguan congress to fill out the term of his father, and when he ran unopposed as the presidential candidate in the 1957 elections, the U.S. government had nothing to offer but congratulations to the new head of state.

The timing of the transition in Nicaragua shows a bit of Somoza luck. By the end of the Eisenhower administration, democracy regained some of its value as a tool of U.S. policy. For the first time since the administration of Woodrow Wilson, the absence of democracy was considered a destabilizing factor that could lead to subversion and outside influence in the area. It is instructive to compare the very different response of the U.S. government to the ouster of Batista in 1959 or the assassination of Trujillo in 1961.[23]

When Kennedy was elected in 1960, a true Wilsonian disposition to export democracy and the conviction that democratic government was infinitely exportable and adaptable returned to U.S. policy. Now, however, it was explicitly tempered by a fear of the Communist menace and manipulated to undercut pressure in Latin America for radical change. As it had been for Wilson, democracy was a reasonable political system that would end the appeal of more radical solutions to the region's problems.[24] Both the Eisenhower and Kennedy administrations tried to get the nations of Latin America involved in a struggle against Cuba in which the presence or absence of democracy would be a critical feature. In the case of Nicaragua, Kennedy was prepared to sacrifice Somoza, if necessary, but he would not act alone. He was surprised and disappointed when there was so little positive response from Latin American leaders.

Luis Somoza realized that his government's good standing in Washington required a boost. The coffee and cotton boom of the 1950s intensified the growth of the export sectors and widened the gap between the rich and the poor. More serious to liberal critics in the United States, the Somozas had used the growth of the Nicaraguan economy to turn Nicaragua into a family fiefdom. Of greatest concern in Washington was the founding of the Frente Sandinista de Liberación Nacional (FSLN) in Havana in 1961. The FSLN made it clear that it would employ armed struggle to rid Nicaragua of the Somozas and that it perceived the United States as the principal cause for Nicaragua's underdevelopment. Castro was attempting to export Marxist revolution the way the United States exported capitalist democracy. To observers in Havana and Washington, the most corrupt dictators were the most vulnerable, and the U.S. government's support for those dictators was a potential cause of embarrassment.

This combination of internal and external events and circumstances prompted Luis Somoza to push for reforms along a number of lines. The regime decided to reform the constitution in order to allow for third-party representation in the legislature, while guaranteeing the opposition at least one-third of the seats in the congress regardless of the electoral outcome. Control of the electoral machinery would remain in the hands of the government party so that there was no real danger of an upset. The regime also decided that it was convenient to place a non-Somoza in the presidency. The person chosen was René Schick, a long-time associate of the Somozas who had occupied a variety of posts in government since the 1930s and who would be completely tractable.25 After Schick's election in 1963, Luis Somoza stepped down to head the Liberal party and participate in legislative affairs.

The government proceeded to enact the first land reform law in Central America since Arbenz's ill-fated attempt of the early 1950s in Guatemala. Extremely mild and cautious, the law did speak about "elevating the standard of living of the peasant masses" and of redistributing land, but stopped short of expropriating private property unless it was totally unused and restricted the land reform program to national lands or those purchased by the land reform institute. To no one's surprise, the results of land reform were quite limited. Agrarian policies tended to favor private export producers, especially those engaged in meat and cotton production.26

These political and socioeconomic measures, together with others that sought to modernize the state's role in national development, were more than sufficient to allow the United States to channel large amounts of Alliance for Progress funds to Nicaragua. Within the alliance vision of a democratized and modernized Latin America, Nicaragua appeared to be doing the right things. Of course, Nicaragua was involved in equally important activities for the United States, such as providing unrestricted use of its territory for anti-Castro activities (including training the troops for the Bay of Pigs invasion) and keeping a very close leash on leftist activities within Nicaragua.

Thus, U.S. interest in democracy in Nicaragua during the 1960s was tempered and limited by security concerns that became paramount after the triumph of the Cuban Revolution and the increasing Soviet presence in the Caribbean. The Guardia Nacional, long the heart of the Somocista regime within Nicaragua, became the most coddled ally of the United States within the Central American region. The creation of the Central American Defense Council (CONDECA) in 1963 gave the commander of the Guardia Nacional of Nicaragua an unrivaled position of influence in the entire region, as well as within Nicaragua. The commander of the Guardia after 1956 was Anastasio Somoza Debayle, Somoza García's younger son. "Tachito" lacked his father's sense of balance and his brother's political skills. These deficiencies together with boundless greed would be his undoing. When Luis Somoza died in 1967, Tachito ran for president in elections held that same year. He won easily despite public expressions of protest, which the Guardia repressed violently, leaving hundreds dead in the streets of Managua in January 1967.

The Johnson administration decided not to protest these activities. It had become so concerned with Vietnam that it did not have the collective energy to engage in a protracted effort to force Somoza to clean up his act. Latin American policy had come under the control of Assistant Secretary of State Thomas Mann, a career official whose decidedly conservative approach led to the rejection of the active thrust of the Alliance for Progress. Members of the Johnson team felt they had been forced to intervene in the Dominican Republic in 1965 to prevent a chaotic situation out of which groups sympathetic to Castro might emerge. In this context, it did not seem to make any sense to Mann and others to destabilize the guardia in Nicaragua.

In the course of the Nixon administration, as the war in Vietnam was brought to an end, opposition in the Congress and in the public to U.S. support for unpopular and corrupt dictators grew in size and vehemence. Nixon and his chief foreign policy advisor, Henry Kissinger, had little interest in Latin America and began to distance themselves from the more reprehensible of the region's rulers. According to Nixon's formula, the dictators would get only a handshake. A warm embrace would be reserved for the region's democrats, the true friends of the United States.

Under increasing internal and external pressure, Somoza decided to repeat a move used successfully by his father in the 1940s. He called on the Conservatives to join his Liberal party in revamping the political system. The Conservatives, under Fernando Aguero, behaved just like they had under Chamorro in 1947 and 1950: they jumped at the opportunity and signed a pact with Somoza's Liberal party in March 1971 that guaranteed them a share of the seats in the legislature, judgeships, and positions on the municipal councils.[27] The deal became known as "Kupia Kumi," the Misquito words for "one single heart" with which Pedro Joaquín Chamorro, the young editor of *La Prensa* and son of the earlier Conservative leader, baptized and ridiculed the agreement. Kupia Kumi was followed by a legislative decision to hold elections in February 1972 for a constitutional convention that would, in turn, choose the three-man junta that would run the country until a new president, elected under the new constitution, took office in January 1974. Somoza resigned from the presidency and turned power over to the junta on which Aguero sat.

In December 1972, an earthquake devastated Managua. Anastasio Somoza Debayle, as commander of the Guardia Nacional, declared himself head of the National Emergency Committee (Coordinador de la Junta de Reconstrucción) to handle relief and reconstruction in the Managua area.

He brought in the entire cabinet to assist him, thus creating a parallel government structure that had no immediate responsibility to the governing junta.[28] Aguero, the Conservative member of the junta, resigned in protest, but a more pliant Conservative was named to replace him. U.S. ambassador Turner Shelton, one of Somoza's most fervent defenders, strongly supported requests by the Nicaraguan government for emergency aid. Within eight months of the earthquake, the Nicaraguan government had negotiated loans with foreign credit institutions worth approximately $100 million to finance the cleaning up operations, reconstruct the infrastructure, and reactivate the economy. Other funds were allocated in the national budget itself. And with Somoza back in the presidential office after an unopposed campaign in 1974, the way was prepared for a veritable orgy of corruption and open, cynical manipulation of the system for the enrichment of Somoza Debayle and his cronies beyond anything perpetrated by any previous Nicaraguan ruler. It was as if Somoza had thrown all caution to the wind, defying the domestic opposition, the United States, and the rest of the world to stop him if they dared.

The legitimacy of the Somoza dynasty, built up with great care by Somoza García and Luis Somoza, careful to accommodate the sensibilities of the U.S. government and operate within the rules of formal democracy and electoral politics, eroded rapidly in the face of Somoza Debayle's civic depravity. The FSLN's campaign picked up steam after some successful operations in Managua and the interior in 1974 and 1975, while the business community, long the dynasty's major civil bulwark, looked with fear and anger at the rapidly growing empire of the Somozas that became engorged on the reconstruction of Managua. In the United States, concern with human rights violations in all of Latin America emerged as one of the most passionately espoused issues in the Congress. Nicaragua began to get its share of accusations as the Somoza regime responded to increasing dissidence with brutal tortures and political persecution. The election of Jimmy Carter in 1976 signaled that U.S. concern for human rights had an advocate in the White House itself.

By the end of 1978, the administration in Washington knew that Somoza's days were numbered unless the U.S. tried to do what it did in 1912 and 1927. But this was out of the question. The struggle against Somoza involved, on the one hand, an enraged populace that had suffered enough corruption, brutality, and injustice, a population that had witnessed enough hypocrisy from its rulers and more than enough repression of its advocates. On the other hand, it involved a set of countries, in Latin America and Europe, now willing to assist in the overthrow of the regime once and for all. If the United States had decided to act on behalf of Somoza, it would have done so completely alone and in defense of a regime that had very little internal support and no international support outside, perhaps, of Paraguay. Not even the military dictatorships in Guatemala and El Salvador were willing to stretch a helping hand to Somoza; they had sufficient problems of their own holding on to power.

The policy debate in the Carter administration over how to handle the collapse of the Somoza regime reflected virtually the same set of priorities and calculations that had infused the policy formulation process since the first intervention in Nicaraguan affairs in 1909: the global perspective of U.S. interests, the presumed responsibilities of the United States in the region, and the likely implications of any decision for the broader foreign policies of the government. Two conjunctural considerations framed the debate: the efficacy of the human rights policy in relations with the Soviet Union, and a determination not to repeat the supposed mistakes made by the Eisenhower administration in negotiating the end of the Batista regime in Cuba twenty years earlier. These two considerations—together with the fact that the nations of Latin America were more united in their determination to push Somoza from power as soon as possible than they had been on any issue in inter-American politics since the Caribbean Legion had urged the United States to take the lead in supporting democratic regimes in the region at the end of the 1950s and the beginning of the 1960s—pushed the Carter administration to assume an active role in getting Somoza to leave Nicaragua. The only countervailing force was the insistent warning on the right that failure to support Somoza, a loyal friend in the struggle against Communism, would play into the hands of hostile forces. None of these considerations took Nicaragua into account or attempted to weigh policy options in the light of the legacy of U.S. relations with Nicaragua in the twentieth century. The result was a clear policy put into effect in a hesitant manner with little public notice: the United States would not save Somoza nor could it get credit for forcing him from power.[29]

Revolution and Democracy after 1979

The overthrow of the Somocista regime in 1979 did not end the debate about democracy in Nicaragua by any means. To the extent that the Sandinista Front for National Liberation took effective control of the new revolutionary state, other groups within the Nicaraguan polity felt left out and began to engage in active opposition to the revolutionary government and its policies. The United States, on the other hand, could not remain indifferent to the course of events in Nicaragua. Under President Carter, the U.S. government agreed to provide economic assistance (to the private sector primarily) and attempted to engage in a correct dialogue with the new revolutionary government. But events in neighboring El Salvador, where the strength of the insurgent Farabundo Marti National Liberation Front (FMLN) threatened to create another revolutionary regime in Central America, put the U.S. administration on guard. Nicaragua again became a country within a region where U.S. security concerns overwhelmed any policy considerations about development, reform, or democracy.

The U.S. election campaign of 1980 dragged Nicaragua back into its traditional role of a geostrategic issue for U.S. policy makers and politicians. As during the early part of the twentieth century, Nicaragua again was reduced to a place on the map that could not be allowed to "fall" into the hands of an extracontinental, hostile power and whose "falling" had nothing or very little to do with internal factors or indigenous causes. Under such a scheme, the "loss" of Nicaragua could be prevented by external forces alone. The elimination of both the shah in Iran and Somoza in Nicaragua became an important topic of Ronald Reagan's campaign for the presidency. President Carter stood accused of "losing" those two countries by not doing enough to help their erstwhile leaders and by insisting on a respect for human rights that undermined the old regimes' strength. While Iran probably could not be returned to the fold by the forceful reinstallation of a pro–United States regime, Nicaragua, much closer and much more vulnerable to U.S. pressure, seemed an ideal place for Washington to work its will.

As explained in the Sante Fe Memorandum that summarized the Republicans' campaign interest in the hemisphere, Central America was a region under attack.[30] The Soviet Union and its allies had taken advantage of U.S. weakness to penetrate into our very backyard. It was time to strengthen the nation's will. To show the Soviets and the rest of the world that the United States was prepared to reassert its dominance and stop and even reverse the falling dominoes, Central America, because of its proximity, would be the ideal place to begin with a quick victory.

The Reagan administration lost little time in putting together a policy toward Central America that sought the military defeat of the FMLN in El Salvador and the overthrow or replacement of the FSLN government in Nicaragua. The second objective was never spelled out publicly in such terms. After all, Washington maintained diplomatic relations with Managua during all the Reagan years and insisted that it only wanted the development of a full-fledged democracy of a Western type in Nicaragua. Still, the extraordinary efforts made by the Reagan administration before Congress to secure funding for the counterrevolutionary forces operating out of Honduras make it clear that the real objective was to achieve some sort of military victory. On the other side, the Sandinista government perceived U.S. objectives in similar terms and proceeded to gear up its forces for a protracted and costly war.

Within this confrontational environment, the space for political expression and competition within Nicaragua became more restricted. The government of Nicaragua had to face both the military attacks of the contras and the severe consequences of the cutoff of U.S. and multilateral aid. The establishment of the military draft proved particularly unpopular, whereas the economic decline that set in after 1983 made it increasingly difficult to maintain the social services and economic subsidies that constituted the basis of the revolution's redistributive and development policies. Politically, the triumphant revolutionary coalition had begun to break apart by 1982 and those who were never much convinced about the Sandinistas' intentions now saw a chance to make common cause with the United States.

The Sandinistas tried to defuse the growing crisis by seeking a political arrangement with the United States through talks with Washington officials held in Manzanillo, Mexico, during 1984. But these conversations led to nothing; on the contrary, the assistant secretary of state for Latin American affairs, Thomas Enders, who thought that a negotiated settlement was possible, was sacked and replaced by Elliott Abrams, a hard-liner who identified totally with President Reagan's beliefs about the inherent evilness of Sandinismo. Within Nicaragua, the Sandinistas attempted a rapprochement with the internal opposition by renewing their promise to hold elections by 1985. Such a promise had been made in 1981 and formed part of the Sandinista pledge to take Nicaragua down the road to pluralist democracy, a mixed economy, and international nonalignment.

Ever since 1981, the Sandinista party had held conversations with the other political parties of Nicaragua in order to reach agreements on the organization of the electoral process. As a result of these contacts, legislation was passed by the Nicaraguan legislature in 1983 and 1984 that set the basis for the holding of elections for president and a constituent assembly in November 1984. The supervision of the electoral process would be in the hands of a five-person Supreme Electoral Council with opposition party representation, remarkably similar to arrangements made between the Liberals and the Conservatives during the Somoza years. The participating political parties were defined as contenders for power and would be alloted material resources by the state in order to carry out their campaigns.[31]

The response to the electoral initiative was mixed. Within Nicaragua, a number of parties decided not to participate, even though they conducted extensive negotiations with the Sandinista Front until only a few weeks before the election itself. One group of opposition parties and business associations, the Coordinadora Democrática, put forth the candidacy of Arturo Cruz, but he dropped out of the race when conversations in Rio de Janeiro with Sandinista representatives broke down. The presidential candidate of the Independent Liberal Party, Virgilio Godoy, also withdrew although many of his party's candidates continued to campaign.

In the cases of both Arturo Cruz and Virgilio Godoy, the United States exercised strong pressure to achieve their withdrawal. By doing so, Washington sought to undermine the legitimacy of the electoral process and of the entire political system. However, seven parties remained in the running, three of them to the right of the Sandinista Front and three to its left. The results gave the Sandinista Front the presidency of the Republic and three-quarters of the seats in the National Assembly in elections that were remarkable for their calm and high voter turnout. Still, the U.S. government refused to acknowledge that elections in Nicaragua had produced a legitimate government. The elections themselves were dismissed as "farcical" by Washington. After 1984, the United States increased the pressure on Nicaragua by openly seeking assistance in the Congress for the contra forces, which by now had been identified as "freedom fighters" and likened to the Founding Fathers of the United States. It was clear that Washington's concern for democracy in Nicaragua was a function of its desire to rid itself of the Sandinistas.

The role of democracy in Reagan's Central American policy grew over time. At the outset, it seemed an afterthought or a cynical use of rhetoric to appease domestic liberal critics. By the end of the decade, it was the driving force behind the administration's policy in the hemisphere.[32] The shift must be attributed to a series of miscalculations by the administration of U.S. public opinion, of the expression of that opinion through the Congress, and of the consistent and stubborn pressure of our European allies. The decline of the Soviet Union, the accommodation of the Sandinistas to their geopolitical reality, and the growing determination of the nations in the region to end the bloodshed also gave democracy greater weight in the policy calculations of the U.S. government.

The Reagan administration thought it could apply force as it chose in El Salvador in its quest for a quick, uplifting victory. As soon as armed Green Berets were shown on the evening news, the public indicated its bipartisan opposition to any adventure that threatened to escalate out of control—what came to be called the Vietnam syndrome. The congressional counterpart of this phenomenon was the reduction in the executive's leverage over the policy process in the aftermath of the war in Vietnam and Watergate, which strengthened the disposition and the capacity of fairly small groups of legislators to question the legitimacy of the executive's policy and its interpretation of events in the region.[33]

The varying interpretations hinged on the relative importance attributed to internal or external factors as causes of the unrest in the region. Reagan and his senior advisers were convinced the problems had external causes and would be solved once those causes were removed. Liberal opposition could be ignored.[34] What could not be ignored was the fact that most of our allies disagreed with the U.S. government's official explanation of what was happening in Central America, rejected its Manichaean association of the struggle in El Salvador and Nicaragua with their security, and insisted with growing conviction that a negotiated settlement was preferable.[35] In each of these factors, the concept of democracy as a goal, as an objective of policy, was crucial. In El Salvador, it became important because it was notoriously absent from the concerns of the government we supported there. In Nicaragua, it was important because our support of the contras, with remnants of Somoza's Guardia Nacional prominent in its leadership, seemed inconsistent with the achievement of that goal. In addition, from the very beginning, the Sandinistas appeared sensitive to the power of democracy as a bargaining chip in its dealings with the United States, with the NATO nations, with its own opposition, and with the nations of Latin America. All of these factors kept democracy on the table for discussion as a policy goal and kept increasing as a priority in the policy process.

The increase in the levels of military confrontation in Nicaragua (and El Salvador) also engaged the attention of a number of Latin American countries, four of which came together to form the Contadora Group. The Contadora peace initiative finally put together a draft treaty by the middle of 1986 but the Central American countries, which had participated in the discussions over the draft, never got around to signing. The United States government, which gave formal support to the Contadora initiative, did not like the form that the final draft took, especially because it recognized the existing governments; set limits on foreign troops, arms shipments, and military maneuvers and bases in the region; and demanded an end to economic sanctions (which the United States had imposed on Nicaragua).[36]

Although Contadora was stillborn, it laid the basis for another regional peace initiative introduced by President Oscar Arias of Costa Rica in early 1987. The Arias Plan succeeded to some extent precisely because it was not as ambitious as the Contadora Plan; it centered on the political aspects of the problem (dialogue, amnesties, elections) and left out the military components, which would have affected the United States most directly. Even though Washington described the Arias Plan as "flawed," it was embraced by the other Central American presidents when they met in Guatemala in mid-1987 and took shape in succeeding meetings.

The Arias Plan bore its most immediate and important fruits in the case of Nicaragua. The agreement signed by the government of Nicaragua and the contras (by then formally known in the United States as the Nicaraguan Resistance) at Sapoa in March 1988 committed both sides to initiate negotiations for a long-lasting solution that included the freeing of political prisoners in Nicaragua, the disarmament of the contra fighters, and a general amnesty for everyone who had left the country for political reasons. At the same time, support in the U.S. Congress for assistance to the contras waned in the aftermath of the Iran-Contra scandal and President Reagan cut a deal with the Speaker of the House, Jim Wright, that included tacit support for a negotiated settlement to the Nicaraguan war. From that moment on, the prospects for the success of the Arias peace initiative in the case of Nicaragua looked especially good.

The government of Nicaragua also was desperate for an end to the war and the economic sanctions that had destroyed the promises of the revolution in the fields of education, health, and employment. For its part, the

Soviet Union made it clear to Nicaragua in October 1988 that further assistance for Nicaragua's development was predicated on a resolution of its differences with the United States. Thus, when the five Central American presidents met in El Salvador in February 1989, President Daniel Ortega of Nicaragua made specific commitments to assure the complete respect for democratic principles and procedures in his country as part of an overall political settlement. He offered to advance the date of presidential and legislative elections from November to February 1990, he promised to reform electoral legislation to satisfy all the political parties, and he announced that international observers from the United Nations and the OAS would be invited to observe the electoral process from beginning to end. In exchange for these commitments, the Central American presidents promised to put together within ninety days a plan to demobilize the contra forces.

At this time, the U.S. policy toward Nicaragua shifted noticeably. Congress allowed further nonmilitary assistance for the contras on condition the administration pressure contra leaders to return to Nicaragua and participate in the electoral process. Bush argued that the efforts to democratize the Sandinistas required the armed threat of the contras. But, the events in Eastern Europe made the Soviet menace pale as an argument in congress and the spreading crisis in the savings and loan industry made spending money on the contras seem frivolous. To assure "a level playing field," the U.S. government assigned funds for the opposition parties and groups through the National Endowment for Democracy and encouraged private citizens to help out in this new crusade against the Sandinistas. Once a viable opponent to the FSLN was organized in the form of the Unión Nacional Opositora (UNO), Washington did little to hide its electoral preference. The fourteen parties that made up a fractious UNO stretched from the Communists on the left to a faction of the Conservatives on the right but Violeta Chamorro, the presidential nominee of UNO, was deemed a strong candidate to face incumbent President Ortega. Mrs. Chamorro was received by President Bush at the White House and she toured a number of U.S. cities with large Nicaraguan émigré populations.

Once the campaign got underway, it became clear that the underlying issue was the United States. The Sandinistas identified Mrs. Chamorro as the candidate of the Bush administration and criticized her willingness to work with contra leaders who had returned to the country. Her promise to end the military draft and dismantle the economic policies of the Sandinista government left her open to the accusation of being a contra herself. Mrs. Chamorro, in turn, accused the Sandinistas of provoking the United States and turning their backs on the Western democracies that had helped them in their struggle against the Somoza dictatorship.

Once committed to the electoral option, it became clear that the Sandinistas would seek a working relationship with the United States to wind down the war and gain access to the credit of the multilateral lending agencies. The same events in Eastern Europe that made them appear less threatening to the United States implied a decreasing commitment of the Soviet bloc countries in Nicaragua's development projects and its military defense, making them more vulnerable to external pressure. In the case of UNO, its strong ties with the principal business groups of Nicaragua effectively mandated a normalization of relations with the United States in order to gain access to U.S. markets for sugar, beef, and coffee. Business groups also pressured for normalization of relations with Nicaragua's Central American neighbors.

On February 25, 1990, Nicaraguans went to the polls to elect a government that would chart a new course for their country. They had heard campaign speeches, watched television debates, participated in numerous rallies and street demonstrations, and discussed among themselves what the best choices might be. During the entire campaign, the country was invaded by hundreds of observers from the United Nations and the OAS, as well as numerous private groups and organizations from the United States, Latin America, and Western Europe. Although some argued that Nicaragua's sovereignty was compromised by the very visible role of foreign political actors in the electoral process, such a presence also helped to assure a high level of participation and to legitimize the results both within and outside Nicaragua.

The election of February 25, 1990, proved a turning point in Nicaraguan political development. After ten years of confrontation with the United States, the people of Nicaragua were tired and poverty-stricken. They knew that to end the war and initiate some sort of economic recovery, they had to come to terms with the United States. The Sandinistas had recognized this for some time. The election results left no doubt that Mrs. Chamorro was seen as the political leader with the best credentials to begin a new relationship with Washington. The Nicaraguan people did not turn their backs on the Sandinistas strictly out of ideological convictions. Mrs. Chamorro got over 54 percent of the vote to Daniel Ortega's 41 percent. In the legislative branch of government, the UNO coalition ended up with fifty-one seats to thirty-nine for the FSLN.[37]

The results surprised most observers. President Ortega commented after the vote that the Nicaraguans had gone to the polls "with a gun to their heads." It was not the first time they had done so. The transition to democracy will not be easy. The Sandinista Front remains the strongest single political organization within the country, with a solid voting bloc in the assembly and considerable support among peasants and workers. UNO, on the other hand, was created with a purely electoral objective. Now that it is in government there is no assurance that it will remain united, even after changing its name from Unión Nacional Opositora to Unión Nacional Organizada. For example, Mrs. Chamorro has no party affiliation of her own nor does she exercise any special authority over the remaining contra forces. Ironically, her government will need the support of the Sandinistas more than from her own political following during the difficult transition from war to peace as the contra forces are demobilized. She will also need the strong economic and financial support of the United States to insure that her promises of a better future for all Nicaraguans do not remain a purely electoral ploy. The decision in May 1990 by the U.S. Congress to reject President Bush's proposal for emergency aid to Nicaragua was not encouraging.

What is really at stake is a new political system for Nicaragua. For the first time in the twentieth century, all political forces in Nicaragua, large and small, made their case before the Nicaraguan people and sought their votes. For the first time, a democratically elected head of state turned over the office to a democratically elected candidate from the opposition. For the first time, no one (except the more recalcitrant contra forces) has denied the legitimacy of the new government. The 1990 election in Nicaragua is the closest that country has ever come to practicing the basic principles of pluralist democracy, albeit within the worst possible social and economic conditions and under severe external pressure. If the U.S. government wants to claim credit for promoting democracy in Nicaragua, it should do so with extreme caution.

The United States intervened in Nicaragua politically and militarily at least once in each of the first four decades of this century to set up a democracy, but the end result was nearly half a century of Somocista dictatorship. In the 1980s the United States intervened again in defense of democracy, but the result is a country with a devastated economy and deep social and political divisions. It is tempting to suggest that if democracy does flourish in Nicaragua during the succeeding decades, it will come to pass not because of the United States but more likely in spite of it. The United States has been remarkably unsuccessful in its efforts to implant its special version of pluralist democracy in Nicaragua. So startling is the historical record that it is tempting to suggest, further, that democracy in Nicaragua will have a better chance if the United States lets it develop on Nicaragua's terms rather than trying to dictate and impose its own version "for export only." But the same historical record suggests that the United States has been a critical actor in Nicaraguan politics for eighty years. There is no reason to believe that it will end that role in the near future. The question that the United States and Nicaragua must face together is how the role of the United States can be made constructive and positive in the effort to create a democratic and just society in Nicaragua. It is a question that will not be easy to answer.

Notes

1. David McCullough, *The Path between the Seas: The Creation of the Panama Canal, 1870–1914* (New York: Simon & Schuster, 1977); Walter LaFeber, *The Panama Canal: The Crisis in Historical Perspective* (New York: Oxford University Press, 1978); and Walter LaFeber, *Inevitable Revolutions: The United States in Central America* (New York: Norton, 1983).

2. Elting E. Morison, ed., *The Letters of Theodore Roosevelt* (Cambridge: Harvard University Press, 1951), 3: 235.

3. Ibid., p. 463.

4. See E. R. May, *American Imperialism: An Interpretative Essay* (New York: Atheneum, 1973), for a synthesis of the contemporary debate over the nature of U.S. imperialism.

5. For a general discussion of the nineteenth century in Central America, see R. L. Woodward, Jr., *Central America: A Nation Divided* (New York: Oxford University Press, 1976). For a discussion of caudillismo in the nineteenth century, see John C. Chasteen, "Twilight of the Lances: The Saravia Brothers and Their World" (Ph.D. dissertation, University of North Carolina, 1988); and Mark Szuchman, ed., *The Middle Period in Latin America* (Boulder, Colo.: Lynne Rienner, 1989).

6. Quoted in LaFeber, *Inevitable Revolutions,* p. 23. For a detailed account of these events, and a very different interpretation from the one offered by LaFeber, see Dana G. Munro, *Intervention and Dollar Diplomacy in the Caribbean, 1900–1921* (Princeton: Princeton University Press, 1964).

7. Arthur Link, *Wilson the Diplomatist* (Baltimore: Johns Hopkins University Press, 1957); and LaFeber, *Inevitable Revolutions.*

8. Only in the case of Mexico would Wilson admit publicly that local players might have to adapt democracy to their own milieu. See Mark Guilderhuis, *Wilson and Mexico* (Albuquerque: University of New Mexico Press, 1985). Link's defense of Wilson is in his biography, *Woodrow Wilson* (Princeton: Princeton University Press, 1960–64), vols. 3 and 4.

9. See Joseph S. Tulchin, *Aftermath of War* (New York: New York University Press, 1971), chaps. 1 and 2.

10. Ibid., chaps. 3 and 7.

11. See the chapter by Paul Drake in this volume.

12. The text of the law is in *La Gaceta/Diario Oficial,* vol. 27, nos. 71–74 (March 3–6, 1923).

13. Richard Salisbury, *Conflict in Central America* (Wilmington, Del.: Scholarly Resources, 1989).

14. It is worth noting that the leader of the Marine force in Nicaragua, Smedley Butler, was convinced that he was fighting to bring democracy to the country and that Sandino was an obstacle to the achievement of that goal. Correspondence cited in James B. McKenna, "Smedley Butler in Nicaragua," unpublished manuscript in the possession of the authors. See also Neill Macaulay, *The Sandino Affair* (Chicago: Quadrangle Press, 1967).

15. This period is described in detail in Bryce Wood, *The Making of the Good Neighbor Policy* (New York: Columbia University Press, 1961).

16. For a detailed account of Somoza's rise to power, see Richard Millett, *Guardians of the Dynasty* (Maryknoll, N.Y.: Orbis Books, 1977).

17. The U.S. reaction to Somoza's continuismo can be found in *Foreign Relations of the United States, 1945,* vol. 9 (Washington, D.C.: U.S. Government Printing Office, 1969), pp. 1215–30. For a discussion of elections in Nicaragua under U.S. influence, see Alvaro Argüello, "Tres modelos de elecciones en Nicaragua," *Envío* 32 (1984).

18. For a comprehensive discussion of this policy, see Wood.

19. For a detailed history of the Argentine episode and the debate within the U.S. government over democracy as a policy priority and the willingness to intervene in the affairs of Latin American states in order to impose democracy there, see Joseph S. Tulchin,

Argentina and the United States: A Conflicted Relationship (Boston: Twayne Publishers, 1990).

20. This period is covered in Knut Walter, *The Regime of Anastasio Somoza García and State Formation in Nicaragua* (Chapel Hill: University of North Carolina Press, forthcoming).

21. The agreement was ratified formally by the Nicaraguan congress as "Decreto convocando a elecciones para Asemblea Constituyente y Presidente de la República," *La Gaceta/ Diario Oficial 54*, no. 75 (April 15, 1950).

22. On the economic situation, see Walter; and V. Bulmer Thomas, *The Political Economy of Central America since 1920* (Cambridge: Cambridge University Press, 1987). On the business approach to development at this time, see R. Harrison Wagner, *United States Policy toward Latin America* (Stanford, Calif.: Stanford University Press, 1970); and Stephen Rabe, *Eisenhower and Latin America* (Chapel Hill: University of North Carolina Press, 1988).

23. The transition in policy during the second Eisenhower administration is chronicled in Rabe.

24. This period is discussed in Tulchin, "The United States and Latin America in the 1960s," *Journal of Inter-American Studies 30*, no. 1 (Spring 1988): 1–36.

25. "Reforma parcial de la Constitución Política," *La Gaceta/Diario Oficial 66*, no. 116 (May 26, 1962).

26. See Robert G. Williams, *Export Agriculture and the Crisis in Central America* (Chapel Hill: University of North Carolina Press, 1986). The land reform law is in *La Gaceta/Diario Oficial 67*, no. 85 (April 19, 1983).

27. The text of the legislation is in *La Gaceta/Diario Oficial 75*, no. 207 (September 11, 1971).

28. See "Decreto de creación del comite de Emergencia Nacional," *La Gaceta/Diario Oficial 77*, no. 30 (February 10, 1983).

29. For discussion of Carter's policy in Nicaragua, see Robert Pastor, *Condemned to Repetition* (Princeton: Princeton University Press, 1987); Anthony Lake, *Somoza Falling: The Nicaragua Dilemma: A Portrait of Washington at Work* (Boston: Houghton Mifflin, 1989); and, on the human rights issue, Lars Schoultz, *Human Rights and U.S. Policy toward Latin America* (Princeton: Princeton University Press, 1985).

30. Roger Fontaine, et al., "Las relaciones interamericanas," *Cuadernos Semestrales 9* (1981).

31. For a general analysis of the 1984 elections in Nicaragua, see the report published by the Latin American Studies Association entitled *The Electoral Process in Nicaragua: Domestic and International Influences* [November 19, 1984] (Pittsburgh: LASA, 1984).

32. See the chapter in this volume by Thomas Carothers and his excellent new book, *The United States and the Resurgence of Democracy in Latin America* (Berkeley: University of California Press, forthcoming).

33. The impact of these factors on U.S. policy has been discussed in Joseph S. Tulchin, "EE UU y la crisis en Centroamerica: una perspectiva histórica," in Juan Del Aguila, et al., *Realidades y Posibilidades de las Relaciones Entre España y America en los Ochenta* (Madrid: Instituto de Cooperación Iberoamericana, 1984).

34. The debate over U.S. policy has produced a flood of books and articles. For a sample that defines the terms of the debate, see Howard Wiarda, *In Search of Policy: The United States and Latin America* (Washington, D.C.: American Enterprise Institute, 1984); Richard Fagen, *Forging Peace: The Challenge of Central America* (New York: Basil Blackwell, 1987); Richard E. Feinberg, *Central America: International Dimensions of the Crisis* (New York: Holmes & Meier, 1982); and Robert Wesson, ed., *Communism in Central America and the Caribbean* (Stanford, Calif.: Hoover Institution Press, 1982).

35. On the European role, see Jordi Solé Tura, et al., *Las relaciones entre España y America Central (1976–1989)* (Barcelona: Asociación de Investigaciones y Especialización

sobre Temas Iberoamericanos and the Centre d' Informació i Documentació Internacionals a Barcelona, 1989); Eusebio Mujal-Leon, *Europe and Central America* (Washington, D.C.: Center for Strategic and International Studies, 1989); and Wolf Grabendorff and Riordan Roett, eds., *Latin America, Western Europe and the United States* (New York: Praeger, 1985).

36. On the Latin American perspective, see Cristina Eguizabal, ed., *America Latina y La Crisis Centroamericana: En Busca de una Solución Regional* (Buenos Aires: Grupo Editor Latinoamericano, 1988); and Luis Guillermo Solis and Francisco Rojas, *¿Súbditos o aliados? La política exterior de Estados Unidos y Centroamerica* (San José, Costa Rica: Editorial Porvenir, 1987).

37. For complete official results of the voting, see *Barricada Internacional* (March 10, 1990). A comprehensive evaluation of the elections has been put together by a commission of the Latin American Studies Association under the title *Electoral Democracy under International Pressure* [March 15, 1990] (Pittsburg: LASA, 1990). For a Nicaraguan appraisal of the parties and of the electoral process, see Elia María Kuant and Trish O'Kane, *Nicaragua: Political Parties and Elections 1990,* Working Paper (Managua: CRIES, 1990).

6 | U.S. Business: Self-interest and Neutrality

Elizabeth A. Cobbs

THE HISTORY of United States relations with Latin America shows a persistent failure on the part of the U.S. government to come to terms not only with what it actually wants from the relationship but also with its own national motives. Does the United States want the challenge of genuinely democratic neighbors or the acquiescence of political pawns, be they nominal democracies or outright dictatorships? Should the nation be guided by clear economic and political self-interest or, as the Puritans' "city on a hill," should the nation place its historic "responsibility" to furthering democracy first, above other motivations?

Going back to its founding during the Enlightenment, the United States has long been at conflict with itself over the competing pulls of its democratic "mission" and economic self-interest.[1] Readers may suggest that this is more of a conflict between Thomas Jefferson and Alexander Hamilton than an issue for modern, materialistic America, yet anyone who has studied the often sorry history of U.S. relations with Latin America might argue differently. At times U.S. policy toward that region seems positively adolescent: characterized by wild mood swings between a grossly calculated desire to use and control, and, as Paul Drake shows elsewhere in this volume, a quixotic, messianic wish to produce democracy on demand—whenever policy makers and the public suddenly feel it essential to find the familiar face of their own political system in the terrain of Latin America, whatever the cost to others in national sovereignty. From the viewpoint of critics, the mood swings sometimes seem to represent a self-perceived Dr. Jekyll and Mr. Hyde complex: when U.S. policy toward that region is guided mainly by economic self-interest, we are being "bad." On those much rarer occasions when the United States idealistically tries to promote democracy, we are being "good." According to both moderate and radical interpretations of U.S.–Latin American relations, business is widely presumed to be at the far end of the self-interested (and therefore "bad") part of the spectrum. And yet, as this chapter argues, in the post–World War II period business has frequently evidenced a stronger commitment to consistent, constructive relations with Latin America than has the U.S. government, and a good measure of self-interest may be precisely the reason why.

Academics have fought battles for years to determine exactly how self-interested or disinterested the Good Neighbor Policy and the Alliance for Progress were, an implicit presumption being that they ended or failed when, alas, self-interest finally won out.[2] The revisionist literature of the 1960s and 1970s gained much of its moral and argumentative force from the successful attempt to show that U.S. policy, while rhetorically idealistic, was in practice self-serving. But even if a disinterested policy were possible, is it best? As is evident from other chapters in this volume, the prodemocracy campaigns of the United States have usually been self-contradictory failures. They are also not as disinterested or idealistic as they may seem: promoting democracy is a policy that builds domestic consensus (it appeals to what North Americans *think* their country should be about), offering an important self-justification for any U.S. administration's other policy goals, however unrelated.[3] U.S. business behavior in Latin America, on the other hand, shows far more evidence of lessons learned over the years than do studies of the behavior of the U.S. government, which is distressingly cyclical in its mistakes and interventionism. Indeed, from the 1950s forward, U.S. business groups, when they have operated at their most organized and coherent, have frequently taken a more neutral stance toward local political decisions than the U.S. government. Although certain individual businesses have gone way beyond the pale in terms of intervention, they may (as I shall discuss later) be more the exception than the rule.

This is not to say that U.S. businesses, on the whole, care whether the countries in which they operate are democratic or dictatorial. Self-interest suggests only two real preconditions for investment: (1) a level of stability that guarantees that the rules of business are not being changed constantly and that possessions are not threatened with expropriation; (2) an orientation toward economic expansion and a market large enough to allow it on the part of the host nation—ruling out politically stable but small nations such as Paraguay, Albania, and Luxembourg. Democracies, right-wing dictatorships, and Communist gerontocracies all have the potential to deliver these conditions. What business does care about is *not* democracy per se, but favorable, untroubled international relations.

One reason for this commitment to consistent, untroubled relations may be that business has an economic stake in Latin America that is far more tangible, immediate, and fragile than the strategic stake of the government. U.S. diplomats from Sumner Welles to Nelson Rockefeller to Cyrus Vance have long fought a losing battle to convince the U.S. government and public that Latin America is important. Yet few political or economic crises south of the Rio Grande have managed to generate sustained attention by North Americans for more than a year or two, especially since 1945. England is important; Russia is important; China, Japan, and Germany are important. Latin America, well, yes, but . . .—*this* has been the persistent attitude of the government and public. They know they should care, but essentially they do not. Indeed, it is precisely this lack of sustained interest in Latin America, combined with the relative weakness of those nations vis-à-vis the United States, that allows each administration to reinvent Latin American policy anew, constrained little by history, by domestic constituencies, or by any threat of effective retaliation from abroad. As Joseph Tulchin once noted about the interwar period, "this insulation from outside forces gives the process of formulating policy [toward Latin America] an academic quality."[4] One might add that insulation tends to give policy a unilateral quality as well.

But for businessmen invested in Latin America the relationship is different in kind. Not only does the topic hold their interest, but the displeasure of foreign governments, local political upsets, debt crises, and hostility toward Americans can have an immediate, direct effect on their economic well-being. For this reason, business has not only a stake in Latin America, but a stake in well-functioning U.S.–Latin American relations. It is precisely this sustained self-interest that has made U.S. business diplomacy in Latin America more pragmatic, attentive, and reciprocal than that of the government.

This chapter considers the evolution of the U.S. business relationship to Latin America in the post–World War II period, with particular attention to its political dimensions. I will not argue that business sought to promote democracy: it did not. But I also do not find a preference for dictatorships. Instead, I find that over this period business has gradually evolved a style of operating that generally offers more concessions to local sovereignty than does the U.S. government. Although concessions to sovereignty, especially in the form of neutrality toward domestic political decisions, do not promote democracy per se, it may be argued that in the long run such a policy is more productive of local self-determination than a policy that oscillates between extravagant demands for democracy and an active support of dictatorships.

Early Twentieth-Century Background:
Interventionism and Omnipotence

It is ironic and revealing that, in the course of the twentieth century, the interest of U.S. business in Latin America has grown as that of the U.S. government has declined. Before 1940, what international power the United

States had was concentrated in one region alone: the Western Hemisphere. And for a time, as world tensions increased in the 1930s and Nazi Germany threatened to overtake and hold all of Europe, it seemed that the U.S. might be closed off permanently to greater influence worldwide. One consequence was a flurry of attention to "Fortress America" and a concerted effort to mend fences with Latin America through the Good Neighbor Policy. This changed with the fortunes of war. By 1944–45, the United States could look forward to an almost unchallenged global power—politically, economically, militarily. Influence in Latin America could henceforth be simply presumed as an adjunct to global preeminence, which in other areas of the world had to be cultivated, paid for, and assiduously maintained. But while regional considerations became less important to government relative to global issues, they became relatively more important to business.

Before World War II, American business was far more likely to stay at home than go abroad. World War I had brought the first opportunities for concerted expansion to the south, as the U.S. government took an active role in seeking to replace British capital and influence with North American. The wartime Wilson administration built merchant ships to take advantage of trade routes neglected by the British during the war and the liquidation of U.S. debts to Europe brought cash with which to make investments in ailing South American enterprises previously controlled by the British and Germans.[5] In the interwar period, the U.S. State Department continued to use its influence to gain for business a dominant position in the strategic areas of Latin American finance, communications, and petroleum.[6] But once this position was gained, State Department interest in coaxing expansion declined, and the core of North American businessmen was not sufficiently motivated toward foreign investment to undertake major new initiatives themselves. Postwar competition from Europe, and especially Germany after 1933, was still stiff, and American manufacturers largely preferred to invest in the domestic economy. U.S. economic activity in Latin America remained concentrated in raw materials, investments such as mining, and tropical agriculture.

Investments in raw materials were more likely to yield "natural monopolies" than investments in manufacturing.[7] Control of a nation's primary export, whether it be oil or bananas, often connected to control of a central transportation and communications network, gave corporations a kind of power and omnipotence not to be matched by investments in products that could be duplicated by other companies in the same country or abroad. As long as U.S. investments remained concentrated in this kind of economic activity, they were likely to yield North Americans an imperious sway over the fortunes of host countries; thus, for example, Commodore Vanderbilt, Minor Keith, and Sam "The Banana Man" Zemurray ran much of Central America for nearly a hundred years. It is notable that the worst examples of political interventionism on the part of U.S. companies in even the late twentieth century have all come from companies in extractive enterprises or other natural monopolies: the United Fruit Company (Guatemala), International Petroleum Corporation (Peru), and International Telephone and Telegraph (Chile).

But this scenario began to change just before and in the aftermath of World War II. Before the war, as part of the Good Neighbor Policy, the U.S. government developed a much more selective policy of intervention than it had previously had. In the late nineteenth and early twentieth centuries, the U.S. had been relatively willing to shell shores or threaten a landing of troops whenever companies or individuals suffered damage at the hands of local governments. This commitment to intervention on behalf of business had been weakening throughout the 1920s,[8] but with the nationalization of Mexican oil in 1938 the U.S. government put business decisively and publicly on notice that it would use force to defend corporate interests only when the executive branch saw fit for broader security reasons—for example, Guatemala in 1954. Since business confidence is predicated on the reliability and predictability of environmental factors over years if not decades, the on-again, off-again interventionism of the government gradually forced most U.S. companies to find their own accommodation with local regimes.

Also, after World War II, U.S. investors entered manufacturing in Latin America in significant numbers for the first time, especially in large-market countries like Brazil. This trend further increased business vulnerability in several ways: production for consumption (import substitution) instead of for export made local perceptions and sensibilities more relevant; investments in manufacturing did not have the advantages of natural monopolies; and the larger the country the less influence any one company was likely to have over policy and direction. In addition, anti-imperialism and increasing nationalism among Third World colonies and nations after the war further heightened the perils to U.S. investors, just as many of them were exploring foreign opportunities for the first time.

The 1950s: Government Inaction and an Emerging Business Code of Behavior

For U.S. corporations a central challenge of the postwar period thus became how to cope with rising nationalism in Latin America in the face of greater inherent vulnerability and a changed (or at least a less dependable) U.S. policy toward military intervention on behalf of business. The solution that some businessmen would begin to evolve was a code of conduct based on political neutrality and cooperation with local economic development goals. Eventually, autonomous business organizations and foreign relations lobbies such as the Council of the Americas would debate these questions, but in the 1950s most initial discussion of the problems of foreign investment went on in trade journals and ad hoc forums organized by government.

The Business Advisory Council's Committee on Latin America, organized by the U.S. Department of Commerce, was one of the most important conduits of business opinion to the Department of State during this decade. Top representatives of the biggest U.S. companies in Latin America participated actively in the committee: David Rockefeller of Chase National Bank; Leo Welch of Standard Oil of New Jersey; Sam Baggett of United Fruit Company; H. W. Balgooyen of the American and Foreign Power Company; and H. A. Davies of International Harvester, among others. In their individual responses to a memorandum on U.S. foreign policy toward Latin America written by Assistant Secretary of State Edward Miller in 1952, the committee members revealed a common anxiety about the future of the U.S. business relationship to Latin America. Thomas Taylor called the situation a "crossroads," noting that the transition from a policy of military interventionism to a policy of negotiated protection for American interests placed business "in the vulnerable position of being in mid-stream," ultimately necessitating "a great deal closer relationship and understanding with those countries."[9]

Most of the representatives on the Business Advisory Council seemed to accept the fact "that the use of physical force is out," while continuing to argue in favor of some sort of "prompt and positive support from the United States Government when its interests are prejudiced or discriminated against." The techniques most suggested for carrying out such a protective policy were a firm and consistent trade program supported by embassy staffs with more than a passing knowledge of business and economics, and the use of such bargaining "chips" as foreign aid, imports of "essential supplies" from the United States, and access to the U.S. market to induce Latin Americans to respect U.S. property abroad.

Only two members of the council advocated a more aggressive stance: Leo Welch of Standard Oil and Sam Baggett of United Fruit. Although he did not openly call for military intervention, Welch characterized U.S. policy as "supine" and "unduly subservient" toward Latin America, and said he could not share Assistant Secretary Miller's assumption that "the so-called 'toleration' of Mexico's expropriation of U.S. oil companies marked an advance in American relations with Latin America." Baggett said that American propaganda was "too defensive," and pressed detailed suggestions for an intense, daily campaign against Communism and the Soviet Union. But Baggett and Welch are notable partly for a vehemence and aggressiveness that are a counterpoint to the more moderate suggestions of the majority of council members.[10]

Committee members also discussed how business could protect itself through modifications of its own behavior, in response to a question by Miller as to whether it might be possible to arrive at a common standard of conduct for business abroad. Although some answered that it would be "hardly possible to have a common standard of conduct at the level of details," the respondents generally agreed (with the exception of Welch and Baggett, who did not even respond to this question) that U.S. businessmen should adhere to a general set of principles modeled on the practices of "responsible" business in the United States.[11] Not only should companies investing in Latin America "conduct their business on the same high standard of conduct and efficiency as they would at home," as the International Packers' representative phrased it, but they should also, as another executive wrote, "treat labor fairly, train and develop local people into positions of responsibility, [and] refrain strictly from meddling in the foreign country's politics."[12]

Other executives stressed that companies could insure good relations only by "recognizing and respecting legitimate local rights and aspirations and by scrupulously avoiding any political action," and that businessmen should "learn more about Latin America . . . study the languages, comprehend the national aspirations of the people and learn to see the parallel between the development of those countries in this century and our own in the 19th century."[13] In all, four out of the seven council members who submitted written responses specifically called for a "minimum standard of decent behavior" and two specifically pointed out that this should include neutrality in local politics.

It is clear that at least on a conceptual level some businessmen had begun to apply notions of "corporate responsibility," specifically political neutralism, to foreign investments by the early and mid-1950s. Importantly, this is not evidence of increased morality on the part of business, just of an increased awareness of the dangers and requirements of the postwar world— one in which foreign nationalism exposed direct investments to increased risks, and in which the political logic of the cold war could easily supersede the economic logic of specific business interests in terms of government priorities. That is, with its relatively new political and military commitments, the U.S. government no longer looked to economic ties as being the only binds to other nations. Indeed, one could argue that economics served politics in the postwar world, not the reverse, as in previous decades.

Various writers for the *Harvard Business Review* echoed the same conclusions in the early and mid-1950s. Jack Butler wrote in 1952 that "The age is dead when commercial enterprises could shatter opposition with a 'whiff of grapeshot.' . . . businessmen will have to calculate on their own the hazards involved in acquiring assets overseas . . . [and] work out some way of mitigating the possibility of failure." One way of avoiding these hazards, Butler counseled, was "to remain neutral, virtually aloof from the political tides that shift so often in most underdeveloped countries."[14]

But "political responsibility" was only one half of the story: international businessmen of the era also seemed increasingly concerned through the 1950s to demonstrate their "economic responsibility," and especially the role business could play in implementing the postwar U.S. goal of political stability and democratization through "modernizing" economic development. On the surface, this point of view fit perfectly with the policy of the Eisenhower administration. But the rather empty rhetoric about development spouted by Washington failed to meet the needs and expectations of Latin Americans (as Richard Nixon and the world discovered in 1958), and by extension the concerns of at least some businessmen who recognized that for its own protection business could not afford to ignore development questions to the extent that perhaps the U.S. government could.

Dwight D. Eisenhower assumed office in 1953 with a predisposition toward military alliances as the basis for relations with Latin America and a distaste toward aid as a tool of economic development. Secretary of the Treasury George Humphrey had one of the strongest voices in the cabinet, and his unequivocal opposition both to grants and soft loans for Latin America set the tone for the first years of the administration's policy. Humphrey made his stand on the premise that economic development was going to happen through business dealings or not at all, and that there was no way that government was going to subsidize the development of foreign industry that might eventually compete against American.[15] Although on the surface this perspective seemed to favor business generally, in fact it represented the views of nationalist businessmen, not internationalists. The business community had long been divided into those who, producing largely for the home market, favored protective trade and lending policies, and those businessmen who favored a "universalist" world order to facilitate world trade and investment.[16] In his opposition to the Export-Import Bank, Humphrey clearly showed himself to be of the nationalist, isolationist camp—a fact not appreciated by those who supported tax and credit incentives for foreign investment.

Secretary of State John Foster Dulles, with Eisenhower's support, ran a foreign economic policy based on free trade, development through private investment, and minimal government-to-government assistance. In the larger strategic scheme, both Dulles and Eisenhower lacked interest in Latin America and believed, as Eisenhower expressed it in a letter to his brother, that as a region not "directly open to assault" it did not merit grant aid for economic development.[17] Whatever external or internal threat Communism posed in Latin America could be best handled by a strengthening of Latin American police forces, thought Eisenhower, who initiated the first U.S.-sponsored program to do just that, using monies earmarked for economic development projects.[18] Since the economic status quo in Latin America presented no problem for the United States, and it seemed that whatever problems the status quo presented for the poor of Latin America could be handled by their police, relying on business to produce "trickle-down" development was perfectly consistent with the administration's political "realism."

But although the Eisenhower administration publicly pronounced its confidence in the ability of foreign investment to produce economic development, the government consistently ruled out proposals for tax concessions that would encourage such investment and made virtually no attempts to educate businessmen about their supposed responsibilities.[19] During the second half of Eisenhower's term (1955–60), foreign direct investment in Latin American grew less quickly than at any point in the thirty year period from 1940 to 1970. While American investments in Western Europe and Canada increased in the second half of the 1950s by 123 and 65 percent, respectively, investments in Latin America increased by only 24 percent.[20] Eisenhower and his advisors were slow to take Latin American development questions seriously. They focused on nonstatist solutions to development as much to avoid these questions as to affirm the role of the private sector. U.S. corporations, and their Latin American partners, were on their own.

American trade journals occasionally reflected an awareness of the role assigned to business by the administration, with relevant articles tending to fall into one of two categories: those that proclaimed *all* American ventures abroad to be a form of foreign "aid," regardless of how or for what purposes the particular businesses were organized, and those articles (consistent with the ethos of the Business Advisory Council during Edward Miller's tenure) that encouraged a harder look at how American business could fit itself within the postwar environment of developing countries.

One of the best examples of the first type, from *The Magazine of Wall Street* in 1958, called America's total overseas investment "a gigantic Point Four program . . . which eclipses in scope and magnitude the more publicized achievements of U.S. and U.N. projects." As evidence of the "silent revolution in living standards" brought about by these investments, the author noted that from billboards the world over "Colgate dentrifice smiles its bright assurance of sparkling teeth" and "Palmolive soap caresses with cosmopolitan impartiality the complexions of dusky Nubian maidens, porcelain Japanese Geishas and alabaster Swedish beauties."[21] Other articles on the automobile and food refining industries made similar claims to private "Point Four" programs based on little more than the sheer presence of American capital.[22] In spirit, these articles matched the vapid rhetoric of the Eisenhower government, which was equally vague in its assertions about what American investments would actually accomplish in the way of development.

In contrast, articles in the "corporate social responsibility" school of thought tended to raise substantive questions concerning the *ways* in which corporations conducted themselves abroad. Business analyst Clifton Wharton, Jr., argued that companies had to initiate specific programs to bring about development and cited examples of various companies that had started projects to "grapple with the basic problems of health, disease, and hunger." Without these programs, he admitted, foreign countries were frequently justified in charging that American business was irresponsible and opportunistic. Wharton quoted the president of Costa Rica as saying, "We resent the pretense of speculators who assert that their motive in investing money abroad is to foster the development of our countries. . . . The sole objective in most cases is to make money, and our economic development is only a doubtful consequence." Wharton concluded that it was "up to the executives of foreign subsidiaries to show . . . that privately financed aid and assistance are not a new form of colonialism and exploitation."[23]

Writers in the corporate responsibility mode also frequently noted in the 1950s that political development could, and even should, be a consequence of economic development. M. C. Conick, a *Harvard Business Review* contributor, pointed out that U.S. business could support the development of a free press in Latin America (and thereby political democracy) by bolstering advertising revenues. Jack Butler, also in *Harvard Business Review,* stated that it was not enough for U.S. companies to pay their taxes abroad when such taxes benefited only the ruling class and tended to "preserve the status quo beyond its natural life." While remaining politically aloof, companies had a responsibility to foster the conditions under which local rulers would be encouraged to direct national revenue into avenues that would "elevate the economic level of the people as a whole." According to Butler, grass-roots educational programs for women (who were often "denied a fruitful role in society"), enlightened labor policies, and a corporate attitude supportive of "the right of political self-determination" were all a part of fostering local goodwill toward foreign companies and of mitigating the dislocating effects of industrialization.[24]

Two practical pioneers in international "corporate social responsibility" who emerged in the 1950s were Nelson Rockefeller and Henry Kaiser.[25] Both Kaiser and Rockefeller were well known in the U.S. business community for innovative programs to share the profits from investments with foreign nationals. Kaiser's ventures in Argentina and Brazil, to establish domestic automobile industries based initially on the manufacture of jeeps, were a common topic in journals like *Business Week.*[26] Rockefeller's International Basic Economy Corporation, which started in agriculture in Brazil and Venezuela and eventually ran companies throughout Latin America, was frequently cited by writers on foreign investment as the foremost model of corporate social responsibility abroad.[27]

The distinguishing trait of the Rockefeller and Kaiser enterprises was their commitment to encouraging local ownership participation. In Brazil in the 1950s, where the Kaiser and Rockefeller activities overlapped, they implemented this commitment through measures that had the effect of promoting small-investor participation in the local stock market and thereby establishing one of the presumed "building blocks" of democracy, American-style: a burgeoning middle class. In the thinking of Kaiser and Rockefeller, public participation in the stock market had political as well as economic ramifications. A share in a company was a vote in the economy in the way that a vote in a democracy was a share in the political process.

By marketing their companies through public sales of stock (a highly unusual practice for either foreign or local companies in Latin America at the time), Rockefeller and Kaiser evidenced a common assumption about developing nations and their prospects for long-term political and economic stability. At a congressional hearing during World War II, a representative asked Nelson Rockefeller, "What does South America need?" Rockefeller responded, "I think it needs a great middle class of people such as we have in the United States."[28] This assumption was widely shared by American intellectuals and policy makers, who predicated much of their thinking during the development debates of the 1950s on the idea that economic growth and "modernization," including distribution of resources throughout a society, were the prerequisites for political democracy in the American, Jeffersonian mode. The thinking of Rockefeller, Kaiser, and many others in business, government, and academia was based on certain liberal precepts. Among these was the notion that democracy is not a matter of will (laws and formal constitutions) but a matter of money (wealth and industrialization)—that is, that economic development is the *first* building block of a stable, free society. A second, related assumption was that a substantial and growing middle class is a prerequisite for a prosperous, democratic society, both because a large middle class represents the spreading of abundance throughout the social structure, and because the middle class (the bourgeoisie) has historically been the strongest support for liberal, democratic principles.[29]

To businessmen of the era it was undoubtedly gratifying to think that by fostering economic development they automatically strengthened civil society, promoted democracy, and enhanced local goodwill toward their own companies. And yet, as Rockefeller, Kaiser, and other businessmen demonstrated by an increasing commitment to political neutrality in the 1950s, and as Rockefeller reaffirmed in his 1969 *Report on the Americas,* a preference for democracy did not stand in the way of working relationships with military dictators.[30] Although U.S. businessmen may have been confident in the ultimate redemptive power of economic development, promoting democracy was a goal that ranked behind maintaining amicable, productive relations with host governments. The informal code of conduct that began emerging in the 1950s sought to create these relations through political neutrality and a promise to aid in economic development.

The 1960s: The Alliance for Progress and Business

There is evidence that, after the Eisenhower administration's relative neglect of Latin America, many segments of the business community welcomed John Kennedy's new initiatives. The intent of the Alliance for Progress to promote economic development fitted well with business concerns about finding ways of proving to Latin American nationalists (be they civilians or generals) that private investment could be responsible and beneficial. Especially welcome were indications that Kennedy's approach might include new tax incentives for foreign investment—incentives that Eisenhower's economically orthodox advisors had ruled out. U.S. investment in Latin America had slowed considerably under Eisenhower and was showing an even sharper downward trend as the sixties got underway. Meanwhile, foreign criticism of business exploitation was becoming noticeably bitter abroad, especially in the wake of the Cuban Revolution.

Business concern about these trends was evidenced in several ways. First was the increasingly active discussion of the concept and possibility of joint ventures with Latin American businessmen as a way of promoting at least partial local ownership of foreign enterprises and circumventing nationalist criticisms. The Kaiser and Rockefeller ventures were often cited in this connection, and in the third year of the alliance, business executives would support a U.S. government vote in favor of an Economic Commission for Latin America resolution encouraging joint ventures.[31]

Second, executives also continued to discuss appropriate codes of conduct and ways in which businesses could improve their public relations through advertising, more thorough financial disclosures abroad, training and promotion of foreign nationals, and contributions to community improvement activities in host countries. Business groups held conferences on the subject, articles were written, and business and Department of Commerce officials actively discussed how business could build trust with local communities. Related to this, the early 1960s saw the proliferation of private groups and government committees devoted in one way or another to coping with the foreign crisis of confidence in U.S. business, including the Business Council for International Understanding, the Latin American Information Committee, the Latin American Business Committee, and the Business Group for Latin America.

Initially it seemed that the Kennedy administration would actively encourage these new departures. In the first Alliance for Progress planning document composed by Kennedy's advisory group, which met even before the presidential inauguration, conferees agreed that:

> A better understanding of the contribution of private enterprise is needed within the Executive and Legislative branches of the U.S. Government as well as within the governments of Latin America. . . . The obstacles to private investment, some of them created by the U.S. Government, must be reduced. . . . support should be given to developing and implementing an international code of behavior to be applied equally to private investors and host countries.[32]

But few of Kennedy's primary advisors were drawn from business, unlike in the previous administration, and business input into the alliance was minimal at first. Representatives of business were not even invited to the Punta del Este founding conference in August 1961, though executives from the Rockefeller and Kaiser enterprises and four or five other companies attended anyway, in spite of the lack of any official sanction.[33] The State Department did not announce the formation of a business Committee on the Alliance for Progress (COMAP) until April 1962, nearly a year and a half after planning for the alliance had begun.

It seems that the Kennedy administration's initial lack of a commitment to business involvement was due more to the political emphasis of the alliance in its early years than to any determination to exclude the private sector. As one official of the era later noted, private sector participation "was largely an afterthought," in part because the administration believed "that it was governments that could win the hearts and minds of the Latin American population and save them from Castro."[34] Kennedy's program explicitly called for agrarian and tax reform as prerequisites to aid, and sought democratization and social reform through support of moderate-left political parties in Latin America. These were not goals of the business community, and there may have been some presumption that business would not be sympathetic, helpful, or perhaps even relevant in devising plans. The prophecy may have been prescient or simply self-fulfilling. Although there is little evidence that business opposed either democratization or social reform, as time wore on business leaders became increasingly vocal about being excluded from the alliance and also about the alliance's economic program being subverted by its insistence on prior political change.

Peter Nehemkis, Jr., a Whirlpool executive who had been one of the few business people invited to participate in the earliest alliance planning group, was particularly articulate about his discouragement. He noted in one speech that although U.S. companies paid one-fifth of all taxes collected in Latin America, there had been almost no attempt to halt the sharply downward slide of investment in the region by changing U.S. tax laws to facilitate investment abroad or by encouraging business input into the alliance. The Punta del Este Conference had set a goal of significantly increased private investment in Latin America, and yet the reality was that net new U.S. investment had gone from an inflow of $141 million in 1961, to an outflow of $32 million in 1962, and was still declining into 1963. There were many in the business community, Nehemkis argued, who understood that "business as usual" was not enough to overcome "the pervasive social injustice . . . [and] the meager benefits of industrialization for the masses"—and yet those who had most power to bring economic change were being given the least role.[35] Rather than being tapped as an ally, business was placed in the role of an outsider, and eventually became somewhat of a critic.

And allies were in short supply, both in the United States and Latin America. The U.S. Congress had been lukewarm on the Alliance for Progress from the start: conservatives did not want to see U.S. dollars financing expropriations required by agrarian reform, and liberals such as Wayne Morse and Ernest Gruening in the Senate wanted to see cuts in the military dimensions of foreign aid. Kennedy's proposed allocations for the alliance were cut by one-fifth to begin with, tied to a yearly review, and never came even close to the level of commitment he had initially indicated the United States would make. Latin American businessmen and politicians, even some of whom had been identified with the "democratic left," also questioned the political aspects of the program. Former Brazilian President Juscelino Kubitschek wrote one of the earliest and most critical outside evaluations of the alliance for the Organization of American States. He said that while reforms had to be carried out in order to eliminate "institutionalized poverty," by putting reform first the alliance had "created a system that might result in the postponement of large-scale external aid"—aid that was essential if reformers were to have any hope of taking their nations in new directions. It was, he said, "a vicious circle." Among other things, Kubitschek recommended "permitting private enterprise [in both the U.S. and Latin America] to take part in the conduct of the Alliance. . . . the program would thereby win additional support in an important sector of public opinion and other element from which to obtain objective suggestions."[36]

At a conference in New York in early 1963, Latin American businessmen from ten nations (almost all democratic) expressed their reservations in private, with a view to avoiding conflict with their own governments and that of the United States. Nonetheless, they made it clear that they saw the alliance as a good idea theoretically, but one that had been oversold and inappropriately politicized. By focusing on reform rather than growth the alliance had actually brought about capital flight. "The Latins feel that agrarian and tax reform is their problem and should be handled without outside dictation," one U.S. businessman reported, and that by "selling socialism in Latin America . . . [the] Alliance is backing the wrong horse in their opinion."[37] While it may be argued, correctly for some Latin American businessmen and incorrectly for others, that they would have fought reform under any circumstances, their arguments in favor of respect for national sovereignty (local solutions to local problems) made sense to U.S. executives for whom political neutrality was part of an emerging, if informal and still inconsistent, code of conduct.

David Rockefeller echoed these particular Latin American sentiments and those of many people in the U.S. business community at a speech to the Economic Club of Chicago, shortly after the New York meeting. Rockefeller argued implicitly for a gradualist approach to sociopolitical reform along with a "swiftly-paced" approach to economic growth, saying that anything else was unrealistic considering the "inescapably slow and tedious" nature of social change. Rockefeller also raised the issue of sovereignty, noting:

> We must not try to force Latin American countries simply to create a society in our image. These countries must adapt their institutions and policies to their own conditions. It is in our interest that they should be both effective in satisfying the aspirations of the people and consonant with democratic processes. Yet our own experience and that of Western Europe have demonstrated . . . that the variety of policies and institutions under which economies can prosper in a free society is a large one.[38]

Whereas Kennedy's advisors may have assumed that, in Robert Packenham's phrase, "all good things go together"—that is, democracy, reform, and economic growth—David Rockefeller, his brother Nelson, and many others in the business community clearly believed that economic growth was the engine that pulled the other cars.

But the most important criticisms of the Alliance for Progress, from the point of view of its long-term survival, came from the conservative U.S. Congress. By 1963, the honeymoon was long over and many of Kennedy's programs were in trouble. In particular, both Republicans and Democrats questioned the proposed allocation for the Agency for International Development (AID), which may be the reason why Kennedy himself, in his 1963 AID message, stressed that increased efforts to promote private investment would be the "major new initiative" of U.S. foreign aid efforts for the future. AID staff and advisors saw this change as being perhaps the only hope for continued high allocations in foreign aid. Franklin D. Roosevelt, Jr., under secretary of commerce, wrote AID chief David Bell that "the central fact is that the Congress is unlikely to continue to support anything like an adequate aid program unless there is some major change in its image and mode of operation." Roosevelt suggested that one way to accomplish this would be through emphasizing the nation-to-nation (rather than government-to-government) approach that Kennedy had announced. Private enterprise was to be the "New Look" of foreign aid.[39]

As part of this, officials from the Department of Commerce actively encouraged a more coherent, stronger business presence in the alliance throughout 1963. Jack Behrman, the commerce official in charge of relations with the alliance, sought to do this by encouraging unification of the many business groups concerned with U.S.–Latin American relations. Before Behrman could engineer such a merger, however, David Rockefeller took the initiative and did it for him, much to the administration's pleasant surprise. In the summer of 1963, Rockefeller wrote to a variety of the most active participants in the Business Council for International Understanding, the Latin American Information Committee, COMAP, and so on, urging the formation of one organization to represent the U.S. business perspective on Latin America. The idea attained support almost immediately from business as well as from the Kennedy administration. While the administration wanted it made clear to the public that the move was entirely at private initiative, "to discourage Latin American speculation that there has been some special relationship newly constructed with the business community with respect to the Alliance for Progress," Kennedy nonetheless agreed to a first official meeting with the new "Business Group for Latin America" on November 21, 1963.[40] The meeting was postponed when Kennedy decided to make a quick political trip to Texas.

Observers would later agree that the Alliance for Progress was in trouble well before Kennedy was shot in Dallas on November 22.[41] The political dimensions of the alliance were not preempted mainly by its later support for private enterprise, or by the conservatism of Thomas Mann, Lyndon Johnson's appointment to the post of assistant secretary of state for Latin America. The prodemocracy, agrarian, and tax reform elements of the alliance lacked solid support against predictable opposition in both the United States and Latin America and were falling of their own weight well before November 1963. Kennedy seems to have realized this reluctantly, as did AID administrators. Undoubtedly, many mistakes were made in the initial design and selling of the Alliance for Progress, which scholarly study has yet to analyze or explain fully. One of them may have been to wait far too long before attempting to woo the support of what conceivably could have been one of the most important sources of support for the program, and what certainly was one of its most interested audiences: business. Ironically, the Kennedy administration failed to heed the successful strategy pursued over a decade earlier by proponents of the Marshall Plan for Europe, which was to engage immediately the support of the internationalist business community—support that, according to historian Michael Hogan, "played an important role in overcoming conservative opposition . . . in Congress."[42] Indeed, while some historical interpretations have suggested that the Alliance for Progress was killed off by its later attention to private enterprise, it may be that this change in focus actually prolonged its life.[43]

A Formal Relationship Evolves: Business Diplomacy in Latin America in the Late 1960s and 1970s

According to David Rockefeller, one reason for forming the Business Group for Latin America, which eventually expanded and became the Council of the Americas, was to avoid U.S. government dictation. As long as the government organized and sponsored business input into policy (through groups like COMAP), public officials could pick and choose the kind of advice and advisors they got. Business needed its own forum, separate from government.[44] Considering the government's hot-and-cold interest in Latin American issues, a forum independent of executive or congressional whim made even more sense. The Alliance for Progress had shown how fickle the U.S. commitment was to either democracy or development. Once again, as under Eisenhower, the lesson learned was that if business were to construct a strong relationship with Latin America, it would have to do so on its own.

The Council of the Americas was specifically organized as a neutral forum for discussion among U.S. executives and government representatives, North and South. In the decades since its formal founding in 1965, the council has taken a public stand in favor of only *one* issue (ratification of the Panama Canal Treaty), otherwise preferring to operate more as a clearinghouse for business views than as a lobby per se. In fact, all exchanges between council members and Latin American government representatives are strictly off the record. At the same time, it has implicitly supported the status quo by trying to foster good communication between U.S. business and Latin American governments, many of which were dictatorships from the early 1960s through the early 1980s. Although some executives may have felt, as one former staff member of the council later commented to the author, that "Democracy is a comfortable system to work within because you know the rules," in practice the conditions that U.S. companies operating abroad have sought are stability and free-market policies, whether in Communist China, democratic Costa Rica, or authoritarian Chile.[45]

The more active public lobby group on behalf of U.S.–Latin American relations that evolved during the same time was the American Association of Chambers of Commerce of Latin America (AACCLA), founded in 1967 by U.S. chambers operating in five Latin American countries: Argentina, Brazil, Colombia, Mexico, and Venezuela. From the mid-1970s through the early 1980s, AACCLA was probably the most active business lobby intervening directly with Congress and the president with regard to U.S.–Latin American relations. What characterized their stands in this period was not an ideological preference for either democracy or dictatorship, but a paramount concern for bilateral relations that were not conflict prone. What this often produced, interestingly, was a predisposition to "give" on those issues that Latin American governments consider the highest priority (even when they conflicted somewhat with U.S. ideology), and a willingness to act as a conduit for pressure from abroad. That is, as the segment of U.S. society whose material interests are most affected by foreign needs and wants, international business had a stake in communicating these needs and wants to the U.S. government—which otherwise has little vulnerability to or interest in foreign opinion, especially from the non-European, nonsuperpower nations. For example, AACCLA was consistently supportive of lobbying efforts to maintain U.S. foreign economic aid to Latin America during the Carter and Reagan administrations. It is of note that while lobbying on behalf of its own interests, business may also at times be one of the most active, consistent domestic lobbies on behalf of Latin American perspectives—or at least those perspectives expressed by governing groups.

The U.S. chambers of commerce in Latin America originally organized themselves into a coalition largely in response to the example set by U.S. chambers in Europe, which had begun an association a few years earlier. In 1966, members of the U.S. chamber in Venezuela thought that a parallel coalition for Latin America might be useful for providing mutual support, and especially for encouraging businesses abroad to open chambers in more Latin American countries than the five that already had them. By 1988, the presence of U.S. chambers of commerce in twenty countries attested to the successful attainment of that goal—and to the consequent growth in U.S. business influence vis-à-vis both the U.S. Congress and Latin American governments. The fulfillment of this organizational objective also meant that beginning in the mid-1970s the association could focus its attention on its more primary purposes, which included "representing its constituency before major governmental bodies, especially the U.S. Congress and the Administration . . . [and] interpreting Latin American developments to the news media."[46]

As a lobby, AACCLA's emphasis on nonconfrontational bilateral relations and an open trade policy led it to take several stands at odds with the more conservative elements in U.S. society and government. Specifically, in 1975, AACCLA began to evidence support for a greater normalization of hemispheric trade relations with Cuba. In particular, AACCLA reported favorably in its newsletter on the vote taken by the Organization of American States to drop its eleven-year embargo of Cuba and allow each member nation to set its own policy for trade with the island. AACCLA went even further to encourage the U.S. government not to punish foreign affiliates of U.S. companies that wished to trade with Cuba.

This stand was consistent, of course, with the commercial interests of AACCLA's membership: if they could earn money in Cuba, so much the better. But there was also an issue of sovereignty, AACCLA argued. If certain Latin American countries decided to renew trade with Cuba, but U.S. law prohibited North American affiliates organized under the laws of those nations from trading with the island, "such a situation would reinforce allegations that decisions affecting the host country's economy are taken abroad."[47] In other words, if a U.S. corporation built cars on Brazilian soil utilizing mostly Brazilian labor, capital, and raw materials, Brazil should be able to export those cars to Cuba and improve its balance of payments thereby. Although the U.S. Treasury Department only slowly adopted aspects of AACCLA's liberal interpretation, the organization continued to lobby quietly for trade normalization, especially at the beginning of the Carter administration when it seemed that an improvement in relations with Cuba might be possible.

Throughout the 1970s, AACCLA consistently demonstrated a preference for giving way on issues that impinged on sovereignty, with the understanding that such issues had the greatest potential for undermining bilateral relations and thus business relations. Of course, again, this could mean respect for the sovereignty of dictatorships just as much as for democracies, and in light of the political makeup of Latin America at the time it was dictatorships that were more likely to benefit. Two issues that demonstrated the variable outcomes of such a policy were the Panama Canal Treaty and Jimmy Carter's human rights policy.

On the Panama Canal Treaty, AACCLA was the first U.S. business organization to take a favorable, vocal stand. The association began in 1975 by sending telegrams urging Congress to approve the allocations that were necessary for the negotiations to proceed. When the treaty became an electoral issue in the campaign of 1976, AACCLA kept its members informed of the candidates' stands on the treaty, including Ronald Reagan's statement in early 1976 that "We bought it, we paid for it, we built it, and it is ours, and we intend to keep it." When conservative forces in the House threatened again to cut off all funds for negotiation in June 1976, AACCLA sent telegrams to 150 congressmen. The move was overturned, leading the assistant secretary of state to thank AACCLA's president personally for his help with this "crushing defeat for the anti-negotiation forces."[48]

Once the treaty had been formulated, the Carter administration again looked to AACCLA for leadership. On November 1, 1977, the AACCLA board, meeting in Costa Rica, voted to support the treaty as written. After this, the Council of the Americas also came out publicly in favor of the treaty, breaking with its traditional neutrality. AACCLA tried to develop further support for the treaty within the business community by asking the domestic U.S. Chamber of Commerce (its affiliate) to take a stand in favor of the treaty as well. Interestingly, the national chamber could not achieve a consensus on the subject, which within the United States was simply "too divisive," according to AACCLA's executive secretary.

Only those U.S. businesses with direct ties to Latin America saw the treaty as a "must," because of the strong feelings about it throughout the hemisphere. Speaking before Congress during ratification hearings in 1978, AACCLA's president Patrick Hughson emphasized that the standing treaty from 1903 "symbolized a paternalistic and interventionist image of the United States." Ratification of the new agreement would affirm the "American values of justice and national self-determination."[49] Failure to ratify, he hardly needed mention, would produce a serious rupture in relations with a number of countries. Even after the Senate finally approved the treaty, AACCLA representatives continued to follow it through 1979 when, for a fourth time, they met with and sent telegrams to congressmen—this time to ensure that the allocations needed to implement the agreement were made.

AACCLA's lobbying effort with regard to Carter's human rights policy was not nearly as active—nor as concerned with "American values of justice." But it was consistent. Above all, the chambers of commerce showed their preference for nonacrimonious relations with Latin America. In this case, business showed a willingness to look the other way that National Security Council officials normally reserved only for strategic allies such as South Korea or China or for use as a bargaining chip with important enemies. As far as AACCLA was concerned, "the whole human rights issue is becoming the greatest irritant in U.S.–Latin American relations," and this was enough to make it a problem. In 1976 an AACCLA representative and the U.S. chamber president from Argentina met with the assistant secretary of state for inter-American affairs to register concern, and twice during 1978 AACCLA urged the Senate and House "not to impose punitive human rights constraints" on loans made by the Eximbank to Latin America.[50] The ruling militaries of countries in violation of U.S. human rights standards had made the issue into one of sovereignty, and as in the case of the Panama Canal Treaty AACCLA lined up behind them, albeit less energetically than in the case of the canal treaty. As usual, local sovereignty and stability in inter-American relations came first for AACCLA, this time to the detriment of democracy and social justice.

Central America in the 1980s: The Case of Revolutionary Nicaragua

Business groups and individual corporations will never be entirely consistent, however, and AACCLA was no exception as the debates over policy toward Central America in the 1980s demonstrated. When President Carter asked for $75 million in aid for Nicaragua in late 1979, the past president of the American chamber in Nicaragua initially testified before Congress in support. Especially attractive to the chamber was that $60 of the $75 million was to go for the encouragement of private sector enterprise. But within six months the Nicaraguan chamber had changed its position, and in the process departed from the usual policy of nonconfrontational relations. In April 1980, the current president reversed his predecessor's stand, testifying before Congress that the U.S. should do more to insure that the Sandinista government restored democracy and specifically stating that the $75 million aid package was not likely to be used for the benefit of the private sector.[51] One result was that the Nicaraguan government declared the chamber president persona non grata, and the chamber's credibility and position in the country were severely strained. AACCLA itself did not take a position on Nicaragua or on policies toward El Salvador or Guatemala, preferring to allow local chambers to take their own stand on the issues. But organizational sentiment was nonetheless "strongly supportive" of the Reagan approach throughout the 1980s, according to one AACCLA official.[52]

What is most interesting, though, is not the consistency or inconsistency of specific organizations, but rather overall trends; and it is clear that the overall trend among U.S. bankers and direct investors was a cautious neutrality toward Nicaragua in the early 1980s evidenced by "a low profile sympathetic to the Revolution," in the words of business analyst John Purcell. According to Purcell, U.S. business in Central America in this period was notable chiefly for its "reactive and adaptive" nature, leading to cooperation with oligarchs in Guatemala and revolutionaries in Nicaragua on the premise that "business can be done within a broad spectrum of national ideologies." Bankers pursued cautious but nonpunitive loan policies, while companies with large fixed investments continued operating in both Nicaragua and El Salvador. The Council of the Americas sponsored meetings in New York with members of the Sandinista directorate in 1979, and in 1980 organized a trip of U.S. businessmen to Nicaragua and Costa Rica to meet with private sector and government representatives.[53]

The neutral, adaptive posture of business was due less to the ideological predispositions of executives, according to Purcell, than to financial pragmatism (the desire to hang onto investments) and to common organizational characteristics that led senior executives to listen carefully to managers and analysts at the local level. As one middle manager said about top executives in an interview with Purcell: "They may be as right-wing as Attila the Hun but they are extremely pragmatic when it comes to business decisions." A part of this pragmatism, Purcell notes, may have been a recognition of the declining regional hegemony of the United States in recent years and thus the decreased ability of the U.S. government to protect business investments overseas. Of course, as already noted, it may be argued that the ability of business to depend *categorically* on government for protection in Latin America has been in question since at least 1938, and that business neutrality and adaptability has increased perceptibly since that time. The decline in U.S. hegemony may have simply accelerated the process.[54]

United Fruit, International Petroleum, and ITT: Exceptions or Rules?

The most important exceptions to a gradual fifty-year trend toward political neutrality on the part of business can be found in the behavior of the United Fruit Company, the International Petroleum Company (IPC), and International Telephone and Telegraph (ITT) in the 1950s, 1960s, and 1970s, respectively. Their stories of gross interventionism have been repeated often and need not be elaborated here.[55] But there are some aspects to these incidents that may actually confirm, rather than deny, the general hypotheses concerning the unreliability of government intervention and the corresponding reinforcement of business political neutrality.

First, in all three cases, there is considerable (if not definitive) evidence that the U.S. government instigated the interventions for its own ideological and geopolitical reasons, not primarily to protect U.S. business interests. In the case of Guatemala in 1954, historians in recent years have tended to emphasize John Foster Dulles's anti-Communism and Dwight Eisenhower's commitment to containment in Latin America to explain the reasons for the U.S. overthrow of Jacobo Arbenz, rather than the specific complaints of United Fruit. Similarly, the Kennedy and Johnson administrations' intervention on behalf of IPC, to many observers, went far beyond what the company itself asked of the government and corresponded more with what officials thought of as being the proper way to make Latins conform to the etiquette of the Alliance for Progress than with the actual interests of the company—which was eventually expropriated in its entirety.[56] Lastly, it is clear that although ITT pressed actively for intervention against Salvador Allende, this would have been the policy of the Nixon-Kissinger administration in any case, committed as it was to preventing the further spread of socialism within the hemisphere. What all this means is that protection of business was a complementary but decidedly secondary goal of the U.S. government, not the raison d'etre for intervention, and thus not something upon which business could rely with certainty. Secondary goals can always be shelved to fulfill primary ones. Indeed, although these three corporations engaged in the most blatant kinds of intervention, what the general business community may have learned from their experiences was that government aid was conditional, and—even more important—that it could backfire, as in the case of IPC. "American business is realizing that Washington and its embassies are of questionable value in a Latin American scuffle," businessman George Lodge wrote in 1970. Expropriation and other expressions of nationalism, he added, "are teaching United States companies that their survival and prosperity in the changing environment of Latin America depend very much on themselves."[57]

Second, what makes the political improprieties of these companies seem more like exceptions to the general rule of behavior rather than examples of it is the response that these corporate interventions provoked in the business community. Although the actions of United Fruit seem to have elicited few complaints by other businessmen in 1954, by the early 1960s companies increasingly voiced the concern that they were paying for the transgressions of a few in the form of escalating nationalism. One result was the founding of key business organizations such as the Council of the Americas and AACCLA, which spent much of the decade discussing codes of conduct and the ways in which companies could improve their public relations abroad. As one council official later said, formulating guidelines for corporate conduct in Latin America was a council priority for "most of the sixties."[58] When the International Petroleum Company and its parent company, Standard Oil of New Jersey, intervened in Peruvian politics in the mid-1960s, other U.S. companies refused to support their actions precisely because, as Levinson and Onís put it, "of the widespread feeling that IPC had hardly been a model of corporate responsibility."[59]

The case of ITT in Chile is perhaps even clearer. In 1970, ITT president Harold Geneen began a three-year effort to overthrow the government of Salvador Allende, which included offering funds for rival political parties, endorsing positions of the opposition newspaper *El Mercurio*, submitting suggestions for political and economic sabotage to National Security

Advisor Henry Kissinger, maligning U.S. diplomats who took a "soft" line on Chile, and offering to contribute up to $1 million to a CIA fund for Chilean destabilization. ITT also attempted to involve major U.S. companies and banks in a coordinated effort to pressure the U.S. government for stronger intervention through an "Ad Hoc Committee on Chile," which ITT convened in January 1971. But the Ad Hoc Committee met only twice, and with little result. Kennecott Copper withdrew after concluding that the meetings "had no particular value," while the president of Ralston Purina expressed basic opposition to the ITT approach and ordered his subordinates not to attend any future meetings "even if invited."[60] ITT officials working under Geneen had encountered similar reactions earlier when they had first sought to drum up opposition to Allende's imminent election. As one memo to Geneen stated: "Our poll of companies with plants, or activities in Chile continued to show an almost complete lack of interest on their parts."[61] Only Anaconda Copper, of all the companies ITT contacted, was willing to make protestations to Kissinger directly, and none evidenced the level of intervention suggested by Geneen.

As it turned out, once ITT's actions became public knowledge, they provided the occasion for a public purging of the U.S. corporate conscience and a public shaming of Harold Geneen. At the Senate hearings on ITT's involvement in Chile, four of the largest banks in the nation vociferously proclaimed their policies of political neutrality. Although representatives stopped short of condemning ITT's intervention, they made it clear that, as one banker said, "we would not do it."[62] The senior vice-president of First National City Bank stated that a fundamental presumption of the bank's operating policy was that "every country must find its own way, politically and economically"—to which Senator William Fulbright responded that he wished the State Department felt the same way.[63] The Bank of America representative stated emphatically that "the unique dependence of a bank on good relations with the host government . . . makes it unthinkable to run the risk of political involvement." The executive vice-president of Chase Manhattan Bank countered the notion that ITT's activities were typical of corporate behavior with the comment that "not only is it not a pattern but it is just not done." Ralston Purina and IBM underscored the banks' testimony, with the IBM official calling political intervention "totally abhorrent."[64]

But going beyond questions of fair play and good conduct, the business representatives also made it clear that specific economic interests were at stake. The companies were almost all involved in delicate negotiations over expropriations and sales with the Chilean government at the time of the ITT intervention. The Allende government had required the banks to sell off their branches, and the banks were eager to get the best price possible. At stake was not only the outcome of the negotiations (which several banks had reason to think would end in reasonable compensation), but also the repayment of millions of dollars in loans that had been made both before and after Allende was elected. As it turned out, some banks did arrive at satisfactory agreements with Allende and noted that the socialist government had made commendable progress on its loan payments. Manufacturers Hanover Trust, First National City Bank, and Bank of America (as well as Ralston Purina) all testified that political confrontation or the creation of economic chaos in Chile would have been directly counter to their immediate financial interests.[65] Clearly, these corporations were trying to avoid the kind of outcome which IPC's interventionist behavior had produced in Peru, and which ITT's behavior produced in Allende's Chile: uncompensated expropriation. In this case, self-interest may have operated as an important constraint on behavior, leading companies to learn (or repeat) lessons in negotiation and flexibility that were lost on the U.S. government.

Conclusion

Although this investigation suggests that business behavior may be more politically neutral than often thought, it also raises questions beyond the scope of one article. Specifically, surveys and case studies that would utilize the records of individual companies are needed to determine what the *range* of corporate behaviors is, without unduly emphasizing those corporations that have long records of intervention at the expense of those which have equally long records of political neutrality. ITT, for example, had a history of generally offensive behavior throughout Latin America, which had been specifically documented in the case of Puerto Rico, Peru, and Brazil even before its forays into Chilean politics.[66] It might be noted that ITT was also a conspicuous violator of antitrust laws and a secret contributor to political campaigns in the United States. The pattern of interventionist behavior that studies of ITT reveal may have to do more with that particular corporation and management than with the general record of U.S. business either in Chile or other parts of the region. Although interventionist behavior is critical to document and understand, it is the broadest historical patterns that give insight into how U.S.–Latin American relations have evolved and in what directions policy may be shaped for the future.

    In addition to a series of case studies that would more accurately reflect the wide range and large number of U.S. companies operating in Latin America than do present "exposés," we also need closer analytical attention to what constitutes appropriate political behavior. Self-interest may act as a constraint on confrontational behavior, but self-interest also dictates that companies do what they can to cut the best deals for themselves and protect their investments. The question, then, is where does lobbying end, and intervention begin?

    Of course, this presumes that lobbying is an appropriate form of political behavior—distinct from and preferable to bribery, covert destabilization, and collusion in the overthrow of governments—and that this is the means by which business legitimately interacts with the political process of a nation. This is not a presumption made by everyone, however, as evidenced by some analyses of U.S. business influence. A telling example is Angela Delli Sante's 1979 contribution to *Capitalism and the State in U.S.-Latin American Relations*. Delli Sante correctly states that a goal of the American Chamber of Commerce in Mexico was to promote acceptance of private enterprise and the capitalist system through its own public relations programs and through encouraging member companies to exhibit social responsibility by endowing university chairs, providing health and educational services to workers, sponsoring sports events, and so forth. She concludes that these activities inherently represented "a direct attempt to tell the Mexican people and the Mexican government what to do."[67]

As far as Delli Sante is concerned (and her viewpoint is not uncommon), it is not legitimate for U.S. business to promote its philosophy of private enterprise in other countries in much the same way that it has in the United States since the advent of welfare and consumer capitalism in the Progressive period. And yet, one might ask, what other philosophy is business supposed to promote, and is it realistic to assume that any human endeavor will exhibit ideological neutrality? The private sector will promote private-sector enterprise by its very nature, and it is logical that it will attempt to do so more overtly when it perceives itself under attack. The truly pertinent question is not whether U.S. business promotes the ideology on which it is founded—of course it does—but whether business does so using measures commonly judged legitimate or illegitimate.

By painting all attempts to cultivate legitimacy and influence within a foreign country as a form of interventionism, one risks perpetuating the false dichotomy between self-interest and virtue. It is an analytical trap that hinders attempts to discover exactly what makes international relations better or worse. Again, Delli Sante's article is helpful as an illustration of this familiar problem. By condemning all types of business influence, the author misses an opportunity to deal with the complexities of the one good example of possibly illegitimate business behavior she is able to cite: the participation of U.S. subsidiaries in a four-month advertising boycott of the newspaper *Excelsior* during 1972 because of its sympathetic coverage of socialist experiments in other parts of Latin America and negative editorials on consumerism, capitalist forms of development, and foreign investment. Private Mexican and U.S. companies both participated in the boycott, which was followed by a negative press campaign in the Mexican media concerning *Excelsior*. It is possible that U.S. companies actually instigated the campaign, although the evidence is sketchy: we know only that U.S. groups participated in the decision along with Mexican bankers and industrialists and that Sears Roebuck held out on the boycott even after other U.S. and Mexican companies had returned to advertising with the paper.[68]

In any case, the story raises important questions. Is participation in a public boycott a legitimate or illegitimate way of attempting to wield influence? Would U.S. participation have been more appropriate if the boycott were organized entirely by the Mexican private sector, or not? Do companies have an obligation to give advertising to newspapers with which they disagree? On the other hand, considering that newspapers represent free speech, is any attempt to use financial power vis-à-vis such a publication, especially a foreign one, politically inappropriate? Of course, going beyond even what jurists or scholars might consider legal or appropriate is the question of what the public of the host country will perceive as fair. This kind of pressure is very likely to be seen as interventionism and may in fact constitute it. Indeed, an interesting point is that one of the largest U.S. corporations in Mexico refused to participate in the boycott on precisely those grounds. Clearly, at least some businesses, in their own self-interest, gave careful consideration to the distinction between business influence and political interference. Scholars need to do the same. Further investigation of the U.S. business role in Latin American politics would give an empirical basis to such analytical distinctions.

Nevertheless, it is to be hoped that the present paper does more than simply raise additional questions; it should also suggest what seem to be important trends and propositions. First is that U.S. business in general has learned some lessons about "correct" and "incorrect" ways of participating in the political life of Latin American nations over the past fifty or so years. These years have taught that U.S. military and diplomatic intervention is not a totally reliable or effective bulwark against anti-Americanism or expropriation; that business has to find its own accommodation with foreign regimes, be they democratic or dictatorial; that conspicuous neutrality on political issues is a useful device for avoiding confrontation with host governments; and that bribery and political contributions are dangerous (and, since the 1977 Foreign Corrupt Practices Act, illegal) ways of cultivating influence abroad. These lessons represent a code of conduct formally supported by organizations like the Council of the Americas, and informally adhered to by probably the majority of corporations. This is not to say that the "rules" are not broken. Clearly they are. But at least business has evolved a widely accepted code of conduct concerning interventionism and political neutrality, which is more than can be said of the U.S. government. As Ernest May once noted, "In appraising the American record in Latin America, one ought to judge either by intentions or results. If by the one, the Government comes off well; if by the other, business does."[69]

A final, related, proposition is that self-interest may (perhaps unfortunately) be a more effective way of directing behavior than appeals to American virtue or democratic ideals. Since 1945, the U.S. government has been able to do pretty much whatever it wanted in the Western Hemisphere with little if any consequences for its global power if U.S. policy failed to please Latin Americans. The fundamental goal of policy has been to maintain the essential acquiescence of other nations in the region on economic and foreign policy questions by whatever means necessary, up to and including physical force. One thing that has made this basic stance tolerable to politicians and a public raised on the principles of the Declaration of Independence is a highly sporadic policy of "promoting democracy" in Latin America. "Promoting democracy" thus becomes a way to cleanse periodically the North American conscience of the tarnish of other less high-minded but more persistent motives in international relations. To accomplish this, North Americans do not actually have to promote democracy, they just need to *think* that is what they are doing. Geopolitically, the United States has been able to do what it wants in the hemisphere because of overwhelming economic and military power. Psychologically, the U.S. government has been able to sell its policy and salve the national conscience precisely because of its supposed democratic ideals.

Individual businesses, however, cannot call on such tremendous power nor can they claim to promote democracy. Governments respond to them based on actual behavior. If subsidiaries are expropriated, parent corporations may suffer losses from which recuperation is not possible. Both logic and observation suggest that business is perhaps more likely than not to be neutral on political questions in Latin America, whereas the U.S. government is more likely than not to be interventionist. That is, it is in the self-interest of business to be nonconfrontational, whereas the U.S. government has only marginal need to get along with its weaker neighbors.

What has this to do with democracy? Perhaps not much. Businessmen on the whole do not "care" whether Latin America is democratic, dictatorial, or some place in between—or if they do care it does not usually affect their investment decisions. But is "caring" of the type represented by episodic, psychologically self-serving "democracy-promotion" programs much better, wedded as they seem to be to a related policy of controlling political change in the Western Hemisphere to our advantage? Sovereignty is not democracy, but it is clearly a prerequisite. The private sector may not have the answer for many things, but with respect to political neutrality it may have a better answer than does the U.S. government.

Notes

1. On the conflict between "republican virtues" and self-interest, see Gordon Wood, *Creation of the American Republic, 1776–1787* (New York: Norton, 1969), and Joyce Appleby, "What Is Still American in the Political Philosophy of Thomas Jefferson?" *William and Mary Quarterly* 39 (1982): 287–309.
2. Works written in this spirit include Lloyd Gardner, *The Economic Aspects of New Deal*

Diplomacy (Madison: University of Wisconsin Press, 1964); David Green, *The Containment of Latin America: A History of the Myths and Realities of the Good Neighbor Policy* (Chicago: Quadrangle Books, 1971); and Jerome Levinson and Juan de Onís, *The Alliance That Lost Its Way: A Critical Report on the Alliance for Progress* (Chicago: Quadrangle Books, 1970). For an exposition of the thesis that the Alliance for Progress failed largely because business ultimately had its way, see Abraham Lowenthal, "United States Policy toward Latin America: 'Liberal,' 'Radical,' and 'Bureaucratic' Perspectives," *Latin American Research Review* 8 (Fall 1973): 3–25; and Ruth Leacock, "JFK, Business, and Brazil," *Hispanic American Historical Review* 8, no. 4 (1979): 636–73.

3. See Thomas Carother's article in this volume. Ronald Reagan's Central American policy provides a good example of the appeal, and nearly independent life, of democracy rhetoric.

4. Joseph S. Tulchin, *The Aftermath of War: World War I and United States Policy toward Latin America* (New York: New York University Press, 1971), p. vi.

5. David Kennedy, *Over Here: The First World War and American Society* (New York: Oxford University Press, 1980), pp. 301–30. Also see Tulchin for a comprehensive overview of U.S. government–planned expansion into South America.

6. Tulchin.

7. A natural monopoly in this sense is any kind of economic activity in which there is normally or frequently only one producer or provider—that is, railroads, utilities, or extractive enterprises requiring investments of capital far beyond the reach of any but one or two of the best-equipped and financed corporations.

8. Tulchin, pp. 242–44; also see Joan Hoff Wilson, *American Business and Foreign Policy, 1920–1933* (Lexington: University of Kentucky Press, 1971), pp. 165–66.

9. A. Thomas Taylor to Edward G. Miller, May 19, 1952, p. 1. National Archives (NA), R.G. 59, Lot file 53D26, Office Files of the Assistant Secretary of State for Latin America, 1949–53, box 3, folder: "Business Advisory Council." Citation hereafter referred to as "Business Advisory Council."

10. Leo Welch to Miller, May 28, 1952, and Sam G. Baggett to Miller, June 4, 1952, "Business Advisory Council."

11. Quotation taken from letter of H. A. Davies to Edward Miller, May 12, 1952, p. 4. Also see letter of H. W. Balgooyen, May 20, 1952, p. 6, "Business Advisory Council."

12. Taylor to Miller, May 19, 1952, p. 3, and F. T. Magennis to George Wythe, p. 4, "Business Advisory Council."

13. Quotation, respectively, from Theodore Weiker, Jr., to Miller, May 12, 1952, p. 6, and H. A. Davies to Miller, May 12, 1952, p. 4, "Business Advisory Council."

14. W. Jack Butler, "Public Relations for Industry in Underdeveloped Countries," *Harvard Business Review* 30, no. 5 (September–October 1952): 64 and 69. For other articles calling for a new type of U.S. business presence abroad, see for example (all in *Harvard Business Review*): J. Anthony Panuch, "A Businessman's Philosophy for Foreign Affairs," 35, no. 2 (March–April 1957): 41–53; H. J. Dernburg, "Prospects for Long-Term Foreign Investment," 28, no. 4 (July 1950): 41–51; M. C. Conick, "Stimulating Private Investment," 31, no. 6 (November–December 1953): 104–12; W. Jack Butler, "Fighting Communism Overseas," 34, no. 4 (July–August 1956): 96–104; and Clifton R. Wharton, Jr., "Aiding the Community: A New Philosophy for Foreign Operations," 32, no. 2 (March–April 1954): 64–72. Also see "Foreign Aid without Tax Dollars," *Nation's Business*, July 1957, pp. 82–88.

15. See *Fortune*, November 1953, p. 114, for a summary of Humphrey's views as expressed during the fight over the Eximbank, in which he sought to diminish the bank's lending power and general authority.

16. Michael Hogan, "Corporatism: A Positive Appraisal," *Diplomatic History* X (Fall 1986): 365; Thomas McCormick, "Every System Needs a Center Sometimes," in Lloyd C.

Gardner, ed., *Redefining the Past: Essays in Diplomatic History in Honor of William Appleman Williams* (Corvallis: Oregon State University Press, 1986), pp. 201–6.

17. Dwight Eisenhower to Milton Eisenhower, December 1, 1954, p. 1. Fundação Getúlio Vargas (Rio de Janeiro), Centro de Pesquisa e Documentação, Eisenhower Library Documents, Code 3, 54.12.01.

18. Eisenhower used discretionary technical assistance funds provided by the Mutual Security Act of 1954 to start a "Public Safety Program" for training foreign police forces in order "to maintain internal security and to destroy the effectiveness of the Communist apparatus in the Western Hemisphere." ("U.S. Policy toward Latin America," National Security Council, August 20, 1956, p. 16; found in *Declassified Documents Reference System,* Carrollton Press, 1982, 333–B.) When the National Security Council established a new operating plan with regard to Latin America in 1956 ("NSC 5613"), the Public Safety Program became the core component in the new "Overseas Internal Security Program." Although Congress attempted to undercut the administration's support for repressive regimes by ruling in 1958 that "internal security requirements shall not normally be the basis for military assistance programs to American Republics," Eisenhower could legitimately claim that no *military* funds were being used for such purposes since the necessary funds were being taken from economic programs instead. For an account of Eisenhower's initiative in suggesting the police programs, see A. J. Langguth, *Hidden Terrors* (New York: Pantheon Books, 1978), p. 48. For the Congressional ruling on internal security programs, see the *Mutual Security Act of 1959,* U.S. Senate Committee on Foreign Relations (Washington, D.C.: U.S. Government Printing Office, 1959), p. 708.

19. According to Burton Kaufman, "The fact was that the White House had never been enthusiastic about any of the provisions for encouraging private investment abroad." Burton J. Kaufman, *Trade and Aid: Eisenhower's Foreign Economic Policy* (Baltimore: Johns Hopkins University Press, 1982), p. 158.

20. Percentages based on investment data for 1955 and 1960 in *Historical Statistics of the United States: Colonial Times to 1970* (Washington, D.C.: U.S. Government Printing Office, 1975), part 2, p. 870.

21. A. W. Zanzi, "$32 Billion Overseas Investment—Capital With a Mission," *The Magazine of Wall Street,* January 4, 1958, p. 442.

22. See "Corn Products Refining: Old Line Company in New Growth Phase," *The Magazine of Wall Street,* October 26, 1957, p. 152, and *Automobile Facts,* February–March 1955, p. 8.

23. Wharton, pp. 65, 72. For similar viewpoints, see Butler, Panuch, Dernburg, and Conick, cited previously. Also see Thomas Aitken, Jr., "The Double Image of American Business Abroad," *Harper's,* August 1960, pp. 12–22.

24. Conick, p. 107; Butler, "Public Relations," pp. 64, 69, 71.

25. See the author's dissertation on this subject, "'Good Works at a Profit': Private Development and United States–Brazil Relations, 1945–1960" (Ph.D. dissertation, Stanford University, 1988).

26. The Kaiser Corporation was frequently praised for its decision to invest in Latin America at all and for its role as a recruiter of foreign capital and technical assistance. See *Business Week,* October 9, 1952, p. 164; and June 21, 1958, p. 108. Also see *Washington Post,* October 10, 1954, editorial, and *Harper's,* August 1960, pp. 12–22.

27. See Butler, "Public Relations," p. 66, where he talks about IBEC; Wharton, p. 68, where he calls the Rockefeller's American International Association "the most outstanding project of all in the field of corporate giving abroad"; and Saville Davis et al., "The Struggle for Men's Minds Abroad," *Harvard Business Review* (July–August 1952): 129, in which Nelson Rockefeller is called "the most far-sighted businessman who has gone into Latin America . . . since the war." It is also noteworthy that, in his widely read *Manual of Corporate Giving* (Washington, D.C.: National Planning Association, 1952), editor Beards-

ley Ruml characterized the Rockefeller projects as the best example of "5% programs" abroad, and that the one article in the book on corporate philanthropy abroad focused on the work of the American International Association.

28. Quotation cited by Representative Lawrence H. Smith (Wisconsin) during the testimony of Nelson Rockefeller in Hearings Before the House Committee on Foreign Affairs, *International Cooperation Act of 1949 ("Point IV" Program)* (Washington, D.C.: U.S. Government Printing Office, 1950), p. 91.

29. Robert A. Packenham, *Liberal America and the Third World: Political Development Ideas and Social Science* (Princeton: Princeton University Press, 1973), esp. pp. 4–5, 199–210. For examples from the era of this outlook, see Max Millikan and Walt W. Rostow, *A Proposal: Key to An Effective Foreign Policy* (New York: Harper, 1957); John J. Johnson, *Political Change in Latin America: The Emergence of the Middle Sectors* (Stanford, Calif.: Stanford University Press, 1958); and David M. Potter, *People of Plenty: Economic Abundance and the American Character* (Chicago: University of Chicago Press, 1954).

30. Rockefeller's *Report on the Americas* has often been remembered as being an endorsement of military involvement in Latin American politics. In actuality, however, Rockefeller's report was considerably more philosophical and objective about such regimes than favorable toward them. Writing at the height of military dominance in Latin America, Rockefeller made the traditional argument of a diplomat: that the United States had to be pragmatic about the existence of governments with which it did not agree, should not isolate itself from them, and should look for and try to reinforce whatever reformist tendencies such regimes might exhibit. Rockefeller argued that military governments might have the one redeeming quality of bringing members of the middle and lower classes into power (and with them a greater social consciousness), but he also concluded that military regimes were ideologically less reliable than democratic, civilian governments and often more xenophobic. The report further emphasized, at the beginning and throughout, that the goal of the United States should be to "strengthen the forces of democracy." In any case, Rockefeller's stand was consistent both with the business code of neutrality and with his own predisposition—going as far back as his support for Peronist Argentina's admission to the United Nations in 1945—to place inter-American cooperation above conformity with U.S. ideological expectations. Nelson A. Rockefeller, *The Rockefeller Report on the Americas* (Chicago: Quadrangle Books, 1969), pp. 20, 31–33, 57–59, 144.

31. Edwin Martin to Lincoln Gordon, August 8, 1963, p. 1. John F. Kennedy Library, Jack Behrman Papers (hereafter JFK, Behrman Papers), box 1, file: "AID and Private Investment Correspondence, 9/63–12/63."

32. "Alliance for Progress," Foreign Policy Clearing House, Faculty Club of Harvard University, December 19, 1960, p. 8. JFK, Behrman Papers, box 1, file: "Alliance for Progress, Origins of the. Reports 1960."

33. Report from Rowland Burstan to Luther Hodges, Secretary of Commerce, on the Punta del Este Conference, August 5–20, 1961, p. 5. JFK, Behrman Papers, box 1, file: "Alliance for Progress, Origins of the. Correspondence."

34. Daniel Sharp, "The Private Sector and the Alliance," in L. Ronald Scheman, ed., *The Alliance for Progress: A Retrospective* (New York: Praeger, 1988), pp. 185–90.

35. Peter Nehemkis, Jr., "Private Investment and the Alliance for Progress," March 21, 1962, pp. 1, 9. JFK, Behrman Papers, box 2, file: "COMAP, Correspondence, 1962." Also see Nehemkis's book, *Latin America: Myth and Reality* (New York: Knopf, 1964). For other statements by executives encouraging an active and reformist role for business in the Alliance for Progress, see Jack Behrman's file, "Foreign Aid and Private Enterprise Correspondence, 1961–1962." JFK, Behrman Papers, box 7. For trade statistics cited, see Peter Grace to Jack Behrman, July 1, 1963, p. 9. JFK, Behrman Papers, box 3, file: "COMAP-Correspondence, 7/63–10/63."

36. Juscelino Kubitschek, "Report on the Alliance for Progress," June 1963, pp. 12, 13, 18. JFK, Behrman Papers, box 2, file with same title.

37. Felix Larkin (W. R. Grace and Co.) to Jack Behrman, March 5, 1963, pp. 1–2 of "informal meetings" summary. JFK, Berhman Papers, box 9, file: "Latin American Business Committee Correspondence, 2/6/63–3/15/63."

38. David Rockefeller, Speech to the Economic Club of Chicago, April 23, 1963, pp. 7–9, 12. JFK, Behrman Papers, box 3, file: "COMAP Correspondence, 3/63–5/63."

39. Franklin D. Roosevelt, Jr., to David Bell, December 2, 1963, pp. 1–10. JFK, Behrman Papers, box 1. The papers of David Bell also reveal the extent to which AID fought an increasingly losing battle against Congress in this period. See, in particular, box 23 of the Bell Papers at JFK.

40. JFK, Behrman Papers: Jack Behrman to Luther Hodges, July 2, 1963, p. 1, box 1, file: "AID Correspondence, 7/63–7/63"; and William Dentzer, Jr., to Jack Behrman, November 7, 1963, p. 1, box 3, file: "COMAP Correspondence, 11/63–12/63."

41. JFK, Oral-History Interviews with Roberto Campos (p. 54) and Lincoln Gordon (pp. 29–31 of Van Grasstek interview).

42. Michael J. Hogan, *The Marshall Plan: America, Britain, and the Reconstruction of Western Europe, 1947–1952* (Cambridge: Cambridge University Press, 1987), p. 140. With regard to the alliance's failure to recruit business support, see Sharp, p. 187.

43. See Lowenthal; and Levinson and Onís.

44. Interview with David Rockefeller, New York City, June 14, 1989.

45. Quote from Alice Lentz, Council of the Americas, New York City, June 14, 1989.

46. Memorandum on History of AACCLA (ca. 1975), p. 2. Obtained from AACCLA, Washington Office, file: "History, AACCLA (Misc.)."

47. Ibid., p. 4. Also see *AACCLA's Washington Letter* for August 4, 1975, September 4, 1975, November 26, 1975, December 29, 1975, and February 1977. AACCLA, Washington Office, file: "AACCLA Washington Letter, 1975–1979."

48. Quote from *AACCLA's Washington Letter,* June 25, 1976, p. 3. Also see October 15, 1975, p. 1, and May 21, 1976, p. 6. AACCLA, Washington Office, file: "AACCLA Washington Letter, 1975–1979."

49. *AACCLA Report,* vol. 8, no. 1 (November–April 1977–78): 3. Information on the U.S. Chamber of Commerce from Keith Miceli, Washington, D.C., June 22, 1989.

50. *AACCLA's Washington Letter,* September 3, 1976, p. 2; April–May 1977, p. 2; and September–October 1977, p. 3. AACCLA, Washington Office, file: "AACCLA Washington Letter, 1975–1979."

51. *AACCLA's Washington Letter,* November–December 1980, p. 1, and April 1980, pp. 1–2.

52. Conversation with Keith Miceli.

53. John F. H. Purcell, "The Perceptions and Interests of U.S. Business in Relation to the Political Crisis in Central America," in Richard E. Feinberg, ed., *Central America: International Dimensions of the Crisis* (New York: Holmes & Meier, 1982), pp. 107, 116, 122.

54. Ibid., pp. 110, 117, 122.

55. See, for example, Stephen Schlesinger and Stephen Kinzer, *Bitter Fruit: The Untold Story of the American Coup in Guatemala* (Garden City, N.Y.: Doubleday, 1982); Adalberto J. Pinelo, *The Multinational Corporation as a Force in Latin American Politics: A Case Study of the International Petroleum Company in Peru* (New York: Praeger, 1973); and "Multinational Corporations and United States Foreign Policy, Hearings on the International Telephone and Telegraph Company and Chile, 1970–1971," parts 1 and 2, U.S. Senate Committee on Foreign Relations (Washington, D.C.: U.S. Government Printing Office, 1973), hereafter referred to as Church Hearings.

56. On Guatemala, see Stephen Rabe, *Eisenhower and Latin America: The Foreign Policy of Anti-Communism* (Chapel Hill: University of North Carolina Press, 1988), and Richard

H. Immerman, *The CIA in Guatemala: The Foreign Policy of Intervention* (Austin: University of Texas Press, 1982). With regard to Peru and IPC, see Levinson and Onís, p. 160.

57. George C. Lodge, *Engines of Change: United States Interests and Revolution in Latin America* (New York: Alfred A. Knopf, 1970), pp. 295, 299.

58. Testimony of Enno Hobbing, Church Hearings, part I, p. 382.

59. Levinson and Onís, p. 160.

60. Testimony of Lyle Mercer, Kennecott Copper Corporation, and William Foster, Ralston Purina, Church Hearings, part I, pp. 320, 375.

61. E. J. Gerrity to H. S. Geneen, September 10, 1970, Church Hearings, part II, p. 595.

62. Testimony of James Greene, Manufacturers Hanover Trust, Church Hearings, part I, p. 361.

63. Testimony of George Clark, First National City Bank, Church Hearings, part I, pp. 343, 353.

64. Testimony of William Bolin, Bank of America (p. 385); William Ogden, Chase Manhattan Bank (p. 371); William Foster, Ralston Purina (p. 376); and Miles Cortez, IBM (p. 379). Church Hearings, part I.

65. Church Hearings, part I, pp. 353, 360–61, 376, 388.

66. See, for example, Levinson and Onís on ITT in Brazil (pp. 143–46) and letter from Don (last name not given) to Teodoro Moscoso, January 14, 1962, regarding political pressures exerted on Puerto Rico. JFK, Moscoso Papers, box 5, file: "Correspondence, 1/62–2/62." In Peru, ITT not only used questionable negotiating tactics with the local government, but attempted to cut a deal for itself at the expense of the North American IPC (Church Hearings, part I, pp. 200–201).

67. Angela M. Delli Sante, "The Private Sector, Business Organizations, and International Influence: A Case Study of Mexico," in *Capitalism and the State in U.S.-Latin American Relations,* ed. Richard R. Fagen (Stanford, Calif.: Stanford University Press, 1979), p. 362.

68. Ibid., pp. 370–77.

69. Ernest R. May, "The Alliance for Progress in Historical Perspective," *Foreign Affairs* (July 1963): 768.

7 | The Impact of U.S. Labor

Paul G. Buchanan

THE ROLE played by organized labor in the conduct of U.S. foreign policy has been a controversial aspect of U.S.–Latin American relations. Accused by the left of being imperialist agents dominated by obsessive anti-Communism and antinationalist perspectives that slavishly respond to the ideological, economic, and security concerns of U.S. government and business, North American labor has also been defended by government and labor leaders alike as a promoter of human rights, shop-floor democracy, equitable socioeconomic and political development, and pluralist labor relations throughout the globe. Since the field of labor relations and union politics can be considered an essential element of any democratic regime, and since promotion of democracy is the announced goal of the U.S. government's Latin American policy, U.S. labor's approach to these issues constitutes the crux of the question about its activities in the region.

This chapter explores the role played by U.S. organized labor in the U.S. government's Latin American policy, concentrating on its ideological and economic foundations, the vehicles and instruments utilized to further its ends, and the overall impact these have had on the prospects for democracy in the region.

Historical Background

U.S. labor's interest in Latin America began in the aftermath of the Spanish-American war. Concerned with potential competition from unorganized labor and craft guilds in the Philippines, Cuba, and Puerto Rico, in 1898 the American Federation of Labor (AFL) announced that it would support unionization efforts throughout the Western Hemisphere. AFL president

Samuel Gompers worked hard to promote the rise of AFL-affiliated unions in the former Spanish colonies, often in opposition to emergent unions that were nationalist, anarchist, or classist. This responded to a political view that saw foreign ideologies as threats to U.S. national security, and an economic view that saw Latin America as the preferred sphere of influence for U.S. capitalist expansion. Opposition on economic and political grounds to Latin American unions guided by different ideologies became a foundation of U.S. labor foreign policy, and was projected throughout the region during the next half century.

Following a series of talks between the AFL and the Confederación Regional de Obreros Mexicanos (CROM), the Pan American Federation of Labor (PAFL) was created in 1918 as a response to the regional activities of the Marxist Industrial Workers of the World (IWW). On matters of substance, the PAFL maintained a "policy squarely in harmony with the policies of the American Federation of Labor."[1] U.S. labor's interest in supporting Latin American labor organizations was thus based upon the latter's support for the AFL position on issues of mutual concern. In turn, U.S. labor initiatives in the region were from the beginning linked to U.S. government objectives.[2] According to Gompers, "the fundamental policy . . . pursued in organizing the Pan American Federation of Labor is based upon the spirit of the Monroe Doctrine, to establish and maintain the most friendly relations between the *governments* of the U.S. and Pan American countries."[3]

Gompers's death in 1924 heralded the end of the PAFL. Without the driving force of its main architect, the last PAFL congress, poorly attended, was held in 1930. The onset of the Great Depression forced a retrenchment of the U.S. union movement that shifted attention away from foreign affairs and led to a drop in AFL financial contributions to PAFL. Affiliated Latin American unions were unable to make up the difference created by the loss of U.S. funding, so PAFL languished. This allowed nationalist and classist sentiment to make inroads among Latin American unions during the interwar period. The anarchist Continental Workers Association (CWA) was established in 1928 as a regional branch of the International Workers Association (IWA). That same year the Latinamerican Union Confederation (LUC) was created as part of the Red Union International founded at the Third Communist International (1920). However, internal cleavages prevented either organization from consolidating, and both collapsed by the mid-1930s. Even so, their presence redoubled U.S. labor efforts to establish its presence in the Latin American union system.[4]

Opposition to independent unionism in Latin America took on special urgency for the AFL following the creation of the Congress of Industrial Organizations (CIO) in 1935. Comprised of a coalition of dissident and independent labor unions who challenged the conservative leadership of the AFL under George Meany, the CIO included anarchists and members of the Communist party. The Confederación de Trabajadores de América Latina

(CTAL) was established with CIO support in 1938 to replace the defunct
PAFL. Since it affiliated with the IWW and later the Marxist-oriented World
Federation of Trade Unions (WFTU), the AFL opposed CTAL as Com-
munist.

At the same time that it struggled with the CIO on the domestic front,
the AFL challenged CIO support for regional unions on issues such as the
1938 Mexican oil nationalization decree and solidarity with the labor opposition to the Mendieta dictatorship in Cuba. This weakened the AFL's position in the eyes of Latin American unionists while simultaneously strengthening that of the CIO. The CIO capitalized on its increased stature by
creating a standing committee on Latin America in 1939 (the AFL created a
Latin American Department in its International Affairs Office after World
War II).

The outbreak of World War II renewed U.S. labor and government
interest in Latin America, again out of a shared sense of political, security,
and economic concerns extending beyond labor issues proper. The need to
combat the fascist threat led U.S. labor and the government into a defensive
tactical alliance with the socialist camp. The AFL and U.S. government
reversed their positions of opposition to the IWW, CTAL, and other socialist or Communist organizations, and extolled their virtues as antifascist
allies. The change in strategic outlook was formalized in 1943, with the
creation of the Antifascist Latin American Labor Front, which included
CTAL and representatives of U.S., British, and Soviet unions, as well as a
host of non-CTAL-affiliated Latin American unions.

The need for tactical expediency did not prevent the AFL, with U.S.
government support, from engaging in efforts to undermine CTAL at the
very same time it was collaborating in the antifascist struggle. During the
war years AFL representatives sponsored by the U.S. government traveled to
Latin America to establish "back door" contacts with non-CTAL affiliated
unionists, who later were included in travel exchanges with U.S. unions.
From 1943 through 1947, a network of pro–United States Latin American
unionists was cultivated as an alternative to CTAL and its affiliates. These
efforts paved the way for an eventual split with CTAL once the antifascist
front was victorious. At the same time, U.S. labor participation in the U.S.
government foreign policy apparatus was formalized with the creation of
labor attaché posts (most originally located in Latin America) and offices in
the Departments of Labor and State that addressed issues of international
labor policy, and which were often staffed by unionists.[5]

AFL cultivation of pro–United States union support bore fruit in 1948,
when the Confederación Interamericana de Trabajadores (CIT) formed as
an alternative to CTAL. A year later, the CIT allied itself with the anti-
Communist world labor federation backed by the AFL known as the International Confederation of Free Trade Unions (ICFTU). After a brief dalli-
ance with the WFTU (to which CTAL belonged), the CIO defected and

joined the AFL at the creation of the ICFTU in 1949. This followed the purge of Marxists from the CIO begun in 1946 and carried out through the early 1950s, which preceded its unification with the AFL in 1955. Following the ICFTU mandate to promote regional organizations, CIT was reincorporated in 1951 as the Organización Regional Interamericana de Trabajadores (ORIT), becoming the ICFTU regional affiliate in Latin America. As was the case with the PAFL, ORIT was more an instrument of the AFL than a regional labor confederation, and in that capacity responded closely to the directives of the AFL's international affairs office.

Another postwar creation that helped promote U.S. labor interests abroad is the network of Free Trade Secretariats (FTS), world groupings of industrial unions arrayed by industrial sector or functional activity that act as international sounding boards for national union grievances. Headquartered in Europe and linked to the ICFTU, the FTS (later known as International Trade Secretariats or ITS) established Latin American offices in the mid-1950s. As with the ICFTU, the FTS/ITS network relied heavily on AFL-CIO affiliates for funding, making them very responsive to U.S. labor's economic and political interests in the region. Where ORIT focused on the national confederational level, the FTS's emphasis was at the level of sectoral or industry federations, complementing the broader thrust of ORIT policy. Their utility as a political instrument was underscored by U.S. Labor Department official George C. Lodge, who noted that "ITS flexibility, inner cohesion, and conviction make the Secretariats especially effective anti-Communist organizations in the so-called neutralist areas, and thus extremely important to U.S. objectives."[6]

Even so, in the 1960s U.S. government officials and labor leaders saw the need to create a purely North American–operated labor vehicle in order to combat more effectively Castroite infiltration of the Latin American labor movement. Concerned that Latin American representation within ORIT and the different FTSs created divisions over matters of policy that would hinder the formulation of an effective anti-Communist regional labor program, in 1962 the AFL-CIO founded the American Institute for Free Labor Development (AIFLD). On political and economic grounds AIFLD was held to reflect "the unique pluralism and consensus in American society: Labor-Government-Business."[7] Beyond institutionally promoting class collaboration, AIFLD was projected as the U.S. labor counterpart to ORIT and the FTSs, in which the North American approach to labor relations could be directly transmitted to Latin America through AIFLD field offices, educational programs, social projects, and extension facilities.

AIFLD's role grew throughout the 1960s. Superseding the activities of ORIT and the FTS/ITS network, "AIFLD became the principal instrument of the U.S. government for supplying technical assistance—education and training and social projects—to Latin American trade unions."[8] The extension of AIFLD's presence responded to the requirements of the Alliance for

Progress, which along with the export of counterinsurgency tactics and military assistance packages included labor-oriented projects as part of its socioeconomic development program. AFL-CIO president George Meany was appointed chairman of the Labor Advisory Committee (LAC) to the Alliance for Progress, which shaped the content of AIFLD's programmatic thrust in the region. Following LAC guidelines, AIFLD projects were implemented throughout the hemisphere in conjunction with U.S. government developmental programs administered by the Agency for International Development (AID), the Peace Corps, the International Development Bank, and other agencies involved in the Alliance for Progress.[9]

Although AIFLD influence among Latin American unions increased considerably throughout the 1960s, opposition to it also grew. In the United States, foreign policy divisions originated in the AFL-CIO over the issue of support for the Vietnam War. Walter Reuther, head of the Union of Autoworkers (UAW), publicly disagreed with George Meany's support for the war, and after withholding dues in protest, the UAW was suspended from the AFL-CIO in 1968.[10] In Latin America, AFL-CIO, AIFLD, and ORIT collaboration with the CIA in destabilizing labor-based elected regimes and supporting antilabor authoritarian regimes fostered serious opposition within Latin American union ranks. Reuther used revelations about these connections to challenge the foundation of the AFL-CIO's foreign policy, its bureaucratic and elitist orientation,[11] and Meany's leadership. The result was an erosion of regional support for ORIT and AIFLD activities beginning in the late 1960s, which coincided with a more general reappraisal of the U.S. role in world affairs in the age of superpower détente.

From the late 1960s through the 1970s, a series of developments outside of Latin America set the stage for a major shift in the AFL-CIO approach toward the region. In 1969 the AFL-CIO Board of Directors voted to withdraw from the ICFTU because of its alleged reapproachment with Communist unions and, more pointedly, because the ICFTU was considering the application for admittance of the dissident UAW. Since the ICFTU would not submit to the AFL-CIO's demands to harden its line on Communism and dismiss the UAW petition, the AFL-CIO eventually withdrew from the ICFTU. The AFL-CIO did not rejoin the ICFTU until 1982, and during the interim major changes occurred with the ICFTU that had a decided impact on ORIT.

The withdrawal of the AFL-CIO from both organizations removed their major sources of funding and ideological influence. In its absence, the ICFTU increasingly came under the influence of European Social and Christian Democratic thought, as these views gained credence in Europe and Latin America as a middle ground between Stalinism and reflexive U.S. anti-Communism. The emergence of this ideological middle road found echo in the political platforms of the Acción Democrática (AD) and Social Christian (Comite Organizativa Para Elecciones Independientes or COPEI) governments of Venezuela and the major Venezuelan labor confederation, the Confederación de Trabajadores Venezolanos (CTV), as well in the positions of various party and labor currents in and out of office in Costa Rica, Colombia, Ecuador, Peru, and Mexico.[12]

At the same time, AIFLD was forced to downscale many country programs in the face of charges that it was a CIA front. AIFLD's prestige was especially tarnished by congressional findings and press revelations that it was involved in the 1973 *golpe* that ousted Salvador Allende in Chile, following on earlier interventionist activities in the region.[13] Placed under the light of suspicion, AIFLD diminished its regional presence during the course of the 1970s, a process eased by the appearance of repressive military authoritarianism in many Latin American countries.

In the mid 1970s, in the wake of these critiques and confronted by a liberal Democratic administration, the AFL-CIO switched to a position of support for individual and collective freedoms, especially rights of association and judicial due process for persecuted labor unionists. The AFL-CIO endorsed the Carter administration's human rights policy, and AIFLD worked with the State Department to support the cause of imprisoned labor leaders in the Southern Cone and Central America. By the late 1970s and early 1980s the AFL-CIO advocated boycotts of Argentine, Chilean, and Uruguayan products, and lobbied hard for restrictions on military and economic assistance to these countries as well as the Central American autocracies.

The shift in AFL-CIO foreign policy perspective followed the traditional pattern of taking the lead from the U.S. government on issues of regional policy for reasons of tactical expediency, rather than as a result of a policy shift of a substantive nature. Even so, when a wave of (re)democratization swept the region in the 1980s, U.S. labor was in a position to reassert its ties to Latin American unions, even if ideological and practical reasons prevented it from doing so in the measure seen previously.

For one thing, the domestic position of U.S. labor had changed. With the advent of the Reagan administration, labor no longer enjoyed the political favor of the U.S. government. Economically, the recession of the late 1970s and early 1980s seriously weakened U.S. labor's structural power. In Latin America, the history of AFL-CIO regional involvement had clarified the nature of U.S. labor's economic and political objectives. These factors mitigated against the AFL-CIO reassuming a major role in hemispheric labor affairs in the reopened political climates of the 1980s. Even today, AIFLD influence is most strongly felt in the later-developing union movements of Central America, and least felt among the mature industrial unions of South America.

Because of the shifts in the U.S. political and economic landscape, there are signs of more durable change in U.S. labor's Latin American policy. AFL-CIO efforts to improve working conditions in Central America have assisted the rise of procedural democracies in the region during the past two decades. Cooperative programs, land reform and educational projects, sanitary assistance and training, plus other efforts coordinated by AIFLD, AID, and the Peace Corps, have promoted limited worker empowerment and some forms of economic and political emancipation in these countries. This was tragically underscored by the murder of two U.S. AIFLD land reform advisors by a right-wing death squad in San Salvador in 1981, a fact that shows that not only the left has reason to oppose AIFLD.[14]

As of the late 1970s, U.S. labor's influence on the U.S. government's Latin American policy and on regional labor organizations waned at the same time that it was forced to abandon its traditional foreign policy stance and adopt less interventionist and manipulative approaches toward labor relations and political issues in the region. The shifting international labor market and ideological climate at home, as well as political and economic realignments abroad, forced the AFL-CIO to reevaluate the ideological foundations of its foreign policy. With the decline of U.S. regional hegemony and the end of the cold war, the AFL-CIO has found it necessary to reconstruct a more flexible international vision in order to better serve its economic and political interests.

Ideological Bases of U.S. Labor's Latin American Policy

The ideological foundations of U.S. labor's Latin American policy can be disaggregated into two distinct perspectives. Although intertwined and reinforcing, U.S. labor's political and economic perspectives are examined separately before being reincorporated into a single ideological framework.

Political Perspective

The political basis for U.S. labor's foreign policy approach toward Latin America has its origins in the strategic posture outlined in the Monroe Doctrine.[15] U.S. labor traditionally viewed Latin America as part of the preferred sphere of influence of the United States, where U.S. economic, military, and political interests would take precedence. This view held that extrahemispheric attempts to make political and economic inroads in Latin America were dangerous to U.S. security. In that light, U.S. labor had a role to play in preventing external threats from finding root in the region's working classes. U.S. labor's political approach toward Latin America was therefore founded on a defensive premise: resistance to extrahemispheric political influences, specifically those of a "totalitarian" nature. This policy of opposition to extrahemispheric forces took on special importance during World War I, and was a major impetus for the creation of the PAFL. To the defensive, "antitotalitarian" political base was added concrete military security concerns about threats from the south instigated from abroad, an emphasis that continued uninterrupted for the next sixty years.

What shifted over time was U.S. labor's perception of the totalitarian threat. This paralleled U.S. government assessments of the global political-military balance, which lent to government-union political cooperation in the field of foreign policy in general, and issues of Latin American policy in particular. During World War I, the emphasis was on the threat of the Axis powers and the Bolsheviks; during the interwar years the focus was on Soviet Communism and its international expansion; from 1939 to 1945 the emphasis moved toward fighting European and Japanese fascism; and from 1946 to the present the thrust has been opposition to international Marxism-Leninism. On a secondary plane, U.S. labor and government have reacted equally adversely to nationalist-populist movements such as Peronism in Argentina, Vargism in Brazil, and, more recently, Noriega's military populist alliance in Panama.

Following its historical line, the AFL remained closely aligned with the foreign policy of the U.S. government throughout the interwar period, particularly during the Roosevelt administration. The CIO was divided between three ideological tendencies with different foreign policies. The right-wing faction adopted a political perspective much like that of the AFL. The left-wing current, comprised of Communist party members, adhered to the Soviet party line on matters of international affairs. The isolationist wing, headed by John L. Lewis, advocated a retreat from European affairs and a consolidation of U.S. ties with Latin America in the interests of securing a steady source of raw materials and a stable market for U.S. industry.[16]

Events on the continent in 1939 forced a shift in U.S. union strategic perspectives. That year the U.S.S.R. and Germany signed a nonaggression pact. The CIO left wing retreated from its previous position of support for a united front against fascism (which had included advocating a quarantine of Germany, Italy, and Japan), and moved to a position of isolationism and neutrality. This aligned the left wing with Lewis's isolationist bloc in the CIO, which lasted until mid-1941. During the course of 1939 and 1940, the increasing threat posed by Nazi aggression in Europe and Japanese militarism in Asia consolidated the alliance of the AFL and CIO right wing in support of the Roosevelt administration's antifascist efforts, with both groups steadily gaining membership support at the expense of the left-wing/isolationist bloc.

In 1940 the CIO right wing defeated Lewis and his supporters in elections for the CIO national leadership. In June 1941 Germany attacked the U.S.S.R., and the CIO left wing abandoned its policy of neutrality and isolationism in order to join the CIO right wing and AFL in calling for total support for war against the fascist powers. With the December 7, 1941, Japanese attack on Pearl Harbor, the last vestiges of isolationist sentiment were swept aside, and the three CIO currents joined with the AFL in support for the U.S. government's move to a war economy. This was done to preserve labor peace at home while fighting on the antifascist front abroad.[17]

After the war, the anti-Communist foundation of the AFL's Latin American policy was reaffirmed. The report of the Committee on International Relations at the 1946 National Convention warned that "we cannot exaggerate the vehemence and vigor with which the communists in Latin America have been conducting their campaign of vilification against the democratic ideals and the champions of the democratic way of life."[18] By "champions of the democratic way of life" the AFL was presumably referring to the U.S. government and labor, since at the time democratic regimes in the region were few and far between. AFL regional activities were consequently directed toward promoting divisions within CTAL so that there would emerge an anti-Communist consensus in support of the "eventual organization of an inter-American labor body composed of free, independent, democratic unions."[19]

Support for democracy and "free" trade unionism was in this fashion introduced as a labor foreign policy objective, but remained tied to a defensive, anti-Communist perspective that saw the eradication of the Marxist threat as the foremost foreign goal of the United States, something especially important on the international labor front. With the purge of Marxists from the CIO and its merger with the AFL, U.S. labor foreign policy coalesced around the anti-Communist objective.

The Truman administration responded strongly to labor's calls for anti-Communist action in Latin America. In 1946 the U.S. government proposed the establishment of military training and exchange programs involving U.S. and Latin American armed forces, an act that paved the way for the establishment of the Inter-American Defense Treaty of 1949. This followed an AFL vilification campaign that accused State Department officials of Communist sympathies, and which resulted in a reorganization in the State Department so as to better align its Latin American and labor branches with the thrust of AFL policy.[20]

In addition to Communism, ideologies such as national populism greatly concerned U.S. policy makers of the time. John Foster Dulles was quoted as saying that "nationalism is the doorway to communism,"[21] a view reaffirmed in the 1960s by AIFLD, which claimed that Communists used "so-called 'national liberation' in a way such that social revindications give way to anti-U.S. action."[22] This view reflected good insight into the thrust of postwar Marxist revolutionary strategy (since both Marxist-Leninist and Maoist thought held that the best form of making a revolution was via a nationalist, anti-imperialist war that could later open the doors to socialist control), but failed to understand the precise nature of nationalist sentiment in many Latin American countries, which was anything but Marxist-inspired. Moreover, it subordinated support for democratic institutions to the lesser evil and relativist dictates of the "antitotalitarian" logic. Anti-Marxist and antinationalist views, not an interest in democracy per se, thus converged to form a "prodemocratic" or "free" U.S. labor foreign policy perspective that was oriented toward steering the Latin American masses away from totalitarian beliefs, indigenous and foreign.

The Cuban Revolution magnified U.S. fears that Marxism was gaining ground in Latin America. AIFLD official William Doherty voiced this alarm in 1966, testifying that "in Latin America, the key question of our times is the future road of their revolution: Toward Communist totalitarianism or toward democracy. For the American labor movement this is one of the paramount, pivotal issues; all other questions . . . must remain secondary. This is the direct challenge confronting free trade unionists."[23] Given the ideological consensus on the part of the U.S. labor leadership, business groups, and the federal government, it was easy for them jointly to advocate international programs that would include anti-Communist union promotion as part of "democratization" efforts.

The conservative political thrust of the AFL-CIO's Latin American policy continued until the mid-1970s. At that time, shaken by the compound effects of Watergate, the Vietnam War, revelations of AFL-CIO involvement in CIA activities in Latin America and elsewhere, and the sequels to the Meany-Reuther clashes over foreign policy, many affiliate unions began to question the legitimacy and utility of the traditional position.[24] Changes in the U.S. economy, particularly in the composition of the unionized work force via the growth of service unions and entrance of women and minorities into the labor market, gave added voice to the foreign policy debate within the AFL-CIO. These differences came to a head after a wave of military-bureaucratic authoritarianism swept South America in the 1960s and 1970s, where AIFLD complicity in their rise was not rewarded with the establishment of "free" and "democratic" unions, but with the wholesale repression of unions in general, regardless of ideological identification (a situation that many U.S. firms took advantage of, having favorably assessed the investment opportunities provided by such "docile" labor climates).

Differences over foreign policy within the AFL-CIO were recently seen with regard to U.S. Central American policy, and were openly voiced during the 1985 and 1987 AFL-CIO conventions. The 1985 debate was the first public floor discussion of a foreign policy issue at an AFL-CIO convention, and in 1987 over 50 percent of the membership opposed the federation's Central American policy platform. Bureaucratic rationales underpinning the foreign policy agenda of the AFL-CIO must now be defended before a more heterogeneous and independent membership, which in turn has forced the AFL-CIO foreign policy hierarchy to open up to new sources of rank-and-file input and compromise on several issues.[25]

Confronted by internal and external pressures for change, in the 1980s U.S. labor began to adopt a more flexible political approach toward Latin American labor relations, recognizing that ideological diversity in the union movement was a major source of sustenance for many of the new democratic regimes. This was particularly the case with Christian Democratic and Social Democratic ORIT affiliates associated with parties in government or in majority opposition. U.S. labor Latin American policy now downplays anti-Communism in favor of a more explicit prodemocratic position centered on support for the institutionalization of International Labor Organization (ILO) sponsored labor relations frameworks that recognize union ideological pluralism as a political good. This has led to the renewal of AFL-CIO involvement in ORIT; direct collaboration with leftist unions on matters of common interest, such as the Chilean plebescite of 1988; and a shift in emphasis within AIFLD toward projects that promote democratization of national labor relations systems.

> The outlook and purpose of the American labor movement's international work . . . rest on the belief that workers must have the right to organize for a measure of control over the conditions of their work. This means they must have the right to strike, and that they must have the right to express themselves politically, for what is won in bargaining can be taken away by the state. For labor there is only one standard for human rights. All people must have the freedom to create, organize, and control their own organizations and institutions independent of the state.[26]

The restatement of labor's vision of the world carries with it a renunciation of the isolationist stance that periodically is resurrected within the rank and file, as well as of the relativist or lesser-evil approaches of the past. According to the AFL-CIO, the achievement of a stable U.S. foreign policy based on the principles mentioned remains in doubt so long as the anti-totalitarian mentality dominates Washington. "Regretfully, such a foreign policy remains only an aspiration. Too often American foreign policy swings widely from reactive interventionism and paralyzing isolationism, between grandiose rhetoric and feeble performance. This disarray in purpose and execution has been all too apparent in the Reagan Administration."[27]

The labor critique extended to U.S. domestic affairs.

> The struggle for democracy abroad is not served by undermining democracy at home. The AFL-CIO is alarmed and repelled by the actions of some officials in the Reagan administration to circumvent the law and lie to Congress while attempting to fund the Nicaraguan contras. . . . We urge the Reagan administration to pursue in good faith a diplomatic rather than military solution to the conflict [in Central America] within the framework of the Guatemala Plan [signed by the five Central American presidents on August 7, 1987], that will provide for guarantees of democratic freedoms along with a halt to outside aid to all armed opposition groups.[28]

The altered AFL-CIO position on Latin America, particularly its reapproachment with leftist and nationalist unions around the issue of democratic institutionalization, for the first time in the postwar era placed it seriously at odds with the political orientation of the official U.S. foreign policy apparatus.[29]

After years of allowing myopic and reflexive antitotalitarianism to dictate its political approach toward labor developments in Latin America, U.S. labor has recently shifted toward a more neutral and flexible prodemocratic stance. The promotion and guarantee of freedom of association and political representation is the announced center of U.S. labor's Latin American policy, following the more general shift of the U.S. government foreign policy position on democratization.

Economic Perspective

The structural features of U.S. trade unionism are summarized by Robert F. Hoxie:

> The dominant philosophy of the American labor movement has been business unionism . . . a trade union movement which is essentially trade conscious, rather than class conscious. That is to say, it expresses the viewpoint and interests of the workers in a craft or industry rather than those of the working class as a whole. It aims chiefly at more, here and now, for the organized workers of the craft or industry, in terms mainly of higher wages, shorter hours, and better working conditions, regardless for the most part of the welfare of workers outside the particular organic group, and regardless in general of political and social considerations, except insofar as they bear directly upon its own economic ends. It is conservative in the sense that it professes belief in natural rights and accepts as inevitable, if not as just, the existing capitalistic organization and the wage system, as well as existing property rights and the binding force of the contract. It regards unionism mainly as a bargaining institution and seeks its ends chiefly through collective bargaining.[30]

Business unionism is oriented toward class collaboration rather than class conflict, the latter serving as the philosophical base for "revolutionary," "militant," or "classist" syndicalism tied to Marxist ideologies. Unlike its radical counterparts, business unionism adopts a cooperative rather than confrontational premise that views capitalism as a public good rather than a social cost. The objectives here are to lower the level of exploitation and increase the material bases of working-class consent, not to question the private ownership of the means of production.

The apolitical nature of U.S. business unionism was quite transparent in the area of foreign relations, given its antitotalitarian focus. Beyond this political orientation lie the material interests that override U.S. labor's ideological perspective on foreign policy. U.S. labor interest in promoting North American-style business unionism in Latin America stems from the economic interest in securing raw materials and expanding markets for U.S. goods. A modern means of expanding markets for U.S. goods is through "trickle-down" increases in working-class wages in importing countries. The promotion of business unionism involving procapitalist labor agents in foreign extractive industries and component manufacturers also ensures a steady supply of the raw materials and parts required for the production of U.S. finished goods. As consumers of U.S. goods, both North American labor and organized workers of U.S. trading partners have a vested interest in insuring the uninterrupted flow of foreign inputs to the United States. This helps maintain high levels of union employment and wages in domestic manufacturing industries, U.S. labor's historic bastion.

Labor leaders, government officials, and the corporate community see extension of the U.S. export market as essential for domestic prosperity and political stability. Controlled promotion of business rather than classist unionism was traditionally viewed as a means for incrementally increasing working-class wages and consumption within capitalist frameworks both in Europe and Latin America, opening input and output markets dependent on U.S. prosperity.[31] According to Walter Reuther, "It is in our self-interest in terms of providing a market for finished goods from American industries, a market for goods manufactured by American workers, to see the living standards of others raised—to see their own indigenous economies developed and strengthened."[32] The 1946 AFL convention anticipated this view.

> Production and prosperity in the U.S. depend to a very large extent on our ability to secure, through fair and square international trade and commerce with our Latin American neighbors, certain vital raw materials. Similarly the improvement of the working and living conditions of the Latin American peoples are, in large measure, dependent upon their ability and readiness to supply us with these materials and at the same time to develop their own countries' modern industrial techniques and skills.[33]

After World War II, an additional strategic concern was added to this structural perspective. "We must also remember that many raw materials come from the underdeveloped countries of the world, areas threatened by the Soviet sphere of influence. If they were under Soviet control, our industries would be hard pressed to continue full production at all."[34] The preoccupation echoed concerns voiced earlier. In 1939, John L. Lewis remarked that "Central and South America are capable of absorbing all of our excess and surplus commodities. . . . Obviously, increased trade volume with the Latin American countries would lead to improved political and cultural relationships and make for increased security for the United States when the day comes that some imperialistic foreign power challenges the Monroe Doctrine."[35]

Beyond its view of the proper role of unions, U.S. labor's economic perspective on Latin America was based on unequivocal support for capitalism in general, and for U.S. business investment abroad in particular. Regional development was to be exclusively pursued within capitalist market frameworks, using U.S. private investment and U.S. government economic assistance as the preferred vehicles for promoting economic change. This perspective came to be known as Wall Street internationalism.

No alternate form of economic structure, be it socialist (even democratic socialist), or endogenously controlled state capitalism, satisfied the requirements of this vision. Both jeopardized the repatriation of business profits in the United States, and therefore threatened the material interests of organized U.S. workers. The structural dependence of organized labor on U.S. capital gave it a vested stake in the private pursuit of profit abroad. Material interest dictated that U.S. labor adopt antisocialist and antinationalist postures in Latin America on economic as well as ideological grounds, since limitations on U.S.-dominated capitalist development abroad diminished labor rewards at home.

Traditionally, the primary Latin American policy objective of U.S. labor was to help promote stable investment climates in which U.S. business profitability was protected. Despite rhetorical championing, political preoccupation with promoting democratic institutions was subordinated to this structural logic. The promotion of anti-Communist business unionism was consequently seen as a means of insuring that working-class demands remained within the confines of "bread and butter" issues resolvable by U.S.-dominated capitalist development, since the attendant logics of labor collective action would not threaten the profitability of U.S. investors upon which U.S. union wages depended.

As with its political perspective, the AFL-CIO economic perspective has changed. The realities of economic competition in the late twentieth century forced a reappraisal of the basic tenets of Wall Street internationalism. U.S. foreign investment no longer necessarily brings with it domestic prosperity. To the contrary, it has spurred capital flight leading to "runaway jobs," a process by which U.S. factories shut down, unionized employees are dismissed, and employers move abroad in search of cheaper labor costs and less restrictive employment climates (in terms of occupational safety, worker benefits, and employment stability). In addition, foreign countries with repressive labor policies, where standard rights of association, petition, and grievance are curtailed along with wage rates, social services, and other public goods, pose an increasing threat to U.S. workers in the form of competition in trade waged on the backs of exploited foreign workers. With this in mind, U.S. labor has sought to include "trade with justice" and "social" clauses in U.S. trade legislation and international trade standards.[36]

The AFL-CIO opposes U.S. business investment that it considers exploitative and constrictive of labor rights abroad. Two examples of phenomena that U.S. labor opposes are the *maquiladora* assembly plants on the northern Mexico border and employer-created "company" unions known as *solidarismo* associations in Central America. In the maquiladora program, U.S.-based firms have established labor-intensive assembly operations in Mexican border towns, importing U.S.-made components from parts warehouses on the U.S. side, exporting the finished product back to the United States. Low transportation rates, coupled with dramatically reduced labor costs of a predominantly female labor force unorganized and subject to high turnover rates in an environment of pervasive unemployment, make the "twin plant" phenomenon an attractive option for labor intensive manufacturers.

The AFL-CIO is pledged to resist the export of jobs to the maquiladoras. According to a 1987 AFL-CIO policy statement,

> A sincere, long-term strategy for making the jobs of American workers more secure does not include racing to a foreign country to take advantage of cheap labor. There can be no shortcuts to "competitiveness" by employing low-wage workers in Mexico in jobs that perpetuate rather than relieve their poverty because of pitifully low wages. Production for export in Mexico does nothing to increase the goods available to Mexican workers that would allow them to raise their living standards.[37]

Company-created "workers associations" and "alternative unions" pose another threat. The principle of these solidarismo associations is simple: workers give up the right to strike over pay and working conditions in exchange for company-determined representation and employer-provided benefits. For U.S. labor, such "yellow" or "company" unions are extremely dangerous not only to working-class interests, but to democracy in the region as a whole. Hence the AFL-CIO had added its opposition to this type of employee association to its long-standing opposition to government-controlled unions.[38]

Promotion of autonomous trade unionism abroad is now seen by the AFL-CIO as an essential step toward evening out gross imbalances in the global labor market otherwise encouraged by such capitalist practices, thereby preserving union employment and wages at home. This places the AFL-CIO at odds with sectors of the U.S. government foreign policy establishment and business community who see the solidarismo movement in a positive light because of its docile anti-Communist, probusiness nature.[39]

The AFL-CIO has also begun to promote the regional use of Employee Stock Option Plans (ESOPs). Making workers co-owners (even if a minority) of the firms in which they are employed is believed to increase their stake in the company's success, as it makes a more direct link between individual worker productivity and overall profitability. It also gives the worker a voice in management decisions, which reinforces individual involvement in the productive process. The concept of joint worker ownership through stock options has gained credence in the United States, although not without some labor skepticism. That is because in many instances ESOPs have been used to break unions rather than strengthen their stake in the productive process. On the other hand, under certain guidelines (specifically, union control of ESOPs), organized labor has found ESOPs to be a beneficial way of maintaining employment, practicing wage restraint, increasing productivity, and expanding worker benefits.

AIFLD proposals outlining the use of ESOPs in Central America include a maximum of 60 percent employee ownership in order to encourage private business collaboration, the use of private management as sources for expertise, the need for worker education as part of the process, the solicitation of government support, the separation of union functions from board of director or management functions, and other labor participatory resources.[40] AID has supported these efforts by issuing a directive to its field offices to encourage broadening of the ownership stake of workers in national economic development.[41] The promotion of ESOPs in Latin America by the AIFLD thus responds to a logic Elizabeth Cobb, elsewhere in this volume, ascribes to progressive U.S. business interests when promoting joint ventures with Latin American investors: a share in the company is the economic equivalent of a vote in the political process, enfranchising the worker at the point of production in a fashion comparable with voter registration in electoral systems.[42]

This is a far cry from the days when the unqualified probusiness mentality pervaded U.S. labor's economic thought. The lessons of the past and the economic challenges of the present and future have forced the AFL-CIO to rephrase its foreign economic policy. Although this economic perspective is ultimately grounded in the defense of worker material interests at home, its reorientation has permitted U.S. labor to play a more productive role promoting the institutionalization of democratic labor relations systems in Latin America.

The Integrated Perspective

Schematically, the traditional perspective underriding U.S. labor's Latin American policy can be represented in the following series: from capitalism, to business unionism, to antitotalitarianism, to a pro–United States position. This progression helps explain why U.S. labor activities in Latin America have seldom advanced the cause of union or political democracy, although they sometimes did improve the material well-being of cooperative unionists. The conflict between U.S. labor material interests and the normative concern with democracy was resolved in favor of support for capitalism over democracy because U.S. labor's material interests were guaranteed by the former, not the latter. Anything that opposed U.S.-led capitalist expansion in Latin America was consequently regarded by U.S. labor, capital, and the government alike as a threat to the welfare and security of the United States.

The foreign policy perspective of U.S. labor should not be surprising. The incorporation of organized labor as a subordinate partner in the U.S. foreign policy establishment fulfills a condition for the maintenance of democratic capitalist hegemony in the United States. The postwar experience has shown that under conditions of advanced monopoly capitalism, organized labor is incorporated, via material and political concessions and inducements, in an alliance with the state and capital in order to guarantee the economic stability needed for consensual political reproduction.[43] The bases of working-class consent to this incorporation are material and ideological: higher standards of living measured in wages, benefits, and the like, in increasing measure derived from corporate profits made abroad, exchanged for class collaboration (and subordination) on foreign policy approaches that deny the material and political interests of workers abroad. In this sense, U.S. labor has been a conservative foreign policy actor. It has sought to conserve its organizational privileges and prerogatives at home at the expense of workers elsewhere.[44]

AFL-CIO president George Meany well understood the basic point: "You can't dictate to a country from any angle at all unless you control the means of production. If you don't control the means of production, you can't dictate. Whether you control them through ideological methods or control them through brute force, you must control them."[45] This is the ideological foundation of the imperialist labor aristocracy criticized in the Marxist literature.[46]

During the last fifteen years U.S. labor has been forced to modify this perspective in light of changed international and domestic realities. Sobered by the results of previous forms of intervention and the changed political and economic conditions of the international system, U.S. labor tempered its strategy and broadened its ideological perspective on Latin America. The AFL-CIO now accepts the notion that working-class consent is essential for successful capitalist reproduction both at home *and* abroad, regardless of stage of development or specific location in the global network.

This shift finds its economic foundation in the worsening condition of organized labor in the United States during the past decade. The reorganization of the U.S. productive apparatus undertaken in the 1980s resulted in the structural weakening of organized labor, paralleling the harsher antilabor measures associated with the implementation of monetarist economic policies throughout Latin America in the 1970s. Strategic weakening gave material foundation to the decrease in political influence U.S. labor was able to wield in the area of domestic and foreign policy. The neoclassical tenets underpinning the Reagan administration's structural transformation project were complemented by a political approach that was overtly antilabor in nature (again, paralleling the exclusionary labor policies of modern Latin American authoritarians).

The reassertion of U.S. government's procapital stance and the shift in the U.S. economic nucleus from heavy industry to high technology and services responded to the competitive exigencies of the evolving international market. The move was facilitated by enforcement of legislation that authorized firing of strikers and "right to work" (no closed shop) statutes at the state level, and which eased bankruptcy reorganization schemes that permitted union busting at the federal level. The political dimension of the Reagan administration's antilabor campaign exploited public antipathy toward the hierarchical, bureaucratic, inefficient, and uncompetitive traits of the U.S. labor movement, and was evident in the composition and rulings of the National Labor Relations Board during the 1980s.

At the level of production, elimination of Taylorist and Fordist productive schemes was countered by cutbacks in employer-provided benefits, real wages, and an increasing recomposition of the work force within a general picture of union membership decline and loss of jobs in traditional industries. Shifts in union membership toward service industries with large female, black, and Hispanic memberships, coupled with the gradual appreciation of class-based solidarity on the part of North American workers placed on the defensive and increasingly forced to shoulder the burden of sacrifice imposed by the structural transformation of U.S. capitalism, helped to force a general reevaluation of U.S. labor's economic and political platforms.

In the 1980s belief in U.S. labor benefit through foreign trade fell hard in the face of an increasingly complex and interdependent international division of labor, with U.S. unions forced to wage a defensive struggle for the preservation of wages and jobs at home. As a result of adverse labor market conditions and the antilabor domestic political climate of the 1980s, U.S. labor began to accept the legitimacy of certain types of nonbusiness unionism and the need for constraints on U.S. investment in Latin America. It did so not because it believed in national self-determination or the autonomous political role of the labor movement in dependent capitalism, but because it believes that increased unionization and class militancy, coupled with union political activity under democratic frameworks, can deter firms from investing abroad or force them to operate under conditions similar to those of the United States, thereby balancing the international labor market equation. Material self-interest in a changing world economy, not altruism, prompted U.S. labor to shift its Latin American policy toward selectively working with nationalist or socialist unions on projects of democratic institution building in the areas of labor relations and national political participation. This has added flexibility to U.S. labor's posture in the region after years of reactive anti-Communist orthodoxy, although its self-interest remains apparent.

Vehicles and Instruments of U.S. Labor's Latin American Policy

U.S. labor has used several vehicles and instruments to promote its Latin American policy objectives. These include union to union bilateral exchanges, regional organizations such as the PAFL, ORIT, and the Free Trade Secretariats; quasi-public agencies such as AIFLD, public agencies such as AID, the International Relations Division of the U.S. Department of Labor, and the Office of International Labor Affairs of the U.S. Department of State (to which are attached labor attachés stationed abroad), and the CIA; regional organizations such as the Organization of American States and the Inter-American Development Bank (IDB); international organizations such as the International Labor Office and its Latin American regional affiliate, the Confederación Interamericana de Administratión de Trabajo (CIAT); and nongovernmental agencies such as human rights organizations, solidarity groups, and religious organizations. The instruments used by these vehicles have incorporated material and nonmaterial resources including educational, welfare, and housing programs; organizational assistance; legal and technical advice; loan, grant, credit, and other financial aid packages; union salary allowance support; and direct payouts in the form of bloc allocations of a discretionary or covert nature. This section highlights some of the more salient vehicles utilized by U.S. labor in pursuit of its Latin American foreign policy objectives.

ORIT

ORIT was created as the ICFTU-affiliated, anti-Communist regional labor confederation through which anti-Communist business unionism could be promoted in Latin America. As the ICFTU regional affiliate, ORIT nominally receives its policy guidance and funding from that organization. However, the AFL-CIO presence in ORIT was very strong from the beginning, and despite having Latin Americans in many leadership positions, ORIT remains largely dependent upon the AFL-CIO for both direction and financial sustenance. Half of ORIT's 25 million affiliates belong to the AFL-CIO.[47] Since delegate representation is proportional, with 16 million members the AFL-CIO continues to hold a majority position in ORIT executive committees. With under 3 million affiliates, the next largest delegations from Mexico, Canada, and Argentina lag far behind in representation in the ORIT hierarchy.

In 1980 ORIT included twenty-four national labor confederations and 38 percent of the unionized work force in Latin America, compared with thirteen confederations and 20 percent for the Christian Democratic, Confederación Latino Americano de Sindicalistas Cristianos–Confederación Latino Americano de Trabajadores (CLASC-CLAT), ten confederations and 16 percent for the Cuban-sponsored Comite Para la Unificación Sindical de Trabajadores Latino Americanos (CPUSTAL), and seventeen independent confederations covering 26 percent of the organized proletariat. The biggest labor confederations in Latin America, the Mexican Confederación de Trabajadores Mexicanos (CTM) and the Argentine Confederación General de Trabajo (CGT), are ORIT affiliates, as are the AFL-CIO, Canadian Labor Confederation (CLC), and numerous other labor federations.[48]

ORIT's primary source of funding is the ICFTU, although over half of the ICFTU funds in turn comes from the AFL-CIO and several non-union sources, including U.S. government agencies and international organizations.[49] Direct AFL-CIO grants to ORIT continue to be sizable. In 1985 and 1986 the AFL-CIO provided over $100,000 directly to ORIT. Even now, with a downscaled AFL-CIO presence in the ORIT directorate, it still contributes nearly two-thirds of the ORIT budget through direct or indirect grants, with the remainder largely derived from the Canadian CTC, the Venezuelan CTV, and the Mexican CTM.

The creation of AIFLD undermined AFL-CIO support for the ORIT mission. Where in the 1950s it received the bulk of AFL-CIO funds directed toward Latin America, funding for ORIT after 1961 was reduced while that of AIFLD rose.[50] Disagreements with ICFTU comptroller regulations led to additional AFL-CIO cutbacks to the ICFTU in the latter half of the 1960s, increasing ORIT's financial dependence on the AFL-CIO at the same time the overall scope of its activities were being reduced or subordinated to those of AIFLD.

Originally headquartered in Havana, ORIT moved to Mexico City after the 1959 Cuban Revolution. Its major activities are oriented toward union education programs. In 1951 it began a trade union school at the University of Puerto Rico, and in 1962 it founded a trade union institute in Cuernavaca, Mexico. When the CTM assumed control of the Cuernavaca Institute for its own "superior syndical education school" in the 1970s, ORIT's training facilities were moved to Guatemala and Costa Rica, where they remain. It runs courses and seminars on the role and function of "free" unions, the organizational necessities of peasants and women, and collective bargaining. In this it has collaborated with outside agencies such as the Alliance for Progress and UNESCO. Yet here again the creation of AIFLD seriously curtailed ORIT activities, as AIFLD educational programs duplicated and eventually replaced many of those initially offered by ORIT.

In the 1950s and 1960s, ORIT drew heavily upon the AFL-CIO and AIFLD for its leadership.[51] The interchange between AIFLD and ORIT positions was commonplace, with individuals moving smoothly from one agency to the other without having to redefine objectives or mission. As a result, ORIT had no independent voice in the formulation and implementation of regional labor projects, but was used instead by the U.S. foreign policy apparatus as a semiautonomous implementary agency. According to a U.S. Senate study, this was a major cause of its diminished prestige in the 1960s.

> More fundamental, perhaps, has been the tendency of ORIT to support U.S. Government policy in Latin America. ORIT endorsed the overthrow of the Arbenz regime in Guatemala and of the Goulart regime in Brazil. It supported Burnham over Cheddi Jagan in Guyana, and it approved the U.S. intervention in the Dominican Republic. To many Latin Americans, this looks like ORIT is an instrument of the U.S. State Department.[52]

In the 1970s, with the infusion of social democratic thought and funding, ORIT began to establish an autonomous identity as a regional labor group. It redefined its mission as prodemocratic and political rather than apolitical and anti-Communist. At its tenth congress in 1981 the ORIT directorate revised its charter to reflect this new orientation, putting distance between its activities and those of AIFLD, the AFL-CIO, and the U.S. government. This helped restore ORIT's credibility in the eyes of Latin American labor while decreasing its utility as a U.S. labor instrument, although ideological battles between Social Democratic "reformers" and pro-AFL-CIO "traditionalists" continue within it to this day.

AIFLD

AIFLD was founded in August 1961 as a private, nonprofit corporation. Its formal objectives were listed as "assisting in the development of free, democratic trade union structures in Latin America through labor leader training centers and social development programs in such fields as housing, worker's banks, credit unions, consumer and producer cooperatives and related socio-economic activities."[53] The probusiness orientation of AIFLD was explicit from the start. According to a member of its original board of directors, "AIFLD urges cooperation between labor and management and an end to class struggle. It teaches workers to help increase their company's business and to improve productivity so that they can gain more from an expanding business. It also demonstrates in a very concrete fashion that workers can have better living conditions within the framework of a free, democratic, and capitalist society."[54] Testifying in 1967 on AIFLD's relationship with the U.S. firms operating in the region, William Doherty (current AIFLD executive director) stated that "we are collaborating with the Council on Latin America, which is made up of the primary U.S. business institutions that have activities in that area. Our collaboration takes the form of trying to make the investment climate more attractive and more inviting to them."[55]

AIFLD recently redefined its mission so that it includes strengthening democratic trade unionism in Latin America, fostering self-reliant and independent hemispheric unions, and thus making trade unionism a powerful force for democratic development and social change. It affirms that strong and democratic unions are necessary to give voice to legitimate demands of workers in Latin America and the Caribbean, as they are believed to contribute to the sectoral pluralism AIFLD maintains is essential for the full development of democracy. According to this view, where workers are denied voice through their unions in the political, social, and economic decisions that affect their lives, democracy itself is at risk. Promotion of democratic labor relations institutions, rather than procapitalist anti-Communism, is now AIFLD's announced foreign policy objective.[56]

In line with its collaborative nature, AIFLD's first board of trustees reflected a tripartite character, with twenty-one labor representatives (including the AFL-CIO president, who doubles as AIFLD president, and eleven Latin American union leaders), four business representatives, and five members drawn from various professions. Business representation on the board was taken from U.S. corporations represented in the Council on Latin America, including W. R. Grace, United Fruit, Pan American World Airways, Anaconda, Kennecott Copper, Bristol Myers, Johnson and Johnson, Monsanto, Union Carbide, Gulf Oil, Mobil Oil, ITT, IBM, several banks, and various Rockefeller family holdings. In 1980, after much criticism of the business presence in AIFLD, coupled with increased differences between the business and labor representatives over the direction of AIFLD policy, employer representatives abandoned the board. AIFLD is now a bipartite labor-government venture in foreign policy implementation, with an increased Latin American unionist presence on its twenty-five-member board of trustees. This helped ease Latin American fears that AIFLD was merely a U.S. business front.

Headquartered in Washington, D.C., in space provided by the Communications Workers of America (CWA), AIFLD has at one time or another established offices in virtually every Latin American country. From time to time AIFLD has been forced to close its field offices, either because it was expelled by the local government (Peru, 1971; El Salvador, 1973; Nicaragua, 1980; Panama, 1988) or because conditions become too hazardous to operate effectively (Argentina, 1974; Colombia, 1987). Today it is represented in every Latin American nation save Cuba, Nicaragua (where an office was re-established after the 1990 Sandinista electoral defeat), Suriname, Panama (where an office was re-established after Noriega's ouster), and Colombia.

AIFLD publishes a broad array of educational periodicals in English, Spanish, French, and Portuguese. AIFLD Reports, along with the more episodic literature, constitute yet another ideological tool in the AIFLD repertoire. Educational programs vary from country to country, depending on the organizational and educational levels of the work force, and the ideological climate of the government and unions in question. Courses last from one week to three months, and are also taught in each of the respective national offices. Outstanding graduates are sent to the United States to receive advanced leadership training in these subjects.[57]

Since 1962 AIFLD has operated labor training institutes in the United States, first at the Front Royal Institute in Virginia, Georgetown University, Trinity College, and Mt. Vernon College in Washington, D.C.; Loyola University in New Orleans; and then, as of 1979, at the George Meany Center for Labor Studies in Silver Springs, Maryland. AIFLD has offered courses in labor economics, collective bargaining, "democracy versus totalitarianism," comparative labor organization, productivity, industrial organization, social security, labor legislation, workplace safety, human relations, union education and financing, organizing tactics, and grievance procedures, both in the United States and through its field offices. In 1965, when AIFLD recognized that the needs of urban and rural workers differed considerably, an Agrarian Union Development Service was launched.

Upon completing their U.S. coursework, AIFLD graduates were sent home under a nine-month salaried internship program in order to disseminate new skills and knowledge among their *compañeros*. The current norm is for graduates to return to their unions without AIFLD financial support. The graduate reenters the local union bureaucracy as a technical expert specialized in aspects of the labor process and relations of production, and also engages in ideological dissemination functions, promoting anticorporatist views of labor relations. In some cases, such as during the tenure of military-bureaucratic regimes in the Southern Cone and Central America in the 1970s, unionists were invited to attend AIFLD courses in the United States as a means of freeing them from the oppressive labor climate at home, and, more important, in order for them to set the foundations for eventual reorganization of their unions once the dictators departed.[58]

In the late 1970s, at the behest of the Latin American members of their board of trustees, AIFLD formally recognized its political role in supporting "free" trade unionism, and now devotes half of its efforts to political activities. The shift to an overt political role was one of the reasons cited for the withdrawal of business representatives from the board. The shift responded to several factors. The conservative anti-Communist language and apolitical probusiness facade needed to survive in the U.S. political climate of the cold war era was replaced by a moderated ideological tone and more overt political role once AIFLD's position within the foreign policy apparatus was consolidated. Second, the postdétente world, particularly the evolving posture of the Socialist International, the failure of Marxist revolutionary movements in Latin America, and the upheaval in the authoritarian socialist world, allowed AIFLD to establish bases for dialogue with Democratic Socialist and Christian Democratic union currents. In this regard, while it continues to employ divide-and-conquer tactics against anticapitalist unions in countries such as El Salvador and Nicaragua, AIFLD has shifted its general posture in the face of changing global and regional political realities.

AIFLD receives the majority of its funding from the U.S. government, an uncommon situation for a private, nonprofit corporation. In 1967 92 percent of the AIFLD budget came from the U.S. government, a total of $4.8 million. Of the $17.4 million allocated to AIFLD from 1962 to that year, 89 percent ($15.4 million) was channeled through AID. This amounted to 67 percent of the total allocated for labor programs under the Alliance for Progress. By 1971 AIFLD was the fifteenth largest recipient of AID contracts worldwide.[59] The majority of appropriated funds go to AIFLD educational activities. The entire Social Projects division of AIFLD (with jurisdiction over all noneducational programs) is also funded by AID. In 1987, over 90 percent of the $14.8 million AIFLD budget came from AID, with the remainder donated by the AFL-CIO (1.5 percent) and the conservative-dominated National Endowment for Democracy (8.9 percent).[60]

Reliance on AID funding has posed a problem for AIFLD, for it limits the freedom of action AIFLD is allowed to exercise when using those funds. Disputes over funding priorities and comptroller responsibilities plagued the AID-AIFLD relationship for years, although today AIFLD has greater control over in-country administration of AID contracts. Much of AIFLD's funding was originally channeled into ORIT and ITSs in order to support educational and social projects. As of the late 1960s, AIFLD increasingly assumed direct control of these projects.

CIA funding of AIFLD activities has been extensively documented in the press and in congressional hearings. Covert funds were directed toward securing the cooperation of key labor leaders, promoting some organizations and destabilizing others, and generally lubricating the means of access to influential government bureaucracies and political personalities. CIA funding for AIFLD was channeled through fronts such as the Gotham, Andrew Hamilton, and J. M. Kaplan foundations, through cooperative ITSs, and through agencies such as the Institute of International Labor Studies and other labor educational facilities installed throughout the region.[61] Revelations of AIFLD-CIA connections led to cutbacks in covert funding in the 1970s, but links between the two agencies remain. The CIA continues to place agents in AIFLD country offices and as labor attachés, since the AIFLD cover provides a convenient means of gathering intelligence on Marxist union factions, individual leaders, dissidents, and anti–United States foci, and generally keeps agency headquarters appraised directly of developments in the labor field.

Beyond these activities, AIFLD's efforts center on various social projects, including housing construction, loan and credit programs, literacy, vocational, health, and sanitation training, and so-called Impact Projects that involve material donations to needy unions.[62] Through its loan and credit programs and Impact Projects, AIFLD has funded consumer cooperatives, credit unions, and worker-operated enterprises.[63] By 1988 a Regional Revolving Loan Fund underwritten by AID grants and administered by AIFLD had 114 projects throughout the region. In addition, a Special Projects Fund established in 1976 for purposes of emergency relief had disbursed $257,000 on 73 projects by 1988.

By the 1970s AIFLD had assumed control of the AFL-CIO's Latin American policy, replacing the Latin American department in the International Relations Office. Today it is virtually autonomous from the AFL-CIO Department of International Affairs with regard to issues of Latin American labor policy input and implementation. More important, although both agencies continue to be guided by the general tenets of the AFL-CIO's foreign policy, they no longer respond instrumentally to U.S. government directives. This distancing was most evident in the 1980s, with AIFLD and the AFL-CIO opposing the Reagan administration on a number of political and economic issues both at home and abroad, and where the thrust of AIFLD approaches toward political and economic questions in Latin America ran counter to many of the policies advocated by the departments of defense and state. At a time when the military commanders of the region were signing a hemispheric security agreement against precisely such groups (the November 1987 Pact of Hemispheric Security signed in Mar del Plata, Argentina, which identifies such groups "as Marxist fronts and infiltrators"), AIFLD was openly working with many democratic socialist unions to stabilize the nascent democratic regimes of the region.

Despite protest by senior AIFLD officials and claims by many critics that it has not changed its orientation over the years,[64] it is clear that the contrary is true. Although it remains a major foreign policy vehicle of the AFL-CIO, AIFLD has moved from a reflexive anti-Communist, probusiness posture toward a flexible prodemocratic, proworker stance when addressing Latin American labor and political issues. It has reemphasized bread-and-butter labor education along with political participation and ideological pluralism within union ranks. No less important, from covertly interventionist it has become openly participatory in the political life of the nations to the south.

Labor Attachés

The responsibility for formulating U.S. government labor policy belongs to the State Department, where the coordinator for international labor affairs, in conjunction with AID's Office of Labor Affairs, communicates policy directives to the labor attachés stationed in U.S. embassies abroad.[65] The Office of Inter-American Affairs for Policy and Coordination oversees labor policy application in Latin America. There is no overarching labor policy in the State Department beyond support for ILO standards on labor rights. There is no discrete labor policy for individual countries either. State Department labor policy in Latin America is postoriented and reactive, taking its lead from both events on the domestic labor front and AIFLD initiatives in-country. Only when labor issues become especially sensitive do policy formulation and approval shift to headquarters in Washington.

Labor attachés serve as official U.S. government liaisons with national labor administrations (labor ministries), ORIT, the ICFTU, and labor unions in their host countries. They also serve as AIFLD contract monitors when AID funds are used for AIFLD projects and, more generally, are classified as technical and political supervisors of both AIFLD and union-to-union activities. This has caused problems of coordination and turf battles with AIFLD administrators, who prefer to operate as independently as possible from embassy scrutiny.[66]

Labor attachés are traditionally drawn from four sources: the AFL-CIO, the State Department, the Labor Department, and the CIA. More often than not, personnel from the first three organizations are recruited from their Department of International Affairs (in the case of the AFL-CIO), or from the International Labor Offices of the respective public bureaucracies. Assigned to embassies as political officers, labor attachés serve a function analogous to that of military attachés—that is, official liaisons and intelligence gatherers who serve as primary points of contact between the U.S. government and local unions. Where trade relationships are important (such as East Asia and Western Europe), many labor attachés come from the Labor Department; where the relationship between the United States and the particular country is of less strategic importance, the position is most often filled by a foreign service officer; where local union relations with the AFL-CIO are particularly good, the position is often filled by a unionist; and where Marxist influence in the local labor movement is strong, the job frequently goes to a CIA officer. In countries with particularly large, politically active, or well-organized labor movements, more than one specialist is assigned to the labor attaché's office. The specifics of each case depend on the precise combination of these factors, mixed in with geopolitical and ideological considerations of a multilateral and bilateral nature.

Even if considerable at times, organized labor's representation in U.S. foreign policy agencies has not been of a uniformly high quality. For every individual of high caliber sent, U.S. labor has sent many more into government service as labor attachés and labor advisors without the proper qualifications, either as a form of reward for their activities in the union movement, as a form of patronage, or in order to remove them from positions of influence in the AFL-CIO hierarchy when they were no longer useful.[67] Most recently, U.S. unionists have not been interested in becoming labor attachés, subordinated to ambassadors with Republican connections. Nor are most ambassadors keen on having non-foreign-service officers in that position, particularly given the current ideological differences between the Republican administration and the AFL-CIO. As a result, unionist presence in the current corps of labor attachés in Latin America is very low. Of the sixteen labor attachés currently stationed in Latin America and the Caribbean, only two—in Jamaica and Argentina—have union-related backgrounds.

Union-to-Union Contacts

One of the more effective ways of promoting U.S. labor foreign policy objectives in Latin America has been through direct contacts between U.S. and Latin American unions. This practice began early in the century, with the AFL-CROM discussion of U.S.-Mexican labor issues, and continued during World War II with exchanges between AFL affiliates and non-Marxist Latin American unions. Whether by travel exchanges between individual labor leaders, formal correspondence between union directorates, the establishment of cooperative programs, educational tours, or financial interchanges, support for boycotts or calls for political pressure to be applied on both the U.S. and foreign governments, U.S. unions have found direct contact with their Latin American counterparts to be an efficient means of promoting their economic and political perspective on the region.

A productive form of exchange has been for Latin American unions to request assistance from their U.S. peers when confronting U.S.-based transnational corporations on bread-and-butter issues. In 1953 the AFL pressured the United Fruit Company and the U.S. State Department to accept a negotiated settlement with agricultural workers for the first time in the history of United Fruit's Honduran affiliates.[68] AFL-CIO and ITS pressure on the U.S.-based parent company was critical for the success of unionization efforts in Guatemalan Coca-Cola plants in the late 1970s and early 1980s.[69] More recently, workers at a Union Carbide plant in Brazil successfully appealed to the AFL-CIO for support when contract talks with the company stalled.[70]

Direct U.S. union support for Latin unions is not limited to organizational and economic demands. Direct contacts on political issues have been made as well. Defense of Latin American unionists confronted by political repression has been one area where U.S. unions have been particularly effective. Unlike the 1950s and 1960s when silence was the norm, the AFL-CIO and a host of affiliate unions regularly protested the violations of unionists' rights under the military-bureaucratic regimes of Argentina, Brazil, Bolivia, Chile, Uruguay, Peru, and Central America in the 1970s and 1980s. U.S. unions have also been quick to denounce human rights violations under the socialist authoritarian regimes of Cuba, Suriname, and Nicaragua. This represents another shift. Criticism of conservative authoritarian regimes historically was not as consistently given as that directed toward the socialist camp. Only as of the mid-1970s, when human rights became a central issue in U.S. foreign policy, did U.S. unions take a more critical position on AFL-CIO foreign activities and adopt a consistent stand against labor repression in Latin America.[71]

During the last two decades there has been a trend toward more direct union intervention on behalf of Latin American labor groups on issues of specific concern. This stems not only from the rise of dissenting voices within the U.S. labor movement and a concern with imposing some ethical content on U.S. labor's Latin American policy, but also out of the past failures of the AFL-CIO and umbrella organizations such as ORIT and AIFLD to address many of the immediate concerns of Latin American unionists. With the need to protect U.S. union jobs in light of the international economic realities of the late 1980s, U.S. unions have been quicker to support directly the demands of their Latin American brethren, if for no other reason than out of a finely honed sense of self-preservation.

Conclusion

This essay is not intended as an attack on U.S. labor and its foreign policy objectives in Latin America during the course of this century. Nor does the absence of an assessment of their policies in the region imply ignorance of Marxist-Leninist attempts to gain control of Latin American labor, which had much to do with shaping the thrust of the U.S. labor approach in the region. What the chapter has endeavored to demonstrate is the contradictory nature of U.S. labor's Latin America policy. It has done so by arguing that the promotion of "free" trade unionism in Latin America has both helped and hindered the cause of democracy in the region.

Such promotion helped by providing Latin American workers with a series of educational programs and other forms of assistance that are designed to empower them in the workplace and community and to improve their general standard of living. However it also has, to a far greater extent, hindered the cause of democracy in Latin America by adopting a doctrinaire antitotalitarian line behind the facade of apolitical business unionism, which left it blind to the realities of class struggle in Latin America and the non-Soviet nature of many Marxist and nationalist union movements in the region. For a half century U.S. labor unquestioningly accepted a developmental logic that saw U.S.-promoted capitalist expansion as the panacea for all social ills, to which democratic advocacy was subordinated. Anything that ran counter to this view brought about a reflexive, reactive response from the North American labor hierarchy, paralleling the U.S. government response, that often served to undermine the cause of democratization in Latin America.

The greater the regional hegemony of the United States and depth of the cold war, the more doctrinaire and rigid was the U.S. labor response to labor developments in Latin America. The less the regional hegemony and U.S. influence over a given Latin American country, the more flexible and progressive U.S. labor's approach, particularly during periods of improved superpower relations. Until very recently, U.S. labor strongly supported U.S. government foreign policy in Latin America. Even if in opposition now, it continues to take its lead from the administration, following time-honored practice.

The AFL-CIO's reversed posture has a structural root. The changing international division of labor, and the shifting U.S. position within it, has forced organized labor to reassess its former position of unqualified support for U.S. capitalist international expansion. The quest for profit abroad no longer brings with it benefits for organized workers at home, but instead has resulted in an increasing tide of "runaway jobs" and unfair competition in trade.

As the U.S. economy adjusts to an era of increased international competition, U.S. labor has assumed a defensive position, protecting rank-and-file wages and employment through opposition to further U.S. corporate investment abroad. This prompted U.S. labor to accept political, classist, and militant unions in Latin America, because it believes that the latter will deter or constrain U.S. investors, equalize labor climates worldwide, promote "fair" trading practices, and thereby protect rank-and-file material interests at home. To that end, organizational tactics and other forms of educational projects oriented toward strengthening working class participation in the political arena and the productive process have been emphasized by agencies such as AIFLD without as much concern over the ideology of the unions involved.

Despite its changed strategic outlook, the AFL-CIO remains guided by one fundamental logic: the logic of material and organizational self-preservation. If it has not entirely abandoned manipulation and intrigue as foreign policy tools, the economic and political circumstances of the international moment require that the AFL-CIO foreign policy apparatus adopt a more flexible approach to Latin American labor and political issues. The rationale behind this approach holds that it is both foolish and counterproductive to play the role of labor foils for a U.S. foreign policy elite seemingly unconcerned with the material and political foundations of domestic union consent to its activities overseas. Instead, the logic of organizational survival compels U.S. labor to become a reluctant agent for the promotion of democracy in Latin America and elsewhere, fulfilling the democratic mantle that it has long claimed but seldom seen fit to wear.

Notes

This chapter is a revised version of a paper prepared for presentation at the conference on "The United States and Latin American Democracy," University of Southern California, April 6–9, 1989. Portions of this chapter were written during the author's tenure as a Visiting Faculty Fellow at the Kellogg Institute, University of Notre Dame. Additional logistical assistance was provided by Paul Chase, whose support is gratefully acknowledged. I am indebted to William Bollinger and other conference participants for their comments. A longer version appears as Kellogg Institute *Working Paper* no. 136 (1990) under the title, "'Useful Fools' as Diplomatic Tools: Organized Labor as an Instrument of U.S. Foreign Policy in Latin America."

1. Santiago Iglesias, former leader of the PAFL, quoted in George C. Lodge, *Spearheads*

of Democracy: Labor in Developing Countries (New York: Council on Foreign Relations, 1962), p. 23.

2. See R. Radosh, *Labor and United States Foreign Policy* (New York: Random House, 1969); and J. Scott, *Yankee Unions Go Home! How the AFL Helped the U.S. Build an Empire in Latin America* (Vancouver: New Star Books, 1978).

3. S. Gompers, *Seventy Years of Life and Labour* (New York: Dutton, 1948), cited in Scott, p. 176.

4. Proceedings of the 1934 AFL Annual Convention, cited in Scott, p. 177, and Radosh, p. 354.

5. On the formalization of U.S. labor and government ties during this period, see Serafino Romualdi, *Presidents and Peons: Recollections of a Labor Ambassador in Latin America* (New York: Funk & Wagnalls, 1967), pp. 72–73; H. Spaulding, "U.S. and Latin American Labor: The Dynamics of Imperialist Control," *Latin American Perspectives* 3, no. 1 (Winter 1976): 48; and U.S. Senate, Committee on Foreign Relations, Subcommittee on American Republics Affairs, *Survey of the Alliance for Progress: Labor Policies and Programs,* Document 17, 91st Congress, 1st Session (12844-2) (Washington, D.C.: U.S. Government Printing Office, 1969) (hereafter referred to as Senate Document 17-91).

6. Lodge, pp. 73–74.

7. American Institute for Free Labor Development, "Progress Report to the President's Labor Advisory Committee on Foreign Assistance," March 1967. Cited in Senate Document 17-91, p. 582.

8. Ibid., p. 581.

9. A summary of these is offered in Senate Document 17-91, pp. 601–55.

10. On this, see A. O. Hero and E. Starr, *The Reuther-Meany Foreign Policy Dispute: Union Leaders and Members View World Affairs* (Dobbs Ferry, N.Y.: Oceana Publications, 1970).

11. A problem shared by many collective agents, particularly labor organizations and political parties. See R. Michels, *Political Parties: A Sociological Study of the Oligarchical Tendencies of Modern Democracy* (New York: Free Press, 1966).

12. J. Godio, *Historia del Movimiento Obero Latinoamericano* (Caracas: Editorial Nueva Sociedad, 1985), 3: 260–70.

13. For recounts of these activities, see among others, H. A. Spaulding, Jr., *Organized Labor in Latin America* (New York: New York University Press, 1977); Spaulding, "U.S. and Latin American Labor"; H. W. Berger, "Union Diplomacy: American Labor's Foreign Policy in Latin America, 1932–1955" (Ph.D. dissertation, University of Wisconsin, 1966); G. C. Ross, *El Neocolonialismo Sindical* (Buenos Aires: Editorial La Linea, 1974); D. Torrence, "American Imperialism and Latin American Labor, 1959–1970: A Study of the Role of the Organización Regional Interamericana de Trabajadores in the Latin American Policy of the United States" (Ph.D. dissertation, Northern Illinois University, 1975); J. Steinsleger, *Imperialismo y Sindicatos en America Latina* (Puebla, Mexico: Universidad Autonoma de Puebla, 1976); F. Hirsch, *An Analysis of Our AFL-CIO Role in Latin America, or Under the Covers with the CIA* (San Jose, Calif.: n.p., 1974); K. P. Erickson and P. V. Peppe, "Dependent Capitalist Development, U.S. Foreign Policy, and Repression of the Working Class in Chile and Brazil," *Latin American Perspectives* 1, no. 1 (Winter 1976): 19–44. A recent summary is offered in H. A. Spaulding, Jr., "Solidarity Forever? Latin American Unions and the International Labor Network," *Latin American Research Review* 25, no. 1 (Summer 1989): 253–65.

14. For a discussion of the AFL-CIO/AIFLD role in El Salvador, see W. Bollinger, "El Salvador," in G. M. Greenfield and S. L. Maram, eds., *Latin American Labor Organizations* (Westpoint, Conn.: Greenwood Press, 1987).

15. Samuel Gompers stated that the PAFL represented a means of safeguarding Latin America's "autonomous independence" from the "insidious attempts of autocratic forms of

government located outside the hemisphere," which if successful in their efforts would ensure that the "Monroe Doctrine and all that it implies (would) be destroyed and thrown to the four winds," S. Snow, "Samuel Gompers and the Pan-American Federation of Labor" (Ph.D. dissertation, University of Virginia, 1960), cited in Radosh, p. 352. Also see the proceedings of the 1913 AFL Annual Convention, cited in Scott, p. 173, and Spaulding, *Organized Labor,* p. 253.

16. Scott, pp. 193–96.

17. Ibid.

18. Memorandum from S. Romualdi to M. Woll, FTUC Chairman, December 18, 1943, cited in Romualdi, p. 8.

19. Proceedings of the 1946 Annual Convention, cited in Scott, p. 213.

20. Romualdi, pp. 71–73.

21. Quoted in Godio, 3: 114.

22. AIFLD, "Educación Sindical. El Movimiento Obrero en las Américas," vol. 1 (Mexico, D.F., n.d.), p. 74, cited in Ross, *El Neocolonialismo Sindical,* p. 74.

23. "Town Hall Speech," *AIFLD Report,* June 1966, quoted in Senate Document 17-91, p. 585.

24. See Hero and Starr.

25. See the discussion in Spaulding, "Solidarity Forever?" esp. pp. 255–57.

26. AFL-CIO, *The AFL-CIO Abroad: Perspectives on Labor and the World,* AFL-CIO Publication no. 182 (Washington, D.C., August 1987), pp. 3–4.

27. Ibid., p. 251.

28. AFL-CIO, *Policy Resolutions Adopted October 1987 by the Seventeenth Constitutional Convention,* AFL-CIO Publication no. 3 (Washington, D.C., January 1988), p. 113.

29. AFL-CIO, *AFL-CIO: Twenty Five Years of Solidarity with Latin American Workers* (Washington, D.C.: AIFLD, 1987), p. 5.

30. Senate Document 17-91, p. 578.

31. Radosh, p. 359; Scott, p. 197.

32. Scott, p. 197.

33. Proceedings of the 1946 AFL Annual Convention, cited in Scott, p. 208.

34. Scott, p. 197.

35. *United Mine Workers Journal,* September 15, 1939.

36. On the AFL-CIO position on the Generalized System of Preferences (GSP), GATT, and the issue of workers' rights, see the June 1, 1987, letter and attachments from AFL-CIO Director of International Affairs Tom Kahn to David P. Stark, chairman of the GSP Subcommittee of the Office of the United States Trade Representative; the *American Federationist* 93, no. 7 (November 8, 1986); and the AFL-CIO *Bulletin of the Department of International Affairs* 3, no. 1 (January 1988): 2.

37. AFL-CIO, *Policy Resolutions, 1987,* pp. 45–46.

38. Ibid., p. 106.

39. See the testimony of John T. Joyce, president, International Union of Bricklayers and Allied Craftsmen, AFL-CIO, before the Subcommittee on International Economic Policy and Trade of the Committee on Foreign Affairs, U.S. House of Representatives, on the formation of the Central American Development Organization (CADO), April 13, 1988, especially appendixes IV (ICFTU Resolution), V, and VI (memorandum and telegrams from USIA officials in Washington, and San José, Costa Rica, proposing invited visitor status for solidarismo leaders with attendant justifications).

40. See the November 23, 1988, letters written by AIFLD official John J. Heberle to two Salvadorean unions, in which he outlines the general program, offers the suggestions cited, and includes literature prepared by and for the AFL-CIO on the subject of ESOPs.

41. Memorandum from Alan Woods, Administrator of AID, to AID Mission Directors and Overseas Offices, May 6, 1988.

42. "The Role of U.S. Business," at the end of her discussion of business activities in the 1950s.

43. This in turn depends on the ideological stance of government incumbents, the extent of state intervention in the economy, the political orientation and strength of working-class organizations, the conditions of the labor market, and the overall state of the economy, using either corporatist or pluralist mechanisms of interest representation of varying degrees of comprehensiveness.

44. On the role of trade unions in advanced capitalism, see L. Panitch, "Trade Unions and the Capitalist State," *New Left Review* 125 (1981): 21–41. For a critique of the view that the AFL-CIO is somehow "conservative" on both domestic and foreign affairs, see D. C. Heldman, *American Labor Unions: Political Values and Financial Structure* (Washington, D.C.: Council on American Affairs, 1977), esp. pp. 14, 38–40.

45. House of Representatives, Committee on Foreign Affairs, Subcommittee on International Organizations and Movements, *Winning the Cold War: The U.S. Ideological Offensive*, 88th Congress, 1st Session, part II, April 30, 1963 (Washington, D.C.: U.S. Government Printing Office, 1963), p. 134.

46. On this, see I. Katznelson and K. Prewitt, "Constitutionalism, Class, and the Limits of Choice in U.S. Foreign Policy," in R. R. Fagen, ed., *Capitalism and the State in U.S.-Latin American Relations* (Stanford, Calif.: Stanford University Press, 1979), p. 35; M. Nicolaus, "Theory of the Labor Aristocracy," *Monthly Review* 21, no. 11 (April 1970): 97; and *Argentina in the Hours of the Furnaces* (New York: NACLA, 1975), pp. 56–77.

47. Torrence, chap. 2.

48. Godio, 3: 284–85.

49. Spaulding, *Organized Labor*, p. 257.

50. Senate Document 17-91, pp. 584, 658.

51. Torrence, chap. 2.

52. Senate Document 17-91, p. 581.

53. Radosh, p. 416.

54. Speech given by J. Peter Grace at Houston's International Trade Fair, September 16, 1965, cited in Romualdi, p. 418, Scott, p. 225, and reprinted in amended form as an AIFLD Pamphlet, September 1965.

55. U.S. Senate, Committee on Foreign Relations, *Foreign Assistance Act of 1967*, 90th Congress, 1st Session (Washington, D.C.: U.S. Government Printing Office, 1967), p. 1096. Also see Ross, pp. 117–49.

56. AIFLD, *Annual Progress Report, 1962–1988: 26 Years of Partnership for Progress* (Washington, D.C.: AIFLD, 1988), pp. 1–2.

57. AIFLD, *The Advanced Labor Studies Program of the American Institute for Free Labor Development* (Washington, D.C.: AIFLD, 1988), pp. 14–20.

58. Interview with Dr. Hugo Belloni, program coordinator, AIFLD Argentina, June 28, 1988. From 1962 to 1988, AIFLD trained 602,484 unionists in Latin America, the Caribbean, and the United States: 597,445 were trained in-country, 4,834 graduated from advanced courses at Front Royal Institute or the George Meany Center for Labor Studies, and 205 were trained as labor economists at the participating U.S. universities. The largest number of students came from Colombia (71,839), followed by Brazil (67,361), the Dominican Republic (63,500), Ecuador (62,291), Peru (56,880), Honduras (41,044), Bolivia (36,437), Guatemala (33,941), Chile (27,952), the Caribbean (23,450), and Uruguay (22,164). The remaining countries, save Suriname and Cuba which do not have any AIFLD graduates, have had AIFLD student enrollments of less than 20,000 but more than 1,000. Most recently (1987), Guatemala had the largest number of students enrolled in AIFLD programs (11,856), followed by the Dominican Republic (9,524), Brazil (3,096), and Argentina, Chile, Costa Rica, Ecuador, El Salvador, and Peru with between 2,000 to 3,000 students each. AIFLD, *Annual Progress Report, 1962–1988*, pp. 1–2.

59. Senate Document 17-91, pp. 582–83; Spaulding, *Organized Labor,* p. 260.

60. AFL-CIO, *The AFL-CIO Abroad,* p. 12.

61. Spaulding, *Organized Labor,* p. 260.

62. Ibid., p. 262; Radosh, pp. 430–31; AIFLD, *Annual Progress Report, 1962–1988,* p. 3.

63. Spaulding, *Organized Labor,* p. 262.

64. In an interview with AIFLD Executive Director William C. Doherty, Jr., on February 7, 1989, this writer was told that global realities, not AIFLD's posture, were what had changed over time. When it was pointed out that the present definition of AIFLD's mission clearly contradicts the stated mission it had in the 1960s, Doherty continued to maintain that this was mere tactical expediency rather than a shift in its fundamental antitotalitarian emphasis.

65. Senate Document 17-91, p. 577.

66. Ibid., pp. 616–17.

67. J. P. Windmuller, "Labor: A Partner in American Foreign Policy?" *Annals of the American Academy of Political and Social Science* 350 (November 1963): 113.

68. P. Taft, *Defending Freedom: American Labor and Foreign Affairs* (Los Angeles: Nash Publishing, 1973), pp. 184–85; Romualdi, pp. 268–69 (FF 17).

69. See Spaulding, "Solidarity Forever?" pp. 262–64.

70. *People's Daily World,* September 29, 1988, p. 7-A. Given that this periodical is a mouthpiece for the U.S. Communist party, the approving tone of the coverage is all the more remarkable.

71. See Hirsch, and the sources cited in Spaulding, "Solidarity Forever?"

Part Two

Conclusions

8 | Economic Forces and U.S. Policies

John Sheahan

THE SURVIVAL of democracies in Latin American countries depends above all on their own internal relationships and actions, but the economic policies of the United States can change the odds either favorably or unfavorably. Such policies gain power by acting on two levels at once. The more immediately visible is the level on which policies implemented by the United States act to change the availability and costs of international financing, the strength of world markets, the terms of import restrictions and acceptable export promotion, and in general the conditions of the external economic environment. The less visible, but at least equally important, is the level on which the United States either directly through its own actions, or indirectly through its leading rule in the international financing and development institutions, exerts pressures to shape the economic strategies of the Latin American countries themselves.

On the first level, it is clearly possible to foster relatively favorable conditions by helping to reduce debt burdens, to promote expansion of international financing, to support growth of world demand, and to allow open access to U.S. markets for Latin American exports. Many questions need to be considered even on this level: hardly any positive move comes without some offsetting problem. But the tougher questions may apply to the second level, that of the goals and methods involved in trying to reshape the economic strategies of the Latin American countries.

Something of the difficulty of being sure exactly what kinds of economic strategy help and what do not is suggested by the radically different orientation of changes sought by the United States in the two periods of most active attempts to influence Latin American economic policies, in the 1960s with the Alliance for Progress and in the 1980s. In the 1960s the objectives included support for government programs to promote industrialization, for economic planning, for land reform and other social programs, and for more effective tax systems intended to support high levels of government economic activity. In the 1980s the main objectives were to get Latin American governments out of intervention in the economy, to reduce taxation in order to favor the private sector, to promote trade liberalization and privatization, and to discourage government spending on social programs and subsidies in the names of efficiency and fiscal responsibility. Each of these contradictory general directions probably included some helpful and some unhelpful components. Which are which, for what countries under what conditions?

The central theme of this discussion is that questions of the effects of U.S. policies on the survival of democracy require directing particular attention to the *character* of economic growth in Latin America, and in particular to the degree to which the gains of growth are widely shared, as distinct from concern with effects on efficiency and the rate of growth of national income. The underlying hypothesis is that a democratic system must include the majority of the country in the gains of growth if the system is to maintain public acceptance. If practically all the gains of growth go to a minority, if major groups in the society are left out, the chances of sustainable democracy are squeezed down to a narrow path between two opposing tensions: between efforts of the upper-income minority to protect their advantages, and efforts of the left-out groups (and of those sympathetic with them) to overturn the inequitable system. The economic side of Latin American difficulties with maintaining democracy is rooted in the fact that structural characteristics of many of these economies make normal market forces work in exceptionally unequal ways. Economic policies that are desirable from the viewpoint of economic efficiency and growth, and in the interests of upper-income groups, become instruments of aggravated inequality and therefore adverse for democracy.

The first section in this chapter explains the basic thesis that common structural characteristics of Latin American economies systematically weaken the chances for democracy, by turning normal market forces in directions adverse for wide participation in the gains of growth. These structural conditions set up direct conflicts between the chances for democracy and the free-market economic strategy that the United States is promoting as a requirement for external financial assistance. In the next two sections, this thesis is applied to some historical examples of U.S. economic policies affecting these countries from the 1940s to the 1970s, and then in the 1980s. A concluding section considers what the United States might be able to do now to foster economic conditions likely to improve the prospects for democracy in Latin America.

Relationships between Economic Structures and Political Outcomes

In the northern industrialized countries, it is a reasonable expectation that free markets and political freedom serve in many respects to reinforce each other. In most of Latin America, to varying degrees in different countries, it is not. The central reason why it is not is that structural factors common in Latin American conditions make the operation of market forces exceptionally adverse for equality. When the preferences of the majority can be expressed in any effective way, they understandably favor intervention to block the operation of market forces or to change property rights. Such intervention could strengthen democracy if it is well directed and the costs are kept down, but if the costs become too high in terms of instability and blocked growth, or of threats to property rights, the middle and upper classes turn against democracy to protect themselves. Sustained support for democracy requires that both the poor and the nonpoor can see it working in their interests. If either side has good grounds for the belief that it does not, democracy will be widely regarded at best as a readily disposable value and at worst as a threat.

Efforts by the United States to improve the chances of democracy in Latin America are more likely to be successful if they are guided by concern for the specific difficulties of the Latin American economies, and less likely to be successful if they are dominated by the objective of promoting reliance on private enterprise and free markets. The themes of liberalization and privatization emphasized in the Baker and Brady plans of the 1980s, and by the International Monetary Fund and the World Bank, include both potentially helpful and potentially damaging possibilities.[1] Many Latin American governments have hurt their own economies and unnecessarily aggravated strains on democracy through ill-directed intervention or lack of concern for macroeconomic consistency, and some aspects of the policy changes sought by the United States could help lessen such damage. The problem is that an uncompromising insistence on accepting market forces in the name of efficiency and growth is highly likely to aggravate existing degrees of inequality and tear down support for any democratic system identified with this result.

The basic economic characteristics that have worked against equality in many Latin American countries have been high concentrations of property ownership, and of access to capital and to skills, in the context of relatively abundant unskilled labor and a rapidly growing labor force. Rapid growth of the labor force relative to land and to opportunities for productive employment exerts downward pressure on earnings of the majority of workers, with high shares of income going to owners of property and to the minority with specialized skills. Concentration of ownership itself then further accentuates the inequality related in the first place to the balance among factors of production.[2] Structures of production and trade can further worsen inequality by favoring export earnings of those who own land and other natural resources and by holding down the growth of the industrial sector through the competition of lower cost imports.

All these economic characteristics are matters of degree and are subject to change. Some changes in the last few decades have been very much for the better. Following the acceleration of rates of growth of population in the first half of the twentieth century, they began to slow down markedly in the 1960s.[3] Historically weak support for public education, except in Costa Rica and the Southern Cone, began to change for the better at about the same time. The secondary-school enrollment ratio for the region—a good index of the share of the population that has some chance of getting valuable skills—was only 14 percent in 1960. By 1981 it had risen to 39 percent, a striking improvement but one that still left out the majority.[4]

Although studies of land ownership patterns have consistently shown extraordinarily high concentrations of ownership for most of the countries in the region, land reforms have made significant changes in this pattern in Mexico in the 1930s, Bolivia in the 1950s, Cuba and Nicaragua following their revolutions, and Peru at the end of the 1960s.[5] Concentration of land ownership would not necessarily have any great effects on inequality if rural labor were scarce, and especially if opportunities for productive employment outside of agriculture made it readily possible to move to alternative work. If the number of workers depending on agriculture were decreasing this would be a fairly good sign of positive alternative opportunities. But the long-term trend from 1960 to 1984 showed that only one of the countries with more than 50 percent of the labor force in agriculture in 1960, Colombia, actually reduced the total by 1984. Percentage increases, suggesting worsening pressures on rural incomes, were particularly high in El Salvador and Guatemala (62 percent in each), Honduras (82 percent), and Paraguay (79 percent).[6]

Given such structural conditions, the pattern of international trade when it was relatively uncontrolled, up to the 1930s, probably worsened income distribution. Exports were dominated by primary products generating high returns for owners of land and of minerals. In the twentieth century, rapid growth of the rural labor force aggravated rural poverty, while imports of manufactures held down the potential growth of industrial employment. The first clear exercise of independent Latin American economic strategy, import-substituting industrialization, was aimed at exactly this set of issues. That strategy was highly understandable but not favorable either for equality or for sustained growth. It favored capital-and-skill-intensive structures of production, dependent on imported supplies for production and equipment for investment, accomplishing little to raise employment opportunities. By discouraging exports this strategy increased dependence on borrowing and worsened the region's repeated foreign exchange crisis.

Under the strategy of import substitution, management of exchange rates raised exceptionally intense political conflicts because of their joint effects on production and on the distribution of income. Governments responsive to popular preferences, or more specifically to the preferences of urban workers and industrialists, persistently favored low prices of foreign exchange, and resisted use of devaluation as a means of correcting external deficits, in order to keep down the prices of primary commodities relative to urban wages, and the costs of imported inputs for the industrial sector. But the effect of low-cost foreign exchange is invariably to encourage imports and discourage exports, generating trade deficits that keep rising until they lead to foreign exchange crises.[7] For democratic governments, a corrective response by devaluation and fiscal restraint is always difficult to implement because they run against the immediate interests of protected industrialists and urban labor. For the side of society more concerned with resumption of economic growth, the repeated impasse aggravates impatience with democracy itself, and builds up support for military intervention.

Since the strategy of import substitution under state-led development proved in practice to add to the strains on democracy, the case for a contrary emphasis on liberalization and free markets can have a strong appeal. It must in some respects be better. The problem is that in some respects it may also be worse: conditions of high inequality were built into these economies before the industrialization strategy started, so merely reversing course can hardly be a promising answer. What alternative strategies might work better? That question cannot be answered in the same general terms for all countries: the likely answers depend on the structural characteristics of the economy and the particular dimension of market opening under consideration. Three key dimensions are considered briefly here: trade liberalization, intervention in labor markets, and the use of subsidies to change structures of output or consumption.

To allow the pattern of trade to be determined by comparative advantage in an open economy can be either helpful or harmful for equality, depending mainly on the structural conditions of the particular country. A thorough econometric study by François Bourguignon and Christian Morrisson makes clear that exports have more favorable effects on income distribution for those countries in which skills are well diffused (as measured by high ratios of secondary-school attendance), in which comparative advantage is on the side of labor-intensive industrial exports rather than traditional primary products, and in which land ownership is widely diffused rather than concentrated (as measured by the share of small and medium-sized producers in export crops).[8] On all these counts, Latin American conditions have been adverse: trade liberalization with existing lines of comparative advantage is likely to aggravate inequality.

Adverse structural conditions need not stay that way forever. Latin America's potential for a more favorable export structure has been improving on the score of access to education and skills. For a growing number of countries, selective export promotion has been changing trade structures toward higher shares of industrial products in total exports. Selective export help has also stimulated new nontraditional primary products (such as fruit, vegetables, and seafood) that are often more favorable for labor and less land-intensive than traditional primary products. The chances of using trade policy in ways favorable for equality are increasing. The most promising path in the 1990s would surely be to continue or to intensify promotion of the newer kinds of exports, even when the means have to include intervention going beyond normal market incentives. Concern for employment and income distribution would also argue in favor of maintaining enough protection to make sure that the industrial sector does not get demolished in the meantime, rather than to opt for anything like complete reliance on open markets.

In labor markets, intervention is in general adverse for both efficiency and employment. But the importance of the adverse effects and the consequences for equality and for the survival of democracy may differ greatly according to the context of the economy and the particular forms of intervention. Intervention to raise relative wages of better-organized workers in the formal sector is bound to have adverse effects on marginal workers with lower incomes: it hurts the poor as well as the economy as a whole. But when the economy is characterized by persistent downward pressure on wages of unskilled workers, with rising ratios of labor to land and a rapidly growing labor force, to leave the course of wages up to determination by markets may imply indefinitely increasing poverty even when the economy as a whole is growing. It is difficult to believe that a democratic society could long survive in a context juxtaposing rising incomes at the high end with worsening conditions for a substantial minority, or even the majority. To combine criteria of efficiency and of achieving wide participation in the gains of growth involves difficult issues of balancing goals that may for a long period run contrary to each other. Without going into all these issues here, a goal of achieving more participatory growth argues for intervention in labor markets to raise the incomes of lower-income workers by at least the rate at which national income per capita is increasing, if normal market forces are not by themselves achieving such a result.[9]

A more efficient way to seek the same goal—to raise real earnings in line with national income—could be to use extramarket redistribution as distinct from action on wage rates. Extramarket redistribution could take the form of progressive taxation to finance general social programs directed toward reduction of poverty, or more specific forms of subsidies to small farmers to increase production of basic foods consumed mainly by low-income groups, and to low-income consumers on the buying side.[10] Such methods can lessen poverty without any necessity of raising wage costs, and therefore should be more favorable both for employment and for the possibility of generating labor-intensive exports. But subsidies require offsetting taxation to protect macroeconomic balance: the main obstacle in practice may well be the political resistance of the upper-income groups to progressive taxation. If that resistance could be at least partially overcome through competition for votes within a democratic system, there would be little or no case for intervention in wage setting; if it cannot, then such intervention could become a positive component of policies to support democracy.

What does all this mean in terms of U.S. pressures to alter Latin Ameri can economic strategies? In general terms, it means that the kinds of changes that would be desirable to support democracy do not line up in any neat way with questions of favoring or opposing liberalization and reliance on free-market forces. Promotion of labor-intensive export industries, and a shift of investment away from highly capital-intensive industries that can survive only with high rates of protection, should help improve employment opportunities and reduce inequality. But that pattern is not the one likely to emerge under anything like all-out trade liberalization because existing comparative advantages in most Latin American countries go in different directions, toward patterns of trade adverse for equality. Similarly, it should be helpful to break away from the kinds of intervention in labor markets that help raise relative earnings of higher-wage workers, but it could hurt badly to leave wages completely up to market forces when the latter act to block any gains in earnings of low-income workers. Subsidies to change incentives and the structure of output can go badly wrong, but it may very well be helpful to provide selective subsidies for output and consumption of foods basic for the poor. Generalized pressure for liberalization and privatization can include some advantages, but may include even more significant disadvantages if the intent is not just to favor growth but, perhaps more important for the sake of helping democracy survive, to favor more participatory societies.

Conflicts in U.S. Policies: From the 1940s to the 1970s

At the start of the postwar period the orientation of U.S. international economic policies provided basically favorable conditions for growth and change in Latin America but at the same time embodied several characteristics that threatened trouble. The favorable conditions were firm support for the new international economic institutions created to help stabilize the world economy, provision of aid for Western European recovery followed by more limited aid for developing countries, and promotion of reductions in trade barriers by the industrialized countries. Two of the problematic factors at the time, and since, were a consistent goal of promoting U.S.-style free-market economic systems no matter what the public preferences or the structural characteristics of other countries, and a growing determination to stamp out any signs of Communist influence, however marginal the influence in the particular case.[11]

For the Truman administration, and for a high proportion of subsequent decision makers, Latin American economic development was a desirable goal both in its own right and as a means to favor more stable societies, less drawn toward the radical left. But the goals that looked jointly reinforcing often proved to be contradictory.[12] The dominant goal of blocking Communism ran against an otherwise promising wish to promote structural reforms, in particular land reform. A growing emphasis on military aid, focused on curbing the radical left (or anyone else who might be mistaken for part of the radical left), reinforced the conservative side within all these countries. It almost surely lessened the willingness of those with all the privileges to negotiate changes toward more participatory societies. On the one hand, the United States offered help to countries wanting to implement changes intended to lessen inequality; on the other hand, it provided powerful support for those within the societies determined to prevent exactly such changes.

The U.S. preference for promoting private enterprise and free markets played a less important role in this period than it was to play in the 1980s. It was manifested in strong support for U.S. investors in any conflicts with host governments, and clearly reduced the scope for national choice in such matters, but it was not extended to a dogmatic position requiring generalized liberalization and privatization as conditions of external credit. The more fundamental problem, of which this was simply a particular manifestation, proved to be the basic conflict between provision of long-term aid and the hope for more independent societies with a sense of capacity to control their own destinies.

Conflict between cold war concerns and support of either structural reforms or democracy in Latin America proved particularly destructive in the first major postwar confrontation, in Guatemala in the 1950s. The newly established democracy in that country started off with a wide range of structural reforms, including land reform. But the interests of a U.S. corporation as the largest landowner in the country, and the fears of the Eisenhower administration about the possible influence of Marxists in the land reform agency, led the United States to put together an invasion by dissident Guatemalan military, a precursor of more such methods to come. The invasion overturned the government, ended democracy in Guatemala, and insured the reversal of land reform.[13] It also insured more than three decades of violent repression in Guatemala, and weakened whatever chances may have existed for nonviolent reform in Central America.

Subsequent efforts through the U.S. aid program to promote agricultural development in Guatemala, and throughout Latin America, have often raised the question of whether advisors working on the basis of U.S. education and experience can provide effective help. That question is given a bitterly negative answer by William and Elizabeth Paddock in a book based on their personal experience in Guatemala: We Don't Know How.[14] The negative answer includes widely applicable issues, but the underlying problem in the particular case may have been less a matter of the technical character of aid and more a matter of having eliminated the kind of government interested in the welfare of the Guatemalan people.

Conflicts between the dominant theme of blocking Communist influence and the secondary goals of promoting structural reform and more participatory societies worsened in the early years of the Alliance for Progress. The much more activist U.S. presence in the 1960s blended increasing military and intelligence operations with increased economic aid. "The number of U.S. government personnel assigned to Latin America jumped, crowding the suburbs of various Latin American capitals with embassy offices, technicians, and cultural and military advisers, and dotting the countryside with Peace Corps volunteers and military special forces."[15] The new activism included sending U.S. Marines to the Dominican Republic to protect the more reactionary side of the military, our side, against a popular uprising and that part of the military trying to restore a democratically elected reformist president. It also included sending U.S. naval forces to Brazil in 1964, just in time to provide possible backup for a military uprising that overturned democracy there.

Whether the economic side of the Alliance for Progress had any potential to strengthen democracy in Latin America can seem an almost irrelevant question, given the accompanying military-strategic interventions counter to democracy. But the Brazilian case helps bring out a general question about the role of economic aid in its own right, a question that applies to many specific issues. This is the possibility that the very existence of a significant aid program, subject to unilateral change or interruption by the United States, can work against the survival of democratic governments.

The context in Brazil immediately preceding the overturn of democracy provides a good illustration of the points discussed in the first section. In the 1950s the country was a fairly spectacular success story in terms of economic growth, and a notable example of the kind of growth that fosters rising inequality. It had a large reserve of unskilled and very low-income labor in agriculture, and did little to provide rural education even at the primary level. The abundance of unskilled labor, backed up in the rural sector with low productivity and earnings, helped hold down wages despite rapid growth. As the hypothesis presented earlier suggests, this inequality-enhancing system was rejected in the first election, that of 1960, in which a populist leader could run on a platform promising radical change. The new government introduced proposals for land reform and tax reforms, went out of its way to support organization of rural labor, and changed the treatment of foreign investors by restricting withdrawal of profits. It also increased social welfare spending despite rising inflation. Foreign investment slowed down greatly. The U.S. aid program, which had been helping to fuel the prior process of unequal growth, was stopped as a protest against economic mismanagement. With many other factors in the picture, including anti–United States statements on foreign policy by the populist government, an uprising by the Brazilian military in 1964 swept the democratic government off the scene in a manner scarcely more dignified than that of Guatemala.[16] To make the message clear, the new military government was warmly welcomed by the economist serving as U.S. ambassador to Brazil, and the aid program was immediately reactivated to serve this more responsible client.

To cut off economic aid to a bungling democratic government may be meant to force that government to adopt more coherent economic policies, but it can be heard as a statement that the government itself should be removed. To restore aid promptly and enthusiastically to a repressive military government that understands the statement in the latter sense could easily be seen as something of an invitation to the military forces of the Southern Cone in the following decade.

When an aid program has been helping to maintain a process of economic growth that is highly valued by private investors, and the program is then shut down as an expression of U.S. disapproval, it is hard to avoid fostering a conviction among private investors, and property owners generally, that they have a strong interest in changing the government. By the same token, the existence of an aid program that may be stopped can serve as a restraint on the ability of democratic governments to respond to popular preferences This was notably true in this period for the sensitive issue of policies toward foreign investment. Two notable cases in the 1960s were the failure of President Belaunde in Peru to take promised action to change the privileges of the International Petroleum Company, and the failure of President Frei in Chile to respond to popular pressures for nationalization of the U.S.-owned copper companies.[17] In Peru, when Belaunde backed away from promised action he was swiftly deposed by a populist military government that nationalized the company in question. In Chile Frei's refusal to act cost his Christian Democratic party considerable popular support, making it easier for Allende to win the next election and gain wide approval by nationalizing the companies anyway. Belaunde and Frei might have refused to follow popular pressures even if they had not faced the probability that action against the companies could mean the end of external aid. But if there is any substantial aid program going on, and it can be stopped immediately by the offended donor, the freedom of democratic government to respond to popular pressures is almost necessarily restricted.

It seems evident that aid programs can and often do aggravate dependency, restricting the choices and weakening the legitimacy of democratic governments. But this is only one aspect of a complex set of possibilities. They can conceivably strengthen democratic governments by helping them to solve specific problems and to correct some of the structural factors that make for inequitable growth. Their effects on public support for existing democracy can be positive in the right conditions, just as they can be negative in the wrong conditions. If the government is trying to carry out changes that work to favor more equitable growth, external aid can serve both as evidence of external support and as direct financial assistance. This is a context totally different from the connotation of subservience when the threat of reduced aid is used to force governments away from desired changes. Some of the mixture of positive and negative possibilities may be illuminated by conflicting strands in the experiences of Colombia in this period.

In the first years of the Alliance for Progress Colombia was a newly restored democracy, under the National Front coalition government. The main objective of the first two presidents under this agreement was to stabilize a political system torn apart by violence in the preceding two decades, rather than to implement any major changes in the economy. But land reform was a particularly live issue. The country's political leadership had long been divided between those who saw it as a way to incorporate peasant support in a more participatory political system, and those who saw it instead as an attack on the elite's traditional base of wealth and political power. U.S. support for such reform in the 1960s provided the extra push needed to tilt the balance toward adoption of a land reform program.[18] Actual results were very limited at first, under the conservative administration in office from 1962 to 1966. A U.S. review of progress in the first years of the Alliance for Progress brought out a dismal picture: the economy was drifting, little or nothing had changed, inequality had probably increased, and the effects of the aid program looked pitiful.[19]

Just at the time that this evaluation of the aid program was prepared, a new Colombian president, Carlos Lleras Restrepo, began to make significant changes in the country's economic strategy. He gave more emphasis to implementation of land reform, revised economic policies toward promotion of employment and new exports, began a shift away from protection as the means of promoting industrialization, and adopted a new exchange rate system to restructure incentives in support of these goals. Economic growth and industrialization speeded up, employment increased even more rapidly, and incomes of the previously left-out rural poor began to gain relative to the rest of the society.[20] The new economic strategy was very much helped in the first instance by the country's favorable treatment under the aid program, and that help did not preclude effective action by the national government. In fact, improvement of export earnings and the growing strength of the economy raised national self-confidence to the point that Colombia took the highly unusual step of deciding in 1975 to renounce any further reliance on economic aid.

The happier side of this experience in terms of reducing poverty and strengthening national autonomy was unfortunately followed by a halt to land reform under the president following Lleras Restrepo. The immediate cause was a problem common to almost any major break in economic and social relationships: a promised change beginning to take place stimulated pressures for faster and more complete reform. The radical side of the peasant movement began to seize land directly, landowners and the police responded violently, and the national political leadership caved in to the fear that revolutionary forces were becoming explosive. The leaders of the two traditional parties agreed to bury any further action under the land reform program and to apply repression to get rid of radical leadership in the peasant movement.[21] It was not the United States that turned off the land reform; it was the nation's political leaders. Still, it might have been relevant that the United States was by then no longer in the business of providing support for land reform but was more than ever in the business of providing military support. The military side became the main Colombian answer to demands for land reform. That change coincided with a sharp upturn of violence, a turn that has not since been reversed.

These experiences in Colombia support a two-sided view of the effects of a reform-oriented aid program: such a program will not be much help, if any, under a government that does not particularly want reform, and may even weaken pressures to take positive measures, but it can reinforce the efforts of governments that want to accomplish changes toward lessened inequality. The balance may have been on the negative side in the 1960s, but it need not be that way for an aid program more specifically designed to help implement programs of governments that are genuinely trying to create more equitable economic systems. And even in the conflict-ridden 1960s, it is possible that U.S. aid improved the chances for more equitable growth. This was the key decade for the long-delayed demographic transition toward family planning and lower fertility rates, promising eventually better conditions in labor markets throughout the region. It was also a key decade in terms of greatly increased efforts to widen access to education, and thereby to increase the share of the labor force likely to be able to enter fields requiring higher skills and paying higher wages. It seems at least likely that U.S. financial and technical support made the changes easier to implement, spread their effects more quickly, and in these respects contributed positively to the chances of greater equity.

The decade of the Alliance for Progress turned out to be one in which the share of the Latin American population living in conditions of poverty was considerably reduced. For the nine countries covered in a research study by the Economic Commission for Latin America, the percentage of people below the commission's specified poverty line fell from 51 percent in 1960 to 40 percent by 1970. Using an alternative measure of people below a much more stringent line of "destitution," the percentage fell from 26 percent in 1960 to 19 percent in 1970.[22] These reductions could be considered too slow to make any great difference in acceptability of existing political systems but at least they go in the right direction. Relatively generous aid in this period must have helped in some degree to make living conditions less awful for many people.

The contradictory effects of the Alliance for Progress do not suggest either that a reform-oriented aid program is useless or that it can be counted on to have strong positive effects on equity and the chances of democracy. The observed shift toward authoritarian governments in so many countries during and after the alliance seems much more closely associated with the cold war, with the military side of U.S. policies toward the region, than with the economic aid program. But it is also true that an aid program has a major potential for harm, by strengthening the conservative side of the society receiving aid and by enabling weak governments to postpone efforts for change. At the same time, it had the positive potential of supporting a considerable range of changes favorable for lower-income groups, and some of that potential was actually realized. The experience does not argue for any return to a regionwide program providing large-scale assistance for all countries that want it, regardless of whether their governments are reformist, reactionary, or simply inactive. But it does argue for something of the generosity of the economic side of the alliance, and for willingness to help with specific reforms that can change economic structures in ways favorable for more participatory growth.

Influences on Latin America of U.S. Economic Policies in the 1980s

The severely deflationary policies of the United States from 1978 to 1982 (and of England at the same time) hit Latin American economies hard by worsening their export markets, driving down prices of primary commodities, and driving up interest rates on their external debts. When the debt crisis broke out in 1982 and new private credit was almost completely cut off, that forced the region into contraction with falling investment, deteriorating public services, and accelerating inflation.[23] If the countries had not borrowed too much when external credit was cheap and plentiful in the 1970s, they need not have been hit this hard; if the United States had pursued more stable monetary policies, and especially if its own fiscal deficit had been reduced sharply when the economy recovered after 1982, the strains on Latin America could also have been much less than they were. It took both sides to make things go as badly wrong as they did.

When the United States and the other industrialized countries use contractionary policies to counteract inflationary trends, they certainly affect the developing countries but the effects are not necessarily negative. If such policies help stabilize the world economy, without creating recession, they could be positive for all sides. It was exactly this issue of maintaining overall balance in the world economy that led to the creation of the International Monetary Fund (IMF) in the first place, to provide credit to countries hit by falling external demand in order to prevent cumulative contraction. In line with this objective, most of the industrialized countries supported a major increase in lending facilities for the IMF and the World Bank at the start of the 1980s, to enable them to help the developing countries deal with recessionary world conditions. But that movement ran counter to the U.S. administration's ideological preference to leave the world economy up to private market forces. The administration fought to hold down any increases in lending power for the international financial institutions, and at the same time used its position within them to exert pressure to tighten up conditions for any new loans. The choice was to use the financial crisis to force a particular set of preferences on debtor countries.

For better or worse, the United States rarely speaks with a single voice. While the administration was resisting proposals for positive steps to deal with the strains on the world economy, the Federal Reserve responded swiftly to the Mexican government's announcement, in August 1982, that it could not maintain scheduled payments on its debts. The Federal Reserve took a leading role in negotiations for emergency credit, and quickly changed the direction of U.S. monetary policy to relieve tightness in world financial markets. The change helped considerably to reduce interest costs for Latin American debtors, but the Federal Reserve's room to move in the direction of monetary expansion and lower interest rates was simultaneously restricted by the administration's macroeconomic policies, or more specifically by its determined effort to force down the role of government by cutting taxes. The series of budget deficits, understandable and desirable in the depressed economic conditions of 1980–82, turned into a persistent factor operating to keep real interest rates relatively high throughout the rest of the decade. The effect on debtor countries was to keep the costs of debt service higher than it would otherwise have been, contributing to pressures for nonpayment in some cases and to severer domestic contraction than would otherwise have been necessary. The poor of Latin America—and much of the middle class as well—were forced to help pay the cost of rising consumption, stimulated by tax reductions, in the United States.

For the world economy as a whole, one of the most important consequences of the budget deficit and associated high interest rates was that international capital began to flow into the United States on a large scale. That had complex effects in many directions, including rapid appreciation of the dollar, swiftly rising imports in response, and intense pressures by U.S. firms to tighten import restrictions.[24] The administration resisted these pressures to some degree but still increased import restrictions through quotas and by exerting pressure on exporting countries to adopt "voluntary export restraints." The controls were aimed mainly at exporters from the Far East but they included tighter restraints on consumer products in which many Latin American countries might have been able to compete, as well as steel for which both Brazil and Mexico were becoming effective competitors. The inescapable effect of blocking some of the key exports otherwise possible for Latin American countries, in conditions of desperate need for foreign exchange earnings, was to exert greater downward pressure on wages in order to become competitive in other products.

U.S. policies on international financial questions gradually turned for the better as the debt crisis wore on. The administration reversed its initial resistance to expansion of lending power by the international institutions, and in the Baker and then the Brady plans began to give at least official support, if little actual money, to the idea that Latin America needed new external credit to resume growth. The more positive thesis became that renewed growth is essential in order to pay for debt service out of rising incomes rather than by grinding down living standards. Although external financing has been extremely modest so far, the change at least suggests recognition that extramarket help for growth is linked to the chances for more sustainable democracies.

In another promising change, the U.S. government quietly toned down its position that exchange rates and interest rates should be left up to private financial markets. Old clichés never die, but the United States began to take an active role in promoting coordination among the major industrial countries to limit conflicts over policies toward exchange rates and monetary conditions, to promote joint consideration of needs for either expansion or restraint of world demand, and to emphasize the needs of the developing countries for greater flows of new credit. The dangers implicit in such coordination by a few of the rich countries, without a voice for the rest of the world, are clear enough to invite debate about how to handle the objective in more participatory ways. But coordination itself, insofar as it reduces the violence of swings in world demand, in the terms of trade of developing countries, and in the conditions of external credit, could in principle do a great deal to lessen the kinds of shocks that have repeatedly upset whatever degree of economic stability Latin American countries have been able to achieve.

Economic Policies to Support Latin American Democracy in the 1990s

The implications of the preceding discussion might be summarized in terms of three groups of questions: first, external debts, conditions of international finance in general, and the ways in which U.S. macroeconomic policies affect those conditions; second, issues of international trade, including protection on both sides and positions toward export subsidies by Latin American countries; and third, the kinds of economic policy changes within Latin America that are encouraged or discouraged by conditions attached to credit either from the United States or from the international institutions in which it plays a major policy-determining role.

Debt and External Finance

Had the Latin American countries been relieved of the burden of external debt in 1982, when the extreme costs of servicing it first became evident, poverty would be less than it is now, employment and output would be higher, greater investment through the 1980s would have provided greater scope for growth in the 1990s, the extremes of inflation sweeping many countries would be much less likely, and democratic governments would probably have stronger public support. On the other side, so to speak, the creditors would have had to find some solution to their loss of financial assets, it is possible that some of the nondemocratic governments that have been replaced in the 1980s might still be holding on, the stimulus to more active opposition parties and possibly more meaningful democracy evident at present in Brazil and Mexico might be weaker, the measures taken under pressure to increase government revenue and reduce inefficiency would have been less likely, and the widespread shift of the region toward development of more diversified exports—and therefore to potentially greater autonomy—would also have been weakened. It is easy to vote in favor of eliminating the debt, but not all its consequences have been negative.

One of the best things that could happen to Latin America would be to learn to live without reliance on external credit. That could force a greater effort to develop domestic sources for capital equipment and inputs into production, encourage the search for domestic technological solutions, and keep up pressure for more diversified exports. Too much and too easy external credit fosters excessive dependence on foreign goods and foreign methods, and lessens pressures for efficiency and for change of any kind. In the words of Alejandro Foxley, the impossibility now of "depending, as in the past, on high levels of external credit would make it possible for Latin America's new leaders to launch an appeal for large-scale nationwide mobilization to solve the debt crisis through domestic savings and internal efforts."[25]

Foxley does not go on to conclude that the present context is optimal in such respects: it is not in fact one of independent growth but instead of near stagnation due in part to the costs of transferring resources to creditors. The intensity of the squeeze on Latin America might be measured by the change from a net resource inflow equal to 3 percent of gross domestic product (GDP) in 1981 to a net resource outflow equal to 6 percent of GDP by 1985.[26] Output per capita, consumption, and investment have all been driven down. Consumption per capita in 1988 was 9 percent lower than in 1980. Investment had averaged 23 percent of GDP for 1970–79, was driven down to 16 percent for 1983–87, and then barely edged back to 17 percent in 1988.[27] The burdens of dealing with the debts in a context of excessive constraint on new credit were clearly too great to allow reactivation of Latin America's capacity for economic growth.

More independent growth requires raising the share of output that can be exported, but to get the extreme inflation rates in Argentina, Brazil, and Peru under control, and to keep inflation from turning up again in Mexico, that objective may need to be made conditional on prior macroeconomic stabilization.[28] Stabilization requires first of all that the countries control their primary fiscal deficits (the deficits for domestic spending as distinct from purchases of foreign exchange to pay service requirements on the debts). But it would be greatly helped by reductions in required debt service to reduce both those domestic financing requirements and the need to generate a trade surplus to earn foreign exchange for external payments.

Negotiations over debt service included for several years a requirement by the IMF that countries continue making interest payments to the commercial banks as a condition of new IMF credit. A key change promoted by the United States, meant only for the special case but still significant, was to come to the rescue of the Bolivian stabilization program by permitting, or inducing, the IMF to stop insisting on this condition. That change made it possible to avoid continuing devaluations aimed at pushing additional exports to get the foreign exchange needed for the interest payments.[29] It allowed Bolivia to concentrate on efforts to stop inflation, uncomplicated by the contrary policy of export promotion. So far at least this approach—coupled with the essential counterpart of restraint on spending in Bolivia itself—has been one of the few instances of success in stopping hyperinflation. How all this will affect democracy remains most uncertain: everyone welcomed the striking success in slowing inflation, but not the accompanying rise in unemployment and fall in real wages. In this case, with poverty levels so extreme and democracy so new, aid that provided net new resources linked to alleviation of poverty might make a great difference.

If inflationary pressures return in the United States, that will rightly call for greater restraint on domestic spending. But the degree to which such a change would hurt debtor countries can be very different according to whether the restraint comes through taxes and reduced government spending or through restrictive monetary policies. To apply restraint on the monetary side alone maximizes the costs to debtor countries. Tax cuts in the United States in the 1980s, not matched by reductions in government spending, increased domestic consumption and had the counterpart effect of reducing living standards and growth in poorer countries. The United States and the international financial institutions are right to insist on the need for more responsible fiscal policy in Latin America; it would be in Latin America's own interest. But the world needs more of a two-way kind of pressure: fiscal irresponsibility by the United States can worsen poverty and destroy macroeconomic balance abroad.

Trade Policies

U.S. policies toward the use of protection and export subsidies by Latin American countries have had increasingly important effects in the 1980s, partly because their heightened need for credit has forced them to pay more attention to conditions established by the international lending institutions, partly because the United States has taken a tougher line within these institutions, and partly because it has adopted more aggressive bilateral negotiating techniques with greater use of retaliatory import restrictions. These pressures respond to real problems of trade restrictions abroad, but the more that the U.S. government gives in to them the more difficult it becomes for Latin American countries to restore growth of income and employment.

To exert strong pressure on Latin American countries to liberalize imports, while deliberalizing them in the United States, is not the kind of policy stance to make one glow with pride. But it is true that past excesses of protection have reduced efficiency and have probably worsened inequality by sheltering monopolistic firms, so reductions in protection clearly could have positive effects. They could be especially significant for actual or potential export industries, if the latter are released from excess costs imposed by being forced to get inputs from protected domestic suppliers. The overall effect would be to drive structures of production closer to the existing pattern of national comparative advantage. If comparative advantage includes a significant share of competitive export industries, as it does in East Asia and now in Brazil as well, the net effect could be to open up better possibilities for growth. Where the underlying pattern of relative costs is on the contrary more favorable to exports of primary products and imports of most industrial goods, then the net result could be to worsen both the distribution of income and the chances of future growth.

A return to comparative advantage could have seriously negative effects because of the structural characteristics explained in the chapter's first section: concentrated ownership of land and other natural resources, combined with growing ratios of labor to land and downward pressure on wages. If increased imports of industrial products act to reduce industrial employment, the most likely consequence is not a rise in more efficient alternative lines of production but a worsening of employment conditions. More positive results would be possible if industrial exports could be promoted through selective incentives, including subsidies. This type of export strategy was a central feature in the dynamic, and relatively egalitarian, styles of postwar economic growth in Japan, Korea, and Taiwan. Export subsidies can have adverse effects when they are given to inappropriate industries, when they are not financed by taxation to offset effects on the budget, or when they reduce the supply of goods because imports are not raised as fast as exports are increased. They need to be kept within a ceiling of maximum stimulus, to be financed by taxation, and to be used for increasing supplies of imports to keep up the growth of supplies for domestic use. Given such conditions, subsidies for industrial exports could be a potent help for any semi-industrialized developing country, including many countries in Latin America.

Relationships between promotion of nontraditional exports and income distribution have two important aspects: (1) if rapid growth of employment can be fostered by promotion of labor-intensive exports, the effects on real wages and income distribution are bound to become positive eventually; but (2), the initial effects on real wages in the formal sector may be negative and, if conditions of excess labor are extremely adverse, these negative effects may continue for a long time. The consequences depend on the degree of initial imbalance, the labor intensity of new exports, and the speed of their growth. Possible conclusion: it would be very much worthwhile to move the structure of production in the right direction for sustained increases in real wages by promoting industrial exports, but negative effects in the first stage point to the need for complementary social expenditure policies to keep up living standards of the poor until market forces become sufficiently positive.

U.S. Pressures on Latin American Economic Strategies

Mutually helpful relationships between the United States and Latin American governments are not likely to be furthered by using a period of intense need for external credit on their part as the time to demand that they remake their economic systems in the U.S. image. Some aspects of liberalization and privatization may be desirable in their interest, and more attention to macroeconomic balance is certainly in their interest, but to insist on detailed internal changes as the price of credit is not in the interest of either side. Negative effects are likely in part because many of the changes that the United States has been trying to sell in recent years would worsen inequality and for that reason could weaken democracy. Negative results are also likely because using a period of extreme financial need to force countries to swallow unwelcome medicine (as distinct from choosing it freely by their own decisions) demeans the governments concerned and sets up a good case for reversal of such policies in the future. Democracies need a minimum of self-confidence and self-value if they are to hold together in the face of strains. To build up such confidence by providing external conditions that help their economic systems function better would be a clear gain. To insist that they change their systems is not.

The central thesis of the chapter's introductory section is that the free operation of market forces acting through private enterprise is in common Latin American conditions systematically adverse to equality and to the minimal levels of personal security necessary for public acceptance of democratic governments. Informed voters will, if given the chance, consistently get rid of governments that follow the main lines of economic policy on which the United States has in the 1980s tried to insist. Our style of economics is not at present favorable for democracy in Latin America.

The other side of the coin is that particular *kinds* of economic strategy frequently practiced by Latin American governments can be just as bad or worse for equality and growth than our free-market themes. Overvalued exchange rates can hurt industrialization and employment by blocking potential industrial exports and by making imports too cheap; fiscal deficits in conditions of supply shortages and inflationary pressure aggravate inflation and turn the public against any democratic government; and high protection for particular firms may worsen inequality at the same time as it wastes resources and takes away the possibility of competition that could help restrain inflation. Changes made from common past practices in these respects, or more generally an increase in attention to the need for both external and internal macroeconomic balance, should be helpful for Latin American economies and strengthen rather than hurt the survival chances of democracies.

The scope for gain by specific changes in economic policies does not mean that it is desirable to insist on reducing the economic role of government in general, either for support to increase economic growth or for efforts to lessen inequality. The case for relying more on market forces is superficially strong because of the multitude of self-inflicted forms of past damage, under both authoritarian and democratic regimes. But the underlying structural context is one in which positive action is essential if growth is to be more equal. The main problem is not government action per se; what counts is the basic set of purposes and the methods that governments actually use. Given a democratic government truly interested in more equitable growth, it can do more to pursue that objective if it has a strong tax base; participates actively in shaping incentives for investment; can keep up its own investment in education, infrastructure, and social programs in general; and can use subsidies when appropriate both for social purposes and for stimulation of new industries and new exports. If by any succession of miracles Latin America is blessed with democratic governments that want to move in directions of more equitable growth, they should be encouraged and helped to act, not discouraged.

Conclusions

Economic conditions do not dictate political outcomes. One of the most promising and in many ways surprising characteristics of both new and established Latin American democracies in the 1980s was the resilience they displayed in the face of severely adverse economic conditions. The strains helped stimulate increased political awareness and activism, but in most cases this has been a positive activism through participation rather than a return toward mutual destruction.[30] That strengthened flexibility may be related to an increase in the value that many Latin Americans place on the survival of democracy.[31] Given greater concern to negotiate solutions acceptable to conflicting interests, response to economic adversity may serve to build up confidence in national ability to handle problems peacefully. But economic strains do not go away just because conflicting groups within societies try to cooperate: it is also essential both that they adopt workable economic strategies and that the outside world does not create intolerably adverse conditions.

The United States can help by providing more resources to alleviate current strains, by promoting greater stability in world economic conditions, by turning back from the trend of the 1980s toward increased protectionism, and by paying more attention to the negative consequences of trying to force on everyone else its own preference for private market solutions. A fundamental change for the better might just possibly be developing now. The United States "may be released from a great fear: the fear of communism that has dominated American society for so long."[32] For relationships with Latin America, that fear has led to persistent reinforcement of the side of their societies opposed to change in the interest of equity. It led to the destruction of reformist democracy in Guatemala, poisoned the Alliance for Progress, and encouraged the right-wing military factions that crushed democracy in the Southern Cone.

The most evident economic constraint holding back growth and aggravating inflation in the majority of these countries throughout the past decade has been tight restriction on external credit combined with the burden of service payments on their debts. Latin America has had to transfer resources to the United States ever since 1982, effectively helping to finance spending in excess of production in the United States at the cost of lower investment and living standards in the region, greater inflation, and slow or no growth in per capita income. If the United States were seriously interested in being helpful, it could provide new external credit and share the costs of writing off most of the debt. How could that be financed when the United States itself has a budget deficit and has been running close to the limits of its productive capacity? It could be done by adopting exactly the same kind of fiscal responsibility recommended for the Latin American countries: raise taxes, restrain consumption, offset any fall in demand by monetary expansion, and raise the share of output that is directed to exports.

It hardly needs saying, but clearly needs changed actions, that import restrictions by the United States go directly contrary to the possibilities for stabilization and growth in Latin America. Domestic pressure for such restrictions could be eased by a more competitive exchange rate for the dollar, and that in turn depends on more responsible fiscal policy.

Coordination of macroeconomic and exchange rate policies among the main industrial countries could reduce the violence of swings in aggregate world demand and monetary conditions, and thereby lessen dramatic changes in the terms of trade of developing countries, in the room for growth of exports, in real interest rates, and in the availability of international credit. Coordination requires that the United States responds to advice of other countries on such sensitive questions as fiscal policy and exchange rates. That may be asking too much: advice is easier to give to others than to hear. But any coordination that might be achieved by the industrialized countries could lessen external shocks and thereby raise the chances of successful economic policies for all developing countries.

The changes that the United States has tried to encourage in the economic policies of the Latin American countries include some features that are almost surely desirable for their own ability to control their economies and resume growth, and a good many that are not. The desirable group includes pressures to keep up exchange rates favorable for exports, to reduce extremes of protection, and to make greater efforts to hold down fiscal deficits. The unhelpful side includes opposition to intervention by governments even when it could foster more equitable growth, to subsidies for new exports, and to the kinds of intervention in the price system that could act to lessen poverty and inequality. To drive governments away from such policies in favor of reliance on private market forces could foster more inequity and more strains for democratic government than can possibly be justified by any gains of efficiency.

Pressures to cut down the role of the public sector can readily be understood in terms of frequent waste and costly actions by governments, but the fact that mistakes are common does not mean that weaker governments are desirable. Democratic governments in Latin America, facing severe constraints on all sides, need a high capacity to carry through decisions, to control the operation of market forces in the interest of lessened inequality without blocking efficiency, to impose taxation effectively, and to act in some degree on behalf of the people in these societies who get left out of the growth process. The U.S. preference for a restricted role of government goes in many respects in the wrong direction for the needs of democratic government in Latin America.

Attempts to induce changes in the economic strategies of Latin American countries by conditions attached to debt relief or new credit involve a contradiction between two important principles. One is that provision of access to valuable resources should not be allowed to serve as a prop allowing governments to continue policies that weaken their economic systems, foster inequality, and compromise the future. The second is that the outside world should not force countries to follow paths contrary to the preferences of their people. Even if the prescribed paths are more productive in economic terms, to be forced into a kind of subservience contrary to national values is bound to weaken confidence that democracies can respond to what their people want, and confidence in the value of the nation itself. Both principles have claims to respect. The conflict between them argues for a difficult balancing act, avoiding ideological prescriptions of the kind of economic institutions and strategy that other countries should adopt, while at the same time trying to help implement the specific kinds of structural change needed for more participatory growth.

Notes

1. The U.S. government has avoided, probably wisely, any detailed official statement of what it would mean to conform fully to the call for liberalization and privatization in the Baker and Brady plans. Statements by the International Monetary Fund (IMF) and the World Bank have been frequent, with a consistent core but varied specifics. For two clear but different statements by IMF economists, see Anthony Lanyi, "World Economic Outlook and Prospects for Latin America," and Vito Tanzi, "Fiscal Policy, Growth, and Design of Stabilization Programs," in Ana Maria Martirena-Mantel, ed., *External Debt, Savings, and Growth in Latin America* (Washington, D.C., and Buenos Aires: International Monetary Fund and Instituto Torcuato di Tella, 1987), pp. 26–50 and 121–41.

2. John Sheahan, *Patterns of Development in Latin America: Poverty, Repression, and Economic Strategy* (Princeton: Princeton University Press, 1987), esp. chap. 12.

3. Alan B. Simmons, "Social Inequality and Demographic Transition," in Archibald Ritter and David Pollock, eds., *Latin American Prospects for the 1980s* (New York: Praeger, 1983).

4. World Bank, *World Tables,* 3d ed. (Washington, D.C.: World Bank, 1983), 2: 158–59.

5. Thomas F. Carroll, "The Land Reform Issue in Latin America," in Albert Hirschman, ed., *Latin American Issues: Essays and Comments* (New York: Twentieth Century Fund, 1961); Solon Barraclough, ed., *Agrarian Structures in Latin America* (Lexington, Mass.: Lexington Books, 1973); Alain de Janvry, *The Agrarian Question and Reformism in Latin America* (Baltimore: Johns Hopkins University Press, 1981).

6. Sheahan, *Patterns,* table 3.1, p. 56.

7. This process is traced through for six Latin American countries in Jeffrey Sachs, "Social Conflict and Populist Policies in Latin America," and Rudiger Dornbusch and Sebastian Edwards, "Macroeconomic Populism in Latin America," National Bureau of Economic Research, Working Papers no. 2897 and 2986 (Cambridge, Mass.: National Bureau of Economic Research, 1989).

8. François Bourguignon and Christian Morrisson, *External Trade and Income Distribution* (Paris: OECD, Development Research Centre, 1989).

9. John Sheahan, "Economic Policies and the Prospects for Successful Transition from Authoritarian Rule in Latin America," in Guillermo O'Donnell, Philippe C. Schmitter, and Laurence Whitehead, eds., *Transitions from Authoritarian Rule* (Baltimore: Johns Hopkins University Press, 1986), pp. 154–64.

10. Marita Garcia and Per Pinstrup-Andersen, *The Pilot Food Subsidy Scheme in the Philippines: Its Impact on Income, Food Consumption and Nutritional Status,* Research Report 61 (Washington, D.C.: International Food Policy Research Institute, August 1987); Harold Alderman, *The Effects of Food Price and Income Changes on the Acquisition of Food by Low-Income Households* (Washington, D.C.: International Food Policy Research Institute, 1986).

11. Robert A. Pollard, *Economic Security and the Origins of the Cold War, 1945–1950* (New York: Columbia University Press, 1985).

12. Robert A. Packenham, *Liberal America and the Third World: Political Development Ideas in Foreign Aid and Social Science* (Princeton: Princeton University Press, 1973).

13. Thomas Melville and Marjorie Melville, *Guatemala: The Politics of Land Ownership* (New York: Free Press, 1971); Richard H. Immerman, *The CIA in Guatemala: The Foreign Policy of Intervention* (Austin: University of Texas Press, 1982); Stephen C. Schlesinger and Stephen Kinzer, *Bitter Fruit: The Untold Story of the American Coup in Guatemala* (Garden City, N.Y.: Doubleday, 1982).

14. William Paddock and Elizabeth Paddock, *We Don't Know How: An Independent Analysis of What They Call Success in Foreign Assistance* (Ames: Iowa State University Press, 1973).

15. Abraham Lowenthal, *Partners in Conflict: The United States and Latin America* (Baltimore: Johns Hopkins University Press, 1987), p. 30.

16. Alfred Stepan, "Political Leadership and Regime Breakdown," in Juan J. Linz and Alfred Stepan, eds., *The Breakdown of Democratic Regimes: Latin America* (Baltimore: Johns Hopkins University Press, 1978), pp. 110–37; Phyllis R. Parker, *Brazil and the Quiet Intervention* (Austin: University of Texas Press, 1979); Michael Wallerstein, "The Collapse of Democracy in Brazil: Its Economic Determinants," *Latin American Research Review* 15, no. 3 (1980): 3–40.

17. Sheahan, *Patterns,* pp. 207, 211, 242–43.

18. Merilee Grindle, *State and Countryside: Development Policy and Agrarian Politics in Latin America* (Baltimore: Johns Hopkins University Press, 1986).

19. U.S. Senate, Committee on Foreign Relations, Subcommittee on American Republics Affairs, *Survey of the Alliance for Progress,* Document 17, 91st Congress, 1st Session (12844–2) (Washington, D.C.: U.S. Government Printing Office, 1969).

20. Although these changes in economic strategy were favorable for earnings of the rural poor and of unorganized urban workers, they were initially adverse for real wages in formal urban sector employment. If one focuses on wages versus profits of industrial workers, the changes were initially adverse for equity; if one focuses on relative earnings of the poor, they were favorable. By 1975, real wages of workers in the formal urban sector began to go up too, and recent studies suggest that the overall distribution of income has become less unequal: Miguel Urrutia, *Winners and Losers in Colombia's Economic Growth in the 1970s* (Oxford: Oxford University Press, 1985), and Eduardo Sarmiento, "El desarrollo colombiano: un proceso de desequilibrio," monografía presentada al Simposio internaciónal sobre la obra de Hirschman y una nueva estrategia de desarrollo para América Latina, Buenos Aires, noviembre de 1989.

21. Leon Zamosc, *The Agrarian Question and the Peasant Movement in Colombia* (Cambridge: Cambridge University Press, 1986); Bruce Bagley, "The State and the Peasantry in Contemporary Colombia," *Latin American Issues* 6 (1988): 1–86.

22. Sergio Molina, "La pobreza en América Latina: situación, evolución y orientaciones de políticas," in CEPAL-PNUD, *¿Se puede superar la pobreza en América Latina?* (Santiago: Naciones Unidas, 1980), p. 23.

23. Andrés Bianchi, "Adjustment in Latin America, 1981–86," in Vittorio Corbo, Morris Goldstein, and Mohsin Khan, eds., *Growth-Oriented Adjustment Programs* (Washington, D.C.: International Monetary Fund and World Bank, 1987), pp. 179–225; Inter-American Development Bank, *Economic and Social Progress in Latin America, 1985 Report: External Debt: Crisis and Adjustment* (Washington, D.C.: IDB, 1985), and following *Annual Reports.*

24. Rudiger Dornbusch and Jeffrey A. Frankel, "Macroeconomics and Protection," in Robert M. Stern, ed., *United States Trade Policies in a Changing World* (Cambridge: MIT Press, 1987), pp. 77–130.

25. Alejandro Foxley, "The Foreign Debt Problem from a Latin American Viewpoint," in Richard E. Feinberg and Ricardo Ffrench-Davis, eds., *Development and External Debt: Bases for a New Consensus* (Notre Dame, Ind.: University of Notre Dame Press, 1988), quotation from p. 81.

26. Inter-American Development Bank, *Economic and Social Progress in Latin America, 1988 Report*, p. 5. The net outflow of resources stayed close to 5 percent of GDP through 1986 and 1987.

27. IDB, *1988 Report*, p. 22, and *1989 Report*, pp. 1, 11.

28. Jeffrey Sachs, "Trade and Exchange Rate Policies in Growth-Oriented Adjustment Programs," in Corbo, Goldstein, and Kahn, *Growth-Oriented Adjustment Programs*, pp. 303–7.

29. Ibid., pp. 316–17.

30. Paul Drake, "Debt and Democracy in Latin America, 1920s–1980s," and Robert Kaufman and Barbara Stallings, "Debt and Democracy in the 1980s: The Latin American Experience," in Robert Kaufman and Barbara Stallings, eds., *Debt and Democracy in Latin America* (Boulder, Colo.: Westview Press, 1989), pp. 39–58 and 201–23; Karen Remmer, "The Political Impact of the Debt Crisis in Latin America," Paper presented at the conference on "Financing Latin American Growth: Prospects for the 1990s," Bard College, October 1988.

31. James M. Malloy and Mitchell A. Seligson, eds., *Authoritarians and Democrats: Regime Transition in Latin America* (Pittsburgh: Pittsburgh University Press, 1987), especially the chapter by Silvio Duncan Baretta and John Markoff, "Brazil's *Abertura:* From What to What?", pp. 43–65.

32. Anthony Lewis, "Free at Last?" *New York Times*, November 23, 1989, p. 27.

9 | The Imposition of Democracy

Laurence Whitehead

HISTORY indicates that democracy is quite frequently established by undemocratic means. This is especially true of the history of U.S. foreign relations, which have frequently involved the promotion of democracy by force of arms. France, Italy, Japan, and West Germany all acquired or reacquired democratic institutions under the tutelage of American armed forces. So, the "imposition" of democracy is no contradiction in terms, at least not in the U.S. political tradition. In fact one feature distinguishing the United States from all previously dominant or hegemonic powers is its persistent and self-proclaimed commitment to the promotion of democracy as an integral element of its foreign policy, and its long-standing confidence that "all good things" (U.S. influence and security, economic freedom and prosperity, political liberty and representative government) tend naturally to go together. With such confidence and assertiveness rooted in the American tradition, and with some remarkable successes available as confirmation of their initial intuition, policy makers in Washington are disinclined to believe that "democracy by imposition" is a concept containing any particularly intractable contradictions. On this issue, however, the perceptions of most Latin American policy makers are strikingly different.

For although a democratic regime may originate from an act of external imposition, it will subsequently be necessary to secure the withdrawal of intrusive foreign influences if the democracy is eventually to take root and to secure the trust and acceptance of the national society in question. Unfortunately this intuitively plausible model of the democratization process assumes the prior existence of a well-defined nation-state in which no major problems of national identity remain pending. It also implicitly views the act of imposition as an isolated event, rather than as one episode in a protracted sequence of interactions between a dominant nation and a subordi-

234

nate one. Neither of these assumptions can be safely made in relation to the United States and Latin America, which is why the imposition of democracy in the region has often proved a problematic and frustrating experience. In fact, as discussed in this chapter, the broad notion of "imposition" may embrace a considerable variety of distinctive forms, each with its own logic and consequences. Three variants are considered here: incorporation, invasion, and intimidation.

For most of the present century, and in particular since the 1940s, the United States has occupied a dominant position in the affairs of the Western Hemisphere. Its ascendancy has been not only economic, demographic, and military but also political, ideological, and to some extent even cultural. In contrast to the position of the majority of dominant ("hegemonic") powers in the course of world history, U.S. ascendancy over its neighbors has been underpinned by a series of shared values, traditions, and assumptions. These were all liberal republics, at least in origin and rhetoric; they were all sheltered by the wide Atlantic from the internecine struggles of Europe, a region from which the dominant elites nevertheless drew much of their inspiration. For the most part these were underpopulated rather than over-populated territories, with corresponding opportunities for geographical and social mobility. Although Latin America contained large areas of poverty, overcrowding, and misery, there were also considerable economic dynamism and modernity. Both private enterprise and public welfare provision, such as that for education, were considerably more advanced than in most of the Third World, and they were well established much earlier.

In short, by world standards this was quite favorable terrain for the implantation of conventional liberal democracy. And indeed democracy *did* flower here—in Uruguay before World War I; in Argentina in the 1920s; in Chile from the 1930s; in Costa Rica after 1948; in Colombia and Venezuela since 1958; and more generally in the 1970s and 1980s. Moreover, throughout this whole period the United States, as the dominant power, proclaimed the promotion of democracy to be one of its enduring regional priorities. So, on the face of it, the subject of this volume should be unproblematic. Both Latin America and North American predispositions favored the generalized establishment of liberal democracy, and that is what we are now witnessing with only a few laggards where extrahemispheric antidemocratic influences are yet to be eradicated (the most important of which is Cuba).

The view just outlined may have some instinctive support (at least within the more conservative circles in the United States); but of course, as the various contributors to this volume make clear, it requires a great deal of qualification and revision. In particular we cannot yet assume a liberal democratic "end of history" for Latin America at the end of the twentieth century. The obstacles to such an outcome remain extremely large and can by no means be encapsulated under the rubric of extrahemispheric subversion.

But if after half a century or more the construction of democracy in Latin America remains incomplete and uncertain, then a critical examination of the limitations of past efforts is required. Why, if the United States has generally favored democracy promotion for so long, and if U.S. influence in the region has been so great, and if the underlying local realities have been relatively favorable—why then have the results been so slow, uneven, and modest? For clarity this chapter concentrates on one aspect of the U.S. record of democracy promotion: its reliance on various methods of imposition, particularly in those countries where the relative power of the United States is most overwhelming.

The point can be put provocatively, but not unfairly, as follows. There is only one place in Latin America where a strong consolidated liberal democracy has been established largely as a result of a sustained U.S. commitment to that end. (The reader unable to identify the place in question may wish to skip a few pages to solve the puzzle.) Apart from this one very clear-cut exception, there is no reason to dissent from the verdict of G. Pope Atkins: "U.S. attempts to extend the practices of representative democracy and protection of human rights have been ambiguous and vacillating. When resources have been committed to the goal of democratic development, it has usually been viewed as an instrumental objective aimed at achieving one or the other of the long-range goals,"[1] namely, the maintenance of political stability and the prevention of foreign control.

The interpretation proposed in this chapter derives from the assumption that not all good things necessarily go together. Where the promotion of democracy reinforces political stability, creates profitable business opportunities, and excludes rival powers from any real influence within a given territory (as in the exceptional case to be discussed), strong and sustained support for democratization may be expected from Washington. But what if democracy promotion might destabilize a key ally (as in Mexico in 1988)? What if the local electorate supports parties or policies hostile to U.S. business interests (Guatemala, 1950; Chile, 1970; almost Brazil, 1989)? What if the "institutionalization of uncertainty" implied by an open democratic contest includes uncertainty over the future international alignment of a strategic neighbor (Jamaica, 1980; or, prospectively, Nicaragua, 1996)? In all such cases both history and theory would suggest that Washington's commitment to the goal of democracy promotion could be expected to waver; and that at least some part of the U.S. policy-making apparatus would be tempted to disregard democratic niceties in pursuit of the more urgent goals of stability, a good business climate, and the preservation of U.S. ascendancy in the region.

In South America during the 1980s the conflict between democracy promotion and other U.S. foreign policy goals was attenuated as the Cold War faded, and as the debt crisis impelled Southern Hemisphere governments of all persuasions to compete in attracting scarce foreign capital.

Even so, many in Washington were reluctant to destabilize friendly author-itarian regimes. In fact, the sharp distinction made in the early 1980s be-tween "authoritarian" and "totalitarian" variants of undemocratic politics had the effect of deflecting pressure against the former. However, the Ar-gentine military regime destabilized itself by precipitating the Falklands/Malvinas war, and the Uruguayans achieved a similar result by holding and unexpectedly losing a plebiscite. As the decade progressed, the argument about destabilization shifted, for it became increasingly clear that rigid defense of an authoritarian status quo was likely to be more destabilizing than a controlled and gradual liberalization. Even where the eventual out-come of liberalization was likely to be full democratization, with all the risks and uncertainties that that might entail, almost any incoming civilian gov-ernment would be driven to mend its fences with Washington by the severity of the socioeconomic problems it would inherit, and by the need to circum-vent the potential veto power of vested interests left over from authoritarian rule. Thus the United States had less to fear from South American democra-tization in the 1980s than would have been the case a decade or two earlier. It also had relatively limited influence south of the Caribbean and therefore prudence dictated that if democratization was coming anyway, Washington would be well advised to anticipate and herald the change.

Conditions were different in the Caribbean basin and on the Central American isthmus, however. There America's Cold War reflexes still pre-dominated during the 1980s. Even after fears of Soviet intentions were assuaged by Gorbachev's new policies, Washington policy makers remained affronted by Castro's Cuba, and by the challenges from Havana that they still perceived in El Salvador, Nicaragua, and Panama. Several of America's allies still seemed vulnerable to destabilization if too much was demanded of them in the areas of human rights and respect for political pluralism. Although by the eighties U.S. investments were generally far less impor-tant than they had been in earlier periods, this part of Latin America had become quite intimately linked to the U.S. economy via migratory flows, the concessionary trade links encouraged under the Caribbean Basin Initiative, and large-scale illegal transactions concerning narcotics, armaments, and money laundering. In contrast to South America, therefore, the promotion of democracy in the Caribbean Basin still had the potential to clash quite fundamentally with Washington's other more traditional foreign policy pri-orities. Moreover the inequalities of power between the U.S. and many of the region's mini- and microstates was far greater than in most of South America, and the interventionist tradition was far more strongly entrenched. It is here that the U.S. capacity to "promote democracy" in foreign lands should be at its greatest; and it is here that the U.S. has the longest track record of "teaching good government," including by direct occupation and military imposition.

This chapter therefore examines three selected examples of the imposition of democracy in those parts of the Caribbean Basin where U.S. ascendancy has been longest and greatest. The object is to determine under what conditions (and with what limitations) Washington has succeeded in achieving this proclaimed policy goal; and therefore *what kind* of democracy is likely to be favored by a massive and unilateral deployment of U.S. power in the region. This is an exercise in recent comparative history, but, as noted briefly in the conclusion, it also has implications for the 1990s, particularly in relation to the still-pending issue of Cuba. Three methods of imposition have been selected for comparison: incorporation, invasion, and intimidation. This highlights the contrast between U.S. and European Community approaches to democracy promotion in adjoining territories. Whereas the decision-making processes of the United States tend to favor democracy promotion by imposition, the European treaty structure precludes such an approach.

Democracy Promotion through Incorporation: Puerto Rico

The one Latin American country with a fully consolidated democratic regime where the United States has played a consistent, sustained, and determining role in the democratization process is of course the Commonwealth[2] of Puerto Rico. Yet this spectacular example is overlooked in the literature, perhaps simply because it is so easy to forget that Puerto Rico is indeed a Latin American country, or more seriously perhaps because the political price paid for this U.S. support—namely, the absence of sovereignty—is unwelcomely high. But in fact the Puerto Rican experience cannot be dismissed at all lightly, for although it is such a rare case of "success," it actually dramatizes in an extreme form processes of imposition that can also as we shall see be observed elsewhere.

In the exceptional case of Puerto Rico there is no ambiguity about use of the term *imposition* to describe the first phase of American policy. Whereas in Cuba and in Panama U.S. intervention was at least nominally in sup port of local forces fighting for national liberation, the U.S. seizure of Puerto Rico from Spain in 1898 was a straightforward act of colonialism. Cuba and Panama were both allowed a degree of semi-independence in the early 1900s, whereas fifty years were to elapse before Puerto Rico's colonial status began to shift. Even now the eventual outcome (labeled here democratization through incorporation) is by no means complete. However, if we take incorporation as the essential pattern, then the U.S. contribution to Puerto Rican democracy can be compared with the experience of Hawaii, or with the French role in Guadeloupe and Martinique, not to mention various British colonies such as Bermuda. In all these instances it seems that the domestic entrenchment of representative institutions has been forcefully promoted by a metropolitan power whose permanent involvement and commitment precludes the possibility of self-determination. In other words, they all appear to involve some kind of trade-off between sovereignty and external support for democracy.

The Puerto Rican experience provides a model case. Here we shall briefly consider the nature and scale of the U.S. contribution to Puerto Rican democracy; the reasons why it was more durable and effective than elsewhere in Latin America; and the consequences for the regime both positive (strong consolidation) and negative (insecurity over political identity, lack of national authenticity). In the light of this discussion some conclusions can be drawn about the *type* of democratization likely to arise from such strong external involvement, and about the applicability or otherwise of this broad approach in other parts of Latin America.

Political parties, representative institutions, and competitive elections existed in colonial Puerto Rico long prior to the landing of U.S. troops in July 1898, although the Spanish imperial authorities retained the right to veto local laws. On the other hand, starting in 1812, Puerto Rican deputies were seated in successive Spanish Cortés and could vote on all legislation (a contrast to the present situation in which the island's commissioner in Washington may vote in committee but has no vote on the floor of Congress). However this system of representation was far too restricted to qualify as a modern democracy. Whether one would have developed in the absence of U.S. intervention is a tantalizing but unanswerable question. (It could also be asked of Cuba, Panama, the Dominican Republic, and other countries.) At any rate, in 1898 the Spanish system of representation appears to have commanded little loyalty, and most Puerto Ricans are said to have welcomed the American troops, accompanied as they were by the promise "to give to the people of your beautiful island the largest measure of liberty consistent with this military occupation . . . to promote your prosperity and bestow upon you the immunities and blessings of the liberal institutions of our government," according to the U.S. military proclamation of July 28, 1898.

From 1900 onward U.S. law guaranteed islanders the right to elect mayors and the lower house of a legislative assembly (on a restricted franchise), but executive power was vested in nominees from Washington. Since 1917 Puerto Ricans have enjoyed American citizenship (including liability to the military draft), and there has been an elected bicameral assembly with some authority over the cabinet. From 1948 onward the governor has been directly elected. However, these American citizens cannot vote in presidential elections, and the island's elected authorities lack various attributes of sovereignty such as the power to set tariffs, to enter into international economic agreements, or to control the immigration of foreign (non-U.S.) citizens. Although the island has its own electoral commission and its own supreme court, the ultimate arbiter of disputed local elections, like that of 1980 (and indeed of all constitutional issues), remains the U.S. Supreme

Court. Other matters of vital concern to the islanders, such as the Internal Revenue Code and the funding of the U.S. welfare system, are also decided in Washington without their participation. It is true that they can vote from time to time in plebiscites to determine possible changes in their constitutional status—for example, in 1967 39 percent voted to apply to Washington for statehood, and more may do so in the next test expected in the early 1990s. But the power of decision on such changes remains vested in the U.S. Congress, and such tests of Puerto Rican public opinion are no more than advisory, albeit of great moral force. This, then, is the current status of Puerto Rican democratic institutionality.

So in what sense does Puerto Rico have a "fully consolidated democracy," and what was the U.S. contribution to the consolidation process? There is as yet no clear consensus on what constitutes the "full consolidation" of a democratic process, but by most criteria Puerto Rico ranks ahead of almost every other Latin American and Caribbean country. The closest rival with full sovereignty is Costa Rica. Elsewhere[3] I have argued that one partial but very revealing test of whether a fragile democracy has become fully consolidated is to ask whether the citizens of a long-established and secure democracy would feel unthreatened by an act of political unification or incorporation. By this standard the European parliament in Strasbourg implicitly judged Portugal, Spain, and Greece to have fully consolidated democracies by the 1980s (but not Turkey). Likewise the U.S. Congress made this judgment about Hawaii in 1959. It seems extremely probable that Puerto Rico would have passed this test in 1967, if the plebiscite of that year had favored statehood, and the same outcome seems even clearer if that situation arises in the 1990s. By this severe test, then, Puerto Rican democracy has long been remarkably "consolidated." This is not a claim that can yet be safely made about, say, the Dominican Republic or Venezuela.

By more conventional criteria Puerto Rico established a modern electoral democracy in successive stages. Female suffrage was obtained in 1932; universal adult suffrage in 1936; the exchange of votes for favors became less common after 1940; promotion by merit began to replace the spoils system of public employment in 1947. The U.S. Congress was of course directly responsible for progress while the island remained a colony. Then with the 1952 constitution the local legislature established a strong legal framework for electoral competition. (It is worth noting that whereas in the British Caribbean democratic structures were created from above by the less-than-democratic method of imperial orders in council, in Puerto Rico this was the work of a popularly constituted constitutional convention.) The organization of a well-structured majority party, the Partido Popular Democrático (PPD), no doubt facilitated this process of institution building. U.S. support was ensured when the PPD politically isolated and neutralized the once-powerful independence movement; thenceforth the best way for

Washington to stabilize the power of its Puerto Rican allies was to back their democratization project.

In due course a second more conservative party, the Partido Nuevo Progresista (PNP), gained sufficient electoral strength to constitute a genuine alternative to the PPD, this time by advocating full statehood. The governorship has alternated between these two parties in successive elections (in 1968, 1972, 1976, and 1984). Control of the legislature has also passed back and forth in a normal manner. Minor parties have also established niches for themselves (in part because Puerto Rican law provides for minority-party representation on local councils), and the political commitment of the electorate is confirmed by the extremely high levels of turnout that characterize most elections, even after the voting age was lowered to eighteen in 1971 (an estimated 88.3 percent in the 1980 governorship election, for example, compared with the 59.2 percent of the U.S. voting age population who reported voting in the presidential election held on the same day).[4] Since 1977 Puerto Ricans have also participated in the primaries organized by the two main U.S. parties to select their presidential nominees. As already noted, the law also provides for the possibility of holding plebiscites, as was done in 1952 and 1967 on the status issue.

In view of this record it is hard to dissent from the conventional judgment that Puerto Rico has established a free and democratic system of political representation. Freedom House, for example, considers that in 1985 Puerto Rico was one of only 10 nonsovereign territories (out of 55) to enjoy full civil liberties (only 20 out of 167 sovereign states met this condition). In the nonsovereign territories of the Caribbean only the Netherlands Antilles and the British Virgin Islands reached the same standard, and in the sovereign states of Latin America and the Caribbean only Belize, Costa Rica, and St. Kitts were rated as highly.[5] For the sake of realism it must also be mentioned, however, that when in 1981 the Puerto Rican supreme court ruled in favor of the PPD and against the PNP in an election dispute, the PNP governor accused it of blatant partiality, arguing that six of the seven judges had been appointed by the PPD. He therefore appealed the case to the U.S. Supreme Court (claiming that the matter was a civil rights rather than an electoral issue and was therefore subject to federal law). Eventually the Washington court upheld the original Puerto Rican court judgment.

As this appeal to the U.S. Supreme Court indicates, the whole process of democratization in Puerto Rico has been continuously stabilized and guaranteed by the institutions of the United States. Certainly the islanders and their political leaders have played leading and for the most part constructive roles in this process, but always within a framework provided from outside. Even the electoral timetable is set by the rhythms of Washington. Indeed one reason why Puerto Rican democracy receives so little international recognition is that gubernatorial election results coincide with and are therefore swamped by simultaneous U.S. presidential results. So this case represents a clear exception to the generalization that in postwar Latin America democratizations are internally driven, with external factors playing only a secondary part.

Why was U.S. support for democracy so much more durable and effective than elsewhere in Latin America? Obviously the 1898 invasion denied external powers access to the island and thus removed a competing foreign policy concern. The key step was the Jones Act of 1917 by which the U.S. Congress conferred citizenship (albeit "passive"—that is, without congressional representation). This was regarded as an irrevocable step. It made young Puerto Rican men liable for U.S. military service and therefore eligible for the benefits conferred on ex-servicemen. Unsurprisingly, then, the island also became an indispensable element in the U.S. naval system. The Jones Act also implied a general right to travel and work on the mainland without fear of deportation. Of course, these political arrangements were linked to an economic settlement. These passive citizens would be exempted from federal taxation as well as from congressional representation. Even prior to the 1952 constitution, therefore, the island possessed a degree of fiscal autonomy (it could raise its own taxes, and grant its own tax exemptions), while at the same time enjoying duty-free access to the huge mainland market for its goods, and relying on the U.S. Federal Reserve to provide its currency and to conduct its monetary policy.

In short, Washington has undertaken a succession of economic, strategic, and political commitments to Puerto Rico that are far more far-reaching and irrevocable than any other obligations it has shouldered in Latin America. U.S. business interests enjoy the full panoply of legal guarantees available on the mainland; so Washington is not cross-pressured between democracy promotion and business promotion. Puerto Rico's small population and peculiar history made it possible for the United States to accept such obligations in this case, precisely because no general precedent would be set. It seems unlikely that American policy makers could seriously have offered similar arrangements to larger or more indigestible Latin republics (such as Cuba). But in the unique case of Puerto Rico, Washington was willing to undertake such massive and durable (if lopsided) commitments that the United States effectively underwrote an American-style democratization of the island.

What, then, were the costs and benefits of this method of democracy promotion for Puerto Rico? The political benefits have already been outlined—a stronger system of civil rights, a securer rule of law, and a more firmly entrenched system of electoral pluralism than almost anywhere else in Latin America. The economic benefits must also be mentioned, for the stability of the political system has been powerfully reinforced by the accompanying experience of considerable relative prosperity. Income levels have risen well above the Latin American norm (and now approach half those of the poorest state in the union, Mississippi): Puerto Rico is sheltered from the inflation, debt crisis, and International Monetary Fund (IMF)-imposed austerity programs of its neighbors (for example, government borrowing benefits from a federal guarantee). Living standards have risen to such a point that by 1982 minimum wages on the island could be raised to the federal level. However, there is a negative side to the economic record. High unemployment is a predictable counterpart to high minimum wages. The federal food stamp program provides a costly safety net for the poor. But the most important cushion has come from the unrestricted right to emigrate to the mainland, where about two-fifths of all islanders now reside. Were it not for some very expensive subsidies to Puerto Rican industry (notably tax breaks for U.S. firms investing on the island), unemployment and/or emigration would be even higher. Federal transfers, welfare payments, and tax concessions account for about a quarter of the island's regional income, and of course the laws governing inflow are written by a legislature in which the islanders have no vote.

The political price of such a democracy is therefore a considerable loss both of sovereignty and of formal representation. Puerto Ricans sent to fight in Vietnam had no voice in America's debate over the war; their rights to abortion may be curtailed or extended by the decision of others; decisive elements of economic policy are fixed by mainlanders without their concurrence; their elected representatives have no voice in international economic forums. From the standpoint of democratic theory these are serious imperfections, signifying that some U.S. citizens have formal rights that are gravely and permanently impaired compared with those of the majority. In place of the ethic of citizen autonomy, with rights and duties conventionally balanced, Puerto Rican democracy rests on a constrained and dependent form of citizenship with special exemptions excused by the provision of unilateral subsidies. In fact this is a democracy based on the acceptance of second-class citizenship. According to theory, such a formula should breed both resentment and irresponsibility. In practice the main result seems to have been to generate a persistent obsession with the status issue, and an associated insecurity over the island's real social identity. Although this chapter has classified the islanders as a Latin American people, in many respects they still find themselves in an international limbo.

What lessons can we draw from this example of strong U.S. involvement in democracy promotion? Above all, the Puerto Rican path to democracy is most unlikely to be repeated. The U.S. Congress will almost certainly not grant citizenship (and the unrestricted right of entry) to any other Latin American people or nation in the foreseeable future. The only wholly democratic outcome consistent with the extension of U.S. citizenship would be full Puerto Rican entry into the union as an additional state. This may eventually come about if the next plebiscite clearly favors statehood, but if so it will only occur after an extremely protracted interregnum. Almost a century has already elapsed since the military proclamation of July 1898, and still opinions remain divided, both within the United States and on the island, about the shape of the eventual constitutional settlement. If Washington is to promote democracy strongly in other parts of Latin America, it will almost certainly seek a shorter route, and one that can be traversed at lower cost to the U.S. taxpayer. For their part Latin American beneficiaries of such strong U.S. support will presumably seek to achieve a greater degree of sovereignty at a lower cost in terms of social identity.

Democracy Promotion through Invasion: Panama

It would be rash to anticipate the unfolding consequences of the December 1989 U.S. invasion of Panama, but some inferences can be drawn from that country's now quite lengthy past. Because of the canal, and because of all the history associated with it, we can be fairly sure that Washington will continue to seek a strong influence over the course of Panamanian politics. If the U.S. commitment to democracy promotion is anything like as strong as declaratory statements suggest, Panama is second only to Puerto Rico (perhaps equal with Nicaragua) as a country where one would expect that priority to materialize.

In November 1903 Panama broke away from Colombia under the protection of U.S. gunboats. The new republic received prompt recognition and financial assistance from Washington, and in return granted the United States extensive concessions over the proposed canal route. In theory U.S. military action responded to Panamanian aspirations and sheltered a sovereign and liberal new regime.

However, on May 16, 1908, Secretary of War Taft wrote to President Theodore Roosevelt about a proposed treaty with Panama:

> We should be given direct control over the elections, so as to permit us, should we desire, to intervene and determine who is fairly elected. This I agree detracts from the independence of the "Republic" but as the Republic has not shown itself competent in this regard, we are justified . . . to protect our own interests.[6]

This American supervision persisted until the Great Depression. But in January 1931 a Panamanian president was surprised to find his appeal for U.S. military assistance against his political rivals unanswered. "The old political hierarchy, which had survived for nearly three decades by periodic threats of American intervention, suddenly found itself discredited. In the ensuing campaign for the Panamanian presidency, no candidate solicited American endorsement."[7]

Under the Good Neighbor Policy of the 1930s Washington to some extent backed away from this degree of external supervision, signing a new canal treaty in 1936 that somewhat increased the Panamanian government's room for maneuver. On the political front, in place of gunboat diplomacy the United States sought to substitute good neighborly abstention from direct involvement in Panama's electoral processes. But this policy proved quite as problematic as the one it displaced, because in Panama as in other former U.S. protectorates the political forces that moved to fill the space created by Roosevelt's self-denying ordinances were less than wholly democratic. By the time of the tense elections of April 1948 Secretary of State Marshall was straining to avoid U.S. intervention.[8]

The 1948 election revealed in the starkest terms the contrast between what Washington could achieve in conditions of direct rule in Puerto Rico and what American policy makers would have to contend with in an ex-protectorate where the national police had been allowed to acquire an identity of its own. At first Colonel Remón of the national police chose to support a fraudulent electoral outcome, and both the electoral tribunal and the supreme court of Panama fell into line with this decision. The United States, following the policy of nonintervention, also accepted this outcome. Within eighteen months, however, Colonel Remón decided that his interests would be better served by a reversal of position. Disregarding Panama's supreme court, in November 1949 he forced the incumbent president to resign and summoned the elections board to recount the 1948 results. "In hours the Board found pro-Arias votes it had been unable to find in weeks after the 1948 ballotting."[9] U.S. Ambassador David was left to fulminate:

> While action [by] Remón and Arias may evidence flattering confidence [in the] reality [of] our non-intervention policy, it shows also a cynical disregard of principles democratic and otherwise, and complete disdain for our oft repeated expressions of policy. It is believed Remón and his gangster associates are incapable of understanding international implications. Apparently it is their idea that they can be brazen about their illegal procedure and yet insist we recognize decisions forced upon their judicial and legislative branches. . . . Since we let it be known we would be guided by action of National Assembly and Supreme Court, it would be logical to do, stating U.S. government therefore recognizes (deposed) Charis as constitutional president and is prepared to proceed with conduct of normal business once illegal interference by force ceases to impede. This course should not, however, be taken unless we are prepared to take a determined stand and see it through.[10]

The ambassador's recommendation was not adopted, however, in part because the internal legality that it invoked was so unreal. Within three days the State Department had concluded that Arias was in control, at which point a very different view of the 1948 election emerged: "There can be no doubt that he won the election last year and was cheated out of the Presidency by the fraudulent actions of the electoral jury."[11] In the absence of full U.S. control over internal political processes, there was no way that even the sincerest and most single-minded Washington supporter of Panamanian democracy could sidestep the reality of competing partisanships and fragmented legitimacy.

In reality, of course, any concern Washington might have felt for democracy in Panama was always overshadowed by the higher priority of preserving the security of the Canal Zone. U.S. policy documents record a close and continuing interest in the internal politics of the republic, but this was always viewed from the standpoint that a friendly and secure pro-American administration would be the best guarantor of Washington's overriding security interests. On the many occasions where that priority conflicted with an even-handed concern for the sovereign democratic order, the issue of democracy took second place. All Panamanian political factions understood that reality and conducted their activities accordingly. Thus, regardless of all the rhetoric in favor of democracy and nonintervention, the objective structure of these power relations was systematically weighted against the consolidation of a democratic order. This goes far to explain why from initially fairly similar points of departure at the turn of the century the Panamanians made virtually no progress in the establishment of democratic institutions, whereas especially since 1950 the Puerto Ricans achieved major cumulative advances.

The Panamanian electoral process of 1948–49 deserves reconstruction because it anticipates so much of the experience of the 1980s. It therefore demonstrates the existence of a systematic pattern of political interaction between the United States and Panama that cannot simply be attributed to the criminality of General Noriega; and since this pattern of political behavior is entrenched, the task of averting future repetitions of the cycle will require far more than just the seizure and imprisonment of one military leader.

In May 1984, as in May 1948, a hard-fought presidential election ended fraudulently. The head of the electoral tribunal resigned rather than certify the results, which were imposed by the National Guard under the direction of General Noriega; international observers described them as rigged, but the U.S. State Department accepted them at face value. The incoming president was more acceptable to Washington than his electorally more successful rival—indeed U.S. policy makers appear to have played an important role in selecting and nominating him. In any case the State Department feared a coup if the progovernment candidate lost the first election held in sixteen years. Even with the benefit of hindsight the chief U.S. policy maker, Elliott Abrams, still defended the endorsement of a fraudulent outcome, which in his view "seemed to help propel Panama into the flow towards democracy that is powerfully moving the hemisphere."[12] In 1985, as in 1984, the illegitimate civilian president attempted to assert his authority against the National Guard that brought him to power. The results were the same, as was the initial U.S. response. Abrams later conceded that the forced resignation of the president was a setback to democracy, but consoled himself with the observation that "constitutional procedures were followed, at least formally, and Panama remained an open society."[13] In the ensuing four years Panama was headed by a succession of nominal presidents while real power was retained elsewhere. As in 1948–51, conflicts of jurisdiction escalated and political institutionality degenerated, until following an even more fraudulent election in May 1989, the United States recognized a government in hiding and finally in December 1989 resorted to armed intervention. The stated grounds for this invasion by twenty-six thousand U.S. troops were, first, to safeguard the lives and property of American citizens; second, to terminate General Noriega's drug trafficking; third, to "restore democracy" in Panama; and fourth, to maintain the normal operations of the canal. It is the contention of this section that the first, second, and fourth goals on this list express the tenor of U.S.-Panamanian relations far more typically than the third; the method they imply is imposition, a method that would be far less appropriate if the principal goal of policy was democracy promotion.

The record of U.S. policy toward Panama in the 1980s culminating with the 1989 invasion leaves plenty of room to argue, with the benefit of hindsight, that some alternative choice of policies would have been more effective, more prudent, more principled, or even more supportive of Panamanian democracy. While that may be so, the critical point is that, despite all the advantages available to Washington policy makers, and despite their strong interest in shaping a favorable political outcome in Panama, their choices were all suboptimal, and their capacity to reshape Panamanian political processes proved once again to be remarkably limited. In the absence of stable and autonomous legal institutions (which might sometimes clash with immediate U.S. security interests), and in the presence of a perverse pattern of reactions established over several generations through which Panamanian leaders learned how to play off what Washington said about their country against what it really meant, the United States was reduced to the starkest and most unattractive of alternatives, either to endure continuing ridicule and defiance from a patently oppressive and corrupt former protégé, or to intervene unilaterally and with massive force in the hope of establishing a fresh beginning.

Although the first eighty-seven years of U.S.-Panamanian relations has not proved very productive from the standpoint of democracy promotion, there are those who regard the December 1989 invasion as the start of a bright new era. Such claims should never be dismissed out of hand. Just as the directly colonial phase of U.S.–Puerto Rican history gave way to a somewhat more equitable relationship in the 1950s, similar possibilities should be considered in Panama. This chapter does not exclude that hypothesis but merely argues that it will take some time before we can judge. Meanwhile the legacy of the past will continue to impede the prospects for authentic and durable democracy promotion in Panama. The security of the canal, although less vital to the United States than in earlier years, will continue to preoccupy Washington policy makers as much as the health of Panamanian democracy. If the two priorities were ever again to conflict the United States would again seek above all else to protect the canal. After all, America's power, its prestige, and even the lives of its soldiers have just been reinvested in that enterprise.

In the wake of *any* invasion, the first priority of the occupying force will naturally be to protect the security of its nationals and to make the outcome of the invasion irreversible. Where the aims of the invasion are temporary, and coincide with the wishes of the local population (as in the Grenada "rescue mission" of 1983), the occupying force may subsequently manage to withdraw leaving a well-functioning democracy behind. But in Panama the situation is not so clear-cut, in part because American nationals are not about to be withdrawn from the Canal Zone; in part because the National Guard or some equivalent military force is likely to retain a degree of local control; and in part because the Panamanian economy will continue to revolve around supplying "services" within this dollar zone and as an adjunct to the entrepôt functions of the canal. Therefore the postinvasion regime will continue to grapple with very similar problems to those that impeded democratization before 1989.

If drug trafficking, money laundering, and arms dealing are no longer to provide the basis of the Panamanian economy, how can an independent democratic government achieve reconstruction and the restoration of confidence after the dislocation caused by the U.S. sanctions and invasion? If the new government (which bases its legitimacy on 1989 election results that were annulled before the count was complete) lacks sufficient authority or resources of its own it will be forced to depend once more on the protection of Washington. But a restoration of the 1903–31 protectorate system is unlikely to work any better at the end of the twentieth century than it did at the beginning. Because Washington has no wish to incorporate Panama (as it incorporated Puerto Rico), the problem of anti–United States nationalism is almost bound to recur in one form or another. It is inherent in the enterprise of promoting the appearance of national sovereignty while intrusively supervising the substance of local politics. Of course the option of nonintervention may eventually return to favor. But unless Panama undergoes a major economic transformation, unless the public administration, the courts, and the military are improbably transformed, and unless the citizens of Panama come to see the legacy of American influence as U.S. opinion makers wish them to see it, then an eventual shift back to nonintervention is unlikely to serve the cause of democracy promotion any better than before.

With the passage of time it could be that these doubts will be dispelled. However, an objective assessment of the effects so far of America's massive presence in Panama offers little encouragement to those who suppose that all good things come readily together. Democracy promotion does not necessarily accompany the projection of U.S. power, least of all when that result is sought on the cheap; without any dilution of Washington's other purposes; and without much understanding of the perverse psychology engendered by a combination of formal sovereignty with real dependency.

Democracy Promotion by Intimidation: Nicaragua

Our third example of democracy promotion in the Caribbean Basin is Nicaragua. Here too the United States has an extremely long track record; again Washington's power in relation to any government in Managua is potentially overwhelming; although in the nineteenth century there was some thought in the United States of incorporating Nicaragua, that notion has had no currency in the twentieth; and since the 1920s the idea of invading Nicaragua has been distinctly out of favor with U.S. military planners. There was a U.S. military presence from 1912 to the Great Depression, and the United States did propose in 1979 that the Organization of American States (OAS) might send a "peacekeeping force" to prevent the Sandinista revolutionaries from seizing full power (along the lines of the successful U.S. intervention with OAS approval in the Dominican Republic in 1965). Throughout all these episodes the defense or promotion of democracy has been repeatedly articulated as a justification of American policy toward Nicaragua. In a similar way it is currently claimed that the February 1990 elections vindicate hotly contested assertions made throughout the Reagan administration concerning the democratic purposes of the "covert" or "contra" war against the Sandinistas, launched in November 1981, and sustained for more than eight years thereafter. So does the recent history of U.S.-Nicaraguan relations demonstrate the efficacy of Washington's strategy of democracy promotion through intimidation, or does it more nearly resemble the pattern just sketched of U.S.-Panamanian interactions?

Once again we are dealing with a long history. Over several generations the United States has exerted its extensive influence in Nicaragua in ways that have not served to generate political consensus or to encourage respect for democratic norms. In the second and third decades of this century, the Marines were used to prop up strongly contested governments in Managua. For example, they supervised and administered the 1928 elections against a substantial military and political challenge from the revolutionary general César Augusto C. Sandino. In American eyes he was a "bandit," but to many Nicaraguans and to a wide swathe of Latin American opinion he was a more authentic political leader than the Nicaraguan party leaders who had consented to elections on Washington's terms. Latin disbelief in Washington's ostensible commitment to democracy in Nicaragua was reinforced by U.S. conduct during the almost half-century of the Somoza dynasty. As in Panama, Washington attempted a stance of nonintervention in Nicaragua's internal affairs, and as in Panama this provided undemocratic armed forces with a license to commit abuses and to pursue personal enrichment with political impunity. Successive American administrations hesitated to criticize such a well-entrenched ally (with good friends in Congress), especially since he could be counted on to endorse Washington's most controversial foreign policy initiatives. To lock in U.S. support the Somozas took care to neutralize the democratic center in Nicaragua, always presenting Washington with the choice between an undemocratic but reliable right, or a radical and potentially "disloyal" left.

The Sandinista revolution of 1979 was a logical outcome of this long history. The many nationalist and radical currents of opinion that had been suppressed by the Somozas resurfaced under the umbrella of the Sandinista Front. Although the bulk of the front's leadership was Marxist-inclined, and although many of the key figures had been Cuba-trained or -influenced, the rigid and repressive nature of the Somoza regime enabled the Sandinistas to build a broad alliance, with centrists attracted by the promise of democratic elections, a mixed economy, and nonalignment. According to the official U.S. view, Washington's policies of "intimidation" during the 1980s were in fact intended to force the Sandinistas to honor these original promises, and that is the result they are said finally to have achieved in the February 1990 elections that displaced the Sandinistas from government.

On closer inspection of the record of U.S. intimidation of Nicaragua during the 1980s the picture is less clear-cut. To avoid misunderstandings it must be stated at the outset that the Sandinista front chose to overplay its hand, attempting to consolidate a far more radical, political, and economic order than that initially promised. Thus it was not only Washington but also Managua that chose the path of continued polarization in the 1980s. Although the Sandinista strategy may seem explicable in view of the long preceding history of U.S.-Nicaraguan relations, it was not entirely forced upon them (certainly not by the Carter administration). They therefore bear considerable responsibility for the ensuing consequences, which included missing the opportunity to promote national reconciliation and democratization.

That said, let us turn to the topic of this chapter, which concerns the U.S. role. Let us consider first the motives, then the methods, then the results of the U.S. response. This policy of intimidation was motivated by a variety of considerations, among which concern over the quality of democratic governance in Nicaragua was not, to put it mildly, always foremost. Initially policy was shaped by the pressures of the Carter–Reagan election campaign in which a dominant theme was the need to reassert American self-confidence and international leadership. In this setting Nicaraguan realities were compressed to fit into the terms of a debate set by the Iranian hostage crisis. After Reagan's victory campaign, perceptions continued to override reality and the "Nicaraguan threat" was inflated to improbable proportions. The genuine issue that underlay mounting U.S. hostility toward Managua was the fear of a second revolution in neighboring El Salvador. It was to cut off supplies to the Salvadoran guerrillas rather than to promote democracy in Nicaragua that the "contras" were initially funded by the National Security Council, in November 1981. (After all, Washington was at that time sheltering a regime in El Salvador whose democratic credentials were at least as dubious as those of the Sandinistas.) As the contra war expanded, U.S. objectives became more complex and difficult to decipher. One possibility was certainly the armed overthrow of the Sandinistas, and it remains extremely questionable whether that would have heralded a new dawn of democracy in Nicaragua. (The precedent of Guatemala in 1954 hardly seems encouraging.) Another was simply to isolate and discredit the Sandinista model, so that no other Central American republic would be tempted to follow that example. (Again, the democratic content of this outcome would seem questionable.)

By 1984, with the Salvadoran regime becoming more stable and respectable, and with the Grenada "rescue mission" accomplished, the theme of democratizing Nicaragua became much more prominent and explicit. To the Reagan administration the promotion of democracy in Nicaragua had one great advantage over all other possible justifications for the "contra" war. With any other war aim, the danger existed that the Sandinistas would accept U.S. demands, and the administration would therefore come under pressure to call off hostilities before the regime in Managua had been toppled. "Democracy," by contrast, could be promoted as an unimpeachable goal that would attract the support of many waverers. Under Reagan the State Department would adhere to a definition of the term designed to ensure that no form of Sandinismo, however toned down, would ever qualify, just as no form of facade democracy in El Salvador would ever be allowed to disqualify.

This may seem a harsh and uncharitable explanation of Washington's motives in the mid-1980s. But we cannot overlook the fact that in November 1984 the Sandinistas did finally honor their 1979 pledge and hold national elections, and that various respectable foreign observers considered these acceptable. If the United States had genuinely sought the strengthening of democracy in Nicaragua, would it have pressured the leading opposition candidate to stand down, and would it have disdained to see any merit in this electoral process? The trouble with these elections from Washington's point of view, was not that they were fraudulent (we have seen that fraudulent elections held in Panama at that very time were praised as a step toward democracy). It was that even under clean elections the United States believed the Sandinistas would probably win.

During the 1980s the Sandinistas were progressively weakened by the long U.S. campaign of harassment against them, but they were never toppled by the contras, and no U.S. invasion ever came. Their response to the demand for democracy was to offer to extend political freedoms if the campaign of harassment abated, but to curtail them if U.S. hostility put Nicaragua's national security at risk. This can be viewed as just a question of tactics, but it also reflected an underlying disagreement about the *kind* of democracy that might be established. The Sandinistas might be willing to move toward democracy-with-sovereignty, but as the very name Sandinista implied they could not contemplate democracy on Puerto Rican terms, or of the post–Panama-invasion variety. The Reagan administration, by contrast, seems to have defined democracy to require congruence with American interests. A sovereignty that clashed with U.S. priorities was unlikely to be regarded as acceptable. Since the end of the Reagan administration the United States has somewhat softened its position on such questions, but it remains to be seen how Washington would react to some future Sandinista electoral victory. Thus it cannot be said that pure democracy promotion motivated U.S. policy toward Nicaragua in the 1980s.

Even if the *motives* for U.S. policy had been straightforwardly democratic, the *methods* chosen were not. As we have seen, there was never any intention to incorporate Nicaragua into the democratic system of the United States, and although invasion may at times have been contemplated this method was also ruled out by the time of the "Irangate" scandal. Therefore Washington resorted to less direct methods of pressure, including covert operations, economic sanctions, and political warfare—"intimidation" for short. But intimidation is inherently a blunt instrument. It does not destroy but merely cows. So the result of a successful act of intimidation is more likely to be purely formal compliance than willing cooperation. In addition, because intimidation stops short of complete destruction of the enemy, it leaves open the option of continuing defiance regardless of cost, so intimidation risks destroying the social prerequisites for democratic compromise and accommodation. Moreover, the Reagan administration's acts of intimidation were also often prima facie undemocratic in domestic U.S. terms (deceiving Congress, misleading public opinion, diverting funds, etc.). Reliance on such methods broadcasts an example that hardly squares with the ostensible goal of democracy promotion. In fact, whereas democracy promotion through incorporation is likely to strengthen the democratic institutions of the metropolitan power (by generalizing and reinforcing them), democracy promotion through intimidation is more likely to damage the qualities of trust, cooperation, and lawfulness in the home democracy, to lower its international reputation, and to breed cynicism and opportunism in the target country.

These are objections in principle to the practice of democracy promotion through intimidation. Nevertheless *in practice,* it may be asserted, the Reagan administration achieved the desired results, and these were unlikely to have been accomplished by any alternative approach. As in the case of Panama, it may be too soon to judge. A great deal will depend upon what is considered to count as a "successful democratization" in Nicaragua—and on who controls the judgment. The foreign observers who authenticated the

1990 election came from many democratic countries—not just from the United States—and it may therefore be that in 1996 the Sandinista electoral opposition will benefit from the same international guarantees that served their opponents in 1990. But the result of the conflict of the past decade has been that many thousands of lives have been lost and the Nicaraguan economy has been ruined. Clearly this does not assist the promotion of democracy, and it seems unlikely that Washington will devote as much resources to reconstruction in the nineties, as it did to destruction in the eighties.

However, defenders of the Reagan administration will argue that there was no other way to "save Nicaragua for democracy." It could be that intimidation was the surest way to break Nicaragua's ties with Moscow and Havana, and with the Salvadoran guerrillas (although the Contadora and Esquipulas initiatives suggest that alternative approaches merited more attention than Washington was willing to concede). But on the question of democracy, the centerpiece of Reagan's strategy was the claim that since the Sandinistas were Marxists-Leninists, by definition *any* political concession they gave was just a stratagem to buy time. This was the argument for seeking to discredit the 1984 election, and for rebuffing all subsequent Sandinista proposals for a political settlement. In view of their scrupulous conduct of the February 1990 election, and of their disciplined acceptance of an unexpectedly adverse result, it remains a serious question whether the Sandinistas were previously as intransigent and antidemocratic as they have been portrayed. The obvious alternative way to promote Nicaraguan democracy would have been to support and reinforce the electoral process of 1984, and to encourage and reward subsequent compliance with the pluralist provisions of the 1987 constitution. Arguably, then, intimidation was not the only possible form of democracy promotion available to the United States in the eighties.

Intimidation was, however, the only form considered, and in the end the Sandinistas were evicted from office by the Nicaraguan electorate. So the policy worked, which on one view is what really matters. As in the discussion of Panama, this chapter does not dismiss that view out of hand but only argues for caution. The legacy of the past will continue to darken the prospects for an authentic and durable democratization of Nicaragua in the nineties. The Sandinistas are likely to remain a major political force, perhaps capable of blocking the reversal of key measures accomplished during their decade of government, perhaps capable of winning a clean election at a later date. Will all their opponents abide by the rules of democratic procedure if this assessment of Sandinista strength and popularity proves correct? After so many years of harassment and political warfare against the Sandinistas, will Washington now become a staunch defender of Nicaraguan democracy, even if their old antagonists stand to gain? One of the greatest dangers of resorting to a policy of intimidation is that it is so difficult to find a clear rationale for stopping. And, as the English discovered when they finally stopped coercing the Irish, it is even more difficult to convince the other side that you really have stopped.

Conclusion

The three instances of democracy imposition reviewed here are extreme, not typical. Other chapters in this volume discuss a much broader range of examples. Here we have selected those cases where the U.S. track record is longest; where the scale of American involvement in shaping the political affairs of its Latin neighbors has been greatest; and where the underlying inequality of power and resources maximizes the likelihood that Washington can have its way. After applying these restrictive criteria, one might expect to find three highly successful cases of democracy promotion, but in fact the results are very mixed. They are also startlingly diverse, with U.S. power being deployed in markedly different ways in each instance. "Incorporation," "invasion," and "intimidation" are quite varied methods for imposing democracy on other countries; when such contrasting methods are used it is perhaps hardly surprising that the outcomes are also various.

The incorporation of Puerto Rico produced the best results. By most normal criteria the islanders live in a well-consolidated political democracy that has received massive and sustained U.S. support over several generations. Even here, however, certain qualifications are called for. Almost a century has elapsed since the United States began reshaping Puerto Rican politics, perhaps half a century since serious democracy promotion began. Yet the process is still incomplete, in that the islanders remain in an international limbo, and viewed from within the U.S. system they are still second-class citizens. Full incorporation, and definitive democratization may well occur in the next few years. But in the meantime Puerto Rico's half-house status requires indefinite transfusions of federal funds, which typically account for around one-quarter of the island's domestic product. Even for those who think that the gain in democracy and prosperity justifies the surrender of sovereignty, the Puerto Rican example hardly constitutes a model, since neither the U.S. government nor the population of any other Latin American nation expect this pattern of democracy promotion through incorporation to be repeated elsewhere.

The invasion of Panama reinstated the authorities chosen in the frustrated election of 1989 and destroyed a tyrannical government. Taken out of context, these two accomplishments can be presented as another major success for democracy promotion. But on a longer view the contribution of the United States to the democratization of Panama is little cause for congratulation. The first eighty-seven years presents a fairly sorry record, and the best that can be claimed is that the invasion could mark a new beginning. The Grenada operation of 1983 offers some encouragement for this view, but the differences should also be kept in mind. In Panama the United States was protecting its long-established vested interests, whereas the population of Grenada viewed the "rescue mission" as an act of altruism by a country with no prior record of intervention there. In Panama the United States acted with the endorsement of neighboring democracies, and against a ruler whose power it had previously built up; its credibility as a disinterested protector of the popular will was accordingly reduced. In Grenada it was possible for the United States to withdraw rapidly and comprehensively leaving a fairly broad-based multiparty democracy to function on its own. Such an outcome is likely to prove far more problematic in Panama. If comparisons are to be made with other instances of democracy imposition through invasion, the Panamanian experience may more realistically be compared with the Dominican intervention of 1965. But in that case twelve years had to elapse before the outcome of the invasion could be subjected to genuine democratic control, and even in 1978 the transition to pluralist democracy remained precarious and unsatisfactory. In view of the continuing U.S. interest in the canal and the nationalist reactions this is still likely to generate, not even the distinctly qualified success of the Dominican democratization-through-invasion can be taken for granted in Panama.

The intimidation of the Sandinistas forced them to accept an unprecedently high degree of international supervision of the 1990 elections due under the constitution they wrote in 1987. For most of the 1980s they had derived political support from their role as defenders of national sovereignty against U.S. provocations, but by 1990 this mechanism no longer worked in their favor. The voters preferred a compromise settlement that would end U.S. harassment, permit national reconciliation, and open the way to economic reconstruction. The Nicaraguan electorate made a democratic choice (albeit constrained from without). Indeed the 1990 result has the potential to trigger a cumulative process of democratization as rival power contenders are forced to recognize that they must work together within an agreed political framework, since none is strong enough to rule alone. However, the election outcome did not signify a general willingness to compromise Nicaraguan sovereignty, nor to abandon all the changes brought in by eleven years of Sandinista government, and the Sandinista army was not defeated by the "contras." The election has given Washington an unexpectedly easy opportunity to reinforce the democratization process in Nicaragua by ceasing all acts of intimidation and by respecting the new political framework. But this requires a clear U.S. understanding of *all* the implications of the 1990 vote. The main test of democracy promotion through intimidation is whether interventionist methods can be convincingly and lastingly foresworn once the democratic transition is underway. In Nicaragua that test has yet to come.

Although the three examples considered here are all extreme, they are unlikely to be unique. Indeed in the 1990s we are likely to witness not only further evidence of the fruits of these three democracy-promotion strategies in the countries studied, but also greater tests of the U.S. capacity for democracy promotion in other parts of the Caribbean Basin. Despite their importance, the difficult cases of El Salvador, Haiti, Guatemala, and even Mexico cannot be considered here but some mention must be made of the largest imponderable, namely Washington's posture toward a prospective post-Castro Cuba.

As is well known, after 1898 the policy of incorporation applied to Puerto Rico was not extended to Cuba, and after the failure of the Bay of Pigs in 1961 Washington also dropped the policy of invasion. Instead for over thirty years Castro's Cuba has been subjected to an unbroken policy of isolation and intimidation, more comprehensive and sustained than that which brought the Sandinista revolution to a halt. Yet Cuba's personalist brand of Communism succeeded in resisting all such pressure, in part because of large-scale Soviet assistance, in part because of Castro's own achievements and determination, and in part because of his success in promoting an anti–United States definition of Cuban nationalism. Following the collapse of Communism throughout Eastern Europe in 1989–90, a widespread impression developed that at long last the U.S. policy of intimidation might be about to pay a massive dividend, in the form of a spectacular collapse of the Castro regime. If this were to occur, it would overshadow all the three cases considered here; indeed, if the outcome were to be the installation of a conventional pluralist democracy in Cuba, then no amount of academic reservations about the past history of U.S. democracy promotion through intervention would dent the surge of American self-confidence. Nevertheless, without foreknowledge of Cuba's route beyond Castroism, an attempt can be made to extend the logic of the preceding analysis to the Cuban case.

The Cuban armed forces have not been, and probably will not be, defeated. Unlike Nicaragua the Cuban people have not been, and probably will not be, offered an internationally supervised electoral forum within which to choose their preferred future. Moscow is probably unable to bring about the downfall of the Cuban leadership (as it appears to have done in several East European cases), even if it wishes to do so. Thus the question is whether a further reinforcement and intensification of Washington's long-standing policy of intimidation is likely to prove an effective instrument of democracy promotion in Cuba. The suggested limitations to this method are that it is too blunt (and may therefore damage rather than build up the social supports for democracy); that it seeks to grind down rather than immediately to destroy (therefore leaving the target regime with a possibility of retaliation, albeit at a disproportionate cost to itself); that it is in its own terms contrary to the spirit of democratic accommodation (therefore potentially harmful to the democratic processes of the country that employs it, and damaging to a nation's democratic credibility); and that great self-control is required to halt practices of intimidation once a democratic transition has begun. These are the reasons for fearing, in advance of the fact, that the long-standing U.S. policy of intimidation may not even now very well serve the cause of democracy promotion in Cuba.

It should not be too readily assumed that the collapse of Communism in Eastern Europe vindicates the U.S. approach to democracy promotion in Cuba. After all, the Federal German constitution of 1949 offered the East Germans the unqualified prospect of reunification whenever they chose to apply for it; this was voluntary incorporation rather than imposition. West Germany also relied heavily on incentives rather than sanctions to win the East Germans round. As for the rest of Eastern Europe (and previously in relation to Southern Europe), the Treaty of Rome offered the permanent incentive of a right to apply for admission to the European Community to any neighboring state that adopted the required standards of political democracy and market liberalization. In contrast to these European incentives to voluntary reform, Washington appears to seek the national prostration of Cuba, an unconditional surrender in return for which the United States offers neither full admission to the union nor any assurance that an independent democratic Cuba would be allowed to exercise its sovereignty.

Thus, however events in Cuba may unfold, this discussion raises an important theoretical issue related to the nature of the democratic outcome being sought or promoted. The traditional view to which most Latin American (and for that matter most European) democrats would probably adhere is that the consolidation of national sovereignty is a precondition for the implantation of a representative democracy. For a government to be securely democratic—answerable to the citizenry through the test of competitive elections—it must establish its authority and policy effectiveness throughout the national territory, and must secure international acceptance of that authority. If extraterritorial authorities not accountable to the local electorate were to exercise decisive power, then according to this view the quality of that particular democracy would be drastically impaired. By this test Puerto Rican democracy falls short, in that San Juan has no say over such critical issues as the waging of war; Panamanian democracy depends on the acquiescence of an occupation force whose first loyalty is to Washington, and whose second priority is the security of the canal; only Nicaraguan democracy appears more or less sovereign. What U.S. efforts at democracy promotion in the Caribbean Basin seem to assume is that democratization can be a *substitute* for what Washington regards as unacceptable or impractical assertions of national sovereignty. Given the overwhelming inequalities of power involved, and the wide range of strategic, economic, and political interests Washington is expected to promote there, such a redefinition of the concept of democracy may be understandable. But from the standpoint of democratic theory it would only be tenable if the relinquishment of sovereignty were to be offset by full incorporation into the American political union. The peculiarity of the form of democracy promotion practiced by the United States in the region where it has the greatest influence is that neither full incorporation nor full democratic sovereignty is consistently envisaged. This peculiarity goes far to explain the apparent paradox presented at the outset of this chapter—why in such favorable conditions such a powerful country, with such a long commitment to democracy promotion, has achieved such modest results. The policy-making process within the United States largely accounts for this peculiarity, in that the American public demands a strong rationale for foreign policy initiatives (democracy promotion), while the Constitution erects formidable barriers against the incorporation of new states, and specific lobbies have frequently induced Washington to exert its power whenever the assertion of sovereignty by small Caribbean states (even the most democratic) seemed likely to clash with their interests.

With the ending of the cold war and the rapid extension of economic and political liberalism, it becomes even more important than before to determine whether (or in what circumstances) democratization involves a trade-off in sovereignty, or whether a new phase of democracy promotion can now begin, with more respect for nonintervention and the formal equality of all democratic states, however large or small.

The three methods of democracy promotion discussed in this chapter (incorporation, invasion, and intimidation) all have one thing in common—they express a radical inequality between the power and rights of the country acting and the country acted upon. They involve unilateral acts of imposition. This radical inequality has deep roots in U.S. history[14] and is a particularly celebrated feature of the U.S. presence in the Caribbean Basin throughout the current century. The U.S. military proclamation of July 1898, already quoted, expresses the central idea common to all forms of democracy promotion by imposition. This is the assumption that one's own domestic political arrangements are secure and beyond reproach. From this starting point, it follows that democracy promotion involves a unilateral transfer that will be best facilitated by maximizing the power and control of the giver, and by minimizing the scope for resistance or modification by the receiver. For this reason the imposition of democracy abroad is likely to prove highly affirming to the status quo at home.

However this is not the only possible model of democracy promotion, as the European Community has recently demonstrated in Southern and Eastern Europe. It is not even the only model of democracy promotion in the Caribbean, as both the decolonization of the British and Dutch West Indies and the incorporation of the French overseas territories in their different ways attest. The broad alternative to democracy promotion by unilateral imposition is democracy promotion by mutual accommodation. In this case the giver may well recognize the imperfection or vulnerability of the home democracy, which may be strengthened by external reinforcement. (This certainly helps explain why the recently restored democracies of Europe engage in democracy promotion.) In this case democracy promotion will involve strengthening the authority of political forces in the receiving democracy (usually this includes enhanced respect for its sovereignty), and may well require some demotion of the agencies of control in the countries engaged in democracy promotion. (For example, European decolonization required a dismantling of imperial institutions, which was often unsettling to the status quo at home but which, once achieved, contributed to the quality of west European democracy.)

Probably the most interesting of these alternatives to the historical U.S. approach is the partial pooling of sovereignty in an enlarged community of democratic nations, as currently envisaged in Europe. This is not an easy alternative for the United States to pursue, in part because the objective inequalities of wealth and power are so much greater than between the European states, in part because it runs counter to strong historical traditions, and in particular because both the U.S. legal system and the policy process would have such difficulty in adapting to any form of supranational constraints. However, recent proposals for a North American Common Market, and eventually even for an America-wide free-trading zone, might seem to imply a new willingness to consider the mutual accommodation of economic policies by agreement with sovereign neighbors. If so, then Washington might also be ready to develop more mutually respectful (more properly *democratic*) methods of democracy promotion than those highlighted in this chapter. As noted at the beginning of this chapter, the republics of the Americas share a number of common liberal features and traditions—more so than the Europeans—that *ought* to facilitate the establishment of a democratic community of nations, provided that nineteenth-century traditions of unilateralism and imposition can be overcome.

Notes

1. G. Pope Atkins, *Latin America in the International Political System,* 2d ed. (Boulder, Colo.: Westview, 1989), pp. 111–12.

2. In Spanish "Estado Libre Asociado," but the literal English translation, "free associated *state*," has connotations unacceptable to U.S. constitutionalists.

3. Laurence Whitehead, "The Consolidation of Fragile Democracies: A Discussion with Illustrations," in Robert A. Pastor, ed., *Democracy in the Americas: Stopping the Pendulum* (New York: Holmes & Meier, 1989), pp. 76–95.

4. For a detailed account, see Fernando Bayrón Toro, *Las Elecciones de 1980* (Mayagüez, Puerto Rico: Editorial Isla, 1982). The statistics on turnout are from p. 33.

5. Raymond D. Gastil, *Freedom in the World, 1985/6* (New York: Freedom House, 1986), pp. 32–40. (By 1989–90, however, twenty-nine sovereign states and thirty-three nonsovereign territories were ranked by the same institution as enjoying full civil liberties.)

6. Quoted in Richard L. Lael, *Arrogant Diplomacy: US Policy Toward Colombia, 1903-22* (Wilmington, Del.: Scholarly Resources, 1987), pp. 18–19.

The following headlines from the *New York Times* give the flavor of the period: "Elections in Panama Must be OK'd by Taft" (May 11, 1906); "Panama Must Make Its

Election Fair" (June 12, 1908); "Want US to Intervene: Panama Parties Would Insure Fair Play at Coming Elections, Says Former President" (May 28, 1916).

7. Lester D. Langley, *The United States and the Caribbean in the Twentieth Century* (Athens: University of Georgia Press, 1980), p. 139.

8. "While we will not permit conditions to reach a stage that could produce another Bogotá, we will not pull anyone's chestnuts out of the fire to maintain a government in power" was how Chargé Hall summarized the conversation with Marshall, in *Foreign Relations of the United States (FRUS) 1948*, vol. 9 (Washington D.C.: U.S. Government Printing Office, 1972), p. 667.

9. Walter LaFeber, *The Panama Canal* (Oxford: Oxford University Press, 1978), p. 111.

10. Ambassador Davis to Secretary of State Marshall, November 25, 1949, printed in *FRUS 1949*, vol. 2 (Washington D.C.: U.S. Government Printing Office, 1975), pp. 725–26.

11. Ibid., p. 729. Subsequently, in May 1951 President Arias dissolved the National Assembly and abolished the 1946 Constitution in an attempt to extend his power. Colonel Remón thereupon overthrew him, and had himself elected president in 1952. Ambassador Wiley wrote to Secretary of State Acheson in December 1951 that "the American eggs all seem to be in one basket, that of Colonel Remón, since he is the sole anti-Communist leader in the entire political panorama. Though the basket, as the Department is well aware, is far from commendable, Colonel Remón still remains an irreplaceable *faut de mieux*"; *FRUS, 1951*, vol. 2 (Washington D.C.: U.S. Government Printing Office, 1979), p. 1567. In January 1955 President Remón was assassinated, apparently in a dispute with the Mafia over control of Panama's narcotics traffic (LaFeber, p. 120).

12. "Panama and the Path to Democracy," a speech by assistant secretary of state, Elliott Abrams, June 30, 1987.

13. Ibid.

14. See, for example, Albert K. Weinberg, *Manifest Destiny: A Study of Nationalist Expansion in American History* (Baltimore: Johns Hopkins University Press, 1935).

10 | The United States and Latin American Democracy: Learning from History

Abraham F. Lowenthal

THIS BOOK tells a cautionary tale. Recurrent efforts by the government of the United States to promote democracy in Latin America have rarely been successful, and then only in a narrow range of circumstances.

From the turn of the century until the 1980s, the overall impact of U.S. policy on Latin America's ability to achieve democratic politics was usually negligible, often counterproductive, and only occasionally positive. Although it is too soon to be sure, this general conclusion may hold true for the 1980s and the 1990s as well. Despite Washington's current bipartisan enthusiasm for exporting democracy, Latin America's experience to date suggests that expectations should be modest.

U.S. officials have tried often to harness the influence of the United States in support of Latin American democracy. The sources and motives of their concern have been mixed, the instruments used have differed widely, and the concepts of "democracy" officials have had in mind vary. But the results of U.S. efforts to promote democracy, with few exceptions, have been equally disappointing.

This chapter, drawing on the others in the volume, summarizes the twentieth-century record of the United States in promoting Latin American democracy, highlights what can be learned from closer looks at a few cases, derives some general conclusions, and offers a few guidelines for U.S. policy. Its aim, like that of the whole symposium, is to gain insights from the past that may illuminate current and future choices. Political leaders and policy makers should reflect upon this sobering history, lest uncritical acceptance of a noble objective once again lead to disillusion and to misguided actions.

Reviewing the Record

From 1913 to 1933, as Paul Drake chronicles, the United States at one time or another promoted democracy in Mexico, Peru, Ecuador, Cuba, the Dominican Republic, Haiti, Nicaragua, Honduras, Costa Rica, and Guatemala. In some cases, U.S. efforts were restricted to rhetorical declarations or halfhearted diplomatic pressure. In others, however, the United States undertook more energetic activities: supervising elections, reorganizing local military forces, pushing for civic and social reforms, favoring those political groups perceived by Washington as most committed to democracy, and offering or withholding financial assistance to Latin American governments on the basis of whether or not they were considered democratic.

U.S. officials sought to nurture democracy in Latin America during this period for various reasons: as a means of pacification to end local civil wars; to help legitimize national regimes in the eyes of the local population, the U.S. public, or international opinion; to permit the extrication of U.S. forces from military interventions that no longer had domestic support in the United States, and thus to counter rising "anti-imperialist" sentiment at home; and to assure that U.S. foreign policy in the border region did not contradict salient U.S. policies elsewhere in the world.

As Drake emphasizes, U.S. officials in the 1920s invariably had in mind a limited and formal institutional notion of "democracy"—that is, constitutional government based on periodic free and fair elections. From time to time, however, individual U.S. officials opined that deeper structural changes might be required in order to assure the preconditions necessary to foster such elections or to permit the elected regimes to govern.

The most strenuous U.S. efforts to promote democracy during this period occurred in the small Caribbean and Central American countries—precisely those nations in which the structural and institutional circumstances for democratic politics were least auspicious. They all lacked political parties, an independent judiciary, an apolitical police and military establishment, broad civic education, and a substantial middle class. Washington concentrated on these countries not from a calculation about where and how democratic politics might likely emerge, but because of U.S. strategic and economic concerns. The promotion of democracy became an end in itself, and was taken seriously as an objective by U.S. officials. But when strategic or economic considerations clashed with the democratic goal, democracy promotion almost invariably got short shrift.

In country after country, from the mid-1920s through the early 1930s, U.S. officials circumscribed and eventually abandoned their direct efforts to promote democracy. U.S. officials faced opposition to their interventionist presence within various Latin American countries and also at home. Often they resented being manipulated by Latin American politicians whose prime motive was not democracy but power. In many cases, they acutely felt the lack of reliable local democratic partners. Aware as well that a strong U.S. presence in the Caribbean Basin was harming U.S. relations elsewhere in Latin America and even in Europe, U.S. officials began to back away from their efforts. They persisted in doing so, indeed, even in the face of evidence that the new local regimes—which were consolidating their holds while the United States was reducing its involvement—were less democratic and more repressive than their predecessors. That was the case in the Dominican Republic, Nicaragua, Cuba, and Haiti.

By the early 1930s, in the absence of any extrahemispheric challenge to U.S. dominance, U.S. officials were ready to embrace the Latin American norm of "nonintervention." After 1934, when President Franklin D. Roosevelt formally pledged the United States to refrain from interference in the domestic affairs of Latin America, the United States gave up the active promotion of democracy in the hemisphere. This recurrent concern of U.S. policy was not to surface again until the end of World War II.

With its triumph in that war, ostensibly fought on behalf of the Four Freedoms, the United States renewed its expressed interest in Latin American democracy. The motives, circumstances, and chosen instruments for this new wave of promoting democracy differed considerably from those of the 1920s, but the results were almost equally meager, as Leslie Bethell points out.

The main impetus for the regionwide move toward political liberalization and at least partial democratization after World War II came from the countries of Latin America themselves. Whereas U.S. efforts to promote Latin American democracy from 1913 through the 1920s concentrated primarily on the Caribbean Basin border nations, after World War II Washington's concern for building democracy extended throughout the hemisphere; indeed, U.S. efforts were especially strong in Argentina, Brazil, and Bolivia, three of the countries farthest from Washington. The prevailing concept of "democracy" was also different; although U.S. policy makers in the 1920s were preoccupied with elections, Washington was more concerned in the 1940s to assure that authoritarian movements—whether profascist or pro-Communist—not come to power in Latin America, through elections or otherwise.

The U.S. desire to promote democracy in Latin America after World War II, again, had mixed sources. The underlying ideological preference for democracy in the United States was strongly reinforced and given broad popular currency as a result of the antifascist wartime campaign. After the difficult and costly antitotalitarian exertion, U.S. citizens no longer felt comfortable about their government's maintaining cordial relations with Latin American dictatorships, and close U.S. ties with such regimes came to be questioned. As Washington began to criticize Soviet policies in Eastern Europe, where undemocratic regimes were being imposed, there was also a natural wish to be sure that the United States could voice such complaints without finding its own record embarrassingly inconsistent with its professed values.

Perhaps most important, the prodemocracy stance of the United States in the years immediately following World War II was a concrete response to the changing internal conditions of Latin America, where strong domestic pressures to open up politics were beginning to build. A generation of urbanization and economic growth was changing the social structure in several Latin American nations. The urban middle class and, to a degree, the working class were now themselves pushing for full political participation.

From 1945 to about 1948, the United States both directly and indirectly reinforced Latin America's democratizing tendency. North American cultural influence became increasingly strong, both because of war-related propaganda efforts and because of the expanding presence of the U.S. media, particularly radio and motion pictures. So did Washington's political influence, especially after the war left the United States unchallenged as the world's greatest economic and military power, with no competitor for hegemonic standing in the hemisphere. The ideological power of the United States and its political system was then at its height.

The strong indirect influence of the United States was reinforced in particular cases by specific U.S. policies—as in Brazil, where Ambassador Adolf Berle pushed for the dismantling of Getúlio Vargas's authoritarian regime; in Mexico, where Ambassador George Messersmith called for competitive elections and briefly promoted the prospective candidacy of Ezequiel Padilla; in Paraguay, where persistent U.S. pressure in 1944–46 led to brief democratizing reforms in 1946; and most strenuously in Argentina, where strong U.S. pressures backfired and the elections held in 1946 were won by strongman Juan Perón.

On the whole, Latin American politics did move in a democratic direction during the immediate postwar years, and the United States seemed generally to support this trend. But by the late 1940s, Latin America's democratic window was closing and the strict limits on Washington's enthusiasm for Latin America's democratic opening became evident. In Argentina, the United States dropped its ideological stand against Perón and instead sought close cooperation with the Argentine caudillo, who was now prepared to cooperate with Washington and with U.S. investors on economic issues. In Peru and Venezuela, where military coups soon overthrew democratically elected regimes, Washington made it clear that it could easily accommodate again authoritarian governments, as long as they respected concrete U.S. interests. And as the wartime antifascist ethos gave way to the emphasis on Europe's reconstruction and to the incipient cold war, the main U.S. concern in Latin America moved from promoting democracy to fostering political stability and economic growth.

The U.S. emphasis on stability and growth was in part a response to the emergence of militant labor unions and strengthened Communist parties in several Latin American countries. Washington's preference for popular democracy did not fully apply when staunch U.S. allies were being challenged, especially by leftists. As U.S. concern grew with the perceived worldwide Marxist threat, Washington's bias for stability strengthened, even when that meant support for nondemocratic or antidemocratic politics. As George Kennan put it, "Where the concepts and traditions of popular government are too weak to absorb successfully the intensity of the Communist attacks, then we must concede that harsh government measures of repression may be the only answer."[1]

It was not much of a leap from this line of reasoning to Washington's orchestration of the successful overthrow of the democratically elected Arbenz government in Guatemala. The covert U.S. intervention in Guatemala in 1954 was possible in part because the U.S. government was no longer according much priority, if any, to promoting Latin American democracy. After 1948, Washington did little to support Latin America's democratizing efforts. The United States attempted to thwart the attempts of the "Caribbean Legion" to overthrow dictatorships in Nicaragua and the Dominican Republic, for example, and took no prodemocracy initiatives of its own.

Promoting democracy was not one of the stated objectives of U.S. policy in the Eisenhower administration's first strategy paper on Latin America, nor was it a major factor in shaping U.S. policy during the first Eisenhower administration.[2] Once again, regional circumstances and U.S. concerns elsewhere in the world combined to overwhelm the impulse to reform Latin America.

During the course of the 1950s, when as many as thirteen out of twenty Latin American states were ruled by dictators, the Eisenhower administration slowly changed its views, however. Authoritarian regimes came to be considered inherently unpopular, thus unstable and perhaps susceptible to subversion by anti-American movements. Pushed by well-informed advice from his brother Milton (who traveled to Latin America several times in the 1950s on behalf of the administration) and from special assistant Nelson A. Rockefeller, President Eisenhower moved during the course of the decade from a policy of indifference toward democracy—and sole reliance on open markets and direct investment as a sufficient foreign economic policy—to a positive interest in promoting both political and economic development in Latin America. This new interest was to be expressed through the transfer of public funds, the establishment of regional economic institutions (especially the Inter-American Development Bank), and the mobilization of U.S. influence in concrete cases in order to promote democratic politics. This policy crystallized in 1957–58 with the crumbling of Fulgencio Batista's long-time dictatorship in Cuba. With some lingering ambivalence, to be sure, the Eisenhower administration pressured Batista to leave office and to make possible a democratic transition. Batista resisted, but the evident withdrawal of U.S. support decisively weakened his hold.

The fall of Batista's regime in Cuba and the coming to power of Fidel Castro, a radical nationalist who was soon to develop close relations with the Soviet Union, precipitated a strong revival of U.S. concern with Latin America. The key preoccupation now was how to assure that the "twilight of the tyrants"—the weakening of a number of personalistic dictatorships—would not revert to another authoritarian night.[3]

The newly inaugurated administration of Pres. John F. Kennedy focused sharply on this challenge, and designed the Alliance for Progress. The idea was to nurture reformist democracies that could steer a middle course between reactionary oligarchs and revolutionaries on the left. The architects of the alliance recognized the revolutionary potential of extreme poverty, inequality, and political repression. Accordingly, Washington undertook to foster economic development, social reform, and democratic politics in Latin America in order to preempt revolution. Based on theories then prevailing in the U.S. academic community, U.S. officials believed that economic growth, the expansion of the middle class, land reform, political democracy, and enhanced stability all went hand in hand, and that the United States could effectively assist these processes from outside.[4]

As initially conceived, the Alliance for Progress called for an infusion of $20 billion in U.S. public and private funds over a ten-year period: to build infrastructure, raise per capita income, reduce illiteracy, improve public health, reform land tenure, and ameliorate income distribution. Because U.S. officials assumed that somehow economic growth and social reform would facilitate democratic politics, they devoted little systematic thought to the actual promotion of democracy. As Tony Smith indicates, the emphasis of policy was on how to nurture economic development; U.S. policy makers believed that democratic opening would follow ineluctably. To the extent that any conscious U.S. effort was made to promote democracy during the early 1960s, it was by not recognizing de facto governments arising from coups, by offering foreign aid as an incentive for democratization, and by providing military assistance and training programs and "public safety" efforts to put down insurgent movements and control instability.[5]

In any case, the Kennedy administration's commitment to democracy was at best conditional. As President Kennedy is reported to have expressed it in considering U.S. policy toward the Trujillo dictatorship in the Dominican Republic: "There are three possibilities, in descending order of preference: a decent democratic regime, a continuation of the Trujillo regime, or a Castro regime. We ought to aim at the first, but we can't really renounce the second until we are sure we can avoid the third."[6] U.S. efforts to promote democracy under Kennedy were often contradicted by programs to strengthen counterinsurgency forces and to shore up the local militaries. Modest efforts to push for land reform in places like northeast Brazil (where land tenure was highly inequitable) gave way quickly when local vested interests opposed the reforms while Communist groups favored them.[7]

Moreover, U.S. attempts to promote democracy during this period were brief and impatient. Disappointed by the lack of multilateral Latin American support for U.S. initiatives to use nonrecognition and political intervention to support democracy, the Kennedy administration backed away from its prodemocracy policy. It remained passive, at best, while Juan Bosch was being overthrown in the Dominican Republic in September 1963, and then edged toward recognition of the Dominican and Honduran de facto governments.

The drift of U.S. policy back toward accepting Latin American governments "as they are," without seeking to reform them, was accelerated and formalized after Kennedy's death, particularly after President Lyndon B. Johnson put career diplomat Thomas C. Mann in charge of Latin American policy. The "Mann Doctrine," a statement of U.S. policy announced by the new assistant secretary in 1964, made it clear that the United States would no longer push for democratic transitions in the hemisphere.

On the contrary, Washington supported the military overthrow of João Goulart's democratically elected government in Brazil in 1964, backed the military coup in Uruguay in 1973, and welcomed General Augusto Pinochet's overthrow of the elected government of Salvador Allende in Chile in 1973. During the late 1960s and early 1970s, Washington seemed comfortable with Latin America's swing toward military rule. Governor Rockefeller, in a report for the Nixon administration, now urged that the United States maintain normal diplomatic and economic relations with military regimes, which he argued could be progressive and reformist, though they were not to be preferred to democratic governments.[8] By the mid-1970s, U.S. relations with the military regimes were so cordial that Washington was widely perceived, indeed, as the champion of authoritarianism in the Americas.

The Vietnam war and its impact on U.S. politics and policy soon reversed this tendency, however. Domestic opposition to U.S. foreign policy, galvanized by the anti-war movement and then by the revulsion against the Watergate political scandal, led to strong criticism of the association of the United States with Latin American dictatorships. A deep current of domestic opinion, crystallized by human rights and religious organizations, pushed during the early and mid-1970s for legislation curbing U.S. economic and military assistance to any country with a record of gross and systematic violations of human rights.

The administration of Jimmy Carter, elected in 1976 after a campaign in which Carter promised to give the United States "a government as good as its people," initially made human rights the cornerstone of its Latin American policy. Convinced that prior U.S. policy toward Latin America and many of the developing countries had been distorted by "an inordinate fear of Communism," the Carter administration initially reduced the prior U.S. preoccupation with stability and anti-Communism in the Western

Hemisphere, and accepted "ideological pluralism" in the region. Its prime concern was with curbing gross violations of human rights—torture, "disappearances," and prolonged incarceration of political opponents—rather than with facilitating general democratic political opening (*abertura,* in Latin American parlance).[9] The administration's efforts were fully consistent with *abertura,* however, and served to reinforce the internal processes in Brazil, Peru, Ecuador, and Uruguay that were impelling those countries back toward democratic politics. In one specific situation, in the Dominican Republic in 1978 (discussed in Jonathan Hartlyn's chapter), the Carter administration pushed effectively to counter electoral fraud and assist a democratic transition. But this was an exceptional case of direct U.S. pressure; in most instances, the Carter administration's support for Latin American democracy was indirect.

Ronald Reagan came to office in 1981 highly critical of the Carter human rights policies, which were said to have destabilized friendly regimes, particularly those of Anastasio Somoza in Nicaragua and of the shah of Iran, without producing democratic (or friendly) governments in their stead.[10] The new administration sought to reverse the perceived mistakes of the Carter period by refurbishing U.S. relations with the "moderately authoritarian" regimes of the Southern Cone, particularly in Argentina, Brazil, and Chile.

The Reagan administration befriended the Argentine military regime, a virtual pariah during the Carter period, and enlisted it as an ally in support of U.S. policy in Central America. Ambassador Jeane Kirkpatrick traveled to Chile to mend fences with General Pinochet. The White House sought, as well, to restore what one National Security Council staff person called a "beautiful relationship" with Brazil. Secretary of State Alexander Haig explained that terrorism from the left would be the new administration's major human rights concern. Indeed, the first Reagan appointee for the post of assistant secretary of state for human rights, Ernest Lefever, was rejected by the Senate because, in keeping with the new administration's thrust, he opposed systematic U.S. efforts to promote human rights in non-Communist autocracies. But despite this initial Reagan approach to Latin America, by the end of the 1980s the U.S. government was once again trumpeting its strong efforts to promote Latin American democracy, and was even taking considerable credit for the region's strides in that direction.

Although promoting democracy was a unifying articulated theme of Reagan pronouncements on Latin America, particularly after 1982, Thomas Carothers points out that in practice there were at least four different subpolicies, each adopted for different reasons and each with diverse effects. At various times and places, the Reagan administration was promoting: "democracy by centrist transition" through the emergence of elected civilian governments in El Salvador, Honduras, and Guatemala; "democracy by force" in Nicaragua and Grenada; "democracy by applause," through limited diplomatic support to the many transitions from authoritarian rule in South America; and "democracy by pressure" to induce the remaining right-wing dictators in Chile, Paraguay, Panama, and Haiti to cede power through elections.

The Reagan administration's first focal point in the Western Hemisphere was Central America, for the new U.S. policy makers believed that the Soviet Union had targeted the region as part of its "master plan" for threatening U.S. interests. The administration's initial aim was simple: to counter leftist gains in Central America by shoring up the governments of El Salvador, Guatemala, Honduras, and Costa Rica—primarily through military and economic assistance as well as by pressuring the Sandinista regime in Nicaragua to cease supporting the left in neighboring countries, if not to give up power themselves. Administration policy makers soon came to understand that it would be easier to obtain congressional approval for these military programs if they were couched in "prodemocracy" terms. The thrust of the administration's policy, however, was not so much to promote democratic openings as to fortify the incumbent regimes, while portraying them in the most favorable light possible.

Late in the Reagan period—after José Napoleon Duarte's regime in El Salvador was safely stabilized and the administration's hard-liners could focus single-mindedly on Nicaragua—the administration concentrated on promoting free and fair elections throughout Central America. Even then, however, the efforts were motivated far more by the aim of mobilizing congressional backing for the anti-Sandinista campaign than by a desire to reshape Central American realities. And whenever a conflict arose among policy objectives in the region, priority went to thwarting the Left.

As part of the effort to isolate Nicaragua, Reagan administration operatives took credit for Central America's democratization during the 1980s, but this tendency merely illustrated the superficiality of that administration's concern with democracy, at least in this context. Washington's efforts certainly did not bring robust democracy to any of the Central American countries, and in most cases the U.S. emphasis on supporting local military establishments arguably reinforced their dominant and ultimately anti-democratic role. Further, the administration's massive economic assistance and its political intervention were so intrusive as almost certainly to reduce the long-term changes for indigenous and autonomous democratic politics.

Although administration officials portrayed the policy toward Nicaragua as intended to induce the Sandinistas to permit free and fair elections, the goal of "democratization" in Nicaragua was actually imposed on U.S. policy by hard-liners within the Reagan coalition who saw it primarily as a way to prevent U.S. accommodation with the Sandinistas by establishing a precondition Managua presumably could not fulfill.[11] Once included in the stated U.S. policy, the objective of democratization in Nicaragua had two effects: to block any negotiated agreement on security issues (just as the hard-liners intended) and to change the terms of the debate in Congress by enabling the administration to sell military aid to the contras as a means of pressuring a nondemocratic government to open up its politics. But this was largely a ploy to strengthen a policy of hostility toward the Sandinistas based on their ties to the Soviet Union and Cuba, not to their lack of full-fledged pluralist democracy.

As an instrument for actually opening up Nicaragua's politics and fostering the conditions for democracy, the Reagan policy of military aid to the contras was surely counterproductive. It was only when the Congress finally forced the administration to drop the contra war that there was space for the Arias Plan, the diplomatic initiative spearheaded by Costa Rica's president, which eventually opened the way to the democratic elections of February 1990.

The striking transitions toward democracy that took place in South America during the 1980s have been cited by former Assistant Secretary of State Elliott Abrams and others as examples of the efficacy of Reagan's efforts to promote democracy. In fact, however, U.S. verbal support for the first few transitions was no more than an overlay on the basic policy of improving relations with the military governments.[12] The administration had no identifiable positive role in facilitating the transitions to democracy in Argentina, Brazil, and Uruguay. If anything, its policy worked against the democratizing trend, as friendly overtures from the United States and the tone of renewed material and diplomatic support temporarily buoyed the military governments.

When the Reagan administration finally did embrace South America's democratic openings, this was mainly in response to the failure of its first attempts to establish durable warm relations with the Argentine and Chilean military regimes and as a belated reaction to indigenous trends in South America; it was also in part motivated by the desire to have a more consistent prodemocracy image in order to build congressional support for the contra aid. The policy of "democracy by applause," although a shift from the earlier stance, was in any case essentially limited to rhetoric. Washington did not provide the economic support the fragile democracies called for. Such verbal backing as was furnished was ineffective or irrelevant in almost all cases.

It was only in the last years of the second Reagan administration that the United States clearly exerted its influence to nurture democratic transitions from the remaining right-wing authoritarian governments in Haiti, Panama, Paraguay, and Chile.[13] In all four cases, the United States did take specific measures, including diplomatic and economic pressure, to try to persuade long-time dictators to cede power. What is most notable about these cases, in turn, is how spectacularly the administration's efforts at democracy promotion failed in Haiti and Panama, how largely irrelevant they were in Paraguay, and that they were apparently successful only in Chile.

And although U.S. officials often cite Chile as an example of the Reagan administration's Democracy Agenda, U.S. policy was not more than a marginal factor in the Chilean transition. As Heraldo Muñoz shows, Chilean opposition groups largely on their own developed the strategy and tactics that brought an end to the Pinochet dictatorship, and they restored national political institutions and practices that were entirely indigenous. Even the exceptional Chilean case thus provides evidence to prove the rule that the United States did not do much during the 1980s that was important and effective in promoting Latin American democracy.

Getting Down to Cases

From the time of Woodrow Wilson to the present, in sum, there has been a recurrent, sincere, but limited U.S. impulse to promote democracy in Latin America. This U.S. drive to export democracy has only rarely had a positive and lasting impact, however. In most cases, in all periods, the strict limits on Washington's capacity to nurture Latin American democracy, even when it wants to do so, have been plainly evident.

These preliminary conclusions are strongly reinforced by focusing on five countries where the United States has repeatedly tried to foster democratic politics: Argentina, the Dominican Republic, Mexico, Nicaragua, and Chile.

Carlos Escudé's comparison of U.S. policy toward Argentina from 1943 to 1955 and from 1976 to 1983 shows that the United States pursued vacillating, contradictory, and indeed incoherent policies with respect to democratic politics and the related issue of human rights in Argentina. At times, Washington pushed Argentine governments hard to respect human rights and constitutional democratic guarantees. But there were also moments, sometimes hard on the heels of a binge of democracy promotion, when Washington subordinated this concern to other considerations, or seemed to abandon it altogether.

Escudé illuminates the divisions in Washington regarding the ends and means of U.S. policy toward Argentina, demonstrating that struggles among policy makers often determined U.S. actions. He hypothesizes that this tendency has been heightened in the Argentine case by the country's peculiar stature as sufficiently large and visible to have some salience, yet sufficiently distant and marginal to the vital interests of the United States to allow full play in the policy-making process to personal idiosyncracies and bureaucratic rivalry.

Whatever the reasons for the cycles in U.S. policy, Escudé's main contention, although perhaps exaggerated, is compelling: the activation and deactivation by the United States of its prodemocracy concerns has had the perverse effect, over time, of helping to undermine Argentine political stability, contributing to further polarization of a divided society, and thus diminishing the country's chances for sustainable democratic politics.

A similar point is made in Jonathan Hartlyn's survey of the relationship between U.S. policy and democratic prospects in the Dominican Republic over a seventy-five-year period, from the U.S. military occupation of 1916 through the 1990 presidential elections. Hartlyn analyzes five different times when the United States was deeply engaged, although to varying extents, in the Dominican Republic's political life: during the military occupation until 1924, at the time of the accession to power of long-term dictator Rafael Trujillo in 1930, in the period of democratic ferment immediately following World War II, in the kaleidoscopic years from the last phase of Trujillo's government through the inauguration of Joaquín Balaguer in 1966, and in the 1978 democratic transition, when Balaguer became the first elected president in the country's history to relinquish power to an elected opponent. Hartlyn demonstrates that the United States has long had great influence in Dominican politics, no matter what its policy, but that Washington has not easily or often determined the Dominican Republic's course. He also finds that Dominican actors invariably try to mobilize the United States as a potential ally in their struggles; that democracy promotion has often been on the U.S. agenda in Santo Domingo, but for sharply changing reasons; and that the extent of U.S. involvement in promoting Dominican democracy has usually been more a function of the general international context than of internal Dominican conditions.

Two points stand out in Hartlyn's account. First, the most effective instance of U.S. democracy promotion occurred in 1978 at a time when Washington was relatively unconcerned about the Dominican Republic, when U.S. actions were confined to supporting local institutions and actors, and when Dominican internal processes played the crucial role in facilitating a democratic transition. Second, the net effect of seventy-five years of U.S. involvement in Dominican affairs, the cumulative impact of three generations of episodic democracy promotion, has been to create a pathology of dependence that will have to be overcome eventually if meaningful democracy is ever to be consolidated in the Dominican Republic. Repeated U.S. efforts to foster Dominican democracy—combined with sometimes abrupt shifts in U.S. policy, as priorities and concepts change— have distorted the Dominican Republic's politics in ways ultimately inimical to democracy.[14]

At many points in this century, U.S. policy makers have articulated the goal of promoting democracy in Nicaragua, as Joseph Tulchin and Knut Walter emphasize, but up to now their efforts have been repeatedly and remarkably unsuccessful. Over and over, U.S. officials have underestimated the difficulty of establishing stable democratic conditions in Nicaragua. Time and again, limited U.S. intervention has expanded until its exaggerated extent has led Washington to curtail its involvement, even at the cost of giving up the democratic policy objective—at which point the nondemocratic dynamics of Nicaraguan politics has taken over once again.

The Nicaraguan presidential elections of 1990, widely recognized as the most open and honest national poll in that country's history, took place to a significant extent because of U.S. pressure, and it is therefore commonly cited as an example of Washington's successful promotion of democracy.[15] What is almost universally accepted in Washington, however, was broadly perceived in Nicaragua as but the latest in a long series of blatant U.S. interventions that have had less to do with democracy than with a continuing U.S. desire to control the country's politics. No one who reads Tulchin and Walter's review of eighty years in Nicaragua's history would entirely discount this interpretation. Perhaps decades of previous experience will be reversed now, but it is certainly much too early to assume that Nicaraguan democracy will be consolidated, or even that the United States would unambiguously and effectively support sustained democracy there.

In Argentina, the Dominican Republic, and Nicaragua, U.S. officials have often talked about promoting democracy and have sometimes tried to do so, but with little positive effect and with some contrary results. In Mexico, however, according to Lorenzo Meyer, U.S. concern about the prospects for democracy, even at the level of rhetoric, occurred only for a brief moment. That was in 1913–14, early in the Mexican Revolution, when President Woodrow Wilson, essentially for ideological reasons, pushed hard but only briefly for democratic opening. Within months, the internal Mexican struggles and intrabureaucratic wrangling in Washington combined to frustrate Wilson's impulse to teach Mexicans "to elect good men." From then until the 1980s, Meyer argues, the United States did little or nothing to promote democracy in Mexico, or even to concern itself about whether Mexico was or could ever become democratic. Washington's overriding concern about Mexico, decade after decade, was not democracy but stability.

Even in the 1980s, when Washington's campaign to promote democracy was applied, if very discreetly, to Mexico, Meyer suggests that the U.S. concern with Mexico's prospects for democracy was at best superficial. During the early and mid-1980s, Washington pursued the goal of democracy tactically, as an instrument for strengthening the rightist opposition party, the Partido Acción Nacional (PAN), and thereby pressuring the government of Mexico to adjust to U.S. preferences on Central America, immigration, drugs, and economic policy. Dramatic evidence that the United States was not fundamentally concerned about democracy in Mexico was provided in 1988, Meyer argues, as the previously fragmented U.S. government quickly and unanimously rallied to support President-elect Carlos Salinas de Gortari despite indications that his election in July 1988 had been marred by fraud.

Ironically, as Meyer briefly suggests, the positive influence of the United States on Mexico's democratic prospects has actually been rapidly expanding since the late 1980s, not because of official policy but despite it. The U.S. media, human rights groups, scholars, and labor and business groups have all become increasingly active in Mexico. For different reasons, all are concerned about the rule of law, free expression, and democratic politics, and their interest is likely to be mobilized with increasing effectiveness by those in Mexico who are pushing for democratic change.

Perhaps the best example of a successful U.S. effort to foster democratic politics in Latin America occurred in Chile beginning in the mid-1980s. From the time of Harry G. Barnes's appointment as U.S. ambassador in Santiago in 1985, the government consistently employed its influence to encourage the authoritarian military regime of Gen. Augusto Pinochet to move toward restoring constitutional democracy. At various critical moments in the late 1980s, U.S. pressures or appeals helped nudge Pinochet toward conducting a national plebiscite under conditions that were sufficiently open and fair to permit the dramatic victory of the opposition coalition and the end of the Pinochet dictatorship. The U.S. also provided encouragement, advice, and assistance to the democratic opposition at a number of points and in different ways—indirectly by supporting the plebiscitary process itself and directly by making available funding and technical help. On some issues and at some critical moments, the U.S. role may well have been significant—in insisting that the opposition campaign have access to television as a condition of U.S. recognition of the plebiscite's validity, for example, and in warning the Pinochet government that an eleventh-hour plan to derail the plebiscite would be strongly condemned.

But, as Heraldo Muñoz argues, even the Chilean success story carries a mixed message about the relationship between the United States and Latin American democracy. Muñoz persuasively argues that Washington has never been particularly interested in democracy in Chile, where the emergence of strong democratic traditions and institutions over the past century had nothing to do with the United States. Indeed, the historic U.S. attitude toward Chilean democracy has been generally neutral and occasionally negative. For several decades, the U.S. approach to Chilean politics was to prevent the left from gaining power, even if it could gain office through democratic means, rather than to bolster democracy as such. The U.S. government conspired against and in some sense contributed to the eventual unconstitutional overthrow of the democratically elected and constitutional administration of Salvador Allende in 1970–73.

The sources and motives of U.S. support for Chile's return to democracy in the late 1980s were mixed, as Muñoz shows: the built-in tension between support for Pinochet and underlying American values; the pressures on U.S. policy exerted by human rights groups and other nongovernmental organizations; the skill of Chilean opposition leaders in taking advantage of the pluralism of U.S. society to mobilize U.S. influence; and, above all, the internal evolution of the Chilean situation, which permitted a consensus to emerge against prolonging the dictatorship and allowed very diverse opposition groups eventually to submerge their differences toward this end. An important ingredient, too, as Muñoz underlines, was career diplomat Barnes, who skillfully transformed U.S. policies to support a democratic transition and thus gave encouragement to many in Chilean society who wanted assurance that an end to the dictatorship was both possible and safe.

In contrast to most of the other cases here reviewed, U.S. efforts at promoting democracy in Chile were effective. But even here, the limits of the case emerge plainly from Muñoz's account. External influence, including that of the United States, helped at the margin to restore democracy, but this was in an already fundamentally democratic nation, under conditions of stability and prosperity, with a strong moderate opposition movement and a weak left mostly committed to peaceful and incremental change. Circumstances as favorable as those in Chile for the nurturing of democracy do not often arise.

Key Nongovernmental Actors

The essays reviewed thus far discuss the impact of U.S. government policy on Latin America's prospects for democracy. Some of the most important ways in which the United States affects Latin America, however, derive not from governmental policy but from the acts and omissions of nongovernmental agents with a strong presence in the region. There are many relevant examples, including religious groups, journalists, scholars, and human rights organizations. All merit more treatment than they receive in this volume, but our symposium does include two chapters focusing on key nongovernmental actors: U.S. business and organized labor.

Elizabeth Cobbs argues, contrary to conventional assumptions, that in the period following World War II U.S. business has often shown a stronger commitment to constructive relations with Latin America, and ultimately to reinforcing the region's democratic movement, than has the U.S. government. This is not because business has particularly noble motives or an ideological attachment to democracy, but rather because the self-interested concerns of business leaders have led them over the past few decades to learn that intervention is often counterproductive and that respect for local sovereignty and neutrality toward local political decisions are ultimately more conducive to political stability and to economic growth than cyclical but short-lived direct efforts to promote their interests.

The contrast between U.S. government policy and that of U.S. corporations in the case of Nicaragua illustrates this point. U.S. firms were willing and able to cooperate with the Sandinista regime at a time when the Reagan administration was determined to undermine it. Even in the most famous cases of political intervention by U.S. corporations—by United Fruit Company in Guatemala in the 1950s and by International Telephone and Telegraph in Chile in the 1970s—the firms were implementing U.S. government policy more than driving it, and the corporate policies were largely opposed by other elements of the business community. On the whole, U.S. companies in Latin America, at least during the past fifty years, have been increasingly respectful of national sovereignty, and thus have contributed to one of the prerequisites for genuine and lasting democratic politics.

Throughout most of the century, the organized labor movement of the United States, by contrast, has been more of an obstacle than an ally to Latin America's democratization. From World War I to the 1970s, U.S. labor pushed pro–United States "business unionism" in Latin America—aimed at guaranteeing profitability for U.S. investors and countering the influence in the region of radical, class-based, nationalist, and independent trade unions. For decades, labor's efforts in Latin America had a consistently conservative and often antidemocratic bias, as its interests were tied primarily to U.S.-led capitalist expansion and to Latin American stability, rather than mainly to political pluralism or social change.

But since the 1970s, Paul Buchanan shows, economic and political changes in the United States, Latin America, and elsewhere have combined to induce U.S. labor to take a positive interest in the political liberalization of Latin America. U.S. labor has come to play a significant role in promoting democratic openings in Latin American nations as different as El Salvador and Brazil, not so much out of ideological conviction as for self-interest. U.S. labor today sees the promotion of economic and political democracy around the world as the best way of equalizing the international labor market, and thus pursuing its own material and organizational objectives. Like U.S. business, U.S. labor has thus come to play a role at least compatible with—and perhaps supportive of—strengthening Latin American democracy. In the 1990s, in contrast with the past, U.S. labor, like U.S. business, may well exert a democratizing influence in Latin America.

General Conclusions

Some tentative propositions may now be advanced about when and where the United States has tried to promote Latin American democracy, why, how, and with what results.

1. The United States Government has often adopted policies intended to strengthen Latin America's prospects for democracy, conceived of in political and institutional terms. These efforts have been most salient in the Caribbean Basin nations close to the United States, and in distant nations (such as Argentina and Chile) large enough to be visible politically and internationally but too far away to be closely

connected with the United States or perceived as vital to its security. Washington's attempts to promote democracy have been least evident in such major nations as Mexico and Brazil, where the overriding U.S. objective has been long-term stability.

2. There is an underlying predisposition in the United States to favor democratic politics throughout the Western Hemisphere (and the world, for that matter), and this fundamental tendency makes unstable and ultimately unviable any U.S. alliance with a repressive authoritarian regime. But the U.S. bias for democracy is rarely sufficient to overcome general and specific constraints on the impulse to promote democracy abroad, or to give the promotion of democracy priority over the other goals of U.S. policy. The impulse to promote democracy may be reinforced in particular situations, however, either for instrumental reasons—as a means of coercion, to achieve consistency in order to bolster U.S. efforts elsewhere to dislodge an antagonistic regime, or to facilitate the extrication of the United States from an unwanted involvement—or because of effective pressures from concerned groups within the United States or in the Latin American nation.

3. The United States has been more likely to push actively for democratic opening in a Latin American nation when:

a. An incumbent authoritarian regime is perceived by U.S. officials as anti-American; or,

b. An incumbent authoritarian regime is pursuing specific policies perceived by Washington officials as contrary to U.S. interests; or,

c. A high priority effort to dislodge or pressure one regime qualifying under condition *a* or *b* requires consistent attempts to promote democratic opening in other nations that can easily be portrayed as comparable; or,

d. Democractic opening, or at least a "demonstration election," is needed as a means of legitimizing a significant diminution of the U.S. presence in and influence upon a country where Washington has heretofore been deeply engaged;[16] or,

e. Local democratic forces by themselves are so close to obtaining power that Washington officials conclude that a timely identification of U.S. policies with their fortunes is opportune; or,

f. Local political forces are particularly adept at mobilizing groups within the United States to pressure for the alignment of U.S. policies with their movement; or,

g. No important U.S. economic or security interests are engaged in the particular country, and the underlying U.S. cultural and ideological preference for democratic politics has recently been strongly reinforced in the minds of policy makers in a broader international context; *and,*

278 · Abraham F. Lowenthal

h. The left in the specific country is either thought to be insignificant or else understood to be committed to democratic and nonviolent forms of political competition.[17]

4. Specific U.S. efforts to promote democracy in Latin America are motivated more often by domestic U.S. or broader international considerations than by particular trends within the affected country. It is largely for this reason that U.S. prodemocracy efforts so often occur in waves and are played out in a number of very different nations within the same period, regardless of whether these nations are themselves evolving toward or away from democratic politics.

5. The United States has used a wide variety of means to nurture Latin American democracy, ranging from quiet diplomacy through pressures and sanctions to outright occupation. Each of these instruments has been useful in pushing for democratic politics in at least one concrete situation. By and large, however, the more interventionist the United States has been in Latin America—by contravening sovereignty and overwhelming local actors—the less it has been able to foster lasting democratic politics, except in the limiting case of Puerto Rico; that is, of outright and permanent imposition.[18]

6. None of the instruments employed by the United States to promote democracy has ever succeeded in an enduring fashion unless local conditions were propitious. By the same token, U.S. influence has been more effective when it could be exercised in support of local actors and even more so when it could back locally controlled processes and institutions rather than specific participants. Similarly, it is easier for the United States to help protect a democracy under siege than to implant democratic practices where they have not previously been rooted.

7. Recurrent U.S. efforts to promote Latin American democracy have not been long sustained. Enthusiasm for active democracy promotion has ebbed and flowed, and the inconstancy of U.S. policy has tended not only to erode the efficacy of U.S. policy but actually to undermine the conditions for democratic politics.

8. The capacity of the U.S. government to nurture democratic politics in Latin America is greatest in those countries where the United States is sufficiently involved to be influential but not so extensively engaged as to warp the domestic fabric of social and political life. Even in such nations, the United States is only likely to be effective in promoting democracy when U.S. influence is consistently exerted.

9. External factors, including U.S. policy, are usually of secondary or tertiary importance in determining a Latin American nation's prospects for democracy, except in highly unusual, very finely balanced circumstances when foreign influence can tip the scale—or else in the small, nearby nations most penetrated by and vulnerable to the United States.[19] In the latter case, however, the immediate prodemocracy influ-

ence of the United States is often overcome by longer-term obstacles to democracy building that derive precisely from U.S. interventionism.

10. The indirect impact of the United States may well be more important in affecting Latin America's prospects for democratic politics than specifically designed U.S. government policies. Among the important ways that the United States affects Latin America's chances to democratic politics are its role as historic model, its cultural and educational traditions, the effect of free-market economics on political institutions and practices, the impact of broad international economic policies and of human rights concerns, the influence of U.S. military doctrines and training on Latin American officers, and the impact of exile in the United States upon Latin American political actors. Of great significance, too, are the activities undertaken by a wide variety of nongovernmental actors: not only business enterprises and labor unions but churches, journalists, scholars, human rights groups, environmentalists, tourists, and others. The U.S. government can probably do more to promote democracy in Latin America by encouraging nongovernmental policies and processes to support the region's democratization than by direct governmental pressures.

11. When U.S. government officials do undertake directly to promote democracy in Latin America, they are most likely to be effective if:

a. The U.S. foreign-policy-making bureaucracy accords a shared sense of priority to Latin American democracy.

b. The goal of nurturing democracy is broadly supported domestically and is undertaken as a bipartisan commitment.

c. The instruments used by U.S. officials are noncoercive and overt, support local processes and institutions, and are carried out with multilateral participation or approval.

Promoting Latin American Democracy: Guidelines for U.S. Policy

Despite its frequent and fulsome rhetoric, the U.S. government has actively promoted Latin American democracy only on occasion. Even when Washington officials have done so, their efforts have often been ineffective and sometimes counterproductive. The few successful instances of democracy promotion by the United States have only rarely been sustained. In the rare cases when U.S. policies to promote Latin American democracy coincided with sustained democratic consolidation, it is unlikely that U.S. influence was determinative.

These sobering conclusions, amply supported in this volume, should not discourage U.S. officials from supporting democracy in Latin America (and elsewhere, for that matter) as a legitimate and significant long-term goal of U.S. foreign policy. The citizens of the United States have good reasons to want their government to foster open, participatory, and constitutional politics throughout the Western Hemisphere. A region of consolidated democracies would be more humane and peaceful than one in which authoritarian regimes predominate. A democratic hemisphere would also be more stable, for effective democracy is the best insurance against guerrilla movements, terrorism, extremism, or anomic violence. The balanced economic social reforms that Latin America must undertake to develop and eventually to expand commercial exchange with the United States are more likely to be sustained under democratic conditions. Perhaps most important, the core values of the American people—tolerance for diversity, respect for fundamental human rights, and the rule of law—are best, indeed only, protected under democracy.

Promoting democracy is not an unworthy, unimportant, or impossible objective, but it is an extremely difficult task. It should be pursued consistently over many decades, not exuberantly chased in short bursts. Because democracy inherently involves self-determination and autonomy, outside efforts to nurture it must be restrained, respectful, sensitive, and patient. These are not qualities for which U.S. foreign policy is generally noted, but they are needed to promote democracy abroad.

Democracy is not an export commodity; it cannot simply be shipped from one setting to another. By its very nature, democracy must be achieved by each nation, largely on its own. It is an internal process, rooted in a country's history, institutions, and values; in the balance of its social and economic forces; and in the courage, commitment, and skill of its political leaders and of plain citizens.

But there is a good deal the United States can do, especially in concert with like-minded countries, to nurture and reinforce democracy in the Americas.

First, the United States should consistently emphasize its concern with the protection of fundamental human rights, for these rights are at the heart of democracy. Through diplomacy that is discreet, tempered, and professional—but not so quiet as to be unheard—the United States, together with the other democracies of the hemisphere, should invariably criticize regimes that grossly and systematically violate human rights. These regimes should be denied military and economic assistance, and they should not be treated as allies or friends. The specter of international isolation may help turn former supporters of authoritarian regimes into influential opponents at a delicate moment in the transition process. Similarly, in the period of consolidation, individual pressure may or may not dissuade backsliding toward the subversion of democratic institutions. U.S. leaders and their counterparts throughout the Americas can, in turn, positively support and reinforce the democratic network that is growing in the hemisphere, involving parties, trade unions, professional associations, women's groups, religious organizations, student federations, and others.

Second, the United States can cooperate with other nations to help strengthen the governmental institutions and practices that make up the very fiber of democracy. The United States should respond positively to requests from Latin American nations for technical assistance to legislatures on such matters as budget, oversight, and civilian control of the military, as well as support programs to improve the training and reinforce the democratic commitments of judicial and law enforcement officials.

Third, Washington should support inter-American efforts to institutionalize an independent and professional capacity to monitor elections, upon request by sovereign governments, and to help assure that elections are—and are accepted as being—free and fair. Elections by themselves do not make democracies; democracies make elections. But periodic and meaningful competition for political power, with a high level of participation and a level of civil and political liberties sufficient to ensure the integrity and legitimacy of the process, is a crucial element of democracy and external monitoring can help assure the proper conditions.

Fourth, the United States, directly through government actions and indirectly through the activities of private groups, can support the network of nongovernmental organizations—economic, social, educational, and civic—that express and mediate public demands and build the pluralism needed to keep democracy vital. Washington can help provide material and moral support to professional associations, trade unions, research centers, and the media in order to reinforce the democratic fabric.

Fifth, U.S. officials can strengthen Latin America's prospects for democracy by providing unambiguous and consistent signals that the maintenance of democratic politics is a high priority goal of the United States. Through the advice of its military missions and the content of its training programs, for example, the United States can help keep Latin America's armed forces out of politics. Latin America's business leaders, too, are likely to be responsive to clear U.S. signals of the importance of democracy.

In all such efforts, multilateral programs are more likely to be effective over time than bilateral ones, which are too easily perceived as partisan and interventionist. The United States should nurture and support cooperative efforts among the democratic governments of the Americas to strengthen democracy region-wide, not go it alone or insist on a leadership role.

It is also wise for Washington to employ mechanisms—such as the National Endowment for Democracy and the affiliated party, labor, and business institutes—that to some extent separate U.S. programs to support democracy from the immediate priorities of the foreign-policy-making bureaucracy. It is equally important that these institutions keep their focus squarely on supporting democratic processes; they should not identify themselves with particular candidates nor parties, or lend themselves to instrumental efforts to press for a specific political outcome.

Probably the most decisive ways the United States can promote Latin American democracy are indirect.

First, the United States can certainly improve Latin America's prospects for democracy by helping countries of the region cope with their fundamental economic problems. U.S. foreign economic policies should reinforce Latin American efforts to make their economies both more productive and more equitable, and thus help to build the underpinnings of democracy. Of all the means available to the United States to strengthen Latin American democracy in the 1990s, this is no doubt the single most important. Democracy is under seige in Latin America after a "lost decade" of depression, declining investment, decaying social services, and worsening inequalities. It is in the interest of the United States—among other reasons because of its commitment to democracy—to help Latin America resume economic growth and development.

Finally, the United States strengthens the democratic cause throughout the hemisphere and elsewhere when it is true to its political values and protects the vitality of its own democratic institutions. Conversely, whenever U.S. officials flout the rule of law, domestic or international—as they did in the case of Nicaragua in the 1980s—they inevitably make the Americas and the world unsafe for democracy. Clandestine, undemocratic, or illegal means are neither justified nor effective as ways of nurturing democracy. The United States should never pretend that it can promote democracy abroad by trampling upon it at home.

Notes

1. The memorandum from which this quotation is drawn is cited at greater length on pp. 64–65 of Leslie Bethell's chapter in this volume; see his discussion and n. 42.

2. Stephen Rabe, *Eisenhower and Latin America: The Foreign Policy of Anti-Communism* (Chapel Hill: University of North Carolina Press, 1988).

3. Tad Szulc, *Twilight of the Tyrants* (New York: Holt, 1959).

4. See Robert Packenham, *Liberal America and the Third World* (Princeton: Princeton University Press, 1973); and Howard Wiarda, "Did the Alliance 'Lose Its Way,' or Were Its Assumptions All Wrong from the Beginning and Are Those Assumptions Still with Us?" in L. Ronald Scheman, ed., *The Alliance for Progress* (New York: Praeger, 1988), pp. 95–118.

5. See, for example, Abraham F. Lowenthal, "Foreign Aid as a Political Instrument: The Case of the Dominican Republic," *Public Policy* 14 (1965): 141–60.

6. See Arthur M. Schlesinger, Jr., *A Thousand Days: John F. Kennedy in the White House* (Boston: Houghton Mifflin, 1965), p. 769.

7. Riordan Roett, *The Politics of Foreign Aid in Northeast Brazil* (Nashville: Vanderbilt University Press, 1972).

8. See Nelson A. Rockefeller, *The Rockefeller Report on the Americas* (Chicago: Quadrangle Books, 1969). A good doctoral dissertation could no doubt be written on the evolution of Nelson Rockefeller's thinking about Latin American democracy from the 1940s to the 1970s.

9. See Lars Schoultz, *Human Rights and United States Policy toward Latin America* (Princeton: Princeton University Press, 1981). Cf. Joshua Muravchik, *The Uncertain Cru-*

sade: Jimmy Carter and the Dilemmas of Human Rights Policy (Lanham, Md.: Hamilton Press, 1986).

10. The classic statement of this view was Jeane Kirkpatrick's "Dictatorships and Double Standards," published in *Commentary* (November 1979). See also Kirkpatrick's "U.S. Security in Latin America," *Commentary* (January 1981).

11. Cf. Constantine Menges, *Inside the National Security Council* (New York: Simon & Schuster, 1988), and Roy Gutman, *Banana Diplomacy: The Making of American Policy in Nicaragua, 1981–1987* (New York: Simon & Schuster, 1988).

12. See Elliott Abrams, "Latin America in the Time of Reagan," *The New York Times,* July 27, 1988. Cf. Andrew Hurrell, "International Support for Political Democracy in Contemporary Latin America: The Case of Brazil," paper prepared for the Latin America Study Group, Royal Institute of International Affairs (London), May 10, 1989.

13. These cases are more extensively discussed in Thomas Carothers, *In the Name of Democracy: U.S. Policy toward Latin America in the Reagan Years* (Berkeley: University of California Press, forthcoming). Cf. Adam Garfinkle, *Friendly Tyrants* (forthcoming).

14. See Abraham F. Lowenthal, "The Dominican Republic: The Politics of Chaos," in A. von Lazar and R. R. Kaufman, eds., *Reform and Revolution: Readings in Latin American Politics* (Needham Heights, Mass.: Allyn & Bacon, 1969).

15. See Robert A. Pastor, "Nicaragua's Choice: The Making of a Free Election," *Journal of Democracy* (Summer 1990): 13–25.

16. See Edward Herman and Frank Brodhead, eds., *Demonstration Elections: U.S.-Staged Elections in the Dominican Republic, Vietnam, and El Salvador* (Boston: South End Press, 1984).

17. With the waning of the Cold War in the 1990s, it may be that this final condition will be relaxed, for the link between the left and a powerful international competitor of the United States has been broken. See Jorge G. Castañeda, "Latin America and the End of the Cold War: A Mixed Blessing for the Left," *World Policy Journal* (Summer 1990): 471–92.

18. In correspondence with the author, Carlos Escudé has pointed out that it is the incompleteness and inconstancy of U.S. intervention in Latin America (see proposition #7) that makes ineffective U.S. intervention for democracy in the region, rather than the fact of intervention itself. He compares the more profound, single-minded, skillful, and effective U.S. intervention for democracy in Italy in 1948. See E. Miller, "Taking Off the Gloves: The United States and the Italian Elections of 1948," *Diplomatic History* (Winter 1983).

19. On the likelihood that external influence will be most significant when the local political equation is delicately balanced, see Robert A. Pastor, "How to Reinforce Democracy in the Americas: Seven Proposals," in Robert A. Pastor, ed., *Democracy in the Americas: Stopping the Pendulum* (New York: Holmes & Meier, 1989), p. 141.

Note on Contributors

Carlos Escudé is a historian at the Instituto Torcuato Di Tella in Buenos Aires.

Heraldo Muñoz is currently Chile's ambassador to the Organization of American States. Previously he directed the program on international relations at Chile's Academia de Humanismo Cristiano.

Jonathan Hartlyn is associate professor of political science at the University of North Carolina at Chapel Hill.

Lorenzo Meyer is professor of history at El Colegio de Mexico and the former director of the Center for International Studies there.

Joseph Tulchin is director of the Latin American Program at the Woodrow Wilson International Center for Scholars and professor of history at the University of North Carolina at Chapel Hill.

Knut Walter is currently a visiting professor at the Central American University in Managua.

Elizabeth A. Cobbs is assistant professor of history at the University of San Diego.

Paul G. Buchanan is assistant professor of political science at the University of Arizona.

John Sheahan is professor of economics at Williams College.

Laurence Whitehead is official fellow in politics at Nuffield College, Oxford, and an editor of the *Journal of Latin American Studies*.

Abraham F. Lowenthal is professor of international relations at the University of Southern California and executive director of the Inter-American Dialogue.

Index

AACCLA. *See* American Association of Chambers of Commerce of Latin America (AACCLA)
Abrams, Elliott, 46, 133, 246, 270
Acción Democrática, 81, 82, 178
Acheson, Dean, 260n11
AFL-CIO, 177, 179, 183–84, 187–88, 190, 192–95, 197–202
Agencia Latina, 15
Agency for International Development (AID), 156, 157, 178, 180, 189, 192, 196–98
Agricultural Trade Development and Assistance Act, 22
Agriculture, 151, 212, 216–17
Agrupación de Trabajadores Latino-americanos Sindicalistas (ATLAS), 14
Agrupación Política 14 de Junio, 73
Aguero, Fernando, 129
AIFLD. *See* American Institute for Free Labor Development (AIFLD)
Alessandri, Jorge, 40–41
Allende, Salvador, 42, 46–47, 163–65, 179, 218, 267, 274
Alliance for Progress: and American Institute for Free Labor Development, 177–78, 196; and business, 152–57; and Colombia, 219–20; conflicts and, 129, 217, 229; Congress's attitude toward, 154–56; goals of, 41, 47, 49, 209–10, 266; and International Petroleum Company, 163; and Nicaragua, 128; and ORIT, 193; and poverty, 220–21; rejection of activist thrust of, 129; self-interest and, 143
American and Foreign Power Company, 147
American Association of Chambers of Commerce of Latin America (AACCLA), 19–20, 158–61, 163
American Federation of Labor (AFL), 58–59, 174–77, 181–82, 186, 200. *See also* AFL-CIO
American Institute for Free Labor Development (AIFLD), 177–80, 182, 183, 184, 189, 191, 193, 194–98, 201, 202, 205n58, 206n64
Anaconda, 164, 195
Anderson, Chandler P., 119
Antifascist Latin American Labor Front, 176
Arbenz, Jacobo, 69, 128, 162, 193, 265

Arévalo, Juan José, 67
Argentina: admission to United Nations, 171n30; Carter's policy toward, 18–28, 30, 37n69; chambers of commerce in, 158; democracy in, 235; democratization in 1980s, 44; dictatorship in, 3, 10–14; economic aid to, 19–26, 30–31, 37n69; economy of, 26–27, 34–35n17, 38n74, 225; Eisenhower's policy toward, 15–17; human rights abuses in, 3, 9–14, 19, 32n1; industrialization of, 151; instrumental use of principle and, 14–15; during 1940s–1950s, 3–17, 28–31; during 1970s–1980s, 3–4, 17–28, 30–31; petroleum industry in, 17; political polarization in, 25–30; postwar boycott of, 18–20, 36n47; quest for free press and free labor unions in, 10–14; Reagan's policy toward, 28, 31, 37n69, 268; relative irrelevance to U.S., 4, 4–5n; review of democracy promotion by U.S., 271–72; U.S. business interests in, 151; during World War II, 5–8
Argüello, Leonardo, 124, 125, 126
Arias, Desiderio, 57
Arias, Oscar, 135
Arias Plan, 135
Atkins, G. Pope, 236
ATLAS. *See* Agrupación de Trabajadores Latino-americanos Sindicalistas (ATLAS)
"Atoms for Peace" agreement, 17
Austral plan, 27
Authoritarian versus totalitarian regimes, 43, 237. *See also* Dictatorships

Baez, Mauricio, 67
Baggett, Sam, 147, 148
Baker plan, 211, 223
Balaguer, Joaquín, 54, 72–74, 77–83, 85, 91n59, 92n69, 272
Balgooyen, H. W., 147
Bank of America, 164, 165
Banks. *See* Eximbank; Export-Import Bank; Inter-American Development Bank (IDB); Multilevel development banks (MDBs); World Bank
Baraona, Pablo, 52n15
Barnes, Harry, 44, 45–46, 49, 275
Batista, Fulgencio, 52n19, 69, 70, 73, 121, 127, 131, 265–66
Bay of Pigs invasion, 91n48, 128